Anti-Racism as a Legal Principle

Anti-Racism as a Legal Principle

SHREYA ATREY

Associate Professor in International Human Rights Law,
University of Oxford, UK

OXFORD
UNIVERSITY PRESS

OXFORD
UNIVERSITY PRESS

Great Clarendon Street, Oxford, OX2 6DP,
United Kingdom

Oxford University Press is a department of the University of Oxford.
It furthers the University's objective of excellence in research, scholarship,
and education by publishing worldwide. Oxford is a registered trade mark of
Oxford University Press in the UK and in certain other countries.

Published in the United States of America by Oxford University Press
546 Fifth Avenue, New York, NY 10036, United States of America.

British Library Cataloguing in Publication Data

Data available

Library of Congress Control Number: 2026939756

ISBN 9780198947615

DOI: 10.1093/9780198947646.001.0001

Printed and bound by
CPI Group (UK) Ltd., Croydon, CR0 4YY

The manufacturer's authorized representative in the EU for product safety is
Oxford University Press España S.A. of Parque Empresarial San Fernando de Henares,
Avenida de Castilla, 2 – 28830 Madrid (www.oup.es/en or product.safety@oup.com).
OUP España S.A. also acts as importer into Spain of products made by the manufacturer.

FSC
www.fsc.org
MIX
Paper | Supporting
responsible forestry
FSC® C013604

The book is dedicated to those who made it possible:

My parents

and

'Ladies who Law'

Acknowledgements

Much of this book was written during a sabbatical at the Trinity Long Room Hub, Trinity College Dublin, Ireland in 2024-2025. The Hub provided the most excellent intellectual community and environment. I am grateful to the Hub team, especially its former Director Eve Patten and my host, Mark Bell, for their exceptional support.

Achas Burin, Hayley Hooper, and Leah Trueblood read too many drafts to justify a mere thanks here. I am lucky to know them and remain in their debt.

I received extraordinary research assistance from Fionn McFadden and Kacper Kryk. I am grateful for their labour and for all the good cheer they brought with their presence.

I have presented draft chapters of the book at the Oxford Public Law Discussion Group; the Uehiro Oxford Institute; the Hertie School Centre for Fundamental Rights; Osgoode Hall Law School; UNSW Faculty of Law; Berkeley Anti-Discrimination Law Group; Trinity Centre for Constitutional Law and Governance; and the UK Government's Equality Hub. I am grateful for the generous feedback I received from colleagues at these places.

This book has benefitted from conversations, comments, guidance, and inspiration I have received from colleagues over many years. My most sincere thanks to Aileen Kavanagh, Alexandra Xanthaki, Anthony Morgan, Anthony Sangiuliano, Antonio Maués, Başak Çalı, Cathryn Costello, Colm O'Cinneide, Daniella Lock, David Kenny, David Oppenheimer, Edward (Long) Lui, Gautam Bhatia, Gideon Basson, Jennifer Koshan, Joshua Castellino, Kate O'Regan, Lia Lawton, Liz Fisher, Lulu Weiss, Manoj Dias-Abbey, Mathias Möschel, Miles Jackson, Naz Ghanea, Nick Barber, Patrick Thornberry, Rosalind Dixon, Sandra Fredman, Silvia Suteu, Sophia Moreau, Sonia Lawrence, Suryapratim Roy, and Timothy Endicott.

Many thanks to Brian Stone, Mirza Rizwaan Ahmad, Paulina Dos Santos Major, and Robert Cavooris at OUP, for their abiding trust in my work.

Finally, my partner, Felix, and my family, Aayan, Archana, Christa, Clemens, Hartmut, Pradeep, Rohit, Vartika, and Vihaan, gently and consistently inquired whether the book was done, and provided considerable assurance that it was not totally silly to write a book on anti-racism in the tumultuous times we live in today. Though in our context, it *is* a bit silly to *thank* family; I did want to acknowledge and appreciate their love and care that sustains me every day.

Brief Contents

Detailed Contents

Introduction

Is there anything like a principle of anti-racism in law?

On the face of it, 'anti-racism' as a term does not appear in law.[1] In domestic law, constitutions, statutory law, and common law do not commonly refer to anti-racism.[2] In international law, treaties, customary international law, and general principles do not commonly refer to anti-racism either. In fact, treaties such as the European Convention on Human Rights (ECHR)[3]—which was adopted in 1950 in response to the atrocities of the Second World War and the Holocaust—and the International Convention on the Elimination of All Forms of Racial Discrimination (ICERD)[4]—which was the first human rights treaty to be adopted by the United Nations in 1965—do not even mention 'racism', let alone 'anti-racism'.

Instead, the term 'racial discrimination' appears. Law, especially discrimination law,[5] is replete with references to racial discrimination—the specific category of legal wrong based on certain racial 'grounds' such as colour, nationality, ethnic or national origins, descent, caste, etc.[6] The assumption that is often made is that the legal category of racial discrimination is meant to address racism and hence is an expression of anti-racism in law.[7]

[1] In contrast, in policy, anti-racism appears frequently, such as in the European Union's Anti-Racism Action Plan 2020–2025 and the Anti-Racism Strategy 2025–2030, which have been followed up by national action plans against racism across European Union countries.

[2] A notable exception is Brazil where the Constitution of 1988 in Article 4, Section VIII, mentions the 'repudiation of terrorism and racism' as a guiding principle for Brazil's international relations, and Article 5, Section XLII declares racism a crime for which bail is not available, and which is punishable by imprisonment. Further, 'The Anti-Racism Act', Law No. 7,716/89, prohibits discrimination based on race, colour, ethnicity, religion, or national origin.

[3] Convention for the Protection of Human Rights and Fundamental Freedoms 1950 (European Convention on Human Rights, as amended) (ECHR).

[4] International Convention on the Elimination of All Forms of Racial Discrimination (adopted 21 December 1965, entered into force 4 January 1969) 660 UNTS 195 (ICERD).

[5] 'Discrimination law' is used interchangeably with equality law, anti-discrimination law, and non-discrimination law and refers to the doctrine and scholarship concerning the prohibition of wrongful discrimination on the basis of certain grounds.

[6] For example, UK Equality Act 2010, s 9 (not applicable to Northern Ireland); ICERD, art 1(1); ECHR, art 14.

[7] John Carson, 'A Matter of Policy: The Lessons of Recent British Race Relations Legislation' (1976) 8 A Quarterly Journal Concerned with British Studies 154, 158; Alastair Bonnett, *Anti-Racism* (Routledge 2000) 69; Erik Bleich, *Race Politics in Britain and France* (Cambridge University Press 2003) 63; Alana Lentin, 'Racism, Anti-Racism and the Western State' in Gerard Delanty, Ruth Wodak, and Paul Jones (eds), *Identity, Belonging and Migration* (Liverpool University Press 2011) 101; Kennetta Hammond Perry, *London is the Place for Me: Black Britons, Citizenship and the Politics of Race* (Oxford University Press 2015) 201; Iyiola Solanke, 'The Race Relations Act @ 50 conference: Where

Anti-Racism as a Legal Principle. Shreya Atrey, Oxford University Press. © Shreya Atrey 2026.
DOI: 10.1093/9780198947646.003.0001

At the same time, this assumption is vehemently refuted. In the first-ever case decided by the UK Supreme Court when it assumed its functions in 2009, *R v JFS*,[8] four individual judges at different points clarified that to be guilty of racial discrimination was not the same as being a 'racist' in the popular sense of the term.[9] This was despite the fact that the Court in *JFS had* found racial discrimination. Likewise, in 2021, the UK Commission on Race and Ethnic Disparities declared that there was no evidence of institutional, systemic, and structural racism in the UK.[10] This was despite its own admission of the existence of both racial disadvantage and racial discrimination.[11] The Commission however was clear that no link between racism, racial disadvantage, and racial discrimination could be made despite the 'strident' attempts of anti-racist movements to do so.[12]

Three questions emerge.

First, if racial discrimination is not racism, then what is it?

Second, if racial discrimination law is not addressing racism, then what is it actually doing?

Third, if racial discrimination law had to address racism, then how should it do so?

This book responds to these questions by offering a systematic account of the relationship between racism and anti-racism on the one hand, and racial discrimination and law on the other hand.

The account is offered at three levels: conceptual, doctrinal, and normative.

Conceptually, the book makes three moves. First, it adopts a meaning of racism which includes racial disadvantage or the vast material gaps between racialized groups. It shows that the severance of racism and racial disadvantage is often the first step in the denial of racism. It finds no principled reason for this severance and thus links racism and racial disadvantage definitionally. Second, the book proposes tripartite typologies of racism and anti-racism. These include interpersonal or individual, institutional or systemic, and structural racism; and liberal, cultural, and transformative anti-racisms. The book hones in on structural racism as the antecedent of all racism. It argues for centring structural racism in thinking about racism as it is the root cause of all racism. Correspondingly, it argues for centring transformative anti-racism in thinking about anti-racism as it is principally about

Were You?' (2015) 20; Simon Peplow, 'The "Linchpin for Success"? The Problematic Establishment of the 1965 Race Relations Act and its Conciliation Board' (2017) 31 Contemporary British History 430; Matthew Vaughan, 'Accepting the "D" Word: Discrimination in 1960s' UK Academic Discourse' (2019) 61 Race and Class 85.

8 [2009] UKSC 15.

9 ibid [9] (Lord Phillips), [54] (Lady Hale), [156] (Lord Clarke), [184] (Lord Hope).

10 Commission on Race and Ethnic Disparities: The Report (March 2021) 77 [hereafter the Sewell Report].

11 ibid 7.

12 ibid 11, 233.

addressing structural racism. Terms such as structural racism, structural discrimination, structural change, anti-racism, and transformation have gained traction recently, especially since the global Black Lives Matter protests against George Floyd and Breonna Taylor's murders in 2020. Yet, few contemporary interventions have clarified the meaning of these terms.[13] In response, the book offers conceptual frameworks of racism and anti-racism which can serve as the baseline for all interventions, in law and beyond.[14]

Doctrinally, the book maps these concepts, especially the concept of structural racism onto existing doctrine in discrimination law. The purpose is to examine how doctrine, as a whole, responds to structural racism. The book takes the example of the UK and surveys the entire labyrinth of British law on racial discrimination under the Equality Act 2010, the Human Rights Act 1998, and the common law. It identifies no outward resistance to anti-racism. Instead, it finds that anti-racism is often resisted in the granularities of how discrimination law is imagined and applied. Consequently, when anti-racism is embraced occasionally, it is not embraced outwardly. The adoption of anti-racism as a legal principle is thus discerned not in the adoption of the locution 'anti-racism', but in the way structural racism is actually addressed, and transformative anti-racism is enacted in judicial reasoning. The book complements this analysis in British law with the discussion of comparative and international law to show a similar pattern therein. In sum, the book presents a root and branch review of law, as laid down and as practised.

Ultimately, *normatively*, the book makes a case for anti-racism as a legal principle. Anti-racism as a legal principle requires the two forms of analyses above. First, it requires a clear sense of the conceptual framework of anti-racism, and second, it needs a clear sense of how that conceptual framework translates into doctrine. The book argues that anti-racism fits the mould of a legal principle which conceptually incorporates the frameworks of structural racism and transformative anti-racism. Anti-racism can be traced in doctrine not by searching for the adoption of the phrase 'anti-racism' but by looking for the resonance of the concept in

[13] Cf the concept of 'structural injustice', which has received greater attention of late: Madison Powers and Ruth Faden; *Structural Injustice: Power, Advantage, and Human Rights* (Oxford University Press 2019); Virginia Mantouvalou, 'Structural Injustice and the Human Rights of Workers' (2020) 73 Current Legal Problems 59; Sally Haslanger, 'Systemic and Structural Injustice: Is There a Difference?' (2023) 98 Philosophy 1; Virginia Mantouvalou, *Structural Injustice and Workers' Rights* (Oxford University Press 2023); Virginia Mantouvalou and Jonathan Wolff (eds), *Structural Injustice and the Law* (University College London Press 2024).

[14] As Paul Kissack, the CEO of the Joseph Rowntree Foundation remarked: 'Definitions matter. Being clear what we mean by certain terms and concepts is essential to meaningful debate and meaningful action. Yet all too often we enter debates without that common understanding, especially in the sphere of social and cultural policy, where concepts can be messy and contested. The debate about racism that followed the publication of the Sewell report ... —"is Britain racist?", "is there institutional racism?"—was a striking example of this. Although the glaring inadequacies of the report itself received some attention, the crux of the political argument were quite different perspectives on what the concept of racism means.' Paul Kissack, 'Coming to Terms with Race and Racism' (15 April 2021) <https://www.jrf.org.uk/race-and-ethnicity/coming-to-terms-with-race-and-racism> (accessed 7 March 2024).

the nooks and crannies of legal practice. In this way, the book makes a case for the normativity of law while treating the legal doctrine seriously.

The central argument of the book is thus twofold. First, anti-racism *should* be conceived as a legal principle which guides the imagination and operation of all law and policy to address structural racism. There is no fundamental legal bar to the invocation of anti-racism as a general principle of law, much like democracy or the rule of law. Without a principle of anti-racism, law, especially discrimination law, seems to operate rudderless in responding to the whole range of racial discrimination claims that are made and the whole range of racism that is out there. Second, anti-racism as a legal principle *can* be located in judicial reasoning in racial discrimination claims, and occasional successes show the difference that anti-racism as a legal principle makes to adjudication.

The argument unfolds in two parts: Part I which proposes frameworks of racism and anti-racism; and Part II which applies these frameworks to legal doctrine on racial discrimination in British, comparative, and international law.

Part I consists of four chapters.

Chapter 1 explores the recalcitrance of racism. It opens with a snapshot of the vast material gaps between racialized groups in the UK. It asks why such racial disadvantage is not considered evidence of racism. It explores the severance of racial disadvantage from racism in the UK's official narrative on racism, especially in the latest and the lengthiest report on racial disparities: the 2021 Sewell Report. In contrast, it argues for racism to be understood in terms which include racial disadvantage and in reference to processes of racialization. This chapter sets the baseline for all references to racism in the book to be indicating some form of racial disadvantage whether social, cultural, political, economic, or psychological.

Chapter 2 maps the understanding of racism along three lines: individual, institutional or systemic, and structural. It distinguishes between the three and then concentrates on defining structural racism for the purposes of this book. It proposes a framework of structural racism to do with who enacts it (state and state-like entities), how it comes about (processes of racialization), and what it does (instate a framework of disadvantage). It explains structural racism as what lies behind all racism and thus what should be the target of all anti-racism.

Chapter 3 maps the understanding of anti-racism especially as developed in the UK along three lines: liberal, cultural, and transformative. While anti-racist theory and praxis have been populated by all kinds of anti-racism, the chapter argues for a preference for transformative anti-racism as that which targets structural racism most precisely. It thus argues for centring transformative anti-racism in law.

Chapter 4 argues that anti-racism as a legal principle guides the imagination and operation of all law and policy to address structural racism. It shows why anti-racism should be conceived as a legal principle as opposed to a legal rule, policy, or value. This is because legal principles provide guidance for action in a deliberative, non-deterministic sense. Anti-racism fits the mould of a legal principle as its action-oriented nature defies a single formula for translation into practice. The chapter goes on to delineate the content, scope, function, and location of anti-racism as a legal principle.

It is important to emphasize that although Part I lays down frameworks for understanding the meaning of racism and anti-racism which are used in the rest of the book, the discussion in this part of the book is meant to be general. The frameworks are suggested as useful per se—beyond their current application to racial discrimination law—to other areas of law and indeed beyond law itself. Part I can thus be perused on its own with a view to understanding the conceptual nature of racism and anti-racism as such. Its most important contribution is in laying down a conceptual framework of structural racism: a fundamental concept of universal appeal.

Part II of the book turns to the law on racial discrimination. Its primary purpose is to understand how structural racism as defined in the book is addressed in discrimination law wherever contained (statutes, common law, constitutions, and international treaties). Can something like a legal principle of anti-racism be gleaned from practice?

Part II consists of six chapters.

Each chapter traces how anti-racism and its various instantiations—liberal, cultural, and transformative—manifest in the current practice across six locations—the Race Relations legislations of 1965, 1968, and 1976 (Chapter 5), the Equality Act 2010 (Chapter 6), the Human Rights Act 1998 (Chapter 7), common law (Chapter 8), comparative law (Chapter 9), and international law (Chapter 10). Finally, the Conclusion considers the implications of the existing doctrine for the adoption of anti-racism as a legal principle.

Chapter 5 considers how anti-racism and discrimination law are related. In particular, it seeks to test the assumption that discrimination law is anti-racist. It traverses the trajectory of development of discrimination law in the UK from the first three race relations legislations in 1965, 1968, and 1976 to the 2010 single consolidated equality legislation which exists today. It shows discrimination law's contemporary commitment to liberal anti-racism and the previous commitment to cultural anti-racism. In contrast, while there is no real explicit rejection of transformative anti-racism and hence of anti-racism as a legal principle, there is no real embrace of it either.

Chapter 6 shows that in the fifteen years since the Equality Act 2010 has been in force, it has hardly operated as a bulwark against racism. It traces how its scope is personally, materially, evidentially, and remedially limited in addressing structural racism. As the main equality legislation today in the UK, its anti-racist record is sparse.

Chapter 7 shows much the same in respect of the Human Rights Act 1998 and how case law on article 14 of the ECHR has developed to exclude structural racism. Though there have been occasional successes under the Human Rights Act 1998 which reflect anti-racism as a legal principle strongly, these successes confirm that the Human Rights Act 1998 is better suited to address structural racism than the Equality Act 2010.

Chapter 8 turns to the common law. It explores the extent to which it addresses structural racism and finds that despite possibilities which exist in principle, there has been little concerted effort to mobilize a common law prohibition of racial discrimination or anti-racism more broadly.

Chapters 9 and 10 then turn to comparative law and international law, respectively. They seek to test whether the patterns in legal doctrine which seem to resist structural racism in the UK are replicated (i) where there are explicit constitutional provisions guaranteeing the right to equality and non-discrimination based on racial grounds; and (ii) international law especially the jurisprudence under the ICERD.

In that regard, Chapter 9 examines comparative constitutional law in Canada, India, and South Africa with a focus on how claims of structural racism are addressed therein. It shows that though constitutions in these postcolonial democracies may seem to commit to anti-racism, they ultimately only do so in a weak sense through a prohibition of racial discrimination and not through a legal principle of anti-racism. Much like the statutory provisions in the UK, the category of 'racial discrimination' in these jurisdictions has developed to exclude structural racism.

Chapter 10 looks at international law especially the practice of the Committee on the Elimination of Racial Discrimination (CERD)—the specialist treaty body tasked with monitoring and enforcing the ICERD, and the UN special procedures such as the mandate of the Special Rapporteur on contemporary forms of racism, racial discrimination, xenophobia, and related intolerance. It shows the distinctive possibility of addressing structural racism through international human rights law especially through inter-state proceedings and through state reporting under treaties, but finds that the inordinate focus on individual communication procedures, and the centripetal force of state sovereignty as the foundation of international law, ultimately impede taking anti-racism seriously.

The Conclusion reminds that though much of the extant body of British, comparative, and international law on racial discrimination fails to address structural racism, examples in doctrine also show how this can be reversed. These examples show that there is no principal resistance to anti-racism as a legal principle and that its adoption is not only doctrinally viable but also makes discrimination law itself viable. Otherwise, discrimination law operates with too little conceptual understanding of or normative commitment to anti-racism, making the legal category of 'racial discrimination' narrow and meaningless. The book closes with a reminder of the importance of adopting anti-racism as a legal principle not necessarily as part of the text of statutes, constitutions, common law, or international treaties, but as part of the normative commitment to high-level legal principles such as democracy and the rule of law. High-level principles guide all law and policy in a fundamental sense. Racism, especially structural racism, can be combatted only with such a high-level and foundational commitment to anti-racism as a legal principle.

PART I

THEORY

Racism and Anti-Racism

1

The Recalcitrance of Racism

1.1 Introduction

Books of the present kind often begin with a recital of statistical evidence on racial disadvantage. The point is to drive home the grim and undeniable reality of differential outcomes of racialized groups across all areas of life.

This book is no different. In the main, it is concerned with racial disadvantage and argues that racial disadvantage is a result of structural racism which lies at the heart of all racism. Anti-racism should then be about attacking structural racism and transforming the conditions which give rise to racial disadvantage. A clear picture of racial disadvantage is thus critical for this project.

The introductory chapter provides this picture. Section 1.2 presents a snapshot of the vast material gaps between racialized groups in the UK. Section 1.3 shows that while these gaps are acknowledged, they are often not considered as evidence of racism. Instead, racism is vehemently denied in the presence of these facts. The paradox between the admission of racial disadvantage and the denial of racism appears to be a definitional issue. That is, the link between racism and racial disadvantage is severed by defining racism as excluding racial disadvantage. Section 1.4 argues that racism should be understood as including racial disadvantage and as a result of processes of racialization. This shift in the understanding of racism is necessary for an eventual shift to understanding racism in structural terms.

This chapter thus lays the foundation for the rest of the book by making both an empirical and a conceptual case for racism to be understood as racial disadvantage.

1.2 Detecting Racism

In her report after a visit to the UK in 2019, the UN Special Rapporteur on contemporary forms of racism, racial discrimination, xenophobia, and related intolerance described 'the structural socioeconomic exclusion of racial and ethnic minority communities in the United Kingdom' as 'striking' and 'alarming' across outcomes in 'education, employment, housing, pay and living standards, health, criminal justice and participation'.[1]

[1] Report from the Visit to the United Kingdom of Great Britain and Northern Ireland Report of the Special Rapporteur on contemporary forms of racism, racial discrimination, xenophobia, and related

Anti-Racism as a Legal Principle. Shreya Atrey, Oxford University Press. © Shreya Atrey 2026.
DOI: 10.1093/9780198947646.003.0003

Indeed, according to the Runnymede Trust, Black and minority ethnic people[2] in the UK are twice as likely to be in 'deep poverty', with Pakistani and Bangladeshi people three and four times as likely, respectively.[3] These groups struggle to meet everyday needs of food and energy. Given the current cost-of-living crisis, everyone has been worse off especially after the austerity measures were introduced in the UK in 2010 and since the Covid-19 pandemic in 2020. But Black and minority ethnic people are worse still. So, while 'white families now receive £454 less a year on average in cash benefits than they did a decade ago … this rises to £806 less a year for Black and minority ethnic families and even higher to £1,635 for Black families. Black and minority ethnic women have been some of the worst affected and currently receive £1,040 less than they did a decade ago.'[4]

Poverty aligns with employment levels. Seventy-six per cent of the UK's working age population is employed. While gap in employment between racialized groups has decreased in the last twenty years, it has not closed. Seventy-seven per cent of white people are employed in contrast with 61 per cent of people from the combined Pakistani and Bangladeshi ethnic group—the lowest percentage of all ethnic groups.[5] The biggest difference in employment is amongst young adults (15–24 year olds) where 58 per cent of white and 39 per cent of ethnic minorities youth are employed. Likewise, while unemployment has remained high since the Covid-19 pandemic, in 2024, the rate was 3.3 per cent for white people as compared to 8.0 per cent for people from Black and minority ethnic backgrounds.[6] There was substantial variation between groups. White (3.3 per cent) and Indian (4.9 per cent) ethnic groups had the lowest unemployment rates, while people from mixed (11.5 per cent) and Pakistani (11.1 per cent) ethnic groups had the highest rates.[7] Similarly, while ethnic pay gap has decreased significantly for white Irish, Indian,

intolerance (27 May 2019), UN General Assembly, Human Rights Council Forty-First Session, A/HRC/41/54/Add.2 [20].

[2] The term 'Black and minority ethnic' includes all non-white ethnic groups who have been 'minoritised' or disadvantaged by their race, colour, ethnicity, nationality, etc. Outcomes for all groups under this umbrella label are not the same. This is especially true for outcomes for Indian and Chinese groups whose outcomes are often on par with the white population. Still, there are some patterns of racialized disadvantages that Asians suffer as such so as to justify their inclusion and the use of the category 'Black and minority ethnic' as a political unifier. Similarly, the label 'Black' refers to both Black African and Black Caribbean groups though outcomes for them are not always the same. Care is taken to present disaggregated data concerning Black African and Black Caribbean as well as Pakistani and Bangladeshi groups were relevant.

[3] Daniel Edminston, 'Falling Faster Amidst a Cost-of-Living Crisis: Poverty, Inequality and Ethnicity in the UK', Runnymede Trust Briefing (October 2022) 2.

[4] ibid.

[5] 'Employment', Ethnicity Facts and Figures, GOV.UK (28 November 2023), https://www.ethnicity-facts-figures.service.gov.uk/work-pay-and-benefits/employment/employment/latest/ (accessed 5 November 2025).

[6] Annalise Murray, 'Unemployment by Ethnic Background', Research Briefing Number 6385, House of Commons Library (16 August 2024) 2.

[7] ibid.

and Chinese ethnic groups as compared to white people, Black employees have the biggest pay gap, earning 5.6–12 per cent less than white employees.[8]

Employment rates in turn align with educational attainment. Though ethnic minorities are more likely to attend university than white people, the latter often outperform the former in attaining higher class degrees.[9] While Gypsy/Roma and Travellers of Irish heritage have the worst educational attainment in the country,[10] Black and Pakistani–Bangladeshi ethnic groups also lag behind at all levels—early years, secondary school, high school, and university education.[11]

Outcomes in health and housing are similar. Black and minority ethnic population has a higher life expectancy but a lower 'healthy life expectancy'.[12] Babies born to Pakistani mothers have the highest rate of neonatal and child mortality,[13] while Black women are five times more likely to die during pregnancy and after childbirth compared to white women.[14]

In housing, all minority ethnic groups, other than Indians, are less likely than white people to be homeowners and in private rented accommodation 'where problems of insecurity, affordability and poor conditions are most common'.[15] All non-white ethnic groups are vulnerable to living in overcrowded conditions with rates of overcrowding highest amongst Bangladeshi (39 per cent), Pakistani (31 per cent), and African (32 per cent) groups and lowest amongst white British (4 per cent) and white Irish (3 per cent) groups.[16] Ethnic minorities also experience disproportionate levels of homelessness.[17]

[8] Carmen Aguilar García and Pamela Duncan, '"Absolutely Shameful" UK Ethnicity Pay Gap Persists, Figures Show' The Guardian (29 November 2023).

[9] 'Inclusive Britain', Report 2023 (last updated 24 May 2024), GOV.UK, https://www.gov.uk/government/publications/inclusive-britain-update-report/inclusive-britain-update-report (accessed 6 November 2025); Equality and Human Rights Commission, 'Is Britain Fairer? The State of Equality and Human Rights 2018', Presented to Parliament pursuant to Section 12 of the Equality Act 2006 as amended by the Enterprise and Regulatory Reform Act 2013 (June 2019) 19.

[10] Nerys Roberts, 'Gypsies and Travellers: Educational Outcomes', Research Briefing Number CBP10016, House of Commons Library (17 May 2024).

[11] Annual Report 2025: Ethnicity, Educational Policy Institute, https://epi.org.uk/annual-report-2025-foreword-executive-summary/ (accessed 5 November 2025).

[12] Pia Wohland et al, 'Inequalities in Healthy Life Expectancy between Ethnic Groups in England and Wales in 2001' (2015) 20 Ethnicity and Health 341.

[13] 'Neonatal and Child Mortality by Mothers' Ethnic Group and Socio-economic Status', Office for National Statistics (June 2024), <https://www.ons.gov.uk/peoplepopulationandcommunity/healthandsocialcare/childhealth/articles/neonatalandchildmortalitybymothersethnicgroupandsocioeconomicstatus/2024-06-05> (accessed 7 November 2025).

[14] 'Black People, Racism and Human Rights', Joint Committee on Human Rights, Eleventh Report of Session 2019–21 Report, https://committees.parliament.uk/publications/3376/documents/32359/default/ (accessed 7 November 2025) [45] [hereafter 'Joint Committee on Human Rights Report'].

[15] David Robinson, 'Race Equality in Housing: Tracing the Postracial Turn in English Housing Policy' (2025) 40 Housing Studies 1967.

[16] David Robinson et al, 'Ethnic Inequalities in Housing: Exploring the Policy Response' in Mark Stephens et al (eds), *2024 UK Housing Review* (Chartered Institute of Housing 2024).

[17] Glen Bramley et al, 'Homelessness Amongst Black and Minoritised Ethnic Communities in the UK: A Statistical Report on the State of the Nation' (2022) (commissioned by the Oak Foundation).

Black people are also overrepresented in crime and policing statistics. Black neighbourhoods have consistently reported over-policing and under-protection.[18] Sixty-six per cent of those subjected to 'stop and search' by the Metropolitan Police in 2023 were Black people.[19] Black people are also overrepresented in statistics of death following use of force by the police.[20] Rates of imprisonment as well as mental health detention under the Mental Health Act 1983 are highest amongst Black men.[21]

Black and minority ethnic people have been disproportionately impacted by schemes to curb immigration ('Hostile Environment'[22]) and radicalization ('Prevent'[23]). The Windrush scandal, for example, revealed the myriad ways in which members of the Windrush generation who had arrived in the UK from the Caribbean after the second world war were systematically denied access to housing, healthcare, welfare benefits, driving licenses, employment, financial services, and right to re-enter the country on the suspicion of being non-British because of their colour.[24] The extent of impact of the Hostile Environment policies such as those at the heart of the Windrush scandal remains unknown. An unidentified number of people were denied access to medical treatment because they could not prove they were British and many have died without having received the compensation they were due under the Windrush compensation scheme.[25]

Likewise, the police have failed to record accurately the ethnicity of those targeted under the Prevent scheme which puts public bodies such as schools and universities under a legal duty to identify people who may turn to extremism and intervene before an incident occurs.[26] This is despite evidence from human rights organizations that the Prevent scheme is predominantly used against Muslim boys and men and against Black and minority ethnic people.[27]

[18] William Macpherson, The Stephen Lawrence Inquiry: Report of an Inquiry, Presented to Parliament by the Secretary of State for the Home Department by Command of Her Majesty (February 1999) [45.7] [hereafter 'the Macpherson Report'].

[19] 'Stop and Search', GOV.UK (3 July 2024), https://www.ethnicity-facts-figures.service.gov.uk/crime-justice-and-the-law/policing/stop-and-search/latest/ (accessed 7 November 2025).

[20] Joint Committee on Human Rights Report (n 14) [70].

[21] ibid [39].

[22] 'Hostile Environment' refers to a set of policies pursued by successive Conservative governments since 2010 to make it life difficult for undocumented migrants, so they leave. They oblige schools, universities, employers, NHS, financial services, license providers, etc to check immigration service before offering a job or providing a service.

[23] The Prevent strategy is aimed at countering terrorism by preventing people from radical or extreme views or activities. It obliges a range of actors to report anyone at risk of radicalization.

[24] Wendy Wiliams, 'Windrush Lessons Learned Review' (March 2020).

[25] Nadine White, 'More than 50 Windrush Victims have Died While Waiting for Compensation, Government Admits' The Independent (21 January 2024).

[26] Rajeev Syal, 'Police Failed to Record Race of Nearly Two-thirds of People Referred to Prevent' The Guardian (6 February 2024).

[27] '"This is the Thought Police" The Prevent Duty and its Chilling Effect on Human Rights', Amnesty International (November 2023); Tufyal Choudhury and Helen Fenwick, 'The Impact of Counter-Terrorism Measures on Muslim communities', Equality and Human Rights Commission Research Report 72 (2011).

The Grenfell fire tragedy too impacted mainly non-white people. Of the seventy-two people who died, when the fire struck the estate in one of the most affluent neighbourhoods in London on 14 June 2017, only eleven were white British.[28]

Other events such as Brexit have both been fuelled by and led to an increase in ethnic tensions targeting Eastern Europeans in general and Gina Miller, the Black British woman, who brought a judicial challenge against Brexit, in particular.[29] The ongoing genocide in Gaza has contributed to a record rise in number of incidents of both antisemitism and Islamophobia in the UK.[30]

Anti-immigration sentiment has been stoked by policies such as the now-abandoned Rwanda scheme proposed by the Conservative government for offshore asylum processing.[31] Not only did the Rwanda Scheme effectively only apply to non-white asylum seekers from the Global South but it also offloaded UK's obligations under international law to be discharged by a country in the Global South.[32] The sentiment has culminated into racist violence on frequent display in far-right anti-immigration demonstrations that have taken place since the election of the Labour government in July 2024.[33]

Evidence can be quoted ad nauseum. But the gap in outcomes between racialized groups is obvious. Racial disadvantage for Black and minority ethnic people is rife and indisputable. Yet, evidence of racial disadvantage is often not considered evidence of racism. In fact, any connection between the two is vehemently denied. The next section explores how this transpires.

1.3 Denying Racism

In the wake of the 2020 protests which swept the world after the murders of Breonna Taylor and George Floyd in the US, the UK government established a Commission to investigate race and ethnic disparities in the UK. The report which followed in 2021, known as the 'Sewell report' named after its Chair Tony Sewell, struck a startling note. Although it found that 'in education, employment, health and crime and policing the UK can be a more inclusive and fairer landscape',[34]

[28] Mark Rice-Oxley, 'Grenfell: the 72 Victims, their Lives, their Loves and Losses' The Guardian (14 May 2018).

[29] *R (on the application of Miller) v Secretary of State for Exiting the European Union* [2017] UKSC 5; *R Miller v The Prime Minister and Cherry v Advocate General for Scotland* [2019] UKSC 41.

[30] 'Islamophobic and Anti-Semitic Hate Crimes Rising' BBC (30 December 2024), https://www.bbc.com/news/articles/cp83p4v4leno (accessed 8 November 2025).

[31] Donatella Bonansinga and Charlotte Forrest, '"Stop the Boats": Populist Contagion and Migration Policymaking in the UK' (2025) Ethnic and Racial Studies 1.

[32] Shreya Atrey, 'Why Offshore Processing of Asylum Applications is Actually Racist' Verfassugsblog (23 October 2024).

[33] David Olusoga, 'There Can Be No Excuses. The UK Riots Were Violent Racism Fomented By Populism' The Guardian (10 August 2024).

[34] Commission on Race and Ethnic Disparities: The Report (March 2021) 7 [hereafter 'the Sewell Report'].

relying on what it considered 'more forensic and rigorous understanding of underlying causes of disparities',[35] it concluded:

> Put simply we no longer see a Britain where the system is deliberately rigged against ethnic minorities. The impediments and disparities do exist, they are varied, and ironically very few of them are directly to do with racism....The evidence shows that geography, family influence, socio-economic background, culture and religion have more significant impact on life chances than the existence of racism.[36]
>
> We found that most of the disparities we examined, which some attribute to racial discrimination, often do not have their origins in racism. Racism has become one of the most potent taboos in the UK, which was not the case 50 years ago. Some argue this has just driven it underground where it operates as powerfully as ever to deny equality to ethnic minorities. That assumption is at odds with the stories of success that this report has found, together with evidence of dwindling White prejudice.[37]
>
> The idea that all ethnic minority people suffer a common fate and a shared disadvantage is an anachronism.[38]

The Sewell Report thus consigned racism to the past. The Commission's understanding was that racism was an ideology, expressed in the form of prejudice by white people against Black people and ethnic minorities in the UK. Such racism was long bygone as the UK had 'fundamentally shifted' to 'become a more open society'.[39] The Commission acknowledged that there was racial disadvantage across its four areas of study—education and training; employment, fairness at work, and enterprise; crime and policing; and health.[40] But it was categorical that racial disadvantage did not mean racism. While more could be done to make Britain, which was already 'a model for other White-majority countries',[41] 'racially fair', there was nothing to be done to make it anti-racist.[42]

Anti-racism, according to the Commission, was pure hysteria. The Commission identified 'an increasingly strident form of anti-racism thinking that seeks to explain all minority disadvantage through the prism of White discrimination'.[43] This form of anti-racism, the Commission averred, 'diverts attention from the other reasons for minority success and failure, including those embedded in the cultures

[35] ibid 8.
[36] ibid.
[37] ibid 11.
[38] ibid 27.
[39] ibid 7.
[40] ibid 10.
[41] ibid 9.
[42] ibid 8.
[43] ibid 10.

and attitudes of those minority communities themselves'.[44] The Commission regretted, that 'too many people in the progressive and anti-racism movements' such as Black Lives Matter, were 'importing bleak new theories about race that insist on accentuating our differences while being reluctant to acknowledge their own past achievements, and they offer solutions based on the binary divides of the past which often misses the point of today's world'.[45] This, the Commission attributed to a generational divide, and the naivety of the young in adopting 'fatalistic' narratives:

> We were established as a response to the upsurge of concern about race issues instigated by the BLM movement. And we owe the mainly young people behind that movement a debt of gratitude for focusing our attention once again on these issues. But most of us come from an older generation whose views were formed by growing up in the 1970s and 1980s. And our experience has taught us that you do not pass on the baton of progress by cleaving to a fatalistic account that insists nothing has changed.[46]

Racism was thus considered not only bygone but also as existing today just as a matter of perception. This perception could be changed, for example, through 'reclaiming British heritage' by showing 'how Britishness influenced the Commonwealth and local communities, and how the Commonwealth and local communities influenced what we now know as modern Britain. One great example would be a dictionary or lexicon of well known British words which are Indian in origin.'[47]

The Commission gave no actual examples of such words. Had the Commission looked, it would have found that one of the first words that entered the British lexicon from Hindi was *loot*. The context of its entry was obviously the loot of the then richest nation in the world—India—first by the East India Company and then by the British Raj. The Sewell Report however said nothing of colonialism, imperialism, or racialized capitalism.

In fact, the Report did not say much about structures at all. 'Structural racism', for the Commission, had its 'roots in a critique of capitalism, which states that racism is inextricably linked to capitalism. So by that definition, until that system is abolished racism will flourish. Many are using "Structural Racism" to mean deep-seated exclusion rather than the tearing down of capitalism.'[48] Yet, the Report went on to define structural racism very much in terms of deep-seated exclusion

[44] ibid.
[45] ibid 233.
[46] ibid.
[47] ibid 8.
[48] ibid 36.

as opposed to capitalism.[49] No justification was offered for conceiving structural racism as either deep-seated exclusion or capitalism. In fact, no other mention of structural racism was made in the 258-page-long Report—the lengthiest and latest official report on racism in the UK to date.

The important point for the Commission was that structural racism had nothing to do with either racism or racial disadvantage. Racism, as understood by the Commission, was 'overt and outright racism' witnessed 'as graffiti on someone's business, violence in the street, or prejudice in the labour market'.[50] Racial disadvantage, as understood by the Commission, signified 'persistent ethnic differential outcomes'.[51] According to the Commission, the use of 'prefixes like institutional, structural and systemic' in describing either racism or racial disadvantage was 'confusing' and 'adding to the problem'.[52] The Commission was firm that it could not 'afford for the term [racism] to become misunderstood or trivialised'.[53]

The simple solution it devised was to define racism narrowly as ideology and specifically as overt prejudice.[54] Structural racism, discussed at mere two places recounted above, had nothing to do with racism then. Importantly, racial disadvantage too had nothing to do with racism.[55] This was despite the fact that the Commission was set up to 'investigate the deeper underlying causes of key disparities'[56] and 'why so many disparities persist'.[57] While admitting that 'the roots of advantage and disadvantage for different groups are complex',[58] the Commission was convinced that the roots had 'often as much to do with social class, "family" culture and geography as ethnicity'.[59] In fact, it found 'much evidence to suggest' that 'more than anything else' 'different experiences of family life and structure can explain many disparities in education outcomes and crime'.[60] In other areas such as health, where disparities were still stark, the Commission rejected 'the common view that ethnic minorities have universally worse health outcomes compared with White people'.[61] Given that on some health indicators, ethnic minorities did better than white people, the Commission was assured that there was 'more than one story to tell'.[62] The story it told was this:

[49] Structural racism, according to the Sewell Report, was 'to describe a legacy of historic racist or discriminatory processes, policies, attitudes or behaviours that continue to shape organisations and societies today'. ibid.
[50] ibid 9, 29.
[51] ibid 36.
[52] ibid 34.
[53] ibid.
[54] ibid 36.
[55] ibid.
[56] ibid 6.
[57] ibid.
[58] ibid.
[59] ibid.
[60] ibid 7, 11.
[61] ibid 199.
[62] ibid 11.

> Another example of overly pessimistic narratives, heightened by the COVID-19 pandemic, has been on race and health. The increased age-adjusted risk of death from COVID-19 in Black and South Asian groups has widely been reported as being due to racism—and as exacerbating existing health inequalities. However many analyses have shown that the increased risk of dying from COVID-19 is mainly due to an increased risk of exposure to infection. This is attributed to the facts that Black and South Asian people are more likely to live in urban areas with higher population density and levels of deprivation; work in higher risk occupations such as healthcare or transport; and to live with older relatives who themselves are at higher risk due to their age or having other comorbidities such as diabetes and obesity.[63]

What lay behind 'an increased risk of exposure to infection'? Why were Black and South Asian people 'more likely to live in urban areas with higher population density and levels of deprivation; work in higher risk occupation such as healthcare or transport; and to live with older relatives who themselves are at higher risk due to their age or having other comorbidities such as diabetes and obesity'? Arguably, structural causes lay behind these by the Commission's own definition of structural racism ('legacy of historic racist or discriminatory processes, policies, attitudes or behaviours that continue to shape organisations and societies today'[64]).[65] But the Commission did not examine this even though its mandate was to understand 'underlying causes of disparities'[66] or 'drivers of ethnic difference'.[67] Having dismissed structural racism from the definition of racism which was restricted to ideology and specifically prejudice,[68] the root causes or drivers of racism were comfortably excluded from the Sewell Report.

This then cleared the path for the Commission to deny racism in the UK.[69] A denial that has been widely condemned as 'divisive',[70] 'disappointing',[71] 'a tone-deaf

[63] ibid 30, 199, 218–222.

[64] ibid 36.

[65] Michael Marmot, 'The Sewell Report Cited My Work – Just Not the Parts Highlighting Structural Racism' UCL News (8 April 2021), https://www.ucl.ac.uk/news/2021/apr/opinion-sewell-report-cited-my-work-just-not-parts-highlighting-structural-racism (accessed 23 October 2025).

[66] The Sewell Report (n 34) 10.

[67] ibid.

[68] In fact, in the only example the Commission gave of the kind of evidence required to prove institutional or structural racism it reduced even those concepts to prejudice: 'Imagine a world with just 2 groups in which both are equally prejudiced, but the minority forms just 10% of the population. When it comes to hiring, the potential prejudice faced by a minority applicant will be much greater than the potential prejudice against an applicant from the majority. But this structural imbalance is measurable through using surveys of individual prejudice, and tests of aggregate prejudices, such as curriculum vitae (CV) studies.' ibid 35.

[69] ibid 45–47.

[70] Aamna Mohdin, Peter Walker, and Nazia Parveen, 'No 10's Race Report Widely Condemned as "Divisive"' The Guardian (31 March 2021).

[71] John Johnston, 'Keir Starmer Is "Disappointed" At Race Report Findings For Failing To Accept "Structural" Problems' PoliticsHome (31 March 2021).

attempt at rejecting the lived realities of people of African descent and other ethnic minorities in the UK',[72] and 'a marked departure from the overwhelming body of evidence of structural racism [that] seeks to turn back the clock on race equality'.[73]

The denial of racism is not new. Narrow definitions of racism as ideology or animus have been used to deny institutional and structural racism only because they do not fit the definitions of racism.[74] This is especially the case when the evidence of racial disadvantage is overwhelming. Narrow definitions which exclude institutional and structural racism come particularly handy in denying the link between racial disadvantage on the one hand and institutional and structural racism on the other hand.

Thus, in the first major report commissioned by the UK Government to inquire into the causes of the 1981 Brixton riots, Leslie Scarman famously proclaimed: '"Institutional racism" does not exist in Britain: but racial disadvantage and its nasty associate, racial discrimination, have not yet been eliminated'.[75] According to the Scarman Report, it was not institutional racism but racial disadvantage and racial discrimination which 'poison[ed] minds and attitudes' and thus were 'a potent factor of unrest'.[76] Racism, understood as 'deliberate bias or prejudice',[77] even if occasionally visible, was ultimately considered absent from the police force as a whole.[78]

Vast socio-economic deprivation concentrated around some racialized communities, such as found in Tony Gifford's Broadwater Farm Inquiry Report which investigated the 1985 riots at the Broadwater Farm Estate in Tottenham, has been opposed but not as a matter of racism which is reduced to racial hatred.[79] In fact, the language of racism has mostly been avoided. For example, John Denham's Building Cohesive Communities Report following the violent racial clashes in Bradford in 2001, skirted around the language of racism while trying to address it all the same by discussing issues of segregation and Islamophobia.[80]

This shifted with the 1999 Macpherson Report following the inquiry into Stephen Lawrence's murder. The Macpherson Report dedicated a whole chapter

[72] 'UN Experts Condemn UK Commission on Race and Ethnic Disparities Report', Statement by independent experts of the Special Procedures of the United Nations Human Rights Council (19 April 2021).

[73] Aubrey Allegretti, 'Equality Watchdog Raised Concerns About UK Race Report, Documents Show' The Guardian (22 April 2021) (quoting Marsha de Cordova, the then shadow equalities secretary) [hereafter Allegretti, 'Equality Watchdog Raised Concerns About UK'].

[74] Ann Dummett, 'Correspondence' (1972) 13 Race 359.

[75] Leslie Scarman, 'The Scarman Report: Report of an Inquiry' (Presented to Parliament by the Secretary of State for the Home Department by command of Her Majesty, November 1981) 209 [hereafter 'the Scarman Report'].

[76] ibid.

[77] ibid 64.

[78] ibid.

[79] Tony Gifford, 'The Broadwater Farm Inquiry: Report of the Independent Inquiry into Disturbances of October 1985 at the Broadwater Farm Estate, Tottenham' (Karia Press 1986) 29.

[80] John Denham, 'Building Cohesive Communities Report' (2001).

to understanding the concept of 'racism'[81] and consciously moved beyond racism understood as 'overt racism or discrimination'[82] and instead understood racism as 'racism in general terms consists of conduct or words or practices which disadvantage or advantage people because of their colour, culture, or ethnic origin'.[83] In particular, it concentrated on the 'more subtle' version of 'institutional racism' and its impact on police delivery 'not solely through the deliberate actions of a small number of bigoted individuals, but through a more systematic tendency that could unconsciously influence police performance generally'.[84] The Macpherson Report today is celebrated for its adoption of the term and acknowledgement of the reality of institutional racism. Its prior move adopting a disadvantage-based understanding of racism is often missed. But it was this prior move marking a shift in the understanding of racism that opened the door to recognizing institutional racism (but still not structural racism).[85]

This shift in the understanding of racism going beyond prejudice and towards racial disadvantage was noted, for example, in the 2007 Equalities Review which investigated the causes of persistent discrimination and inequality in British society, in the following terms:

> In 1999, the gradual trend towards *focusing less on individual acts of prejudice* and *more on the way in which systems and organisations routinely disadvantaged entire categories of people* reached its most radical, and controversial, stage. Prompted by a sustained community campaign led by the family of the murdered teenager Stephen Lawrence, the report of the Macpherson Inquiry introduced the term 'institutional racism' to Britain. Though widely misinterpreted to mean that all individuals in an institution should be regarded as racist, a close reading of the report shows that the idea behind the term was exactly the reverse: that even where there was good will and substantial effort by individuals to eliminate different kinds of discrimination, *the rules, culture and habits of a particular body could frustrate efforts to stamp out disadvantage.*[86]

Yet, despite the Macpherson Report, while official studies dedicated exclusively to racial issues discuss racial disadvantage at length, they steer clear of the language of racism itself. Where racism is invoked, it is invoked in pre-Macpherson terms of understanding racism as ideology or animus.

For example, in the 2017 Lammy Review dedicated to studying the treatment and outcomes of Black, Asian, and Minority Ethnic (BAME) individuals

[81] The Macpherson Report (n 18).
[82] ibid [6.3].
[83] ibid [6.4].
[84] ibid [6.5].
[85] Chapter 2 maps the difference between institutional and structural racism.
[86] 'Fairness and Freedom: The Final Report of the Equalities Review' (2007) 35 (emphasis supplied).

in the UK's criminal justice system, the term racism appears only three times in 108 pages, and is preceded by the words 'perceptions', 'accusations', and 'covert', giving the impression that racism is a mirage.[87] Similarly, the 2017 McGregor-Smith Review on race in the workplace uses the term racism four times prefaced with 'outright' and 'overt'.[88] While it distinguishes such racism from 'unconscious bias' which it considers 'much more pervasive and potentially more insidious' in the twenty-first century,[89] it does not bring up terms such as institutional or structural racism at all.

In contrast, the 2017 Report of the Independent Review of Deaths and Serious Incidents in Police Custody by Elish Angiolini is more liberal in its references to terms like 'systemic racism' and 'institutional racism'.[90] Yet, once again, it explains away the disproportionate number of Black people dying following use of force by police, as falling outside its understanding of racism:

> It is difficult to be able to prove that racism was a factor in deaths in police custody unless sufficient evidence exists and racism can be inferred from the specific facts and circumstances of that case or from a series of such cases of a similar nature arising from the conduct of the suspended officer. Racial stereotyping may or may not be a significant contributory factor in some deaths in custody.[91]

The latest and most comprehensive review of the Equality and Human Rights Commission (EHRC) completed in 2023 makes no mention of systemic, institutional, or structural racism, except in its reference to the Sewell Report which was understood as acknowledging that:

> Poverty and geography are important factors in inequalities experienced by all ethnic groups. These factors can be compounded by others that disproportionately affect some ethnic minorities, such as cultural differences, stereotyping, power imbalances and discrimination, some of which can lead to structural racial inequalities.[92]

[87] The Lammy Review: An independent review into the treatment of, and outcomes for, Black, Asian, and Minority Ethnic individuals in the Criminal Justice System (2017) 52, 69.

[88] Department for Business, Energy and Industrial Strategy, 'Race in the Workplace: The McGregor-Smith Review – Report' (2017).

[89] ibid.

[90] Giles Lindon and Stephen Roe, 'Deaths in Police Custody: A Review of the International Evidence', Research Report 95, Home Office (2017) 84, 85, 89, 93, 244.

[91] ibid 87.

[92] 'Equality and Human Rights Monitor', Equality and Human Rights Commission, Presented to the Parliament pursuant to Section 12 of the Equality Act 2006 as amended by the Enterprise and Regulatory Reform Act 2013 (November 2023) 152.

In fact, before the publication of the Sewell Report, the EHRC's guidance to the Commission was to:

> understand the persistence of structural inequalities, we need to look beyond the prejudices held by individuals and consider the role of systemic factors, including systemic racism—which can be seen in what might be thought to be neutral policies or practices that operate to the disadvantage of certain groups in a number of areas, such as health, employment and justice.[93]

Indeed, shortly after the publication of the Sewell Report, even Tony Sewell admitted that: 'We believe racism exists. It exists in institutions, it exists in structures, it exists across the piece. And we have found that in the report.'[94] A similar admission was made forty years ago in the Scarman Report regarding the 'structural causes' for employment, which were considered 'deeper and more complex'.[95]

The official narrative of racism in the UK is thus marked by the paradox where racism is denied but racial disadvantage is not. Furthermore, while at some points the relationship between the two is also denied, at other points it is accepted. Occasionally, when the relationship is accepted, it is often accepted, in structural terms. The denial and the admission of racism as structural racism are thus co-extensive, distinguished only by definitional preferences for racism as either ideology or disadvantage, respectively.

1.4 Defining Racism

This book is dedicated to developing an anti-racist framework in law which addresses structural racism. To do that, the next chapter develops a tripartite framework of racism as including interpersonal, institutional, and structural racism. But as Section 1.3 argued, such a framework of racism relies on a prior understanding of racism which is broader than racism as ideology or animus and includes racism as racial disadvantage. This section explains the preference for the latter. However, in understanding racism as racial disadvantage, this section does not seek to define racism in any essentialist or exclusive way. It only seeks to stabilize the reference to the term 'racism' as including and not excluding racial disadvantage. It thus explains racism as including racial disadvantage (Section 1.4.1), defined not by ideology (Section 1.4.2) but by processes of racialization (Section 1.4.3).

[93] Allegretti, 'Equality Watchdog Raised Concerns About UK' (n 73).
[94] 'Racism Exists in Structures, Says Sewell' (30 April 2021), https://www.britishfuture.org/racism-exists-in-structures-says-sewell/ (accessed 26 October 2025).
[95] The Scarman Report (n 75) 205, 110.

1.4.1 Capturing Disadvantage

It is useful to take the understanding of the Macpherson Report as the starting point: 'racism in general terms consists of conduct or words or practices which disadvantage or advantage people because of their colour, culture, or ethnic origin.'[96]

This general understanding of racism has two elements: first, of disadvantage; and second, of racial grounds, such as colour, culture, ethnic origin, etc. Racism in this sense is simply *disadvantage which accrues on racial grounds*. This disadvantage-based understanding of racism can serve as the baseline for discussions around race, racism, and anti-racism.[97]

The disadvantage-based understanding of racism marks a break from the now debunked biology-based understanding where racism 'generally refers to the belief that there are clearly distinguishable human races; that these refer not only to physical characteristics, but also to psychological traits and that races can be arranged in a hierarchy of superiority and inferiority relative to one another'.[98]

The disadvantage-based understanding of racism also marks a break from the ideology-based understanding where racism is understood as 'prejudice, antagonism, or discrimination by an individual, institution, or society, against a person or people on the basis of their nationality or (now usually) their membership of a particular racial or ethnic group, typically one that is a minority or marginalized'.[99]

Much of the intellectual history of the term racism is traced back to either biology-based or ideology-based understandings. For example, Benjamin Bowser traced the term racism in social sciences first to Ruth Benedict's *Race and Racism* (1945) and then Edmund Soper's *Racism: A World Issue* (1947),[100] both primarily directed at describing treatment motivated by prejudiced beliefs often based in turn on false ideas of biology. In the following decades, much of the usage of the term continued along similar lines especially in the context of Nazi Germany, apartheid South Africa and Jim Crow US. Though gradually, attention turned towards using racism to understand the vast advantage gaps between racialized groups. This was because racism as biology was now debunked, and racism as prejudice was increasingly being prohibited through constitutions, statutes, policies, etc. Yet, the material conditions of some racialized groups did not look much better

[96] The Macpherson Report (n 18) [6.4].

[97] Michael Banton and Robert Miles in Ellis Cashmore (ed), *Dictionary of Race and Ethnic Relations* (Routledge 1994) 308–309 ('racism denotes the whole complex of factors which produce racial discrimination, and sometimes, more loosely, designates also those which produce racial disadvantage'); Shirley Better, *Institutional Racism: A Primer on Theory and Strategies for Social Change* (Rowman and Littlefield 2008) 10 ('Racism is an individual act or institutional practice that perpetuates inequality, based on racial membership.').

[98] Sheila Allen, 'The Institutionalization of Racism' (1973) 15 Race and Class 99.

[99] 'Racism', Oxford English Dictionary, <https://www.oed.com/dictionary/racism_n?tab=meaning_and_use#27242931> (accessed 5 March 2024).

[100] Benjamin P Bowser, 'Racism: Origin and Theory' (2017) 48 Journal of Black Studies 572, 573 [hereafter Bowser, 'Racism'].

than when racism was not formally condemned.[101] This is where the meaning of racism started to shift from denoting biology of or prejudice against racialized groups to the predominance advantage gaps between racialized groups.[102]

There is then a broad understanding of racism in the contemporary discourse where racism denotes the predominance of disadvantage for some racialized groups as compared to others (where disadvantage is defined broadly to connote disadvantage which is social, economic, material, political, cultural, psychic, legal, etc).[103] In other words, racism implies inequality of outcomes between racialized groups—whether it is indiscriminate police brutality against Black and minority ethnic people or the predominance of people from the Global South in the global migration numbers or differential health outcomes or attainment gaps in education of Black and minority ethnic people. In this sense, racism conveys 'an empirical fact'[104] about racial disadvantage.

It is in this very sense that I have used the term racism so far and will continue to in the rest of the book.

1.4.2 Rejecting Ideology

A disadvantage-based understanding of racism does not denote racism as ideology, not because racism cannot be based on ideology but because the basis of racism in ideology appears both limited in capturing all possible instances of racism and immaterial to the consequences of racism. It is thus unhelpful to focus on ideology-based as opposed to empirically and materially grounded disadvantage-based understandings of racism.

Defining racism as a state of mind or ideology makes it appear as if racism arises out of an entity's—often an individual—mental processes divorced from the social, cultural, political, economic, geographical, or other context. In this frame, racism becomes entirely aberrational—there being little connection between different instances of racism since their origin lies solely in the minds of particular entities. Defining racism thus devolves into a search for racists or entities with racist ideologies.[105] How racial ideologies come to arise—or be embedded in minds of

[101] Peter B Levy, *The Civil Rights Movement* (Greenwood Press 1998).

[102] Kwame Ture and Charles V Hamilton, *Black Power: The Politics of Liberation in America* (Random 1992).

[103] A Sivanandan, 'Race, Class and the State: The Black Experience in Britain' (1976) 17 Race and Class 347, 358 ('But racism is not its own justification. It is necessary only for the purpose of exploitation: you discriminate in order to exploit or, which is the same thing, you exploit by discriminating. So that any other system of discrimination, say on the basis of nationality, would – if available – do equally well.').

[104] Bowser, 'Racism' (n 100) 580.

[105] Ali Rattansi, *Racism: A Very Short Introduction* (OUP 2007) 2 ('one of the main impediments to progress in understanding racism has been the willingness of all involved to propose short, supposedly water-tight definitions of racism and to identify quickly and with more or less complete certainty who is really racist and who is not.').

individuals or within institutions and the larger society—is then treated as a separate matter of failure of socialization or education in the case of the particular entity, or as a sheer inexplicability.

Such a treatment of racism is underinclusive because of its focus on a subjective view of racism based on animus (malice, prejudice, stereotypes, stigma, etc). It excludes benign, paternalistic, or well-reasoned racism from its ambit. For example, it would exclude a pub owner's rational decision to not employ a Black bartender for concern over their safety from a predominantly white clientele which the owner knows to be hostile towards Black people. It would also exclude a police force's decision to patrol only low-income neighbourhoods because it believes that poverty and depravation lead to crime, even though this leads to over-policing of predominantly Black and minority ethnic neighbourhoods.

These examples can be explained as examples of racism via an objective view which is not dependent on the motives—benign or malign—of the perpetrator. This objective view may be found in the way race or racial grounds are invoked by the perpetrator irrespective of their motives. That is, one could look into explicit/implicit or overt/covert ways in which race or racial grounds appear in the perpetrator's reasoning. Racism could then be identified by a perpetrator's reliance on racial grounds.

The first example may now be explained as racism because irrespective of the pub owner's motive, they seem to deploy colour explicitly in their decision not to hire the Black person. An objective view may also explain instances where a pub owner uses names or immigrant status as proxies for race or colour.

But whether racial grounds are apparent or concealed, an objective view will not help explain the second example as an example of racism. Where a police force is led by higher statistics of crime in a low-income neighbourhood, their decision to patrol only that neighbourhood may not have anything to do with race or racial grounds, other than in its effect on a racial group. Thus, neither a subjective nor an objective view of racism seems to explain racism in this instance, or in instances where racism seems to have taken effect as a result of the Hostile Environment Policy, Brexit, the Windrush scandal, or the Rwanda scheme. It appears that neither prejudice nor reliance on race or racial grounds may be key to the enactment of racism in cases such as when the police use income levels or crime statistics to effectively patrol only Black and minority ethnic neighbourhoods, or when passports are to be shown before receiving NHS treatment or renting a house, or when only asylum seekers from the Global South are subjected to the Rwanda scheme.

A perpetrator's subjective or objective view thus does not seem to be a criterial element for understanding racism after all, or at least all cases of racism. What seems instead to be the case is the statistical evidence of a pattern of disparity in outcomes between racialized groups where members of some racialized groups are rendered worse off than members of other racialized groups.[106] This disparity—which is an empirical fact—in each of the instances in the previous section is what is at the heart of the conception of racism as disadvantage, where disadvantage is broadly conceived to include all kinds of disparities to do with physical, mental, material, psychic, political, economic, social, and cultural well-being of people.

This empirical view of racism as disadvantage is however just the starting point. While it is true that, 'in its most general and unspecified way, the term [racism] refers to any situation in which groups, socially defined as races, are systematically disadvantaged in respect of social rewards, capacities or opportunities',[107] it is also the case that the term then becomes, as David Mason correctly observes, 'simply another way of describing the situation. It adds nothing to our understanding of the mechanisms of such disadvantage or of the means of combatting them.'[108] Likewise, as Floya Anthias observes, 'in order to understand racism (as opposed to sorting out empirically who are its targets at any particular point of time), it is important to focus on processes, structures and outcomes'.[109]

I will turn to 'the means of combatting' racism as anti-racism in Chapter 3 but here, in order to give some conceptual foundation to the meaning of racism, it is useful to think about the 'mechanisms' or 'processes, structures and outcomes' of racism, including the racial grounds on which racial disadvantage comes about.

1.4.3 Regarding Racialization

The mechanisms which give rise to racism have been described as 'processes of racialization'.[110] Racialization (also referred to as racialism) is racial definition or racial classification, that is, the placement of people in racial categories.[111] Racialization as a term represents processes through which race and racial hierarchy come into being. Racialization is thus the precursor to both race and racism. This idea deserves some unpacking.

106 Robert Staples, 'Race and Colonialism: The Domestic Case in Theory and Practice' (1976) 7 The Black Scholar 37, 42 ('Racism refers not to individual attitudes but to the pattern of domination in a society.').

107 David Mason, 'After Scarman: A Note on the Concept of 'Institutional Racism' (1982) 10 Journal of Ethnic and Migration Studies 38, 43; Sandra Fredman (ed), *Discrimination and Human Rights: The Case of Racism* (OUP 2021) 10 ('Racism is ... about relationships of domination and subordination').

108 ibid.

109 Floya Anthias, 'Institutional Racism, Power and Accountability' (1999) 4 Sociological Research Online [5.10].

110 Stephen Small, *Racialised Barriers: The Black Experience in the United States and England in the 1980s* (Routledge 1994).

111 David Theo Goldberg, *Racist Culture* (Blackwell 1993) 50 (describing racialization as 'the ordering of human groups on the basis of putatively natural (inherited or environmental) differences') [hereafter Goldberg, *Racist Culture*].

First, racialization is how race comes into being. Although race is often identified as phenotype or colour or through certain physical characteristics like hair texture or facial features, it is not a characteristic which is inherent in or intrinsic to humans in any biological or physical sense. As Bonilla-Silva remarks: 'the selection of certain human traits to designate a racial group is always socially rather than biologically based.'[112] What makes race or racialized groups is then the processes of racialization which induct meaning into physical and other characteristics which define human body and life such that *that* induction then *becomes* race. Racialization thus mediates the creation of race. Without it, racial markers, such as colour, hair texture, or facial features, have no inherent racial meaning of their own. It is racialization which codes racial meaning into phenotype, which then results into race as an idea, and in turn racialized groups based on different races.

Still, some may argue, phenotype carries some objective truth. For example, colour is something observable and provable as a matter of optics. Likewise, descent or lineage can be traced back and to particular families and clans or physical locations and parts of the world. Irrespective of what meaning we ascribe to colour, lineage, and location, it is arguable that these are indeed physical properties.

That though appears irrelevant in these categories serving as the basis of racialization in a social sense as there is no correlation between physical properties and their hierarchical categorization in terms of superiority and inferiority. That is, colour, lineage, and location in a physical sense do not themselves reveal anything which aids in hierarchizing different phenotypes, physical features, ancestry, or places of origin as per se better or worse in a social sense. Such a correlation does not exist and has been conclusively debunked as the falsehood of biological or scientific racism.

Just as race as physical characteristics or aesthetics (colour, hair texture, facial features, etc) has no inherent racial meaning, other racial grounds such as ethnicity or ethnic origin too have no biological basis, but are based on, as Max Weber argued, *the subjective perception* of a common trait,[113] or as Richard Jenkins put it 'the *belief* shared by [members of a so-called ethnic group] that, however distantly, they are of common descent'.[114] Membership in ethnic communities are a result of communities organizing themselves around racialized beliefs.[115] Indeed, all 'cultural stuff'[116]—language, ritual, religion, kinship, economic division of labour,

[112] Eduardo Bonilla-Silva, 'Rethinking Racism: Toward a Structural Interpretation' (1997) 62 American Sociological Review 465, 469.

[113] Max Weber, *Economy and Society* (Guenther Roth and Claus Wittich (trans), University of California Pres 1978) 385.

[114] Richard Jenkins, *Rethinking Ethnicity: Arguments and Explorations* (2nd edn, Sage 2018) 10 (emphasis in original).

[115] Floya Anthias, 'Connecting "Race" and Ethnic Phenomena' (1992) 26 Sociology 421, 433 ('A group does not have to be depicted as a "race" ... to be subjected to racist practices or effects. My view is that all those exclusionary practices that are formulated on the basis of the categorisation of individuals into groups, whereby ethnic or 'racial' origin are criteria of access or selection, are endemically racist.').

[116] ibid 10–11.

lifestyle, familial relationships, etc—provides the basis for communities to form and for ethnic groups to generate, circulate, and proliferate. This does not mean that ethnicity—lacking objectivity of its own—can simply be identified through proxies of cultural artefacts like language, clothing, or diets. That would be unnecessary reductionism.[117]

The point is this: culture, ethnicity, and ethnic origin (also relatedly, nationality and national origin), like phenotype, are empty to begin with and indeed *become* racialized categories of social analysis through processes of racialization or meaning-giving in racial terms.[118] This racialization spans across registers including moral, religious, political, legal, linguistic, religious, psychic, economic, cultural, etc. These registers play on each other to produce what ultimately emerges as race—an umbrella category or 'a "code" that takes on specific meanings and obtains its social force only in particular contexts of use and utterance'.[119]

Therefore, there is no reason for us to make a distinction between racial grounds which are physical and those which are not. All racial grounds are 'virtually vacuous'.[120] Conceptually, race as a family concept—which embodies all racial grounds—should thus be understood as a result of processes of racialization which hierarchize people into racial categories based on a whole range of markers which are often physical and cultural but could also be moral, religious, political, legal, linguistic, religious, psychic, and economic markers.

This version of race—which leaves open the meaning of race to the particular context of racialization under consideration—may leave some discomfited. It may be said that this version generalizes to the extent that any category such as gender or disability could be collapsed into race if race is after all a result of processes of hierarchization based on a range of variables. And this is actually correct (though not collapsible).

Gender and disability are the same as race though the exact variables and their use in the processes of hierarchization based on each varies. Thus, while racial categorizations may be based on variables such as colour or hair texture, gender-based categorizations may rely on sex characteristics, appearances, social roles, etc, and disability-based categorizations may be based on a range of physical and mental attributes of embodiment and their interaction with social barriers. The variables and how they matter to render categories like race, gender, and disability

117 Chapters 2 and 3 critique the 'cultural' turn in understanding racism and anti-racism.
118 Ian F Haney López, 'The Social Construction of Race: Some Observations on Illusion, Fabrication, and Choice' (1994) 29 Harvard Civil Rights–Civil Liberties Law Review 1.
119 Julian Go, '"Racism" and Colonialism: Meanings of Difference and Ruling Practices in America's Pacific Empire' (2004) 27 Qualitative Sociology 35; Paul Gilroy, 'The End of Anti-Racism' (1990) 17 Journal of Ethnic and Migration Studies 71, 72 ('Culture and identity are part of the story of racial sensibility but they do not exhaust that story. At a theoretical level "race" needs to be viewed much more contingently, as a precarious discursive construction.').
120 David Theo Goldberg, 'The Semantics of Race' (1992) 15 Ethnic and Racial Studies 543. It should be obvious that this argument cannot be equated with the denial of race in a social sense and the demand to banish race and racial categories semantically from the discourse of law.

alive differ, but the mechanism is the same: that variables are being brought up and into being *as categories* like race, gender, and disability through processes like racialization. These categories are not really categories which are out there in some objective sense existing in an unmediated or pre-discursive way. They are instead created across social, political, economic, and cultural registers and made to seem like objective categories to begin with. Ultimately, race is only that which is 'invoked in the name of race'.[121]

With all that said about racialization and race, it is useful to turn to racialization and racism. Although racialization is the basis of the idea of race and racial groups, it need not automatically imply racial hierarchy or racism. As Anthias has argued: 'the separation of human populations according to a notion of human stock difference, the characteristic mark of the construct of race, need not posit a hierarchy of groups.'[122]

While that may be conceptually accurate, the reality is that the construction of race through processes of racialization has been for the project of dividing people into superior and inferior races.[123] Goldberg explains the seamless way in which this has transpired:

> classification is central to scientific methodology, and scientific method has long been taken as the ideal model of rationality. The capacity for rationality, in turn, was considered the mark of humanity. It seemed obviously to follow that the anthropological ordering into a system of races in terms of rational capacity would establish a *hierarchy* of humankind. The race represented by the classifiers was assumed as a matter of course to stand at the hierarchical apex. Racial ordering accordingly implied a racial hierarchy and a behavioral expectation. The rational hierarchy was thought to be revealed through its physical, its natural, correlates: skin color, head shape, body size, smell, hair texture, and the like.[124]

Race then emerges as a result of racist articulation via the processes of racialization. In this formulation, racism as prejudice precedes race because racialization which is the placement of actors in racial categories, that is, races, may itself be considered racist because it is brought up for the purpose of hierarchizing and elevating dominant racial groups at the expense of others.[125] The result is that

[121] Goldberg, *Racist Culture* (n 111) 2.

[122] Floya Anthias, 'Race and Class Revisited - Conceptualising Race and Racisms' (1990) 38 Sociological Review 19, 22.

[123] Michael Banton, *The Idea of Race* (Routledge 2019) chs 2–3 (presenting a historical account of racialization in Europe and the World).

[124] Goldberg, *Racist Culture* (n 111) 50 (emphasis in original).

[125] Bhikhu Parekh, 'The Future of Multi-Ethnic Britain: Reporting on a Report' (2001) 90 The Round Table 691, 693 ('Racism creates races by turning open, overlapping, loosely structured and internally differentiated groups into closed and rigid natural or quasi-natural types, and hierarchically grading them on the basis of what are mistakenly believed to be neutral and universal criteria.').

race ultimately is, as David Mason says, 'predicated on the existence of racism',[126] or as Goldberg says, 'a discursive object of racialized discourse'[127] which 'creates the conceptual conditions of possibility, in some conjunctural conditions, for racist expression to be formulated'.[128]

Either way, whether race precedes racism or vice versa, the basis of both is racialization. The specificities of how racialization comes about in actuality, to create race, racist ideology, and racial disadvantage, are what make studies on racism revealing in both an empirical and epistemic sense.[129] This book contributes to unravelling the specificities of racialization in the legal register to understand how law partakes in the production, reproduction, and also deproduction of race, racist ideology, and racial disadvantage, that is, how law serves as a site for processes of racialization.

Because the specificities of racialization differ a great deal, the book neither assumes nor shows that the legal discourse represents a single, coherent, or fixed understanding of racism that applies transhistorically across contexts. Instead, it conceives of racism (and later anti-racism) as a polysemic and intersectional concept. This means that, first, racism is subjective and represents an empirical fact in the particular conditions in which it arises through processes of racialization and thus is capable of multiple meanings not only across time and context but also at any given point in a particular context.[130] Second, racism is co-determined by disadvantages based on other categories—such as gender, class, disability, age, and sexuality—such that there is no pure or authentic category of racism which is distinct from how other hierarchical systems of oppression, such as sexism, classism, ableism, ageism, homophobia, and transphobia, transpire.[131]

These features, far from rendering racism unstable and irrelevant, render it potent and eternal. The very fact that racism can have multiple meanings across time and context and that those meanings are interspersed by other forms of oppression makes it difficult for racism to be pinned down as one thing. Likewise, since racism exists not as a sealed social category of experience but one that is shaped by other

[126] David Mason, 'On the Dangers of Disconnecting Race and Racism' (1994) 28 Sociology 845, 849.

[127] Goldberg, *Racist Culture* (n 111) 42.

[128] ibid.

[129] Floya Anthias and Nira Yuval-Davis, *Racialized Boundaries: Race, Nation, Gender, Colour and Class and the Anti-Racist Struggle* (Routledge 1992) ('Racism ... cannot be seen as derivative of race or ethnic phenomena but needs to be understood with reference to the discourses and practices by which ethnic groups are inferiorized, excluded and subordinated. These meet a diverse number of political and economic projects.').

[130] Devon W Carbado and Cheryl I Harris, 'Intersectionality at 30: Mapping the Margins of Anti-Essentialism, Intersectionality, and Dominance Theory' (2019) 132 Harvard Law Review 2193, 2214 ('There *is* a social force we might call "racism" (though its content and effects, and the technologies through which it is expressed, are neither transhistorical nor predetermined)' (emphasis in original)); Goldberg, *Racist Culture* (n 111) 74 (racism is 'a fluid, transforming, historically specific concept parasitic on theoretic and social discourses for the meaning it assumes at any historical moment.').

[131] Michael Omi and Howard Winant, *Racial Formation in the United States* (1st edn, Routledge 1986).

forms of advantages and disadvantages, it also gets disguised *as* other things such as sexism or classism rather than being appreciated only as implicated *in* these other things.[132] By existing at once *as* many things (polysemic) and existing *in* many things (intersectional), racism conveniently metamorphoses and proliferates.

Contrary to the expectation announced at the start of this section, this discussion may seem to *destabilize* rather than *stabilize* the understanding of racism. This destabilization and its accompanying discomfort are however essential, especially for lawyers. That the field of equality or discrimination law—which is, to put it simply, dedicated to addressing *discrimination based on grounds*—is not about recognizing grounds such as race, gender, disability, etc, as if there is such a thing *as* race, gender, or disability which is not a construct. All grounds are constructs in reality.

Our interest as discrimination lawyers is firmly, much like that of scholars of race, is in addressing that which is *ending up* as looking like discrimination based on race and racial grounds such as descent, ethnicity, nationality, national origin, colour, caste, etc, including their intersections with other grounds such as gender, class, age, disability, sexuality, religion, etc. Discrimination law is however not delivering any biological, physical, or objective truths about grounds or discrimination based on grounds.[133] Not because discrimination lawyers lack disciplinary expertise to do that but because we possess disciplinary expertise to do something else: appreciate and address discrimination based on grounds in terms of ontology rather than metaphysics, that is, about the actual lived reality of discrimination out there rather than some truth about the categories or grounds such discrimination may be based on. Sandra Fredman's reminder remains forever apt in this context:

> Anti-discrimination law is necessarily a response to particular manifestations of inequality, which are themselves deeply embedded in the historical and political context of a given society. Discrimination laws are only effective if they are moulded to deal with the types of inequality which have developed in the society to which they refer.[134]

This is also what Tarunabh Khaitan calls 'the big-picture, systemic, concern of discrimination law' or 'the overall purpose' of discrimination law whose practice '*on the whole*, is geared towards'—the goal 'to reduce (and ultimately remove) any significant advantage gap between a protected group and its cognate groups'.[135]

[132] Michael Dummett, 'The Nature of Racism' in Michael P Levine and Tamas Pataki (eds), *Racism in Mind* (Cornell University Press 2004) 30.

[133] Shreya Atrey, 'Grounds in Equality Law: Before and After *For Women Scotland*' (2026) 89 Modern Law Review 379; Shreya Atrey, 'The Grounds of Affirmative Action' (2025) 47 Human Rights Quarterly 189.

[134] Sandra Fredman, *Discrimination Law* (2nd edn, OUP 2011) 38.

[135] Tarunabh Khaitan, *A Theory of Discrimination Law* (OUP 2015) 121 (emphasis in original).

If the removal of group-based disadvantage is the aim of discrimination law, then the disadvantage-based understanding of racism makes particular sense in this context.

1.5 Conclusion

This chapter has argued that racism is an empirical, polysemic, and intersectional category which denotes race-based disadvantage, where race and racism are both a result of processes of racialization. This skeletal framework should provide the scaffolding for the discussion in the next two chapters which turn to developing typologies of racism and anti-racism, respectively.

This understanding displaces the biology and ideology-based understandings of racism which are either false or fractional. More importantly, this understanding captures the verified empirical reality of the vast advantage gaps between racialized groups. Racism as racial disadvantage takes seriously the profound, persistent, and pervasive material disadvantage suffered by some racialized groups, making it impossible to deny racism as real.

2
A Framework of Racism

2.1 Introduction

The previous chapter argued for understanding racism in terms of racial disadvantage or the material gaps between racialized groups in social, cultural, economic, political, and psychological terms. What gives rise to such racism?

This chapter builds a multilevel framework of racism for understanding the sources of racism or where its roots lie. In showing that its roots are in structural racism, as opposed to individual/interpersonal or institutional/systemic forms of racism, the chapter identifies the form of racism which should be the subject of anti-racism as a legal principle. The chapter thus becomes the basis for examining how law tackles structural racism and how it should tackle structural racism.

A multilevel source-based typology of racism is important because, as David Theo Goldberg observes:

> In order to disavow our social life of a set of social relations as destructive as racism, it is necessary to comprehend it in its full complexity ... The prevailing accounts of racism institutionalized by the mainstream academic perspectives have created an 'object' corresponding only in part to the wide range of racism's manifestations in our daily experience.[1]

This is true of the mainstream perspective in law too. As this book shows, law's understanding of racism and anti-racism is narrow and barely scrapes the surface of racism as it manifests today. So before turning to law in the rest of the book, this and the next chapter take a cue from sociology and political theory to build a conceptual basis for talking about racism not as a legal artefact ('racial discrimination') but as a social phenomenon that is constantly being made. It is the mechanics of racism's making that this chapter unravels.

Section 2.2 explains the basis of the classification offered in this chapter, in particular, justifying the need for a source-based typology of racism. Section 2.3 develops this typology of racism as interpersonal, institutional, and structural.

[1] David Theo Goldberg, 'Raking the Field of the Discourse of Racism' (1987) 18 Journal of Black Studies 58.

Anti-Racism as a Legal Principle. Shreya Atrey, Oxford University Press.
DOI: 10.1093/9780198947646.003.0004

Section 2.4 centralizes structural racism as the paradigmatic case of racism to focus on when thinking about anti-racism. Section 2.5 concludes.

2.2 Conceiving Racism

Chapter 1 showed that there is little consensus that there is a thing out there that may be called racism. While considerable effort is spent denying racism, there is also plentiful evidence of racism, understood in terms of the racial disadvantage suffered by some racialized groups as opposed to others.

This broad understanding of racism can be further understood through a range of frameworks. Some understand racism as directed against historically disadvantaged groups, viz. Black people, Indigenous peoples, Dalits, Irish Travellers, and Roma people, or as specific forms of racism such as anti-Semitism, anti-Black racism, anti-Dalit racism or casteism, anti-Asian racism, anti-Latinx racism, and anti-Roma racism, or as its specific manifestations in slavery, segregation, apartheid, untouchability, and miscegenation. Others study racism with a focus on the meaning of race or racial characteristics such as colour, ethnicity, descent, nationality, or national origin. Some study racism through a psychological perspective as the presence or absence of prejudice. Yet others study racism through disciplinary perspectives which are chiefly legal, social, political, cultural, regional, historical, economic, etc.

All approaches are illuminating and help understand racism in specific contexts and for specific purposes. For example, anti-Dalit racism or casteism concerns the hierarchization and the resulting subordination and exploitation of 'lower' or 'out' castes by Hindu 'upper' castes.[2] It explains forms of racism specific to caste such as the practice of untouchability.[3] Likewise, anti-Black racism brings into focus the subordination of people of African descent as shaped by colonialism, capitalism, and imperialism.

[2] The term 'Dalit' means 'broken' in Marathi language and is used as a term of assertive pride by those belonging to those oppressed and marginalized by the Hindu caste systems. See 'What's in a name?: on the use of the term "Dalit"' (6 September 2018) *The Hindu* <https://www.thehindu.com/opinion/editorial/whats-in-a-name/article59780463.ece> (accessed 5 April 2024).

[3] Untouchability is practice of avoidance of touch by Hindu upper castes against members of lower caste groups or Dalits. It is widely practised by South Asian communities wherever they are based, though it is explicitly prohibited in some countries such as India which, in article 17 of its Constitution, declares that: '"Untouchability" is abolished and its practice in any form is forbidden. The enforcement of any disability arising out of "Untouchability" shall be an offence punishable in accordance with law.' See Amit Thorat and Omkar Joshi, 'The Continuing Practice of Untouchability in India: Patterns and Mitigating Influences' (2020) 55 Economic and Political Weekly 36; Rohit Chopra and Ajantha Subramanian, 'Caste Discrimination Exists in the U.S., Too—But a Movement to Outlaw It Is Growing' *Time* (11 February 2022) <https://time.com/6146141/caste-discrimination-us-opposition-grows/> (accessed 5 April 2024); 'No Escape—Caste Discrimination in the UK', Dalit Solidarity Network UK Report July 2006 <https://idsn.org/wp-content/uploads/user_folder/pdf/New_files/Other_documents/No_Escape_-_Caste_Discrimination_in_the_UK.pdf> (accessed 5 April 2024).

Different typologies are thus variously useful in studying racism through the perspective of specific victims, perpetrators, practices, effects, and methodologies. Yet, although they may illuminate how racism comes about, none of them are devoted to studying racism through its sources per se. That is, if racism is broadly understood in terms of material gaps between racialized groups, then who and what causes these gaps?

Take for example four scenarios:

(i) an individual doctor who refuses to treat Roma, Gypsy, and Irish Travellers whom the doctor believes do not have the right to receive medical treatment;
(ii) a hospital which preferentiates out-patients who live within its vicinity and thereby ends up excluding asylum seekers and refugees;
(iii) a policy which requires healthcare providers to check the right to remain in the country which leads to delays in treatment of people of colour; and
(iv) a pandemic, which has a disproportionate impact of sickness and death amongst Black and minority ethnic population.

In scenario (i), the doctor's belief that Roma, Gypsy, and Irish Travellers do not have a right to be treated because of their transitory lifestyle may be the cause of denial of treatment to Roma, Gypsy, and Irish Travellers at the doctor's clinic. Assumptions or stereotypes around Traveller communities though are not generated by the doctor. While the denial of treatment to Roma, Gypsy, and Irish Travellers may be due to the doctor's own stereotypes, the stereotypes themselves are not exclusively the doctor's own and are part of a much wider social, cultural, economic, and political context. The root cause of the stereotypes which inform individual behaviour are thus elsewhere than in the doctor's mind alone.

Similarly, in scenario (ii), the hospital's policy may be seen as the direct but perhaps reasonable and justified cause of denial of treatment to refugees and asylum seekers who live in the outskirts, but it does not explain why refugees and asylum seekers have come to inhabit the outskirts of the city. While the immediate cause of the denial of treatment may be the hospital's policy, the root cause of spatial segregation of racialized groups of migrants in a city lies elsewhere.

Likewise, in scenario (iii), the government's policy of requiring a right to remain-check before providing medical treatment may be the immediate cause of delays in treatment of people of colour who may have the right to be treated but may be asked to produce evidence, such as a British passport, prior to receiving treatment. That may have the effect of excluding non-white British citizens, such as members of the Windrush generation, who have never applied for a British passport. But what explains the equation of passports with citizenship and citizenship with whiteness in the first place?

Finally, in scenario (iv), a pandemic, which is caused by a virus, affects everyone. Yet, those with poorer prior health or fewer resources to protect themselves from the virus may be affected more than others. What explains poorer health outcomes and material conditions of Black and minority ethnic people for them to be disproportionately affected by the pandemic?

Focussing on stereotypes and prejudices, the specific racial ground involved, the particular groups targeted or impacted, or the severity of impact, may reveal something about the immediate act or omission through which racism transpires or the consequences thereof. But it does not reveal the full story that leads up to these immediate causes or consequences. Why are individuals prejudiced, why are cities segregated, why is healthcare linked to citizenship and citizenship to race, and why do pandemics have unequal effects?

To understand racism fully, the pressing question is thus not about the immediate or the most proximate cause in the chain of events which lead to a specific instance of racism, but the root cause of that instance. Causation, straightforwardly, gets at the former—the immediate or the most proximate cause, while the latter is really about a full explanatory account of the root causes, the sources, or the conditions which give rise to eventual, more proximate causes. It is the latter which we call *sine qua non*, without which racism cannot exist.[4]

Law, traditionally, has only focussed on causation for apportioning legal liability on the actor responsible for the cause which is contiguous to the effect under question.[5] This focus, as Susan Marks says, helps answer 'whether a particular actor can be held answerable for a legal wrong. It does not address the question of why that wrong occurred, how it relates to other wrongs, or what its enabling conditions were.'[6] The latter set of questions which go beyond causation and towards the *why*, *how*, and *what* of legal wrongs require us to probe into 'the reasons behind violations'.[7] That is, probe not only the immediate causes of violations but the explanatory forces which generate the conditions for immediate causes, 'to consider why they are occurring' at all.[8]

Analyses of racism need to be 'conducted at the level of background conditions'[9] to conceive how racism comes about. Instead of studying racism exclusively through who is wronged or by whom or by what kind of intentions or by which actions or omissions, fuller explanatory accounts of racism can consider *all* these dimensions and channel them into understanding what lies at the heart of racism, that without which discrete instances of racism would not exist.

4 See for the range of uses of 'causation' as terminology: Stephen Mumford and Rani Lill Anjum, *Causation: A Very Short Introduction* (OUP 2013) ch 7 [hereafter Mumford and Anjum, *Causation*].

5 HLA Hart and Tony Honoré, *Causation in the Law* (2nd edn, OUP 1985) <https://global.oup.com/academic/product/causation-in-the-law-9780198254744?cc=ie&lang=en&>.

6 Susan Marks, 'Human Rights and Root Causes' (2011) 74 Modern Law Review 57, 60.

7 ibid 59.

8 ibid 59.

9 ibid 72.

2.3 Classifying Racism

How does racism come about?

This section is dedicated to answering this question by developing a tripartite framework for understanding racism through its sources: (i) individual beliefs, acts, and omissions; (ii) institutional norms, practices, and culture; and (iii) state laws, policies, and governance.[10]

Although these sources, at first blush, appear to be about types of actors or actions, as this section shows, equally they reveal *why* and *how* and not only by *whom* and through *what* racism comes about. This dual emphasis is particularly relevant for lawyers as it helps to both apportion legal liability by correctly attributing racism to its sources and, more importantly, advance the understanding of how racism comes about at each source. A source-based framework of racism activates the latter by focussing on the processual account of racism's making or how the root causes of racism are generated.

2.3.1 Interpersonal Racism

At the most microscopic level are individuals whose *beliefs*, *actions*, or *omissions* may be classified as racist. If an individual *believes* that members of an ethnic group are lazy and underserving of jobs, they may well continue to believe so without it being law's business to correct those beliefs. People's beliefs, howsoever problematic, may be protected as a matter of freedom of thought. But some beliefs, when expressed and when capable of expressing a demeaning or violent point of view, may be characterized as racist. Herein law may intervene if a person expresses a view that members of an ethnic group are lazy and should be exterminated.

Likewise, an individual's *actions or omissions* may be classified as racist. For example, someone may prefer to make friends only of people of the same colour or to dine at a place where everyone belongs to a single ethnic group. An individual can

[10] Others have proposed similar typologies. Malcolm Saunders (1982) discusses four forms of racism—individual, institutional, cultural, and structural. But he does not discuss them from a causal perspective. Coretta Phillips also uses a tripartite typology which is similar to the one being suggested here and is discussed in Section 2.4. Malcolm Saunders, 'Education for a New Community' (1982) 10 New Community 64; Coretta Phillips, 'Institutional Racism and Ethnic Inequalities: An Expanded Multilevel Framework' (2011) 40 Journal of Social Policy 173 [hereafter Phillips, 'Institutional Racism']. There has also been a focus on 'systemic racism' which, at least in international human rights law (where this term is prevalent), denotes the widespread or pervasive nature of racism in terms of its scale and intensity. The book avoids the terminology in both the colloquial and the specific sense in which it is used in international human rights law. Where the terminology of 'systems' is used, it is used as coinciding with institutions. That is, institutional racism and systemic racism are used interchangeably. Institutions and systems are thus treated as different from structures because, as Stewart Shapiro explains, a system is a 'collection of objects with certain relations' such as a family, a chess configuration, etc, while a structure is 'the abstract form of a system, highlighting the interrelationships among the objects'. Stewart Shapiro, *Philosophy of Mathematics: Structure and Ontology* (OUP 1997) 73.

also rely on neutral grounds such as preference for a cuisine or for dating people with a particular accent. Although race-neutral on the face of it, preference for a cuisine or accent can act as proxies for race-based preferences. These though may be personal preferences often outside of the realm of law's intervention. But when preferences start affecting other people's interests, law intervenes. For example, where an employer starts dismissing employees belonging to a particular ethnic group, labour law would kick in to protect employees from unfair dismissal on grounds of race.

Irrespective of whether law intervenes in a specific case, the racism at the source of these examples is individual-driven. The source of such racism may be ideological—viz. stemming from 'dogma',[11] 'set of beliefs',[12] 'doctrine',[13] or 'attitudes'[14] of superiority of one race or racial group over another; or non-ideological—viz. choices based on taste, pragmatism, public opinion, economic assessment, etc.[15] Such racism can be malign or benign, or rational or irrational. But, causally speaking, interpersonal or individual racism is initiated by something that the individual thinks or does or fails to do that has a disproportionate negative impact on people from some racialized groups.

Interpersonal or individual racism is thus the simplest type of racism which the law can attack. This is perhaps the reason why it is seen as the paradigmatic form of racism in law.[16]

But as Philomena Essed observed, individual racism 'is a contradiction in itself because racism is by definition the expression or activation of group power'.[17] As Floya Anthias explains:

> It is power that renders the symbols of inferiorisation effective … This is not simply a sophisticated restatement of the argument that racism equals prejudice plus power … The term prejudice locates the issue in subjectivist terms ie. as emanating from individuals. *Racist ideas about groups are the products of discursive and material forces and emerge in a field of contestation and negotiation in society.*[18]
>
> Power is not locatable within individual 'whites'… The issue of power is not one about a power that is exercised by *all 'whites' over all 'blacks'* but is about *the power of the dominant group represented in the state to reproduce its own values*

[11] Ruth Benedict, *Race and Racism* (Routledge 1945) 87.
[12] Pierre Van den Berghe, *Race and Racism: A Comparative Perspective* (Wiley 1967) 11.
[13] Richard Schaefer, *Racial and Ethnic Groups* (4th edn, Little Brown Higher Education 1990) 16.
[14] ibid 53.
[15] For an early (but contested) view of this kind, consider Gary Becker, *The Economics of Racism* (Chicago 1957), and Derick Bell's interest convergence theory proposed in 'Brown v. Board of Education and the Interest-Convergence Dilemma' (1980) 93 Harvard Law Review 518.
[16] Consider Part II of the book for evidence of this view.
[17] Philomena Essed, *Understanding Everyday Racism: An Interdisciplinary Theory* (Sage 1991) 36.
[18] Floya Anthias, 'Institutional Racism, Power and Accountability' (1999) 4 Sociological Research Online [4.1] (emphasis supplied) [hereafter Anthias, 'Institutional Racism'].

and practices on its own terms, despite the discontinuous and shifting nature of the processes.[19]

What this means is that individuals in their individual capacity do not have the power to effectuate racialization to generate racialized groups or racial disadvantage. In other words, individuals acting *as individuals* cannot exert power to demarcate and disadvantage people at the *group-level*. In fact, individual racism assumes the prior existence of both racialization and racial disadvantage.[20] Individuals exist within the larger institutional, social, cultural, economic, or political context in which racism exists. Individuals rely on racism to perpetuate racism, but they cannot be said to give rise to racism *eo ipso* or by their thoughts, actions, or omissions all on their own. Even in the case of scenario (i) in the previous section, where the doctor refuses to treat Irish and Roma Travellers explicitly on the basis of negative stereotypes about those racialized groups, the doctor relies on stereotypes which already exist and cannot be said to engender stereotypes autonomously. Interpersonal racism is thus regenerative but not inventive of racism.

Conceptually, we are thus none the wiser. This is because of the circular nature of interpersonal racism, where racism is meant to be 'established by racist behavior, which itself is proven by the existence of racism'.[21]

So, even though an individual may be the simplest unit capable of giving effect to racism, which can well be addressed in law as interpersonal racism, racism itself is an a priori for interpersonal racism. What is that a priori racism and where is it emanating from?

2.3.2 Institutional Racism

Individuals exist within public and private institutions (organizations or systems) in charge of government, local council, public transport, postal service, police, healthcare, hospitality, supermarkets, etc. These institutions have an identity of their own—in that they have their own set of norms, practices, and culture which determine their behaviour and the impact they have on people. *Norms* can be thought of as formal rules, mostly written, on the basis of which the institution defines and runs itself. *Practices* can be imagined as informal, often unwritten, but informing the way in which formal rules have come to be applied actually, thus

[19] ibid [4.3] (emphasis supplied).

[20] Jenny Williams, 'Redefining Institutional Racism' (1985) 8 Ethnic and Racial Studies 323 ('Racial attitudes cannot *directly* account for racial inequality ... Ideologies predate the individuals or professional groups that use them; they are part of the general social formation, but are used by groups to articulate together different elements of experience into a chain of meaning which works to produce different forms of social consciousness.') (emphasis supplied).

[21] Eduardo Bonilla-Silva, 'Rethinking Racism: Toward a Structural Interpretation' (1997) 62 American Sociological Review 465, 469 [hereafter Bonilla-Silva, 'Rethinking Racism'].

reflecting a degree of individual discretion and agency in how institutions function. *Culture* is the frame of reference which envelopes both norms and practices as well as other beliefs, assumptions, values, interactions, customs, etc within which an institution operates and dictates what is considered commonplace or ordinary within the institution.[22] These three elements represent the institutional apparatus, or that through which an institution operates or functions. Institutional racism occurs when an institution's norms, practices, or culture leads to racialized effects.

Institutions are however not self-executing and are after all run by individuals who effect the institutional norms and practices or make up the institutional culture. That does not mean that individuals give effect to institutional norms, practices, and culture *as individuals*. Instead, individuals within institutions use their agency to act *for* the institution when they activate the institution's norms, practices, and culture.

Importantly, although individual agency activates the institution's norms, practices, and culture which may give rise to institutional racism, once institutional racism is set in motion, it can become the basis for racism between individuals at an interpersonal level. That is, institutional racism can provide the conditions for interpersonal or individual racism to thrive by providing the baseline for a commonsensical view of how things are or meant to be in terms of racial hierarchy and racial disadvantage.[23]

Thus, for example in the case of scenario (ii) in the previous section, a hospital's catchment policy may result in doctors treating mainly white people. The absence of migrants or people of colour in the hospital and the eventual refusal of treatment to refugees and asylum seekers—based on the assumption that their absence is justified by their lack of entitlement to be treated at the hospital—may become part of an internalized culture of whiteness which individual doctors may then start relying on in their own private medical practice or even personal sphere to deny medical treatment to or mistreating, say, Roma, Gypsy, and Irish Travellers; refugees; asylum seekers; and migrants.

Institutional cultures can thus set the norms and standards not just for institutional interactions but also interpersonal interactions between individuals, by providing a baseline of rationality or reason which predetermines the choices of individuals.[24] It is in this sense that institutional racism may be understood as an

[22] As Stuart Hall asserts, in the final analysis, it is actually *culture* which regulates *conduct* because culture forms the 'indestructible part of the institutional *habitus*' and becomes far more effective in regulating conduct of individuals within and beyond institutions, than formal norms are. Stuart Hall, 'From Scarman to Stephen Lawrence' (1999) 48 History Workshop Journal 187, 195 (emphasis in original) [hereafter Hall, 'From Scarman to Stephen Lawrence'].

[23] ibid; Ann Dummett, *A Portrait of English Racism* (Penguin 1973) 131 ('institutions which effectively maintain inequality between members of different groups [do it] in such a way that open doctrine is unnecessary, or even if operated partly by individuals who are not themselves racist in their beliefs, still has the effect of making and perpetuating inequalities').

[24] Louis L Knowles and Kenneth Prewitt, *Institutional Racism in America* (Prentice Hall 1969) 143.

explanatory force behind individual racism. Thus, although the boundaries between individual and institutional racism are porous and the direction of influence is not unidirectional, institutional racism's sphere of influence over individuals is far greater than the influence of individual agency over racialized institutional norms, practices, and culture, or the influence of interpersonal racism (within or beyond institutions) on institutional norms, practices, and culture.[25]

The question remains as to how racism actually gets *institutionalized* from agentic individuals acting within an institution to being produced by the institution's *own* norms, practices, and culture. The answer lies in understanding how individual agency within an institution interacts with institutional norms, practices, and culture and how that dialectic could produce racialized outcomes.

Take for instance the case of a neighbourhood where police stop and search Black people. While section 60 of the Criminal Justice and Public Order Act 1994 in the UK permits suspicionless stop and search, it does not sanction race-based stop and search. The practice of stopping and searching Black people in a neighbourhood thus may have emerged, say, in writing or in oral instructions of a superior officer in charge of the neighbourhood, or may have developed over time as part of institutional culture in formal trainings or during on- or off-duty interactions between officers which stereotype Black people as a threat. The practice may even have started with a single officer's instructions or a single remark made by a discrete individual within the police. If the practice were conjured up and adopted by only a single officer who profiled Black people, the practice may be seen as aberrational and not institutional if it were unknown to others. But the moment the practice is known by others and left unchallenged or adopted and given effect to by more than a single individual within the police, it starts representing more than just an individual and part of the wider institutional practice and culture of the police. There may even be officers who oppose the practice. The fact that the practice operates (even if not practised by every single person within the police) more widely than a single individual and as a practice not of an individual but of the institution itself—in which individuals partake not as themselves but as part of the institutional apparatus—is when the practice becomes institutionally racist.

This understanding of institutional racism chimes in with how the term was first used by Carmichael and Hamilton in 1967 where they described it in contrast with individual racism as that which was perpetrated by 'established and respected institutions in society'.[26] Their description of the term was for the purposes

[25] Anthias, 'Institutional Racism' (n 18) [4.2]. ('Although there are few, if any, situations in which people are wholly powerless and they are not mere victims, having of course agency, this does not mean that they will be able to counter the power of institutions. Unequal power relations, particularly vis a vis the state (and in the actions of the state, such as the police force), but also in terms of class and gender, produce racist effects even where no explicit racist intentionalities can be identified ... Racism without the means to make it effective is like an invention without a maker.')

[26] Stokely Carmichael and Charles V Hamilton, *Black Power: The Politics of Liberation* (Vintage 1967) 4.

of describing the *consequences* of institutional racism, especially the racial disadvantage suffered by Black people in the US. Much of the early discussion around institutional racism followed this trajectory of measuring advantage gaps between racialized groups, in terms of housing, employment, policing, education, etc, to campaign for social and political change.[27]

This discussion shaped the *conceptual* understanding of institutional racism as focussed on the sources of racism, which, as recognized by William Macpherson in his 1999 report on the Stephen Lawrence inquiry, indicated a shift towards institutional or organizational 'rather than simply [the] individuals who represent it'.[28]

The Macpherson Report remains one of the most detailed formal analyses of institutional racism in the UK which provides a framework for the concept against which the Metropolitan Police was evaluated in its handling of Stephen Lawrence's murder. The most cited part of that report is perhaps its definition of institutional racism itself:

> The collective failure of an organisation to provide an appropriate and professional service to people because of their colour, culture, or ethnic origin. It can be seen or detected in processes, attitudes and behaviour which amount to discrimination through unwitting prejudice, ignorance, thoughtlessness and racist stereotyping which disadvantage minority ethnic people.[29]

The definition makes a genuine attempt to refocus the attention from individuals to institutions/organizations/systems. But the attention to 'unwitting prejudice, ignorance, thoughtlessness and racist stereotyping' in the definition and throughout the report[30] claws back not only to individual racism but to a very particular version of it which reduces racism to a state of mind or animus.[31] The only real difference the definition makes is that institutional racism appears to be not out of *outright* but *unwitting* prejudice, ignorance, thoughtlessness, or racist stereotyping. But that is animus all the same. Institutional racism thus becomes a guilt-free version of individual racism where racism is after all being driven by individuals though with less morally culpable animus because it is unwitting.

Despite wanting to shift the attention from individuals to institutions as the source of racism, the Macpherson Report fails to do any such thing. Its definition leaves institutional racism intact within institutions by only attacking individual

[27] Derek Humphry and Gus John, *Because They Are Black* (Penguin 1972); Terry Jones, 'Institutional Racism in the United States' (1974) 19 Social Work 218.

[28] William Macpherson of Cluny, 'The Stephen Lawrence Inquiry Report' Cm 4264-1, TSO, London, 1999 [6.32].

[29] ibid [6.34].

[30] ibid [6.13] [6.14] [6.15] [6.16].

[31] The claw back is to the Scarman Report of 1981 on the Brixton Disorders which, as Dr Oakley put it in the Macpherson Report, understood racism as 'overt acts of discrimination or hostility by individuals who were acting out their personal prejudices', ibid [6.14].

racism within institutions.[32] It was perhaps this which got Stuart Hall to remark that 'the idea of "institutional racism" strikes at the heart of one very English kind of racism, which thrives, not against, but cosily inserted within, liberalism'.[33] As Hall explained, this was because, while the concept of institutional racism 'conceives racism as arising through social processes' it sits at odds with 'the English imagination since (as a former Prime Minister, Mrs Thatcher, once gloriously observed) the latter has no concept of "the social" which cannot be reduced to "individuals and their families"'.[34] Institutional racism's social dimension thus remains subsumed within the liberal framework of individual racism which underpins the Macpherson definition.

How do we exhume the social dimension of institutional racism? The starting point is to observe how norms, practices, and culture of the institution shape the processes which create the conditions for institutional racism.[35] For example, how police officers interact with their superiors versus contemporaries and juniors; how they interact with their colleagues in the canteen and off-duty versus on site and on duty; how they interact with people from different neighbourhoods, genders, ages, sexualities, colour, etc; and how they interact with their own families and wider community within which they operate—all collectively define the social relationships through which the police's norms, practices, and culture are set in motion and indeed, through which, institutional racism comes about. Hall provides a helpful example of this:

> It is perfectly possible for young officers—whose promotion up the ranks and acceptance as 'regular cops' depends on imbibing as an unreflected practice this folk-wisdom of 'how to be a good copper'—to love reggae, eat Vindaloo curry every Saturday night, have a few black friends, and still think that 'good policing' requires them to act on the assumption that a young black man carrying a holdall at a bus-stop after dark almost certainly just committed a robbery and should be 'sussed'—stopped and searched.

In this example, institutional racism as expressed through stop and search of the young Black man operates not as an aberration or as being at odds with other

[32] Sarah Ahmed, *On Being Included: Racism and Diversity in Institutional Life* (Duke University Press 2012) 43; Karim Murji, 'Sociological Engagements: Institutional Racism and Beyond' (2007) 41 Sociology 843, 849; John Lea, 'The Macpherson Report and the Question of Institutional Racism' (2000) 39 The Howard Journal 219; Lee Bridges, 'The Lawrence Inquiry—Incompetence, Corruption and Institutional Racism' (2000) 26 Journal of Law and Society 289; Jenny Bourne, 'The Life and Times of Institutional Racism' (2001) 43 Race and Class 7.

[33] Hall, 'From Scarman to Stephen Lawrence' (n 22) 194.

[34] ibid 195.

[35] Anthias, 'Institutional Racism' (n 18) [5.6]; John Solomos, 'Social Research and the Stephen Lawrence Inquiry' (1999) 4 Sociological Research Online [2.4].

social relationships and interactions. Rather, it is very much nested within social interactions which on the one hand show positive engagement with some parts of Black and minority ethnic culture while on the other hand stereotype and punish Black and minority ethnic people. This duality—which belies individual, especially, animus-level analyses where racial disadvantage can be traced back to an individual and their state of mind—of racism existing within seemingly unracialized, race-neutral, or even race-positive spaces is the hallmark of institutional racism in a liberal society. It requires close and detailed observation of how institutional norms, practices, and culture come to be shaped by a whole range of interactions and interrelationships between people. It is this dialectic which acts as the source of institutional racism which is ultimately about social relationships within, between, and beyond institutions.[36]

That said, while institutional racism exceeds the focus on individual actors and instead focusses on collectivities, it is still limited to 'a narrow perspective of analysing [how] the actions of governments and political institutions [deal] *with a specific issue*'.[37] Ultimately, institutional racism captures only social dynamics of institutions and does not explain the totality of forces surrounding and influencing institutional racism. For example, institutional racism by the hospital in scenario (ii) cannot explain the economic and political forces behind the spatial segregation of asylum seekers and refugees which in turn leads to refusal of treatment by the hospital based on its catchment policy. Likewise, it would be difficult to explain scenarios (iii) and (iv) through the lens of a specific collectivity—an institution or an organization—which brings about the racial disadvantage in these cases.

As Leslie Scarman remarked in his 1982 report, institutions do not create racial deprivation and disadvantage by themselves.[38] But he did not say how exactly institutions (re)produce racism, a possibility that he himself acknowledged. What was left unexplored then and later in the Macpherson Report in 1999 was how institutions operate within the broader social, economic, political, and cultural structures in which they are located. There is an 'indissoluble'[39] link between institutions and broader structures of the society, just as there is an indissoluble link between individuals and institutions.

What are these broader structures?

[36] Sheila Allen, 'The Institutionalization of Racism' (1973) 15 Race 99, 100–101.

[37] John Solomos, *Race and Racism in Contemporary Britain* (Macmillan 1999) 15 (emphasis in original) [hereafter Solomos, *Race and Racism*].

[38] Leslie Scarman's Report into the Brixton Disorders (1981) 135.

[39] Simon Holdaway, 'The Scarman Report: Some Sociological Aspects' (1981) 9 Journal of Ethnic and Migration Studies 366.

2.3.3 Structural Racism

Structures, according to Joseph Whitmeyer, are 'the networks of relationships among actors [and] aggregates of actors'.[40] That is, the overarching social, political, economic, cultural, and psychological networks of relationships which in their totality constitute the structure or the framework within which all human relationships and social life transpire. In the same vein, structural racism is 'the complex totality of forces in British society which have produced racialised political ideologies and practices',[41] or simply, 'the whole complex of factors which produce racial discrimination'.[42]

The question arises as to how this really transpires. Who is controlling or influencing structures and how are structures actually producing structural racism?

First, if individuals perpetrate individual racism and institutions perpetrate institutional racism, structural racism may be perpetrated by the state. The source of power which fuels the structure is the state; the *laws*, *policies*, and *governance* of which make up the structure that shapes the social, economic, political, cultural, and psychological relationships in societies. *Laws* may be constitutional or statutory—as enacted by the legislature of the Parliament and as enforced by the judiciary, or in the form of delegated legislation passed by the executive, who may also be responsible for *policy* at the local, regional, or central level. *Governance* too may be led by the executive and may dictate the government at the local, regional, or federal levels, within its many institutions and departments, and also as a whole in terms of its overall ideational and operational outlook. But why focus on the state at all?

State, according to Michael Omi and Howard Winant, is a constellation 'of institutions, the policies they carry out, the conditions and rules which support and justify them, and the social relations in which they are imbedded'.[43] And at the broadest level, individuals and institutions exist within states, 'which commonly generate and utilize large concentrations of power and which are usually relatively near the surface of social life'.[44] This concentration of power and proximity to social life is what makes states particularly relevant in studying a social phenomenon like racism.[45]

[40] Joseph Whitmeyer, 'Why Actors Are Integral to Structural Analysis' (1994) 12 Sociological Theory 153, 154.

[41] Solomos, *Race and Racism* (n 37).

[42] Michael Banton and Robert Miles, 'Racism' in Ellis Cashmore (ed), *Dictionary of Race and Ethnic Relations* (4th edn, Routledge 1996) 308.

[43] Michael Omi and Howard Winant, *Racial Formation in the United States* (2nd edn, Routledge 1994) 83 [hereafter Omi and Winant, *Racial Formation*].

[44] William H Sewell, 'A Theory of Structure: Duality, Agency, and Transformation' (1992) 98 American Journal of Sociology 1, 24 [hereafter Sewell, 'A Theory of Structure'].

[45] Michel Foucault, 'Society Must Be Defended': Lectures at the College de France 1975–1976 (D Macey trans., Picador 2003) 258 [hereafter Foucault, 'Society Must Be Defended'] ('The specificity of modern racism, or what gives it its specificity, is not bound up with mentalities, ideologies, or the lies

Secondly, states are inherently and centrally implicated in processes of racialization.[46] As Goldberg argues, modern states are in fact 'racial states' as they are:

> engaged in definition, regulation, governance, management, and mediation of racial matters they at once help to fashion and facilitate. For one, racial states *define* populations into racially identified groups, and they do so more or less formally through census taking, law, and policy... in and through bureaucratic forms, and administrative practices. Second, racial states *regulate* social, political, economic, legal, and cultural relations between those racially defined, invariably between white citizens and those identified as neither white nor citizen ... Relatedly, racial states *govern* populations identified in explicitly racial terms... Fourth, racial states *manage economically*. They oversee economic life, shape the contours of racially conceived labour relations, structure the opportunities or possibilities of economic access and closure.[47]

As a comparative matter, no other entity may be considered to be *as* centrally implicated in racialization by defining, regulating, governing, managing, and mediating racial matters *as* the state.[48] So centrally implicated are states in racial matters that the state itself becomes, as Goldberg says, 'racially conceived, on the historical co-definition of race and the state in their modern manifestations'.[49] Both race and the state are thus conceived through processes of racialization.

of power. It is bound up with the technique of power, with the technology of power. ... The juxtaposition of—or the way biopower functions through—the old sovereign power of life and death implies the workings, the introduction and activation, of racism. And it is, I think, here that we find the actual roots of racism.'); A Sivanandan, 'RAT and the Degradation of Black Struggle' (1985) 26 Race and Class 1, 27–28 ('Racism, strictly speaking, should be used to refer to structures and institutions with power to discriminate. What individuals display is racialism, prejudiced attitudes, which give them no intrinsic power over non-whites. That power is derived from racist laws, constitutional conventions, judicial precedents, institutional practices—all of which have the imprimatur of the state ... The fight against racism is, therefore, a fight against the state, which sanctions and authorises it—even if by default—in the institutions and structures of society and in the behaviour of its public officials.'); Leah Trueblood, 'Political Parties and the Rule of Law' ('the state, directed by the government, has a monopoly on the coercive use of force') (manuscript on file with the author).

46 David Theo Goldberg, *The Racial State* (Blackwell 2002) 2 [hereafter Goldberg, *The Racial State*]. ('Not just the way the state is implicated in reproducing more or less local conditions of racist exclusion, but how the *modern* state has always conceived of itself as racially configured. The modern state, in short, is nothing less than a racial state'); Omi and Winant, *Racial Formation* (n 43) 76–77 ('The state is inherently racial. Far from intervening in racial conflicts, the state is itself increasingly the pre-eminent site of racial conflict... Every state institution is a racial institution, but not every institution operates in the same way. In fact, the various state institutions do not serve one co-ordinated racial objective; they may work at cross-purposes. Therefore, race must be understood as occupying varying degrees of centrality in different state institutions and at different historical moments.').

47 Goldberg, *The Racial State* (n 46) 109–110 (emphasis in original).

48 Foucault, 'Society Must Be Defended' (n 45).

49 Goldberg, *The Racial State* (n 46) 3.

For example, at the highest level, it is the state which decides who can access the National Health Service (NHS) in the UK. The state has decided that access to NHS be based on residence. Residence can be proven by a range of evidence, but the state can specify that British passports be produced before receiving treatment. It can do so through its laws as enacted by the Parliament, delegated legislation enacted by those bodies or administrators empowered by the Parliament, governmental policy or ministerial orders or guidance directed at or developed by NHS as an institution. One result of such a policy, as reflected in scenario (iii), was what emerged during the Windrush scandal: that the insistence on showing a British passport before receiving NHS treatment meant that thousands of Black people of the Windrush generation were denied treatment.[50] The actual dynamics of denial is not apparent in the state's residence-based NHS entitlement or its insistence on using British passports as proof of residence. Neither is the denial directed at race or Black people.

Instead, the disproportionate impact on the racialized group of Black people may be explained by the prevailing structure within which this result comes about. This prevailing structure is one that came to be made in the post-war years when people from existing or erstwhile colonies arrived in Britain as the metropole. These new arrivals were already racialized as a consequence of colonization which had relied on racialization as a technique of imperial rule.[51] So upon arrival, they came encoded as white people from the 'old commonwealth' and Black and brown people from the 'new commonwealth'.[52] It was in direct reaction to the growing presence of the latter that restrictive immigration laws in the UK first came to be enacted.[53] The underlying and overwhelming message was clear—that while arrival of white immigrants from Australia, Canada, or New Zealand was acceptable, arrival of too many 'races' from other commonwealth countries was a problem to be fixed.[54] It was in this context that British citizenship came to be racialized as normatively white.[55]

Within this background, when citizenship coincides with whiteness, citizenship can also be assumed with whiteness. Per contra, citizenship cannot be assumed

[50] Wendy Williams, Windrush Lessons Learned Review Report (2020) <https://www.gov.uk/government/publications/windrush-lessons-learned-review> (accessed 5 April 2024).

[51] Tayyab Mahmud, 'Colonialism and Modern Constructions of Race: A Preliminary Inquiry' (1999) 53 University of Miami Law Review 1219; Renato G Mazzolini, 'Colonialism and the Emergence of Racial Theories' in Nick Hopwood, Rebecca Flemming, and Lauren Kassell (eds), *Reproduction: Antiquity to the Present Day* (Cambridge 2018); Nadine El-Enany, *(B)ordering Britain: Law, Race and Empire* (Manchester University Press 2020).

[52] Ann Dummett and Adnrew Nicol, *Subjects, Citizens, Aliens and Others: Nationality and Immigration Law* (Weidenfeld & Nicolson 1990).

[53] Michael Dummett and Ann Dummett, 'The Role of Government in Britain's Racial Crisis' in Lewis Donnelly (ed), *Justice Denied* (Sheed and Ward 1969).

[54] John Solomos, *Race and Racism in Contemporary Britain* (Macmillan 1999).

[55] Kathleen Paul, *Whitewashing Britain: Race and Citizenship in the Postwar Era* (Cornell University Press 1997); Devyani Prabhat, *Britishness, Belonging and Citizenship Experiencing Nationality Law* (Policy Press 2018).

for Black and brown people, who need to show/prove citizenship as no implicit colour-based assumption of citizenship applies in their case. They thus require evidence of citizenship through something like a passport. But passport is simply the evidence of citizenship, not citizenship itself which is a fact.

Many from the Windrush generation never applied for British passports, which are essentially a document for mobility across borders, something not everyone needs or desires, even when they are entitled to one. But lacking both whiteness and British passports, people from the Windrush generation were left entirely vulnerable to exclusion from medical treatment which they were rightfully entitled to as citizens because they arrived in the UK as British subjects. Against this structure where citizenship—legally, socially, culturally, politically, and psychologically—is racialized, that is, has race encoded within it, the possibility of instating racial disadvantage was naturally activated as a consequence of that structure. Thus, against this prevailing structure which was primed for racism, not *deliberately* but *structurally*, state intervention for producing British passports for receiving NHS treatments ended up producing structural racism.

Scenario (iii) is perhaps too straightforward. State intervention in scenario (iv) may be less straightforwardly explained. Herein, the intervention is of the virus, and not the state per se. It is the pandemic—the exponential spread of a virus—which may be said to affect the health outcomes for Black and minority ethnic people disproportionately. Can racism in this case also be explained as structural racism perpetrated by the state?

Potentially yes. The line of inquiry to be pursued here is again the unearthing of the prevailing structure against which the virus—the immediate and most proximate cause of death or illness—transpires in a society. If in a society Black and minority ethnic populations have generally worse health outcomes, say, in terms of cardiovascular health and it is clear that poor cardiovascular health in turn affects ability to fight off the virus, then it is worth asking why Black and minority ethnic populations have poorer health outcomes. Is it genetic predisposition? Is it socio-economic conditions which in turn affect nutrition and health? It is worth interrogating what the state has *done* preceding the virus that has enabled or worsened poorer health outcomes for Black and minority ethnic populations. Similarly, it is worth asking what the state *does* in response to the pandemic which does *not* give due regard to the poorer health outcomes for Black and minority ethnic populations and thus fails to prevent and even exacerbates the unequal impact of the pandemic. Either way, what the state does or does not is an intervening force in the pandemic and racism may be entailed as a consequence of it. Such racism could well be sourced back to the state depending on what a close examination of state laws, policies, and governance reveals.[56]

[56] Fay Faraday, 'Intersectional Feminism, Racial Capitalism, and the Covid-19 Pandemic' (2021) 72 University of New Brunswick Law Journal 222.

This is of course not to say that state laws, policies, and governance are the *only* sources of structural racism or that structural racism is basically state racism. Just as interpersonal and institutional racism are not only driven by individuals and institutions respectively and in fact operate in relation to each other, structural racism also operates relationally. As Omi and Winant argue, while the state

> may represent the core of a given racial regime [no] state can encompass all of civil society. People conceive of, operate, and inhabit their own racial projects (within broader constraints) and 'experience' race in distinct and varied ways... the boundary between state and civil society is necessarily porous and uncertain where race is concerned.[57]

More importantly though, structural racism may have other sources than state laws, policies, and governance alone. That is because structures are more diffuse than the state. Structures may be equally defined by social relationships between and within families, neighbours, workers, religious communities, online communities; or economic relationships between classes of owners, consumers, producers, labourers, sellers, distributers, bankers, lenders, policy-makers, etc; as well as cultural relationships as determined by who has access to education and arts, locally, regionally or globally. Psychic (psychological) or symbolic power relations in terms of who has high or low status may also be a source of structural racism.

These structures may relate equally to race as they relate to gender, sexuality, age, disability, religion, etc. In fact, structures may be co-constituted and indeed co-constitute all these dimensions of group power and identity in way that these forces cannot be disentangled.[58] Structures as a whole may thus exceed both the state and its governance of racial matters in any discrete or essentialist sense. So, an account which takes state (and state-like entities) as the source of structural racism is a chiefly political account of racism. It does not, in fact *cannot*, discount other sources of discursive power which make up the structure as a whole. Structural racism thus does not compel a mono-causal view of racism as if racism is either all related to racial structures or led by the state alone. It however does underscore the complex totality of what constitutes structures (as co-constituted by race and other axes) and the relevance of state and state power in fashioning that totality.

Indeed state-like entities such as regional and international collectivities of states viz. European Union or the United Nations may also be considered as implicated in 'structuring structures'[59]—in terms of setting the tone or the foundation of racial matters at the highest level. Likewise, some private corporations may also be

[57] Omi and Winant, *Racial Formation* (n 43) 137–138.

[58] Cf Marta Jorba and Maria Rodó-Zárate, 'Beyond Mutual Constitution: The Properties Framework for Intersectionality Studies' (2019) 45 Signs 175.

[59] Pierre Bourdieu, *Outline of a Theory of Practice* (Cambridge University Press 1977) 72 [hereafter Bourdieu, *Outline*].

considered state-like when they are capable of enacting and effecting racial matters like the state. Alphabet, Meta, Amazon, and X may thus be considered as acting state-like when they appear engaged in definition, regulation, governance, management, and mediation of race and racism through their platforms. They have immense power in shaping not only, and obviously, technology especially through digital social media but also social and cultural relations (by reengineering forms of engagement), economic relations (through monetizing the attention economy) and political relations (by shaping electoral politics and democracies directly and indirectly).[60] Their impact in shaping the skeletal or framework structure within which all human relationships transpire cannot be overstated. Thus, whether it is the states defining race or racism in law, or the EU or the UN addressing racial matters, or the social media platforms which become sites for organizing racist or anti-racist movements—all end up shaping the way in which race, racism, and anti-racism ideate and circulate in the world. States and state-like entities thus have the power to set the tone for structural racism and in turn individual and institutional racism, and indeed also, anti-racism.[61]

Thirdly, in setting the tone through processes of racialization, states and state-like entities, ultimately contribute to structural racism not only by advantaging some racialized groups at the expense of others but also by instating a framework of disadvantage which can be relied upon by individuals and institutions for advantaging some racialized groups at the expense of others. Because structures which give rise to structural racism are essentially, ultimately, disadvantaging some racialized groups, structural racism becomes the framework for perpetuating and proliferating that disadvantage.[62]

For example, racialized structures—such as social norms around who is considered a citizen, or economic norms around who is considered deserving of support, or cultural norms around who is considered educated and what accents are preferable—which inscribe whiteness into British citizenship essentially instate a framework of disadvantage into citizenship where only some racial groups are considered citizens and others not. Once instated, citizenship can be used by individuals and institutions to reinscribe disadvantage on racial groups which are already disadvantaged. Thus, when individuals or institutions rely on citizenship to

[60] Karen Hao, *Empire of AI: Inside the Reckless Race for Total Domination* (Allen Lane 2025); Dipayan Ghosh and Ramesh Srinivasan, 'The Future of Platform Power: Reining in Big Tech' (2021) 32 Journal of Democracy 63; Lucie Green, *Silicon States: The Power of Politics of Big Tech and What it Means for Our Future* (Counterpoint 2018); Aurélie Leclercq-Vandelannoitte and Emmanuel Bertin, 'How to Deal with Big Tech power? The "Big Tech Raj", A New Form of Biopower in the Digital Age' (2024) 208 Technological Forecasting and Social Change 1.

[61] Bonilla-Silva, 'Rethinking Racism' (n 21) 474 ('Racial contestation is the logical outcome of a society with a racial hierarchy. A social formation that includes some form of racialization will always exhibit some form of racial contestation.').

[62] William M Wiecek, 'Structural Racism and the Law in America Today: An Introduction' (2011) 100 Kentucky Law Journal 1, 5; Stuart Hall, 'Race Articulation and Societies Structured in Dominance' in Stuart Hall (ed), *Essential Essays, Foundations of Cultural Studies* (vol 1, Duke University Press 2018).

offer rentals or to provide medical treatment, they do not need another causal variable for that reliance to be disadvantageous to some racial groups. All they need is to rely on the status quo where a framework of disadvantage has been inscribed into the structures which have established a racialized paradigm of citizenship.

It is in this way that structural racism 'prestructures' racism perpetrated by individuals and institutions. Looking at how structural racism works allows a processual view of 'the way the race relations issues enter into the structures, strategies, and ideologies'[63] and actually become a 'recurring pattern' of 'ordered interrelationships' between people.[64]

This is the critical point then. That the way individual and institutional actors come to be and act is predetermined in part by the structures surrounding them. As William Sewell put it insightfully, 'the notion of structure does denominate, however problematically, something very important about social relations: *the tendency of patterns of relations to be reproduced*, even when actors engaging in the relations are unaware of the patterns or do not desire their reproduction.'[65]

Structures are thus self-perpetuating, or as Pierre Bourdieu said, have the means for their own reproduction.[66] Yet this does not mean that structures are impervious to human agency or change. As Anthony Giddens argued, structures are dualistic in nature, such that they are both 'the medium and the outcome of the practices which constitute social systems'.[67] This formulation allows for structures to be conceived as mutable and responsive to human agency which is constantly colliding with structures in that human agency is both being shaped by and shaping structures. Neither structures nor human agency are automated. They are instead constantly interacting and, as a result, co-determined. So, the reason why structures are considered self-perpetuating is not because they operate irrespective of human agency and are unchangeable, but because by their very nature, they tend to self-perpetuate and hence proliferate disadvantage which is encoded into them.

To sum up, structural racism represents the complex totality of forces which bring about racial disadvantage in a society. It has three salient features. First, structural racism is ideated and effected by the state at the highest level: the Parliament, the government or the executive, and the judiciary, rather than private actors, but including large-scale private corporations such as Alphabet, Meta, Amazon and X which can act 'state-like'. Second, it comes about through racialization which is the process of assigning racial meaning to different groups based on ethnicity, colour, national origin, nationality, language, etc. Third, it puts in place a framework of

[63] Sami Zubaida, 'Sociologists and Race Relations' in Proceedings of a Seminar: Problems and Prospects of Socio-Legal Research (Nuffield College, Oxford, 1972) 141.

[64] John Scott and Gordon Marshall, *A Dictionary of Sociology* (3rd edn, OUP online 2015).

[65] Sewell, 'A Theory of Structure' (n 44) 3 (emphasis supplied).

[66] Bourdieu, *Outline* (n 59).

[67] Anthony Giddens, *A Contemporary Critique of Historical Materialism* (vol 1, Macmillan 1981) 27.

disadvantage for certain racialized groups at the expense of others, a framework which can in turn be adopted and deployed by everyone whom the state governs.

2.4 Centring Structural Racism

This chapter has presented a source-based framework for understanding racism at three levels: interpersonal, institutional, and structural. The book will go on to present an account of anti-racism as well to complement this framework. For now, it is important to create a bridge to that account of anti-racism by emphasizing that any account of anti-racism will have to take seriously and respond to racism understood through this multilevel framework which isolates the sources of racism in different types of racism.

As Coretta Phillips has argued, a multilevel framework of racism 'clearly specif[ies] the mechanisms and interacting processes through which ethnic inequalities are reproduced and sustained in a cumulative fashion.'[68] Focussing not on the consequences or symptoms but the processes of (re)production of racism helps lawyers, amongst others, to understand where racism comes from and not just how it manifests.[69] Responding to the processes which reproduce racism thus becomes important in the anti-thesis of racism. Although much more is required to build an account of anti-racism later, at a minimum, the conceptual work in this chapter establishes that the opposite of racism has to be conceptualized as the opposite of multiple levels of racism, especially structural racism. But why especially structural racism?

The practical answer that the book provides in the next part is that structural racism remains largely unacknowledged in law. Little has been done to address structural racism through discrimination law even when cases of structural racism have so obviously confronted lawyers and judges. Institutional racism is also under-acknowledged and dormant in practice. On the other hand, individual or interpersonal racism is considered the paradigmatic form of racism to be addressed in law. This state of affairs requires course correction because as this chapter has shown racism is not one thing and should be dealt with more broadly than is dealt currently in racial discrimination law.

More importantly, this requires course correction because even though racism is multilevel, the root cause of all racism is in fact structural racism which is left entirely unaddressed in law. Law's focus on individual or interpersonal racism is in

[68] Phillips, 'Institutional Racism' (n 10) 175.

[69] Sarah Ahmed, *On Being Included: Racism and Diversity in Institutional Life* (Duke University Press 2012) 43 ('racism should not be seen as about individuals with bad attitudes (the "bad apple model"), not because such individuals do not exist (they do) but because such a way of thinking underestimates the scope and scale of racism, thus leaving us without an account of how racism *gets reproduced*.').

fact ending up addressing racism which is derivative not generative of racism itself, ultimately letting racism to continue to generate and persist endlessly. To break this cycle of regeneration, law's attention may instead be distributed across all three levels of racism, including and especially structural racism.

The three levels of racism can be understood, as Phillips suggests, as micro, meso, and macro levels, such that

> Existing conceptualisations of institutional racialisation would place it at the meso level, with microlevel racialisation constituted by individual-level practices and interactions. Macro-level racialisation takes into account structural forces beyond individual practices and institutional processes[70].

Visually, the relationship can be depicted as a stacked Venn diagram (Figure 2.1) where structural racism encompasses institutional and interpersonal spheres such that all types of racism are actually, at a macro-level, explained as forms of structural racism as they form part of structural racism.

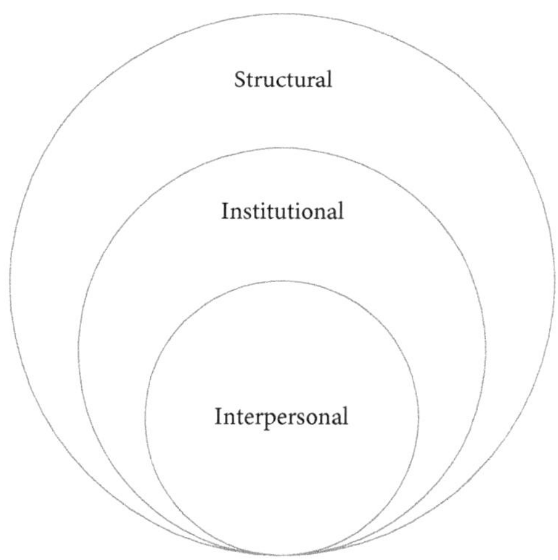

Figure 2.1 A Stacked Venn Diagram Depicting the Relationship Between Different Types of Racism

While interpersonal relationships and institutional dynamics can zoom into specificities of circumstances between individuals and collectivities, structural racism zooms out of 'single, intra-institutional setting to inter-institutional arrangements and interactions'[71] and instead provides a complex view of how multiple

[70] ibid.
[71] John A Powell, 'Structural Racism: Building upon the Insights of John Calmore' (2008) 86 North Carolina Law Review 791, 796.

forces produce racialized structures which then get reflected in interpersonal and institutional racism.

This does not mean that structural racism matters in some causally deterministic way such that all racism is reduced to structural racism. Structural racism instead shifts attention to causal complexity (not reductionism); and to the causal necessity (not sufficiency) of structures in not only structuring structural racism but also structuring interpersonal and institutional racism.

Yet, the necessity of structures or structural racism in other forms of racism does not mean that structural racism *necessarily* leads to other forms of racism. That is, scenarios (iii) and (iv) do not *necessitate* that individual doctors start declining patient-care to people of colour or hospitals operate as white spaces exclusively. Structural racism such as in scenarios (iii) and (iv) merely provides the necessary conditions for interpersonal and institutional racism. Their eventual form is also shaped by individual agency as well as the specific institutional norms, practices, and culture at stake.

Which is why addressing each level of racism matters as the source of each type of racism can be isolated more precisely than collapsing everything into structural racism—even though structural racism is, as this chapter has shown, the *sine qua non* of racism.[72] Centring structural racism allows us to appreciate that *all* racism has structural antecedents, not that all racism is either structural simpliciter or necessitated by structural racism.

2.5 Conclusion

This chapter has presented a tripartite source-based typology of racism as interpersonal, institutional, and structural. It showed that, depending on context, racism can be understood as each of these. But it showed that what is more instructive is to understand the relationship between these. This relationship is best characterized as a stacked Venn diagram where interpersonal racism is nested within institutional racism and then both interpersonal and institutional racism are in turn nested within structural racism. This means that structural racism ultimately defines both interpersonal and institutional racism and without it neither form can exist.

[72] Mumford and Anjum, *Causation* (n 4) 61–62 ('*Sine qua non* means *without which not*, which does not look to be the same as a causal connection ... the gap between a necessary condition and a true cause looks to be quite wide.') (emphasis in original); Paul Kissack, 'Coming to Terms with Race and Racism' Joseph Rowntree Foundation (15 April 2021) <https://www.jrf.org.uk/race-and-ethnicity/coming-to-terms-with-race-and-racism> (accessed 7 March 2024) ('a society is racist if it produces different, inequitable outcomes for different ethnic groups, as a result of the structures, rules, norms and policies that help to define that society. In this definition the concept of 'institutional racism' or 'structural racism' is meaningless—all racism is structural and institutional.').

This chapter will serve as the conceptual backbone for Part II of the book in answering whether and how racial discrimination law addresses racism. Before that, it is useful to reflect on the nature of anti-racism as well. Because for racial discrimination law to address racism, there must be a prior understanding of not only racism, but also the stance against it. This stance, anti-racism, needs its own conceptual framework before it can be traced in racial discrimination law. The next chapter turns to this.

3
A Framework of Anti-Racism

3.1 Introduction

Although accounts of race and racism are central to anti-racist theory and praxis, anti-racism as such is not simply the anti-thesis of racism. This is for two reasons. First, saying that anti-racism is the opposite of racism is hardly revealing enough. It tells us little about what anti-racism actually is or aims to achieve. Second, it does not align with the discourse which has developed, used, critiqued, abandoned, and reclaimed anti-racism both as a theory and as praxis consciously.[1] The syntax and debates surrounding the discourse on anti-racism are thus specific and sophisticated enough to merit their own rendering. This is why, having discussed race and racism in the previous chapters, the need for an account of the meaning of anti-racism itself remains.

This chapter addresses that need. It draws on two main sources to conceive anti-racism. First, the scholarship on anti-racism that developed in the UK in the post-war years. Second, the anti-racist praxis of social movements and civil society organizations in the post-war years. Together, they inform the account of anti-racism presented here, which is conceived as an account equally informed by theory and praxis.[2] It is the account developed in this chapter that this book treats as material in answering the central question posed: is there such a thing as a principle of anti-racism in law?

Section 3.2 below defines the contours of sketching the account of anti-racism for the purposes of this book. It justifies the interest in complementing the source-based typology of anti-racism developed in the previous chapter from the perspective of where racism really emanates from, with a typology of anti-racism defined from the perspective of what anti-racism should really target and who should be

[1] Alastair Bonnett, *Radicalism, Anti-Racism and Representation* (Routledge 1993) [hereafter Bonnett, *Radicalism*]; Alana Lentin, *Racism and Anti-Racism in Europe* (Pluto Press 2004) [hereafter Lentin, *Racism and Anti-Racism in Europe*].

[2] Alastair Bonnett, *Anti-Racism* (Routledge 2000) 4 [hereafter Bonnett, *Anti-Racism*] (describing anti-racism as 'forms of thought and/or practice that seek to confront, eradicate and/or ameliorate racism' and as 'ideologies and practices that affirm and seek to enable the equality of races and ethnic groups'); David Gillborn, 'Anti-racism: From p=Policy to Praxis' in Bob Moon, Sally Brown, and Miriam Ben-Peretz (eds), *Routledge International Companion to Education* (Routledge 2000) 484 ('Anti-racism is not a *gift* bestowed by intellectuals and liberals; it is a vital, developing and changing combination of activism and opposition that must continually involve diverse groups and be sensitive to its own limitations in vision and action. The best anti-racism seems likely to reflect a dynamic mix of experience and critical reflection—*praxis*.' (emphasis in original)).

Anti-Racism as a Legal Principle. Shreya Atrey, Oxford University Press.
DOI: 10.1093/9780198947646.003.0005

held responsible for change. Section 3.3 deals with three kinds of anti-racisms from this perspective—liberal, cultural, and transformative. Section 3.3.1 shows that liberal anti-racism mainly focusses on changing the minds and behaviours of individuals or individuals within institutional settings. Section 3.3.2 shows that cultural anti-racism mainly focusses on changing the collective experience of race and racism between racialized groups. Section 3.3.3 shows that transformative anti-racism focusses on neither and instead targets actors in whom power is concentrated—especially the state—for socio-economic, political, and cultural transformation of relations between people. Section 3.4 argues that transformative anti-racism is the most important kind of anti-racism if the law seeks to address the paradigmatic form of racism, which the previous chapter identified as, structural racism. Section 3.5 concludes with a reminder that while transformative anti-racism may not exclude liberal and cultural anti-racism, liberal and cultural anti-racisms are neither necessary nor sufficient in addressing structural racism.

3.2 Conceiving Anti-Racism

The anti-racist movement in the UK started to develop in the post-war years from the 1960s onwards and cut across contexts and spaces in the initial decades. From the celebration of the Caribbean culture at the first Notting Hill Carnival in 1966 to Rock Against Racism started in 1976 to fight racism through music; from the organized anti-fascist and anti-racist street demonstrations to the targeted advocacy of the Campaign Against Racial Discrimination set up in 1964 and the Anti-Nazi League set up in 1977; from the clamour for multicultural education to the adoption of Racism Awareness Training programmes by local councils since the 1980s; and from the establishment of the Institute of Race Relations in London in 1958 to the establishment of the Birmingham School of Cultural Studies in 1964; different versions of anti-racism have co-existed in social movements, civil society organizations, political parties, public authorities, schools, universities, and workplaces.

Yet, in comparison with racism, anti-racism as a concept remains relatively underdeveloped in scholarship.[3] In fact, the first comprehensive major work on anti-racism in the UK[4] appeared at the same time as when the obituary of 'what was once an anti-racist *movement*'[5] was being written. This was the early nineties, which makes both critiques and defences of anti-racism seem just over thirty years old.

[3] In most major accounts of racism, such as of WEB Du Bois, Frantz Fanon, Derrick Bell, and Stuart Hall, a self-standing inquiry on anti-racism was largely incidental.

[4] Bonnett, *Radicalism* (n 1).

[5] Paul Gilroy, 'The End of Anti-Racism' (1990) 17 Journal of Ethnic and Migration Studies 71, 72 (emphasis in original) [hereafter Gilroy, 'The End of Anti-Racism'].

This timeline though is misleading because it belies just how much work, scholarly and otherwise, had preceded these decades, which could be classified as anti-racist even though no clear or singular account of 'anti-racism' ever existed. Accounts of anti-racism now explicitly regard the anti-slavery and anti-colonial movements as part of anti-racist theory and praxis.[6] Historical accounts of resistance to racism in everyday life are also documented as 'everyday anti-racism'.[7] Likewise, theories of race and racism, considerably more prolific, are considered part of theories of anti-racism, even when they do not theorize on anti-racism independently.[8] The theory-making and practice of anti-racism thus appear to have been well underway long before dedicated accounts of anti-racism emerged in the last decades.

So, what do accounts of anti-racism entail?

As David Theo Goldberg says, anti-racism is basically 'a general but open-ended theory concerning race and racism ... [which] must also enable and encourage opposition to racist expression, for ultimately the efficacy of a theory about race and racism is to be assessed in terms of the ways in which it renders possible resistance to racisms'.[9] Similarly, as Abigail Bakan and Enakshi Dua put it: 'pivotal in advancing anti-racism, defined as a theoretically informed political praxis that can effectively challenge and overcome racism, is the capacity to explain the complex processes that generate race and racism.'[10]

Goldberg, Bakan, and Dua point to three components of anti-racism: race, racism, and change. Theories of, first, race, and second, racism, are central to anti-racism. That is why the discussion in the previous chapters was dedicated to this. How different accounts of race and racism feed into specific types of anti-racism will be discussed below. Third, no account of anti-racism is simply ideological or conceptual. Anti-racism is, as Alastair Bonnett argues, not simply, 'a "cause", fit only for platitudes of support or denouncement'.[11] Anti-racism is action-oriented and clear in respect of enacting change, and thus remains incomplete without a theory and praxis of change.

[6] Amanuel Elias, *Racism and Anti-Racism Today: Principles, Policies and Practices* (Emerald Publishing 2024) ch 7 [hereafter Elias, *Racism and Anti-Racism Today*].

[7] Kristine Aquino, 'Anti-Racism and Everyday Life' in John Solomos (ed), *Routledge International Handbook of Contemporary Racisms* (Routledge 2020); Peter A Hall and Michele Lamont, 'Why Social Relations Matter for Politics and Successful Societies' (2013) 16 Annual Review of Political Science 1; Philomena Essed, *Understanding Everyday Racism: An Interdisciplinary Theory* (Sage 1991).

[8] Robert Miles, *Racism* (Routledge 1989); Frantz Fanon, *The Wretched of the Earth* (Richard Philcox trans, Grover Press 2005); WEB Du Bois, *The Souls of Black Folk* (OUP 2009). For more recent scholarship in the UK, consider especially the collective work done in describing and analysing British racism as part of anti-racist theorizing: Gargi Bhattacharya et al, *Empire's Endgame: Racism and the British State* (Pluto Press 2021) [hereafter Bhattacharya et al, *Empire's Endgame*].

[9] David Theo Goldberg, *Racist Culture: Philosophy and the Politics of Meaning* (Wiley-Blackwell 1993) 41.

[10] Abigail B Bakan and Enakshi Dua (eds), *Theorizing Anti-Racism: Linkages in Marxism and Critical Race Theories* (University of Toronto Press 2014) 6.

[11] Bonnett, *Anti-Racism* (n 2) 2.

It is the relationship of anti-racism with change that forms the basis of the typology of anti-racism in this chapter.[12] Different accounts of anti-racism differ on this precise issue.[13] From these accounts, as with the accounts of racism considered in the previous chapter, we see that anti-racism is not one thing.[14] Corresponding to the source-based typology of anti-racism, this chapter classifies anti-racism from the perspective of what (the phenomenon) and whom (the entity) anti-racism targets as the source of racism to effect the change it aspires to.

Recall the four scenarios considered in the previous chapter:

(i) an individual doctor who refuses to treat Roma, Gypsy, and Irish Travellers whom the doctor believes do not have the right to receive medical treatment;
(ii) a hospital which preferentiates out-patients who live within its vicinity and thereby ends up excluding asylum seekers and refugees;
(iii) a policy which requires healthcare providers to check the right to remain in the country which leads to delays in treatment of people of colour; and
(iv) a pandemic, which has a disproportionate impact of sickness and death amongst Black and minority ethnic population.

In scenario (i), anti-racism could target the individual doctor and aim to punish and prevent the doctor and others in a similar situation for refusing medical treatment. In scenario (ii), anti-racism could target hospitals to demand a justification and an expansion in eligibility for services. In scenario (iii), anti-racism could target policymakers to retract identity-checks as a requirement for medical treatments. In each of these scenarios, there is an identifiable perpetrator whose actions or omissions may be made the target of anti-racism. How effective would these targeted actions be in actually addressing the stereotypes, prejudices, and policy preferences in a society? In contrast, in scenario (iv), the disproportionate impact of a pandemic may be variously attributable to a range of factors and actors responsible for health, education, etc. What and whom would anti-racism target here?

It is useful to interrogate how anti-racism justifies what and whom to target to address racism. Specifically, it is useful to interrogate what targeting individuals, collectivities or groups, and states or state-like actors does in addressing stereotypes, prejudices, policy preferences, and differential outcomes that affect racialized groups.

[12] Or, as Amanuel Elias asks more elaborately, '[t]o what extent are the objectives of anti-racism, such as racial justice and the dismantling of institutional racism/privilege, compatible with existing sociopolitical order?' Elias, *Racism and Anti-Racism Today* (n 6) 162.

[13] It is useful to note that despite significant differences, no anti-racism is simply a statement or declaration of the absence or rejection of race and racism. Anti-racism in any form is not simply a condemnation of racism. Each kind of anti-racism seeks to enact some positive change in addressing racism, though how that change is to be enacted is peculiar to each. What seems to distinguish different anti-racisms is basically what they consider racism and how they think it can be addressed—not whether racism exists and needs to be addressed.

[14] Ann Dummett, 'Anti-Anti-Racism' (1987) 9(13) London Review of Books.

3.3 Classifying Anti-Racism

The previous chapter developed a source-based typology of racism. This chapter develops a similar typology of anti-racism from the perspective of who anti-racism mainly targets or responsibilizes for change and what that targeting actually aims to change or achieve.

Section 3.3.1 discusses liberal anti-racism which is mainly directed at individuals, and their minds and behaviours. Section 3.3.2 discusses cultural anti-racism which aims to address the collective experience of race and racism of racialized groups. Section 3.3.3 discusses transformative anti-racism which targets wider social, economic, political, and cultural change through state and state-like entities who have the power to effect such broad-based change.

3.3.1 Liberal Anti-Racism

Liberal anti-racism targets individual psyche and behaviour. It takes individuals as the unit of attention to affect how individuals act interpersonally and within broader institutional settings.

It is more than an inverse of interpersonal racism which was identified in the previous chapter as the most rudimentary version of racism. Liberal anti-racism solely focusses on individuals and assumes that this focus can correct not only interpersonal racism but also racism in institutional, governmental, and corporate settings or wherever racist individuals are located. The idea is that racism within institutional settings can be addressed by changing the hearts and minds of individuals within them.

Importantly, liberal anti-racism does not target those at the helm of racial power relations, viz. the state and its institutions. Instead, it targets individuals operating on their own or within institutions through—consciousness and awareness raising campaigns,[15] unconscious bias trainings,[16] leadership and mentorship programmes,[17] and bystander response trainings,[18] with programmes like Racism Awareness Training (RAT) or Training in Racism Awareness (TIRA).[19] While leadership and mentorship programmes encourage greater representation of

[15] Marguerite Anne Fillion Wilson, 'A Pedagogy of Critical Consciousness and Anti-Racist Activism: Possibilities and Limitations of a Community-Based Whiteness Workshop Series' (2022) 194 Whiteness and Education 7.

[16] Judy H Katz, *White Awareness: Handbook for Anti-racism Training* (2nd edn, University of Oklahoma Press 2003). Cf Mike Moon, 'Pointless Diversity Training: Unconscious Bias, New Racism and Agency' (2017) 32 Work, Employment and Society 198.

[17] Sarah Diem and Anjalé D Welton, *Anti-Racist Educational Leadership and Policy Addressing Racism in Public Education* (Routledge 2020); Charmaine Roche and Jonathan Passmore, 'Anti-racism in Coaching: A Global Call to Action' (2022) 16 Coaching 115.

[18] Jacqueline K Nelson, Kevin M Dunn, and Yin Paradies, 'Bystander Anti-Racism: A Review of the Literature' (2011) 11 Analyses of Social Issues and Public Policy 263.

[19] Critiqued in Ambalavaner Sivanandan, 'RAT and the Degradation of Black Struggle' (1995) 26 Race and Class 1.

racially disadvantaged individuals in spaces, training programmes seek to prevent individuals from enacting racism in how they treat people from different racialized groups.

In particular, the training model of liberal anti-racism intends to rewire how people think about the Self and the Other, especially by targeting 'the behaviours and dispositions of the dominant racial group'.[20] It aims to derationalize and deincentivize discriminatory behaviour towards the Other especially in employment settings where race is considered irrelevant to job performance. It is this personalization of the struggle against racism that defines liberal anti-racism where anti-racism is equated with 'fighting an addiction [and] requires persistent self-awareness, constant self-criticism, and regular self-examination'.[21] If only the Self can be changed, the racialized Other can also be changed and deracialized in the process.[22]

But it is more than just its commitment to individual as the unit of change that justifies liberal anti-racism's 'liberal' tag. The critical mark of distinction of liberal anti-racism is that it seeks change but within the existing structural constraints, especially economic constraints set by neoliberal capitalism. That is, liberal anti-racism has at its heart a commitment to neoliberal capitalist structures, such that anti-racism operates without challenging the prevailing economic exploitation of or inequality between classes.[23] It thus does not target the vast disadvantage gaps between racialized groups. Liberal anti-racism instead takes structural racism to be the common sensical view of things—unfortunate but inevitable, and ultimately reconcilable. Liberal anti-racism thus acknowledges the existence of structural racism alright, but does not think of it as a target of anti-racism. Likewise, liberal anti-racism remains comfortable with political change so long as it is not structural but individual, that is, aimed at the inclusion of individuals belonging to diverse racial groups in existing political order rather than a shift in political power to those who have hitherto lacked it. Liberal anti-racism is in fact 'founded on the idea that to oppose racism does not necessitate doing more than upholding the fundaments—democracy, human rights, the rule of law, etc.—upon which the (western) state is purported to be based'.[24] It is these commitments, rather than its focus on the individual, that explain liberal anti-racism's 'liberal' tag.

[20] Sam Binkley, 'Anti-Racism Beyond Empathy: Transformations in the Knowing and Governing of Racial Difference' (2016) 9 Subjectivity 181, 183.

[21] Ibram X Kendi, *How to be an Antiracist* (One World 2019) ch 1.

[22] For the conception of white identity as against the racialized other, consider: Alastair Bonnett, 'Constructions of Whiteness in European and American Anti-Racism' in Pinina Werbner and Tariq Modood (eds), *Debating Cultural Hybridity: Multicultural Identities and the Politics of Anti-Racism* (Zed Books 2015).

[23] Arun Kundnani, *What is Anti-racism? And Why it Means Anti-capitalism* (Verso 2023) [hereafter Kundnani, *What is Anti-racism*]; Ambalavaner Sivanandan, *Communities of Resistance: Writings on Black Struggles for Socialism* (Verso 2019); Abigail B Bakan and Ekanshi Dua (eds), *Theorizing Anti-Racism: Linkages in Marxism and Critical Race Theory* (University of Toronto Press 2014).

[24] Alana Lentin, 'After Anti-Racism' (2008) 11 European Journal of Cultural Studies 311, 311.

The obvious downside of liberal anti-racism is that it misdiagnoses where the roots of racism really lie and instead attacks its symptoms as they manifest in individual actions and omissions. That is, liberal anti-racism ignores power structures and thus misunderstands racism as basically an individual problem. In doing so, it actively assumes the legitimacy of existing power relations and rationalizes them as the necessary and inevitable structure within which anti-racism must transpire. Even where it 'involve[s] the criticism of individual state actions ... such criticism is perceived separately from a general belief in the just nature of the principles upon which the dominant political thought is founded'.[25] Liberal anti-racism is not just complicit in but actually enables 'the reproduction of modern economies and the establishment of internationally accepted principles of political legitimacy'.[26]

The change liberal anti-racism seeks to enact is thus a limited one and, in any case, not one which targets structural racism.

3.3.2 Cultural Anti-Racism

Cultural anti-racism targets the cultural indicators attributed to racial groups and seeks to influence the understanding, acceptance, affirmation, and sometimes, even revision and repudiation, of people's religion, language, accent, dress, food, etc.[27] It can occupy the whole spectrum between overwhelming celebration and outright rejection of cultures of racialized groups.

Much like liberal anti-racism, cultural anti-racism seeks mainly a mindset change in how members of racialized groups perceive each other by engaging with the perceived differences between their cultural identities. Though the main difference between liberal and cultural anti-racism is that the former focusses on changing individual minds and behaviours whilst the latter is primarily interested in changing the collective experience of race and racial matters within communities, institutions, and broader public discourse and popular culture. Cultural anti-racism seeks to change the culture and how we engage with racialized cultures across these contexts through mass and social media, events, advertisements, etc. With a difference in what the two seek to change, liberal and cultural anti-racisms seem to run alongside as parallel tracks of anti-racism.

It is useful to dwell on the origin of cultural anti-racism and indeed its 'cultural' framing.

25 Lentin, *Racism and Anti-Racism in Europe* (n 1) 3–4.
26 Bonnett, *Antiracism* (n 2) 26.
27 ibid 88 ('the affirmation of multicultural diversity as a way of engaging racism'); Alana Lentin, '"Race", Racism and Anti-racism: Challenging Contemporary Classifications' (2000) 6 Social Identities 91, 95 ('to combat racism by insisting upon the equal valorisation of all cultures and a respect for difference').

Cultural anti-racism is often traced back to the United Nations Educational, Scientific and Cultural Organisation (UNESCO) which in 1950 was tasked with drawing up a 'statement on race and racial prejudice'.[28] UNESCO's Declaration on Race and Racial Prejudice was ultimately released in 1978. In the main, the Declaration did two things: first, it debunked any biological basis of 'race'; second, it linked racism to difference in lifestyles and cultures.[29] It then proceeded to say how such racism was to be defeated. Its answer lay firmly in culture:

> Culture, as a product of all human beings and a common heritage of mankind, and education in its broadest sense, offer men and women increasingly effective means of adaptation, enabling them not only to affirm that they are born equal in dignity and rights, but also to recognize that they should respect the right of all groups to their own cultural identity and the development of their distinctive cultural life within the national and international contexts, it being understood that it rests with each group to decide in complete freedom on the maintenance, and, if appropriate, the adaptation or enrichment of the values which it regards as essential to its identity.[30]

The Declaration was clear that while human rights and freedoms were essential to combatting racism, they could yet prove insufficient, and thus 'broadly based education and research programmes designed to combat racial prejudice and racial discrimination and ... programmes of positive political, social, educational and cultural measures calculated to promote genuine mutual respect among groups' were needed.[31]

In the UK, this broad-based educational and programmatic approach to anti-racism has been adopted gradually by local authorities, and councils from the 1960s onwards. It has involved targeting community relations by dedicating resources to inter-group engagement through events, festivals, campaigning, etc in schools, neighbourhoods, towns, and cities. The point is to share and generate a positive understanding of the cultural identities of racialized groups, but especially those whose cultural identities are marginalized or vilified. For example, the Oxford City Council Anti-Racism Charter commits to, inter alia:

> Actively promote and celebrate the history and achievements of ethnic minorities and people of colour in communities, schools, colleges, universities, workplaces

[28] Bonnett, *Anti-Racism* (n 2) 69; Lentin, *Racism and Anti-Racism in Europe* (n 1) 112.
[29] UNESCO, Declaration on Race and Racial Prejudice 1978, art 1.
[30] ibid, art 5(1).
[31] ibid, art 6.

> and through arts and cultural events to realise our shared history as core to British history.
>
> Nurture, showcase and award the talent in our diverse communities, so that people of colour and ethnic minorities are recognised and celebrated as role models too, not just by ethnic minorities, but also the wider community.[32]

A similar framing has been adopted by public and private entities for promoting equity, equality, diversity, inclusion, and integration or 'EDI'/'DEI' initiatives as they are often called. Civil society organizations, schools, universities, workplaces, etc make explicit declarations committing to these values. They seek to realize these values through representation-enhancing initiatives to bring in more individuals from different racialized groups within their spaces but also often through cultural exchange and engagement across members of racialized groups in these contexts. This is especially visible in the national curriculum adopted in the UK since the Education Reform Act 1988 which prioritized cultural anti-racism above other versions of anti-racism in education.[33]

The flaw in cultural anti-racism is that it mistakenly assumes that the racialization of culture can be addressed by valorizing culture. It thus adopts the very framing that it seeks to oppose and in turn generates an interminable cycle of racialization of culture.

This critique requires some explanation.

Cultures can indeed be racialized, and thus represent a distinct form of racism as cultural racism.[34] For example, Muslim cultural identity—perceived through religious norms, dress, food, language, lifestyle, national origin, etc—when seen as

[32] Oxford Anti-Racism Charter <https://www.oxford.gov.uk/anti-racism-charter> (accessed 7 October 2024).

[33] Peter Figueroa, 'Multiculturalism and Anti-racism in a New ERA: A Critical Review' (1999) 2 Race Ethnicity and Education 281.

[34] As Michael Wieviorka explains: 'To speak of cultural racism is legitimate if it is being argued that the sources of certain prejudices are cultural, but not if one contends that the definition of "race" by the racist refers exclusively to cultural characteristics—to customs or religion, for example. To dislike Islam to the point of violence, for example, is racist, if Muslims themselves are constructed as a natural category, and their behaviour, real or imagined, is presented as informed in some way or another by an essence, by innate attributions or an almost genetic cultural heritage. That contemporary racism should appeal to cultural factors, to the nation, to tradition, to historical or religious identity, and encompass the idea of a natural (or "racial") substratum, believed by racists to underlie culture, ethnicity and religion, is quite possible, and it is in no way exaggerated in these instances to speak of racism; but we should be careful not to confuse intercultural tensions, abject or violent as they may on occasions be, with racism, which implies, of necessity, an idea of nature. Racism ... is a social construction, a spontaneous or doctrinal representation; in no way can it be based on an external, objective reality of race, even if it is obviously facilitated by a number of—for example—phenotypical characteristics of the racialised group. It is associated with the subjectivity of the actors, and if the latter refer uniquely to nation, religion, traditions and, more generally, to culture, with no references to nature, biology, genetic heritage or blood, it is preferable not to speak of racism.' Michael Wieviorka, 'Is it so Difficult to be an Anti-Racist?' in Pnina Werbner and Tariq Modood (eds), *Debating Cultural Hybridity: Multicultural Identities and the Politics of Anti-Racism* (Zed Books 2015) 142.

conveying something *inherently* backward or dangerous about Muslim people, becomes the paradigmatic case of anti-Muslim racism or Islamophobia.[35]

Cultural anti-racism seeks to respond to such racism by either generating positive images of the tolerant and liberal Muslim or by rejecting aspects of Muslim identity deemed extreme. The former is captured, for example, in the popular representation of Muslims in local and national politics through Sadiq Khan, the longest serving Mayor of London and Humza Yousuf, the first Muslim First Minister of Scotland. The latter is captured, for example, in the UK government's Prevent policy which seeks to address the supposed radicalization of people by Islam.[36] In either case, by insisting on the affirmation or rejection of Muslim identity, cultural anti-racism ends up fossilizing Muslim identity as intrinsic to those who are considered Muslim because of their faith, name, dress, national or ethnic origin, etc. Cultural anti-racism thus ends up endorsing culture as a thing which carries racial meaning.

However, as Chapters 1 and 2 argued, culture, or for that matter, religion, do not carry racial meaning a priori. Muslims are racialized not because their culture or religion signifies their race but through the process of racialization which entails Muslims being banded together *as a* race or a racial group on the basis of religion or culture. Religion or culture become racialized *as a consequence of* racialization. Racialization can occur on any basis—actual, perceived, or mistaken—biological, cultural, religious, etc. What distinguishes racialization from other forms of hierarchy-instating processes related to gender, disability, or class is simply what comes to be called race *as a result of* racialization.[37]

To sum up, cultural anti-racism enacts cultural racism by uncritically adopting the problematic notion of culture or cultural identity as race. Analytically, this adoption is meaningless. Practically, it is ineffective because it not only (i) enacts cultural racism but also (ii) ignores structural racism. That is, first, unlike liberal anti-racism, which neutralizes, even expunges, race from the anti-racist discourse by reducing racialized groups to individuals, cultural anti-racism maintains a psychedelic vision of the world where individuals from different racialized groups, ethnic groups, religions, castes, and communities are painted in the cultures of their groups rather than their political causes. Cultural anti-racism thus often

[35] Nasar Meer and Tariq Modood, 'Islamophobia as the Racialisation of Muslims' in Irene Zempi and Imran Awan (eds), *The Routledge International Handbook of Islamophobia* (Routledge 2019); Tariq Modood, 'British Muslims and the Politics of Multiculturalism' in Tariq Modood, Anna Triandafyllidou, and Ricard Zapata-Barrero (eds), *Multiculturalism, Muslims and Citizenship: A European Approach* (Routledge 2005).

[36] Shamim Miah, 'The Prevent Policy and the Values Discourse: Muslims and Racial Governmentality' in Máirtín Mac an Ghaill and Chris Haywood (eds), *Muslim Students, Education and Neoliberalism Schooling a 'Suspect Community'* (Springer 2017); Imran Awan, '"I Am a Muslim Not an Extremist": How the Prevent Strategy Has Constructed a "Suspect" Community' (2012) 40 Politics and Policy 1158.

[37] Paul Gilroy, *After Empire: Melancholia or Convivial Culture* (Routledge 2004) 37 (describing race as a 'discursive arrangement, the brutal result of the raciological ordering of the world, not its cause').

reduces the 'radical political agenda [of anti-racism] to superficial efforts to serve international foods, wear ethnic clothes, and decorate corporate complexes and airports with native colors and art'.[38] With its focus—variously on tolerance, celebration, assimilation, integration, rejection, or reformation of cultures—cultural anti-racism represents an essentialized discourse where cultures are rendered stolid, impermeable to change, and permanently affixed to individuals as immutable badges of racial identity.[39] Secondly, by adopting a reductive conception of race and racism which privileges culture and identity over politics or history, cultural anti-racism ultimately privileges identity politics over socio-economic change.[40] In fact, it has very little to do with improving the material conditions of racially disadvantaged groups and along with liberal anti-racism represents what may be called neoliberal anti-racism.[41]

3.3.3 Transformative Anti-Racism

Transformative anti-racism seeks to fundamentally transform the totality of racialized relations between people defined in social, economic, political, psychological, and cultural terms.

It can be understood along three dimensions: first, its resistance to prevailing institutions and structures which produce racial disadvantage; second, its call for disruptive, proactive, and preventive action, rather than ex-post, remedial, and incremental change; and third, its commitment to intersectional justice and coalitional politics.

First, transformative anti-racism exceeds the liberal and cultural focus on individuals and communities or racialized groups for reform. It instead targets institutions—its norms, practices, and culture; and structures—especially state laws, policies, and governance. That is, it targets where the source of racist power lies and seeks to diminish and dismantle the power structures which give rise to racialization and racial disadvantage. Inevitably, this means a focus on state

[38] Gloria Anzaldúa, 'The New Mestiza Nation: A Multi-cultural Movement' in Carole McCann, Seung-Kyung Kim, and Emek Ergun (eds), *Feminist Theory Reader: Local and Global Perspectives* (Routledge 2013) 278.

[39] Sara Ahmed, *On Being Included: Racism and Diversity in Institutional Life* (Duke University Press 2012); Walter Benn Michaels, *The Trouble With Diversity: How We Learned to Love Identity and Ignore Inequality* (Henry Holt 2007); Etienne Balibar, 'Is There a Neoracism?' in Etienne Balibar and Immanuel Wallerstein (eds), *Race, Nation, Class, Ambiguous Identities* (Verso 1999); Gilroy, 'The End of Anti-Racism' (n 5) 72; Pierre-André Taguieff, 'The New Cultural Racism in France' (1990) 83 Telos 109.

[40] Ambalavaner Sivanandan, 'Challenging Racism: Strategies for the "80s"' (1983) 25 Race and Class 1; Paul Gilroy, *There Ain't no Black in the Union Jack: The Cultural Politics of Race and Nation* (University of Chicago Press 1991).

[41] Jacqueline Nelson and Kevin Dunn, 'Neoliberal Anti-Racism: Responding to 'Everywhere but Different' Racism' (2017) 41 Progress in Human Geography 26.

power as state is often where power is concentrated in societies. Transformative anti-racism is thus distinguished from liberal and cultural anti-racisms as a form of anti-state anti-racism. Likewise, transformative anti-racism is particularly concerned with improving the material conditions of racially disadvantaged groups and is often distinguished from liberal and cultural anti-racisms as a form of radical anti-racism which is also anti-capitalist.[42]

Yet, secondly, transformative anti-racism is not simply about opposition to state or capitalist structures. It is about opposing *and* replacing the dominant structures. It seeks a fundamental rupture and not incremental change in the totality of social, economic, political, psychological, and cultural relations which bring about racism, and is thus

> more than a discourse. It is a call to make the theoretical discourse of empowerment real, a call for a fundamental restructuring of power relations within the institutional structures of society ... to interrogate and rupture systems of power and privilege in order to effect global social transformation.[43]

To achieve this, transformative anti-racism is both action- and process-oriented. It has its roots in activism and social movements which employ subversive vocabulary (emancipation, liberation, freedom, justice, etc) and tools (pamphleteering, sloganeering, campaigning, disruption, sit-ins, marches, protests, strikes, etc) to challenge racism.

For example, the Black Lives Matter movement UK uses Thomas Sankara's words in large font on its website landing page:

> Our revolution is not a public-speaking tournament. Our revolution is not a battle of fine phrases. Our revolution is not simply for spouting slogans that are no more than signals used by manipulators trying to use them as catchwords, as codewords, as a foil for their own display. Our revolution is, and should continue to be, the collective effort of revolutionaries to transform reality, to improve the concrete situation of the masses.[44]

London Black Revolutionaries or Black Revs, in a statement from 2014, describe themselves as:

> We are a democratic-militant organisation that encourages self-leadership but strictly adheres to fighting oppression and exploitation in non-abstract forms. We combine practical versatility, modern methods for organising, self-emancipation,

[42] Kundnani, *What is Anti-racism* (n 23); Bonnett, *Anti-Racism* (n 2) 88; Lentin, *Racism and Anti-Racism in Europe* (n 1) 129.

[43] George J Sefa Dei, 'Integrative Anti-Racism: Intersection of Race, Class, and Gender' (1995) 2 Race, Gender and Class 11, 15.

[44] Black Lives Matter UK <https://ukblm.org/> (accessed 7 October 2024).

> direct action, militant defensives and offensives and full commitment to the struggle as cornerstones of London Black Revolutionaries. Our organisation is for those who see nothing else but struggle and will not settle for anything less than a world rid of oppression and exploitation.[45]

The Runnymede Trust, which has advocated for racial justice for over fifty years in the UK, describes itself as:

> Proudly independent, we speak truth to power on race and racism without fear or favour. We are not swayed by political agenda, profit or popular opinion. We are authentic, led by an ethnically diverse team we draw from our lived experience and that of our wide and inclusive community and partnership networks.[46]

The self-descriptors of anti-racist civil society organizations and social movements are thus characteristically insurgent and articulated as an expression of collective power. Equally, they call for action for disruptive and total, rather than simply piecemeal and incremental, change.

Thirdly, transformative anti-racism considers race and racism to be co-constituted by other forms of oppression and exploitation such as patriarchy, poverty, classism, ageism, ableism, homophobia, transphobia, etc. Its anti-racist politics is coalitional and based on solidarity across groups fighting for all forms of injustice. Consequently, it is opposed to identity politics which limits political alliances to those who belong to or are seen as belonging to a particular group alone. Rather, politically conscious use of identity categories associated with race, colour, ethnicity, caste, etc is preferred.

Transformative anti-racism is best reflected in the radical anti-racist movement in the UK in the 1960s and 1970s which brought together anti-racists under the political banner of Black struggle—where 'Black' was used purely as a political signifier rid of its descriptive connotations of colour or national or ethnic origin—and instead represented 'all people who have experienced and have a common history of: imperialism, colonialism, slavery, indentureship and racism.'[47] In Sivanandan's emphatic words:

> my experience in the black, anti-racist struggles of the '60s and '70s—when we made black the colour of our politics and not the colour of our skins—when we

[45] London Black Revolutionaries <https://en.wikipedia.org/wiki/London_Black_Revolutionaries#:~:text=The%20London%20Black%20Revolutionaries%20(also,political%20organisation%20centred%20in%20London> (accessed 7 October 2024).

[46] Runnymede Trust UK <https://www.runnymedetrust.org/about/about-us> (accessed 7 October 2024).

[47] Bonnett, *Anti-Racism* (n 2) 127 (quoting from Clark and Subhan's undated work); Stuart Hall, 'Old and New Identities, Old and New Ethnicities' in Stuart Hall (ed), *Essential Essays, Volume 2: Identity and Diaspora* (Duke University Press 1991) [hereafter Hall, 'Old and New Identities'] ('Anti-racism in the seventies was only fought and only resisted in the community, in the localities, behind the slogan of a Black politics and the Black experience.').

> fought on the factory floor and in the community, as a people and a class, and as a people for a class—tells me that only in being involved and supporting each other's struggles can we forge an organic relationship between us, not just ad hoc coalitions. We cannot let ourselves be bogged down in our particularities and miss the wood for the trees. We need to have an international perspective, even as we take on national or local issues. We need to move, in our thinking, from the particular to the general and the general to the particular, both at once. And it is then that we can successfully turn individual cases into social issues, social issues into civic causes, and civic causes into a national movement.[48]

This dual focus on the general and the particular and the local and the global defines transformative anti-racism's all-embracing remit as a grand intersectional coalition of movements fighting for justice.[49] It is captured befittingly in the work of Southall Black Sisters who have worked tirelessly to oppose violence against women and girls since 1979, especially women from immigrant and minoritized backgrounds who have few economic resources and little political power. Their work is thus informed by a keen awareness of how patriarchy, poverty, migration, and racism all intersect such that no single force can be isolated and held up as the sole basis for violence against women.

It is in these three ways that transformative anti-racism targets structural racism. Its focus lies in sharp contrast with liberal and cultural anti-racisms which focus on the minds, behaviours, and cultural experience of individuals and social groups. Transformative anti-racism instead focuses on the drivers of racial disadvantage and aims to transform how racial disadvantage comes about in the first place.

The difficulty with transformative anti-racism is threefold. First, although it seeks to address drivers of racial disadvantage, those drivers are not often transparent. It is challenging to identify structural racism in a causal sense, given the nature of structural racism. Meaningful data and research—which is reliable and comprehensive—is hard to come by. Second, the desire for radical change rather than incremental reform, although admirable, ultimately transpires incrementally in reality. Transformative anti-racism takes seriously the idea that structures are, after all, self-perpetuating and do not permit anything like an overnight overhaul or instant revolution. The change it enacts is thus slow rather than immediate, despite its insurgent and urgent-sounding rhetoric. Thirdly, while intersectional politics may be analytically justified and strategically suitable, it may be impractical in fact. Working across barriers of identity politics and commitment to particular

[48] Ambalavaner Sivanandan, *Catching History on the Wing: Race, Culture and Globalisation* (Pluto Press 2008) xviii–xix.

[49] Floya Anthias and Nira Yuval Davis, *Racialised Boundaries – Race, Nation, Gender, Colour and Class and the Anti-Racist Struggle* (Routledge 1992).

causes, including spatial, lingual, and cultural barriers requires exceptional leadership, organization, and resources.

These though are not analytical challenges in how transformative anti-racism is imagined and conceptualized. They are operational challenges which may be assailed if favourable conditions prevail. But analytical challenges do exist. The next section responds to three such challenges before turning to argue that transformative anti-racism should be treated as normatively central to all anti-racist efforts, including in law.

3.4 Centring Transformative Anti-Racism

As Section 3.3 argued, different types of anti-racism attack different types of racism. However, only transformative anti-racism attacks the drivers of racism, that is, the very structures from which racism emanates. Three questions arise here. First, should transformative anti-racism be considered the only or the main anti-racism worth pursuing? Second, given that structures are self-perpetuating, how does transformative anti-racism actually transform structures and ultimately structural racism? Third, can law, especially discrimination law, which itself is a structure, be considered both open to and also a tool for transformative change?

First, consider the relationship between different kinds of anti-racism. For this purpose, it is instructive to learn from how radical or transformative anti-racist work itself has defined its relationship with liberal and cultural anti-racisms. For example, Southall Black Sisters' work entails specific and individualized support for survivors as well as broader campaigning targeting law and policy. They thus do not exclude liberal and cultural efforts and indeed organize individualized services and community-related events. What has made them iconic is the 'national impact in changing social, cultural and religious norms, and in influencing policy and practice as well as legal reform'.[50] Their work cuts across different anti-racist frameworks much like the work of the Minority Rights Group which works to support minoritized and racialized groups with 'no one-size-fits-all approach'.[51] They pursue international advocacy and strategic litigation as much as media programmes and training. But they also work with indigenous groups and racialized minorities directly for co-designing programmes and strategies for enhancing direct and indirect democratic participation, strengthening public accountability mechanisms, seeking reparations for slavery, and capacity-building and activism.

[50] Southall Black Sisters <https://southallblacksisters.org.uk/our-impact/> (accessed 7 October 2024).

[51] Minority Rights Group International <https://minorityrights.org/about-us/> (accessed 7 October 2024).

Transformative anti-racism thus need not reject liberal and cultural anti-racism. As Alistair Bonnett's empirical research in education has deftly shown, this non-rejection can be reflexive and strategic.[52] It is neither a co-optation by nor a slippage into liberal and cultural anti-racism, but a self-conscious choice of transformative anti-racists to avoid inaction and to generate possibilities of change within the existing structures.

This reflexivity is manifest in transformative anti-racism given that it not only works *against* the structure which is the source of all racism but also inevitably *within*, and also, sometimes *with* it. The subversive possibility for transformative change thus exists within this relational configuration between transformative anti-racism and the existing hegemonic structure.[53] Transformative anti-racism cannot realistically lie outside the hegemonic structure and in a different universe where structural racism does not exist.

It is the location of transformative anti-racism within the hegemonic structure that creates an unstable relationship between the two from the outset. While by its very nature, transformative anti-racism cannot exist in alignment with the very structures it fundamentally opposes, it can exist in perfect or productive discord with structures such that its opposition becomes dualistic—one critical of the structures but also open to using them for transformation.

Transformative anti-racism can thus co-exist with liberal and cultural anti-racisms where the latter two are critiqued and yet seen as exploitable in the fight against structural racism. But it does challenge the preoccupation with individuals and cultures as the mainstay of anti-racism. So, while it enlarges the remit of anti-racism to not exclude liberal and cultural anti-racism, it orientates our attention properly towards tools for critiquing and correcting structural racism mainly.

Once again, the best way to visualize the relationship between different types of anti-racism (Figure 3.1) is to imagine liberal anti-racism as nested within cultural anti-racism and both in turn to be nested within transformative anti-racism. This means that transformative anti-racism encompasses other forms of anti-racism but that other forms of anti-racism are not transformative and hence, alone, cannot fight against structural racism. Liberal and cultural measures to fight racism would thus fail to address the sources or drivers of racial disadvantage and would merely address its symptoms or manifestations as they reflect in interpersonal and institutional racism. Importantly, they would fail to enact change, especially change which is broad-based and uplifts not only those who are racially disadvantaged but everyone who is intersectionally disadvantaged.

[52] Bonnett, *Radicalism* (n 1) 192–193.

[53] William H Sewell, 'A Theory of Structure: Duality, Agency, and Transformation' (1992) 98 American Journal of Sociology 1, 16.

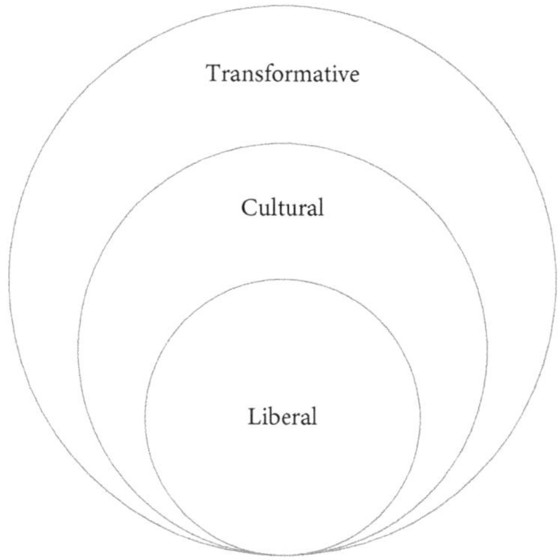

Figure 3.1 A Stacked Venn Diagram Depicting the Relationship Between Different Types of Anti-Racism

But as Chapter 2 showed, structures are self-perpetuating and capable of reproducing themselves until perpetuity. Thus, second, how can transformative anti-racism *actually* transform structural racism?

Structures are durable because they are self-perpetuating but they are not permanent because of the following qualities William Sewell highlights. First, structures vary greatly such that kinship and familial structures operate differently from educational and employment structures which operate differently from religion and law and so on. Structures are also overlapping and create their own intersectional modalities. This heterogeneity and intersectionality of structures and the resulting information asymmetry and incommesurability within them make exact reproduction of structural racism between them contingent as opposed to inevitable. Secondly, structures reproduce through agentic individuals who ultimately translate structural racism from one day to next, from one case to another, from one context to another, etc. These individuals, on their own or acting collectively, carry the 'capacity to engage in highly autonomous, discerning, and strategic actions'[54] and should not be written off as either lacking in agency and hence ineffective against structural racism, or as co-opted agents and hence complicit in structural racism. The reproduction of structures though predictably strong is thus neither certain nor measurable in form or extent. This is what makes transformation

[54] ibid 15, 20 ('Such enactments of structures imply a particular concept of agency-one that sees agency not as opposed to, but as constituent of, structure. To be an agent means to be capable of exerting some degree of control over the social relations in which one is enmeshed, which in turn implies the ability to transform those social relations to some degree.').

possible in the face of self-perpetuating character of structural racism. As the conditions of reproduction of structures variate, structures are not reproduced exactly, and so the reproduction of structural racism is disrupted.

This is ever more possible with states, because, as Sewell argues: 'state and political structures are consciously established, maintained, fought over, and argued about rather than taken for granted as if they were unchangeable features of the world.'[55] Neoliberal entities, such as Meta, Amazon, Alphabet, and X, are similarly negotiating their scale of power in the public discourse. The constant making, unmaking, and remaking of the state and state-like corporate actors generates points of intervention for individuals and collectivities to rearrange the social, economic, political, and cultural relationships around them. This rearrangement too happens on a constant basis and over time can transform the social, economic, political, and cultural relationships between people.

Third, can law produce such transformation? Or, as a structure which is wielded by the state, does law only produce structural racism?

Law, especially discrimination law, has been considered 'fundamentally ambiguous' to accommodate this duality especially for racially marginalized and minoritized groups whose interests are mostly desecrated but sometimes also served by law.[56] As Kimberlé Williams Crenshaw remarks, discrimination law cannot be considered a 'permanent pronouncement of society's commitment to ending racial subordination'.[57] But it does represent 'an ongoing ideological struggle in which the occasional winners harness the moral, coercive, consensual power of law'.[58] It is useful to unpack this duality.

Consider the rejection or prohibition of racial discrimination in constitutional and statutory law. According to Crenshaw, this itself cannot mean that law as a structure is fundamentally transformative. That is, the prohibition of racial discrimination per se cannot be considered as opposed to structural racism. It would be duplicitous if law conveyed its fundamental opposition to structures, including itself. But in conveying *some* opposition to racial discrimination, law leaves open the possibilities for conceiving this opposition broadly. These possibilities can be exploited not only by the state and its institutions which wield law, but also people themselves as they respond to law, mobilize the law, activate legal mechanisms, etc. People's tryst with law, individually and collectively, thus throws open the possibilities of conceiving and operationalizing law in a transformative sense. Even if state's power over law exceeds people's power over law, as explained above, structural asymmetry and human agency allow 'occasional winners' to stake a claim to transformative anti-racism.

[55] ibid 24.

[56] Kimberlé Williams Crenshaw, Race, Reform, and Retrenchment: Transformation and Legitimation in Antidiscrimination Law (1988) 101 Harvard Law Review 1331, 1135.

[57] ibid.

[58] ibid.

Given that this possibility exists, law, including racial discrimination law, can be considered open to transformative anti-racism, that is, a rejection and indeed reversal and replacement of the current social, political, economic, and cultural order which racializes and disadvantages people.

Needless to say, transformative anti-racism is hardly exhausted at law's altar. Its remit is by no means confined to its opposition to law. As Sally Haslanger explains, 'law can function as a means of social reproduction as much as it disrupts it. Legislation depends on elites who, for the most part, have been disciplined to perform their "proper" social function and have an interest in maintaining the system. Moreover, legal activism, even if justified, tends to be ineffective unless there is a corresponding cultural change, over which law has limited control.'[59] Quite rightly, as Haslanger argues, 'structural change requires a multipronged approach'.[60] So, any change through law alone is ultimately going to be limited and should be accompanied by social, economic, political, and cultural change in order to be complete. But to the extent that law shapes social, economic, political, and cultural relations between people, law has a role, significant but not sufficient, in transformative anti-racism.

Hence, while disenchantment with law is part of transformative anti-racism as law is, after all, a 'structuring structure',[61] disengagement is not.

3.5 Conclusion

This chapter confirmed that while there is 'a profound heterogeneity'[62] or 'the concomitant plurality of anti-racisms',[63] transformative anti-racism accommodates this plurality within itself. Still, other forms of anti-racism do not become transformative simply by virtue of this accommodation. In fact, they remain neither necessary nor sufficient in transformative anti-racism's threefold focus on attacking drivers of racial disadvantage, intersectionally defined, through disruptive change. It is this threefold focus that addresses structural racism rather than liberal or cultural anti-racist measures.

Given this relationship between liberal, cultural, and transformative anti-racisms, it is arguable that liberal and cultural anti-racisms, where they exist, are superfluous and ultimately a distraction from addressing structural racism. Yet, the relationship between liberal, cultural, and transformative anti-racisms as explained in the nested-Venn diagram shows that liberal and cultural anti-racisms

[59] Sally Haslanger, 'How to Change a Social Structure' <https://www.ucl.ac.uk/laws/sites/laws/files/haslanger_how_to_change_a_social_structure_ucl.pdf> (accessed 7 October 2024).
[60] ibid.
[61] Pierre Bourdieu, *Outline of a Theory of Practice* (Cambridge University Press 1977) 72.
[62] Lentin, *Racism and Anti-Racism in Europe* (n 1) 3–4.
[63] Yin Paradies, 'Whither Anti-racism?' (2016) 39 Ethnic and Racial Studies 1, 2–3.

can legitimately exist *within* transformative anti-racism. That is, where transformative anti-racism exists, other ways of tackling racism can also exist without it taking anything away from broader efforts targeting structures; where transformative anti-racism does not exist, liberal and cultural anti-racisms appear neither necessary nor sufficient in tackling structural racism.

Thus, it may be argued that liberal anti-racism when existing alongside transformative racism contributes to transformative anti-racism by attacking racism holistically—its drivers and its consequences. For example, EDI measures, such as to train individual healthcare providers to make more inclusive decisions, may be helpful. But when such measures exist only on their own and against a framework of law and policy which is highly restrictive, they will be insufficient in actually broadening access to healthcare. Moreover, such measures may be unnecessary on their own. This is because in the absence of transformative measures, liberal anti-racism's sole focus on changing individual minds and behaviours would only address a form of racism which is clearly not the root or the source of the problem but merely a manifestation. Thus, on their own, EDI measures would be 'a non-solution to the problem of racism'.[64]

Though, in the final analysis, both liberal and cultural anti-racisms get the wrong end of the problem by targeting people's minds, behaviour, and experiences to be opened, redeemed, and restored with equality, tolerance, and empathy and rid of prejudice and bias. They rely on psychologization of anti-racism which has little to do with actual material conditions which sustain racism. This mismatch between the solution that liberal and cultural anti-racisms offer, and the problem of racism, ultimately proves the futility of liberal and cultural anti-racisms existing independently. But alongside transformative anti-racism, liberal anti-racism can be justified (or at least not be considered futile) because another form of anti-racism is actually tackling structural racism. Likewise, cultural anti-racism may have a place within transformative anti-racism. Cultural anti-racism can, for example, challenge how citizenship is conceived along racialized lines through measures for integration of racialized migrants. Art and culture can play a role in shaping a reformed idea of the nation-state which is neither racialized nor nationalist.[65] But in the absence of broader efforts, viz. to reform existing citizenship laws, cultural anti-racism sits against a framework of structural racism which actually disciplines cultural anti-racism. Despite its avowed aims, the limit of cultural anti-racism is thus stymied in the absence of a challenge to the very framework of structural racism within which it exists. Such a challenge can only be provided by transformative anti-racism which then emerges as the key to all anti-racism. For this reason, unless otherwise specified, henceforth in this book, anti-racism refers only to transformative anti-racism because it is only that that is anti-racist in a complete sense.

[64] Bhattacharya et al, *Empire's Endgame* (n 8) 85.
[65] Hall, 'Old and New Identities' (n 47) 404.

4
A Framework of Anti-Racism in Law

4.1 Introduction

The previous chapter explained that the relevant framework of anti-racism is one of transformative anti-racism because it goes to the very heart of attacking racism in the form of structural racism. Thus, while other 'anti-racisms', such as liberal and cultural anti-racisms, can exist within this framework; 'anti-racism' in a complete sense is simply transformative anti-racism.

The previous chapter also explained that law is indeed an apposite site for such anti-racism. The question that arises now is: in what form should anti-racism exist in law?

It is useful to pause to answer this normative question for three reasons. First, because it is often glossed over. Unblinkingly and overwhelmingly, the question is answered: 'but of course, in the form of a prohibition of racial discrimination!'. This answer elides the divide between the normative and the descriptive. The fact that there *is* a relationship between anti-racism and racial discrimination law does not explain what relationship there *should* be between anti-racism and law. Thus, before turning to the descriptive claim about racial discrimination law in Part II of the book, it is worth pausing to reflect on the normative aspect. Furthermore, secondly, given that this book goes on to show that racial discrimination law largely fails in addressing structural racism, it is worth considering how it could. Relatedly, thirdly, since the remit of anti-racism is wider than racial discrimination law, it is also worth considering what else can help enact anti-racism beyond the extant body of racial discrimination law.

This chapter suggests that anti-racism should be conceived as a legal principle. This suggestion is arrived at: first, by tracing the normative contours of legal principles as such (Section 4.2); then, by mapping the frameworks of racism and anti-racism explained in the previous chapters, against the framework of principles as a legal standard as opposed to other kinds of legal standards such as rules, policies, and values (Section 4.3); and finally, the features of anti-racism as a legal principle especially its content, scope, function, and location (Section 4.4).

The central argument is that anti-racism as a legal principle guides the imagination and operation of all law and policy to address structural racism.

To expand, not only ideation, drafting, and promulgation, but also all activities related to law and policy, including interpretation, application, and enforcement, should be guided by an imperative to oppose and redress structural racism. This

Anti-Racism as a Legal Principle. Shreya Atrey, Oxford University Press. © Shreya Atrey 2026.
DOI: 10.1093/9780198947646.003.0006

means, as Chapter 2 argued, paying attention to the three aspects of structural racism in terms of how (i) the state and state-like entities (ii) racialize (iii) to instate racial disadvantage. Further, as Chapter 3 argued, anti-racism in a transformative sense includes an imperative to not only (i) address structural racism, but also to do so to effect (ii) broad-based and (iii) intersectional change, as opposed to individual, incremental, and isolated change. Anti-racism as a legal principle thus embodies the tripartite understandings of both structural racism and transformative anti-racism developed in Chapters 2 and 3, respectively.

Needless to say, anti-racism as a legal principle does not exhaust anti-racism. It should be amply clear from the previous chapters that race, racism, and anti-racism do not exist exclusively or predominantly in the legal register. The claim then is not that a legal principle should be the *only* form in which anti-racism should exist. The claim is that *in law* the most suitable mould for anti-racism is as a principle.

While this is a normative claim, it is not necessarily a prescriptive one. That is, while anti-racism *ought to be considered* a legal principle, whether *it must exist as such*, is a different matter that we only turn to in the conclusion of the book, after considering the descriptive claim of whether anything like anti-racism as a legal principle can be gleaned from doctrine in British, comparative, and international law. The normative claim thus only extends to justifying the possibility of existence of anti-racism as a legal principle.

4.2 Legal Principles

What is a legal principle?

There is far too much debate about legal principles for this question to be answered straightforwardly. The complexity and scale of this debate cannot be conveyed in this chapter. This section mainly provides a working understanding of legal principles to be able to justify the claim about anti-racism as a legal principle.

One understanding of principles was proposed by Ronald Dworkin according to whom a principle 'states a reason that argues in one direction, but does not necessitate a particular decision'.[1] In contrast, rules 'dictate the result, come what may'.[2] That is, a rule applies 'in an all-or-nothing fashion. If the facts a rule stipulates are given, then either the rule is valid, in which case the answer it supplies must be accepted, or it is not, in which case it contributes nothing to the decision.'[3] Principles thus differ from rules 'in the character of the direction they give'.[4] While

[1] Ronald Dworkin, 'The Model of Rules' (1967) 35 University of Chicago Law Review 14, 26 [hereafter Dworkin, 'The Model of Rules'].
[2] ibid 35.
[3] ibid 25.
[4] ibid 35.

rules are deterministic of particular outcomes, principles are not. Instead, principles guide the reasoning behind outcomes.

Principles also differ from policy. A policy is 'that kind of standard that sets out a goal to be reached, generally an improvement in some economic, political, or social feature of the community'.[5] While a principle is a 'standard that is to be observed, not because it will advance or secure an economic, political, or social situation deemed desirable, but because it is a requirement of justice or fairness or some other dimension of morality'.[6] This distinction between principles and policies too is based on the character of direction each standard provides. While policies are directed towards achievement of specified outcomes, principles are directed towards advancement of broader moral, ethical, or political commitments. Both policies and principles may be based on values which are standards which are deemed morally desirable or important such as equality, justice, and fairness. But they differ from values in their specificity. For example, while equality, justice, and fairness are values, principles based on those values are articulated as 'everyone shall be treated equally before the law', 'no one shall be a judge in their own cause', and 'no one shall be deemed guilty without a trial'.

These distinctions are however not clear-cut.[7] Standards such as rules, principles, policies, and values may all form part of a legal system.[8]

Consider the following four statements:

(a) No one shall treat another less favourably on the basis of race.
(b) Free healthcare shall be provided to those in need.
(c) Diversity shall be celebrated.
(d) Structural racism shall be addressed.

Statement (a) may be considered a rule because it stipulates a result (prohibition of conduct) when a condition is fulfilled (less favourable treatment based on race).

[5] ibid 23.

[6] ibid.

[7] Joseph Raz, 'Legal Principles and the Limits of Law' (1972) 81 Yale Law Journal 823 [hereafter Raz, 'Legal Principles']; Torstein Eckhoff, 'Guiding Standards in Legal Reasoning' [1976] Current Legal Problems 205 [hereafter Eckhoff, 'Guiding Standards']; David Lyons, 'Principles, Positivism, and Legal Theory' (1977) 87 Yale Law Journal 415 [hereafter Lyons, 'Principles']; Robert Alexy, 'Zum Begriff des Rechtsprinzips' in Werner Krawietz (ed), *Argumentation und Hermeneutik n der Jurisprudenz* (Duncker and Humblot 1979) [hereafter Alexy, 'Zum Begriff']; Mark V Tushnet, 'Following the Rules Laid Down: A Critique of Interpretivism and Neutral Principles' (1983) 96 Harvard Law Review 781; Donald L Beschle, 'A Matter of Principle' (1985) 19 Marshall Law Review 237; David A Strauss, 'Principle and Its Perils' (1997) 64 University of Chicago Law Review 373; John Braithwaite, 'Rules and Principles: A Theory of Legal Certainty' (2002) 27 Australian Journal of Legal Policy 47; Michel Rosenfeld, 'Dworkin and the One Law Principle: A Pluralist Critique' (2005) 59 Revue Internationale de Philosophie 363; Willliam Twining and David Miers, *How to Do Things With Rules* (5th edn, Cambridge University Press 2010) [hereafter Twining and Miers, *How to Do Things*]; Mitchell N Berman, 'How Practices Make Principles, and How Principles Make Rules' (2024) 28 Journal of Ethics and Social Philosophy 299 [hereafter Berman, 'How Practices Make Principles'].

[8] HLA Hart, *The Concept of Law* (2nd edn, OUP 1994) 238–276.

Statement (b) may be considered a policy intended to achieve a particular outcome (free healthcare for those in need). Statement (c) may be considered a value-based statement about the importance of celebrating diversity.

The last of these, statement (d), may be considered a principle because it provides guidance in general. It asks for structural racism to be addressed in all contexts. Statement (d) does not ordain a specific result such as is ordained in statement (a). Likewise, while statement (b) seeks to promote or achieve a specific socio-economic goal, statement (d) is not so oriented. While statement (c) is overtly value-laden, statement (d) goes beyond the statement of a value and towards guiding action based on a concrete yet general objective of opposing structural racism. However, both statements (c) and (d) may be considered general statements of ideals.

The distinctions between these standards appear more a matter of degree than kind.[9] Statement (d) could, like statement (a), be considered as an imperative to prohibit structural racism. It could also be considered, like statement (b), a policy objective for addressing structural racism. It could also be considered, like statement (c), to be a statement of value, indicating the importance of addressing structural racism.

What *kind* of a standard a standard is cannot thus be determined either lexically or normatively. That is, it may not be possible to pin down a standard simply by observing how it is framed semantically or by observing it against a strict normative but ultimately artificial standard.

But it is possible to distinguish between standards based on their function. Roughly, a sense of what each standard was trying to do guided the categorization above. In this categorization, statement (d) emerged as a kind of principle because it is guiding action in a more deliberative way by orienting the decision maker in opposition to structural racism and is hence different from a rule (which ordains an outcome), a policy (which focusses on a goal), and a value (which conveys a judgement).

What statement (d) is trying to do is to provide general guidance by introducing the need to address structural racism in all reasoning. It is not that other statements are not providing guidance, but their extent of *this* kind of general deliberative guidance is limited.[10] Statement (a) obviously does not provide general guidance as it applies only to facts which relate to less favourable treatment based on race. Statement (b) is not simply guiding reasoning but is aimed at the provision of and hence achievement of a specific objective. Statement (c) is guiding but in a more

[9] András Jakab, *European Constitutional Language* (Cambridge University Press 2016) 369, 377; Twining and Miers, *How to Do Things* (n 7) 83.

[10] Joseph Raz, *Practical Reason and Norms* (OUP 1999) 49 [hereafter Raz, *Practical Reason*] ('"Principles" and "rules" are often used interchangeably, though the word "principles" usually carries an implication of greater generality and greater importance than the word "rules"').

vague and idealistic sense. Only statement (d) guides in a specific but broad sense such that the particular concept or phenomenon of 'structural racism' is invoked and directed to be 'addressed', that is, confronted, corrected, reversed, repaired, and resolved, without necessitating a particular way in which this must be done or a particular outcome.

As a legal principle, statement (d) thus provides deliberative, non-deterministic guidance for action. The next section explains why a legal principle is better suited to address structural racism as opposed to other legal standards.

4.3 Anti-Racism as a Legal Principle

In the previous chapters, we considered the following four scenarios:

(i) an individual doctor who refuses to treat Roma, Gypsy, and Irish Travellers whom the doctor believes do not have the right to receive medical treatment;
(ii) a hospital which preferentiates out-patients who live within its vicinity and thereby ends up excluding asylum seekers and refugees;
(iii) a policy which requires healthcare providers to check the right to remain in the country which leads to delays in treatment of people of colour; and
(iv) a pandemic, which has a disproportionate impact of sickness and death amongst Black and minority ethnic population.

Chapter 2 argued that behind each scenario was structural racism, that is, no scenario could be explained fully without reference to how the state and state-like entities racialize to instate racial disadvantage in social, economic, cultural, political, and psychological terms. Further, while the first three scenarios could be explained partially as interpersonal or institutional forms of racism, the final scenario could only be explained as structural racism.

Chapter 3 argued that the anti-thesis of racism, or anti-racism, involves opposition to structural racism, which lies at the heart of all racism. By addressing structural racism, we thus address interpersonal and institutional racism but not vice versa. What Chapter 3 did not do was to explore what kind of a legal norm can respond to structural racism. In particular, what kind of a norm can respond to structural racism of the kind reflected in scenario (iv) above and hence to all forms of racisms in scenarios (i)–(iii).

Which of the following four statements can address scenario (iv)?

(a) No one shall treat another less favourably on the basis of race. (rule)
(b) Free healthcare shall be provided to those in need. (policy)
(c) Diversity shall be celebrated. (value)
(d) Structural racism shall be addressed. (principle)

Statement (a) is too specific and does not directly control the poor health outcomes of Black and minority ethnic population during a pandemic. Only when facts stipulated in statement (a) intersect with scenario (iv) such as when Black and minority ethnic population are denied medical treatment, does statement (a) apply. It applies deterministically, that is, it dictates a particular outcome—prohibition of less favourable treatment based on racial grounds. Statement (a) represents an anti-racist rule which has the potential to address individual and institutional racism in scenarios (i) and (ii). Furthermore, the anti-racism reflected in the rule in statement (a) is liberal anti-racism. As Chapter 3 explained, liberal anti-racism is directed at changing individual behaviour, institutional policy, or practice. It does not address the underlying causes which give rise to structural racism such as in scenario (iv).

Statement (b) is a broad policy objective which can help address poor health outcomes for Black and minority ethnic population generally through free healthcare. But healthcare does not determine the totality of health outcomes which are equally to do with education, environment, income, class, culture, etc. Statement (b), as an anti-racist policy, does not fully address scenario (iv), and much like statement (a) remains at the level of liberal anti-racism.

Statement (c) is a statement of value: celebration of diversity. It can be said to indirectly oppose a range of things: racial discrimination, structural racism, racial disadvantage, racial conflict, and racial disharmony. So, it can oppose structural racism in scenario (iv) but may be limited in doing so meaningfully because its guidance (to celebrate diversity) is rather amorphous and hence weak. It thus reflects anti-racist values of cultural anti-racism which, as the previous chapter explained, targets racial relations or the collective experience of race and racism within communities. Cultural anti-racism of the kind reflected in values such as in statement (c) do little to actually address the drivers of racial disadvantage behind scenario (iv).

Statement (d) reflects an anti-racist principle because it provides general guidance: to address structural racism. It can be applied to scenario (iv) to understand the determinants of health outcomes for Black and minority ethnic population. Their needs can thus be better catered to for improving health outcomes *before* pandemics, and to prevent worsening of health outcomes and providing better necessary healthcare *during* pandemics. This in turn can prevent the disproportionate impact of sickness and death amongst Black and minority ethnic population due to pandemics. In this way, statement (d) could attack structural racism in scenario (iv).

Importantly, in attacking structural racism in scenario (iv), the principle in statement (d) would also attack interpersonal and institutional racisms in scenarios (i)–(iii). It would prevent the individual doctor in scenario (i) from refusing medical treatment to some because of his beliefs. Instead, the individual doctor would be guided by the opposition to structural racism and the imperative to not only not worsen but actually to improve the racial disadvantage suffered by Roma, Gypsy, and Irish Travellers, by providing healthcare to them. The doctor would be guided to do so directly through a legal principle if the doctor is working in a public hospital. Importantly, statement (d) would guide the actions in scenario (i) even when no rule like in statement (a) exists, that is, even without an explicit prohibition of racial discrimination in the form of a rule. The generality of statement (d) as a legal principle of anti-racism would apply to all actions and omissions of public employees and agents of states and state-like entities. It could thus exist independently or could exist alongside rules and hence orientate rules to oppose structural racism.

Likewise, the legal principle of anti-racism will prevent the hospital in scenario (ii) from preferentiating on any basis such as geographical proximity if it affects people on a racialized basis. This is because it would be particularly vigilant to how hospitals can racialize (instate racial order and hierarchy) and in turn disadvantage some racialized groups while advantaging others. This is the very essence of structural racism as identified in Chapter 2 which is not captured in anti-racism as a rule, policy, or value.

Finally, the principle would prevent enactment of a policy such as in scenario (iii) which requires medical treatment to be offered on the basis of production of evidence of right to remain in a country. Anti-racism as a legal principle would thus address scenario (iii) when an anti-racist rule, policy, or value would be either too specific or too broad in providing guidance for how a policy should be framed to avoid unnecessary delays in or denial of treatment to people of colour.

In this way, the principle of anti-racism can address all scenarios (i)–(iv) and thus all forms of racism: individual, institutional or systemic, and structural. It could do so by existing independently or by existing alongside other norms (rules, policies, and values) and thus helpfully supplementing them by orienting them to address structural racism.

That anti-racism is best captured as a legal principle as opposed to a legal rule, policy, or value—has equally to do with the form of these standards as it is about the substance of anti-racism. Following the argument made in the previous chapter, this section assumed that anti-racism as a legal principle is about addressing structural racism. There is more to be said about what this means. The next section outlines the substance of anti-racism as a legal principle.

4.4 Features of Anti-racism as a Legal Principle

This section defines the content, scope, function, and location of anti-racism as a legal principle. The content of anti-racism as a legal principle embodies the tripartite understandings of structural racism and transformative anti-racism explored in Chapters 2 and 3 (Section 4.4.1). The scope of anti-racism as a legal principle is general and applies across all areas of law and policy (Section 4.4.2). The function of anti-racism as a legal principle is to guide all deliberations for action within the legal system (Section 4.4.3). The location of anti-racism as a legal principle is diffused within the legal system as such it can be found in legislation, judicial decisions, policy, etc (Section 4.4.4).

4.4.1 Content

The content of anti-racism as a legal principle coincides with the understandings of structural racism and transformative anti-racism offered in Chapters 2 and 3. So, even though anti-racism as a legal principle appears in an abbreviated form in this chapter as being about *addressing structural racism*, considerable content is packed within this abstraction. It is important to appreciate the full wherewithal of what it means to address structural racism.

Chapter 3 argued that anti-racism in a complete sense refers to transformative anti-racism because it attacks (i) structural racism in a (ii) broad and (iii) intersectional way. Structural racism, in turn, was defined in Chapter 2 as the complex totality of forces which bring about racialized outcomes in a society. Structural racism has to do especially with how (i) state and state-like entities (ii) racialize (iii) to instate racial disadvantage. While anti-racism can include liberal and cultural forms of anti-racism, it is primarily geared towards attacking the drivers of racial disadvantage and thus goes to the very heart of the causes of racism rather than its symptoms. In doing so, it addresses all other forms of racism such as individual or interpersonal and institutional or systemic forms of racism. Importantly, anti-racism is about addressing structural racism in such a way that it is transformative, that is, it brings about, first, broad-based change which is disruptive, preventive, and proactive as opposed to ex-post, remedial, and incremental; and second, intersectional justice across patterns of racism, sexism, homophobia, transphobia, classism, ableism, communalism, ageism, etc.[11] But because structures by their very nature are complex and co-constituted, addressing structural racism is perforce transformative. That is why anti-racism in an all-encompassing sense is simply that which addresses structural racism. Corollarily, the content of anti-racism as a legal principle too is about addressing structural racism.

Structural racism is not one thing. It is, as Chapter 2 argued, the result of the complex totality of forces which bring about racialized outcomes in a society. Thus, the opposition to structural racism in the form of an imperative to 'address' structural racism is not a command which can be actioned *in one way* to *achieve anti-racism*. Instead, as argued in the previous chapters, opposition to structural racism

[11] Consider Chapter 3, Section 3.3.3 in this book.

requires actions contributing to the continuous process of anti-racism. Again, this is simply due to the very nature of structures which are self-reinforcing or self-perpetuating and belie any possibility of overnight overhaul. Structural change or transformation is thus a process forever in motion and not a result to be achieved once and then terminated.[12]

In this context, 'addressing' structural racism must entail a range of possibilities—such as confronting, denouncing, correcting, repairing, reducing, remedying, replacing, reversing, and resolving structural racism—rather than a single result. Even if that single result means the closing of the material gaps between racialized groups, anti-racism or the imperative to address structural racism cannot be terminated at this result. Anti-racism would continue to work to maintain that result and to prevent racialized gaps from reappearing through structural racism.

For example, addressing structural racism of the kind in scenario (iv)—where a pandemic has a disproportionate impact of sickness and death amongst Black and minority ethnic population—entails not a single but a range of measures. These can include addressing the factors affecting the health outcomes through education, healthcare, environment, income, class, culture, etc. These measures can be both preventive and proactive as well as reactive and remedial. No complete list of measures can be generated to exhaust the range of possibilities to address structural racism in scenario (iv). Importantly, even the termination of disproportionate impact on Black and minority ethnic population cannot exhaust anti-racism which must continue to prevent the regeneration of such impact, including by memorializing the past when such impact existed and by preparing to address such impact if it arises in the future.

Anti-racism as a legal principle would thus give rise to a range of possibilities for enacting transformative anti-racism. This could include rules, policies, and values which can be adopted to address structural racism such as norms (a), (b), and (c) discussed in this chapter. The converse however may not be possible. That is, rules, policies, and values cannot generate a general principle like a principle of anti-racism for the reasons explained in the previous section.

Still, it is worth considering, for example, if anti-racism can be inscribed onto a legal rule such as a prohibition of racial discrimination so as to replace anti-racism as a legal principle? Indeed, if the prohibition of racial discrimination can be considered a prohibition of structural racism, then the need for a principle of anti-racism would recede. As Ludwig Wittgenstein said, 'the rule, once stamped with a particular meaning, traces the lines along which it is to be followed through the whole of space'.[13] If we could 'stamp' the rule—the prohibition of racial

[12] Consider Chapter 2, Section 2.3.3 in this book.

[13] Ludwig Wittgenstein, *Philosophical Investigations* (Blackwell 1953) 219.

discrimination—with anti-racism—then we could trace anti-racism along the length and breadth of discrimination law.

This idea has traction. In fact, much of the field of discrimination law has taken up this suggestion and sought to give meaning to equality/discrimination in a specific sense. The field has thus been preoccupied with debates about what equality means—formal, substantive, anti-classification, anti-subordination, anti-stereotyping, equality of opportunity, equality of results, egalitarianism, etc;[14] or what discrimination is—stigma, stereotyping, prejudice, demeaning, undignifying, autonomy-depriving, loss of substantive freedoms, etc.[15] Scholars, practitioners, policymakers, judges, civil-society organizations, etc all stake claims to particular visions of equality/discrimination including to racial equality and conversely racial discrimination.[16] In this tradition, one could give meaning to rules prohibiting racial discrimination as rules prohibiting structural racism or rules of anti-racism.

The difficulty with this idea is this. The concept of anti-racism cannot be inscribed onto a legal rule so precisely. As Chapter 3 argued and as this chapter has reiterated, anti-racism is not a concept with a concretized inscription to be inscribed on to something. As an action-oriented norm, it can guide reasoning for action, but it is not *determinative* of a result. This is because anti-racism involves

[14] Herbert Wechsler, 'Toward Neutral Principles of Constitutional Law' (1959) 73 Harvard Law Review 1 [hereafter Wechsler, 'Toward Neutral Principles']; Frank Michelman, 'The Supreme Court, 1968 Term—Foreword: On Protecting the Poor Through the Fourteenth Amendment' (1969) 83 Harvard Law Review 7; Owen M Fiss, 'Groups and the Equal Protection Clause' (1976) 5 Philosophy and Public Affairs 107; Paul Brest, 'In Defense of the Antidiscrimination Principle' (1976) 90 Harvard Law Review 1; Cass R Sunstein, 'The Anticaste Principle' (1994) 92 Michigan Law Review 2410; Jack M Balkin and Reva B Siegel, 'The American Civil Rights Tradition: Anticlassification or Antisubordination?' (2003) 58 University of Miami Law Review 9; Christopher McCrudden, 'Equality and Non-Discrimination' in David Feldman (ed), *English Public Law* (OUP 2004); Bob Hepple, *Equality: The Legal Framework* (Hart 2011); Kate O'Regan, 'Undoing Humiliation, Fostering Equal Citizenship: Human Dignity in South Africa's Sexual Orientation Equality Jurisprudence' (2013) 37 NYU Review of Law and Social Change 307; Alexandra Timmer, 'Toward an Anti-Stereotyping Approach for the European Court of Human Rights' (2011) 11 Human Rights Law Review 707; Sandra Fredman, 'Substantive Equality Revisited' (2016) 14 International Journal of Constitutional Law 712; Catharine A MacKinnon, 'Substantive Equality Revisited: A Reply to Sandra Fredman' (2016) 14 International Journal of Constitutional Law 739.

[15] Denise G Réaume, 'Discrimination and Dignity' (2003) 63 Louisiana Law Review 1; Deborah Hellman, *When is Discrimination Wrong?* (HUP 2008); Kasper Lippert-Rasmussen, *Born Free and Equal? A Philosophical Inquiry into the Nature of Discrimination* (OUP 2013); Deborah Hellman and Sophia Moreau (eds), *Philosophical Foundations of Discrimination Law* (OUP 2013); Benjamin Eidelson, *Discrimination and Disrespect* (OUP 2015); Tarunabh Khaitan, *A Theory of Discrimination Law* (OUP 2015); Iyiola Solanke, *Discrimination as Stigma* (Hart 2017); Hugh Collins and Tarunabh Khaitan (eds), *Foundations of Indirect Discrimination Law* (Hart 2018); Sophia Moreau, *Faces of Inequality: A Theory of Wrongful Discrimination* (OUP 2020).

[16] Seminal scholarly contributions include: Laurence Lustgarten, *Legal Control of Racial Discrimination* (MacMillan 1980); Derrick A Bell, *Faces at the Bottom of the Well: The Permanence of Racism* (Basic Books 1992); Linda S Greene, 'Race in the 21st Century: Equality through Law' (1989–1990) 64 Tulane Law Review 1515; Iyiola Solanke, *Making Anti-Racial Discrimination Law: A Comparative History of Social Action and Anti-Racial Discrimination Law* (Routledge 2009); Nancy Leong, 'Racial Capitalism' (2012) 126 Harvard Law Review 2151; Mark Golub, *Is Racial Equality Unconstitutional* (OUP 2018).

transformation of social, political, cultural, economic, familial, religious, and psychological structures. Anti-racism thus does not 'stipulate' facts or 'dictate' a result like a rule can.[17] Thus, if a rule is meant to achieve a result, anti-racism is not such a result to be achieved. We cannot, as Paul Gilroy says, 'anatomise from this distance' what anti-racist futures truly look like.[18]

Instead, the content of anti-racism fits the mould of principles because they are, as Robert Alexy argues, optimization requirements which can be fulfilled to varying degrees.[19] Importantly, and perhaps in contrast with Alexy, this does not mean some quantifiable or mathematical variance which can be measured as more or less against a standard of full optimization. Because there is no blueprint of full optimization in the context of anti-racism, it is more accurate to say that anti-racism as a legal principle can be fulfilled in varying *ways* than varying *degrees*.

However, just because anti-racism can be fulfilled in varying ways does not mean it is result-agnostic. To recall, the content of anti-racism as a legal principle is specifically oriented to achieve transformative anti-racism which, in shorthand, is about addressing the drivers of racial disadvantage. It *has* a particular end goal: to end racial disadvantage. As already argued, given the very nature of structural racism through which racial disadvantage arises, structural racism needs not one but several pathways to be surmounted. Structural racism can thus not be addressed via a rule which stipulates facts to yield a particular result. Only a legal principle of anti-racism can accommodate multiple pathways to transformation.

In sum, a legal system's commitment to anti-racism must exist in the form of a legal principle and not only as a rule prohibiting racial discrimination. In fact, as the rest of this book shows, prohibition of racial discrimination in discrimination law *needs* a principle of anti-racism in order to work optimally against the whole range of racism, especially structural racism. Without anti-racism as a legal principle, a legal rule prohibiting racial discrimination becomes rudderless and substantially limited in its personal, material, evidential, and remedial scope as we will see across British, comparative, and international law.[20]

4.4.2 Scope

A legal principle of anti-racism is specific in its content (addressing structural racism) but general in its scope of application because it is not contextually limited to a specific area of law or policy or activities relating to them, such as legal interpretation.

[17] Dworkin, 'The Model of Rules' (n 1) 25, 35; Raz, 'Legal Principles' (n 7) 841 ('Principles, because they prescribe highly unspecific acts, tend to be more vague and less certain than rules.').
[18] Paul Gilroy and Adam Shatz, 'The Absurdities of Race' (2020) London Review of Books Podcast.
[19] Alexy, 'Zum Begriff' (n 7) 59–87.
[20] Chapters 6, 7, 8, 9, and 10 of this book.

A legal principle is a norm facing the legal system. This means that it applies to the legal system (as opposed to private entities and individuals directly) and to all law and law-related activities.[21] Accordingly, anti-racism as a legal principle would be a norm which applies primarily to the legal system and to all state action which must be in conformity with the law, including policymaking, which must also be in conformity with the law. After all, a legal system is part of the state. So, as a state-facing norm, the scope of anti-racism as a legal principle directly complements its content which focuses on the role of state and state-like entities in enacting structural racism.

But within this legal scope, anti-racism as a legal principle would be general in its application. It would be general in that it would guide the imagination (ideation, drafting, and promulgation) and operation (interpretation, application, and enforcement) of all state law and policy in such a way that they address structural racism. There are two levels of generality here. First, the sphere of application of anti-racism is not limited to particular areas of law (administrative law, constitutional law, discrimination law, human rights law, tax law, tort law, etc) or policy (education, environment, health, housing, labour, security, trade, transport, etc). Instead, anti-racism as a legal principle applies generally across these contexts. This distinguishes anti-racism as a legal principle from the statutory prohibition of racial discrimination which is limited to the context of discrimination law and its well-defined sphere of operation such as in the Equality Act 2010 in the UK (which does not apply to all state action).[22] Second, what kind of legal activity anti-racism applies to is also general. This means that anti-racism as a legal principle applies not only when drafting or interpreting a law, but also to all activities related to law (and policy) including its imagination or ideation, its drafting or formulation, its promulgation or enactment, its interpretation or application, and its administration or enforcement.

The latter is particularly important because there is often a misunderstanding that legal principles are either limited to or are predominantly for interpretation of laws alone. For example, Joseph Raz identified five uses of legal principles—(i) as grounds for interpreting laws, (ii) as grounds for changing laws, (iii) as grounds for certain exceptions to laws, (iv) as grounds for making new rules, and (v) as the sole

[21] Raz calls legal systems 'comprehensive' and explains: 'By this I mean that they claim authority to regulate any type of behaviour ... legal systems ... do not acknowledge any limitation of the spheres of behaviour which they claim authority to regulate.' Raz, *Practical Reason* (n 10) 150.

[22] Colm O'Cinneide, 'Fumbling Towards Coherence: The Slow Evolution of Equality and Anti-Discrimination Law in Britain' (2006) 57 Northern Ireland Legal Quarterly 57, 75 [hereafter O'Cinneide, 'Fumbling Towards Coherence'] ('anti-discrimination legislation does not apply to acts done under the authority of an Act of Parliament, nor can it override other statutory provisions. By itself, it is insufficient to protect against unfair discrimination in vertical relationships. There is a need for "constitutional" equality norms that will steer the interpretation of legislation in a way that maximises protection against discriminatory impact, and provide for the possibility of judicial review challenges to state action that results in unequal treatment.').

ground for action in particular cases.[23] It is the first of these that he called the 'most extensive and least inhibited use' of principles.[24]

But the scope of a legal principle, such as of anti-racism, can neither be limited to these five instances nor to interpretation or hermeneutics alone. That a legal principle of anti-racism *does* apply in these ways and in particular in interpretation *does not* mean that they exhaust its scope of application. The whole point of its generality vis-à-vis the legal system is that it applies to a whole range of legal activities.

As we saw above, anti-racism as a legal principle can be applied in determining the legitimate purpose of institutional or governmental policy or their tools for implementation such as in scenarios (ii) and (iii) above. Likewise, remedial or programmatic measures such as those addressing attainment gaps or variance in health outcomes can be imagined from an anti-racist perspective to address scenario (iv). Tax laws can be drafted from an anti-racist perspective, for example, for the state to lower tax rates for postcodes with a high concentration of racially marginalized groups. Judges could review all of the above against anti-racism as a legal principle, in particular to check that the decision maker has addressed the drivers of racial disadvantage and in turn the racial disadvantage between racialized groups.

The general scope of application of anti-racism is coterminous with its broad function which is to provide deliberative guidance for all state action. This is explored below.

4.4.3 Function

Aligned with the general scope of application of anti-racism as a legal principle is its broad function for guiding all state action.

Anti-racism as a principle provides the 'normative raw material'[25] for thinking through all state action. As state action must be in conformity with law (rule of law), if anti-racism is a legal principle, then all state action must also be in conformity with anti-racism. But as we have seen, anti-racism is not a prescriptive norm. It does not dictate *a* particular result. Instead, it is a deliberative norm which provides guidance for action. Its function is to provide a normative framework for action.

For example, when a government is trying to curb immigration, it must consider the steps it seeks to take against the principle of anti-racism. One of its steps may be to introduce right to remain checks for individuals before they receive medical treatment [scenario (iii)]. Those without permission to remain in the country

[23] Raz, 'Legal Principles' (n 7) 839.
[24] ibid.
[25] Eckhoff, 'Guiding Standards' (n 7) 206–207, 211.

may thus be found out, returned to their home country, and immigration numbers lowered as a result. Likewise, landlords, city councils, electricity providers, phone providers, etc may all be asked to perform right to remain checks to ensure that they are providing services only to those who have permission to remain in the country.

In assessing these options against anti-racism as a legal principle, the government must consider if it is addressing structural racism in the process. This means that it would need to consider that it, as the state, is not racializing people, to disadvantage them. Racializing, as we saw in Chapters 1 and 2, is to instate racial divisions and hierarchies, based on some criteria. In the present case, right to remain checks are particularly vulnerable to racialization as they may be bypassed by those who may seem to have permission to stay in Britain but do not. This sense of perception may be predominantly driven by skin colour and accent such that those who seem white and sound British may not be subjected to right to remain checks as they are presumed to have such a right. Naturalized citizens, second- and third-generation citizens, migrants, refugees, and asylum seekers, who are likely to be non-white or do not speak English, may be subjected to these checks (based on racialization), leading to delays in accessing medical treatment, tenancies, or other public services (racial disadvantage).

To avoid structural racism, the government will need to be particularly aware of how processes of racialization work on a quotidian basis. Once aware, it would not only seek to avoid such racialization but actively redress it. It may do so by targeting immigration at the borders as opposed to within civilian life. It may thus remove the possibilities of racialization in everyday life. It may also take up active promotion and appreciation of immigration in industries which have made a particular contribution to British life, while curbing immigration in industries which are shrinking or with a high volume of labour already available.

The operational significance of anti-racism as a legal principle thus extends beyond deliberation for its own sake and towards deliberation for action and indeed action itself.[26] Anti-racism as a legal principle cannot be observed by a decision maker by deliberating alone.[27] Anti-racism as a legal principle is both action and

[26] That we cannot deliberate rationally about ends has been shown to be false. As Richardson remarks, '[t]o assume in a blanket fashion that rational deliberation cannot extend to adopting ends is wrongly to suppose that intellectual effort cannot be fruitfully brought to bear upon what matters to us most.' Henry S Richardson, *Practical Reasoning about Final Ends* (Cambridge University Press 2012) 6.

[27] Anti-racism as a legal principle is thus distinct from norms such as the public sector equality duty (PSED) embodied in section 149 of the Equality Act 2010 which obliges public authorities to have 'due regard to the need to'—(a) eliminate discrimination, harassment, victimization, and any other conduct that is prohibited by or under this Act; (b) advance equality of opportunity between persons who share a relevant protected characteristic and persons who do not share it; and (c) foster good relations between persons who share a relevant protected characteristic and persons who do not share it. PSED is purely deliberative, while principles require action towards a certain goal or purpose. For example, principles such as 'no one shall be a judge in their own cause' and 'no one shall be deemed guilty without a trial' require the justice delivery system to actively do things to prevent bias and to ensure a

ends-oriented and requires the decision maker, first, to take its normative guidance and then, second, to act to end racial disadvantage. It cannot be simply processual or symbolic in nature.

While anti-racism as a legal principle provides normative guidance for action, it does not deliver 'a knockout punch'.[28] This is what is meant by anti-racism as a legal principle as a non-deterministic norm. It provides a normative framework against which both reasoning and action must take place.[29] With this, it provides decision makers such as the government and the judiciary 'genuinely principled' basis for reasoning and action.[30]

Anti-racism as a legal principle may provide reasons for action in a particular direction in a particular case, but it may provide reasons for action in a different direction in another case. The state may yet choose to follow a different course in either case, but it must show how its actions address (as opposed to retain, reproduce, or exacerbate) structural racism. This is because there may be other principles of equal or greater weight which may provide a different set of reasons for action.[31] Conflicting principles would each seek their own optimization without negating the effect of the other. For example, a highly contagious disease may require a government to impose lockdowns on grounds of public health and security. Lockdowns may have a severe impact of crowding and contamination in tenements housing lower income and racially disadvantaged groups. Under anti-racism as a legal principle, the government may not be required to abandon lockdowns but may be required to act to mitigate the impact on lower income and racially disadvantaged groups. Anti-racism as a legal principle would thus perform the function of providing guidance for action, in this case and in every other case of public administration, with the purpose of achieving the end goal of closing the vast material gaps between racialized groups.

4.4.4 Location

In a parliamentary democracy such as the UK, the parliament is sovereign and declares the law of the land in the form of legislation. So, the parliament could enact a legal principle of anti-racism. But parliaments typically enact rules. Principles, in contrast, are recognized judicially because they are common sensical, ethical,

fair trial such as providing free legal aid and translation services, requiring declaration of conflict of interests, assuming presumption of innocence, and observing other rules of evidence.

[28] Ronald Dworkin, 'The Forum of Principle' (1981) 56 New York University Law Review 469.
[29] Eckhoff, 'Guiding Standards' (n 7) 205, 207; Hyman Gross, 'Standards as Law' [1968–69] Annual Survey of American Law 575, 578.
[30] Wechsler, 'Toward Neutral Principles' (n 14) 21.
[31] Dworkin, 'The Model of Rules' (n 1) 27.

moral, just, or simply expedient in a certain context. Even so, they do not arise from the judiciary. In fact, principles 'cannot be traced to any explicit adoption or enactment'.[32]

Instead, principles arise from legal practice over time.[33] They emerge from a 'sense of appropriateness developed in the profession and the public over time'.[34] Principles can thus be formed in judicial reasoning, and in how law is applied and enforced by state officials, understood by legal academics or the public generally. As Torstein Eckhoff remarked:

> It is often impossible to say when a guiding standard first came into being. The reason to which it refers and have been taken into account several times by judges and other decision makers without even being mentioned in any court opinion. And it can have been mentioned several times and in several different ways before it was linked to a particular verbal formulation.[35]

So, while anti-racism can be positivized, extracted, and articulated as a legal principle in legislation or in a judicial decision, it can also remain diffused. As legal principles underlie the legal system as a whole, they can be found in the crevices of how law is practised across contexts.

In the UK, two peculiarities shape where anti-racism as a legal principle can be found.

First, discrimination law is believed to often be a statement of principle.[36] However, in the UK, discrimination law, as embodied in the principal legislation, the Equality Act 2010, reflects a 'combination of agreement about mid-level operating principles, and strong disagreement about foundational and guiding principles'.[37] Thus, the text of the Equality Act 2010 does not reflect an agreement over foundational principles like equality or anti-racism.[38] That is, no 'constitutional conception'[39] of equality or anti-racism can be gleaned from the text of the Equality Act 2010 even though discrimination law is often the site for the recognition of these concepts.[40]

[32] Lyons, 'Principles' (n 7).

[33] Berman, 'How Practices Make Principles' (n 7) 299 ('legal practices fully ground legal principles, and legal principles partially ground legal rules.').

[34] Ronald Dworkin, 'Is Law a System of Rules?' in Robert S Summers (ed), *Essays in Legal Philosophy* (University of California Press 1968) 39.

[35] Eckhoff, 'Guiding Standards' (n 7) 209–210.

[36] Ronald Dworkin, *Taking Rights Seriously* (Duckworth 1977) 22, 82.

[37] O'Cinneide, 'Fumbling Towards Coherence' (n 22) 64.

[38] ibid.

[39] Nicholas Bamforth, 'Conceptions of Anti-discrimination Law' (2004) 24 Oxford Journal of Legal Studies 693.

[40] Chapter 5 discusses how racism and anti-racism came to be linked to discrimination law in the first place in the UK. Chapter 8 discusses the case for a constitutional conception of equality in the UK.

Second, in a common law system such as the UK, the development of legal principles over time is best observed in judicial decisions. Principles take shape gradually over a period of time when they are applied and articulated across a range of contexts. Principles are thus a product of incrementalism or 'enlightened gradualism'.[41] So, even though principles need not be located in judicial decisions exclusively, judicial decisions are an appropriate site for their development. Again, their development can be discursive. A principle may be applied in cases without being articulated explicitly. It can also be articulated explicitly and once articulated, 'it ought to be applied to all subsequent matters to which it is relevant even if the new facts are different from those of the case in which the principle was first laid down'.[42] But it is important to underscore that explicit articulation is not necessary in judicial decisions for a principle of anti-racism to exist. In line with its deliberative function, anti-racism as a legal principle is meant to justify or explain judicial decisions.[43] As Joseph Raz explained:

> A court can establish a new rule in a single judgment that becomes a precedent. Principles are not made into law by a single judgement; they evolve rather like a custom and are binding only if they have considerable authoritative support in a line of judgments. Like customary law, judicially adopted principles need not be formulated very precisely in the judgments that count as authority for their existence. All that has to be shown is that they *underlie a series of courts' decisions, that they were in fact a reason operating in a series of cases.*[44]

This is exactly what will be tested in the rest of the book. Can anti-racism as a legal principle as articulated in Part I be traced in Part II as *underlying judicial decisions*, as *in fact a reason operating in a series of judicial decisions*? What will not be tested is whether a piece of legislation or a single judicial decision has explicitly stated a principle of anti-racism or not. What will be tested is whether legal practice especially in discrimination law, as a whole, reflects such a principle.

4.5 Conclusion

This chapter underscores that anti-racism as a legal principle makes a difference to how the state acts. Part II of this book is dedicated to understanding the difference

41 PS Atiyah, 'Common Law and Statute Law' (1985) 48 Modern Law Review 1.

42 *Gelyke Kanse and Others v Chairperson of the Senate of the University of Stellenbosch and Others* [2019] ZACC 38 [58] (Mogoeng CJ).

43 Lyons, 'Principles' (n 7) 423 ('judges regard as embedded in the law those principles that justify past judicial decisions, statutes, and constitutional arrangements. Such principles need not be laid down as law by any sort of adoption or enactment. They become law by virtue of their role in justifying past decisions.').

44 Raz, 'Legal Principles' (n 7) 848 (emphasis in original).

between when public action is guided by anti-racism as a legal principle and when it is not. The difference, as the succeeding doctrinal analysis will show, is significant, and one that should matter a great deal to lawyers.

This difference can be traced back to the very nature of anti-racism as a legal principle as set out in this chapter in terms of both its form and substance. The form of anti-racism as a *legal principle* matters because it best fits the nature of anti-racism itself as a deliberative and non-deterministic yet actionable norm. The substance of *anti-racism* as a legal principle, especially its content, which is about addressing structural racism, centres[45] both structural racism and transformative anti-racism. Moreover, the general scope of application, the guidance function, and the diffused location of anti-racism as a legal principle ensure a wide and effective reach throughout the legal system. It is this framework of the form and substance of anti-racism as a legal principle that will serve as a guide in Part II of the book.

[45] Consider Sections 2.4 and 3.4 in Chapters 2 and 3 which make arguments for 'centring' structural racism and transformative anti-racism, respectively.

PART II
DOCTRINE
Racial Discrimination Law

5
Anti-Racism in Racial Discrimination Law

5.1 Introduction

Where shall one begin the search for a principle of anti-racism in law?

The obvious contender, as this chapter shows, is discrimination law, not because of an agreed theoretical, principled, conceptual, or logical reason but because of what transpired historically. The chapter explores this historical congruence between anti-racism and discrimination law, and in particular the type of anti-racism reflected in discrimination law at different points in time. It argues that while the legal regulation of racial discrimination *was* conceived as an anti-racist measure, the precise nature of anti-racism varied across successive 'race relations' legislations. But at no point was racial discrimination law actually transformative in nature, that is, aimed at addressing the material conditions of racially disadvantaged groups in a broad-based (as opposed to piecemeal or incremental) and intersectional way. Thus, despite being the primary site of anti-racism in law, racial discrimination law was conceived to leave structural racism intact.

The chapter proceeds as follows. Section 5.2 shows that racial discrimination law, as originally conceived, was anti-racist in that it intended to address racism against non-white people who had arrived in the UK from the Caribbean and the subcontinent since the 1950s. That said, the choice of the precise mould—or a rule prohibiting racial discrimination—in which anti-racism was cast, is not immediately explicable, precisely because it regulated 'racial discrimination' and not 'racism'. This section explicates the conversion of racism to racial discrimination.

Section 5.3 shows that the trajectory of development of racial discrimination law, through its first instantiation in the Race Relations Act 1965 (RRA 1965) and later the Race Relations Act 1968 (RRA 1968), the Race Relations Act 1976 (RRA 1976), and the Equality Act 2010 (EqA) traverses from cultural anti-racism to liberal anti-racism but never quite arrives at transformative anti-racism to attack racism holistically and especially its structural roots. Racial discrimination law in the UK has thus lacked anything like general principle of anti-racism.

Given that the 'race relations' legislations (RRA 1965, RRA 1968, and RRA 1976) are now repealed, the chapter is concerned not with the minutiae of the text or doctrine of these legacy enactments, but the legacy of these enactments broadly. The succeeding chapters in Part II of the book will turn to legal doctrine. This chapter should help appreciate the anti-racist legacy of the current legal doctrine as embodied in the EqA (Chapter 6), the Human Rights Act 1998 (Chapter 7), and

Anti-Racism as a Legal Principle. Shreya Atrey, Oxford University Press. © Shreya Atrey 2026.
DOI: 10.1093/9780198947646.003.0008

the Common Law (Chapter 8). More importantly, however, the chapter should help understand why the focus on discrimination law is merited at all in a search for a principle of anti-racism. It clarifies why this focus is justified and indeed pre-eminent, in that, no other area of law appears as closely concerned with anti-racism as racial discrimination law. The chapter does both then: it explains *and* queries the legacy of racial discrimination law as anti-racist.

5.2 Racism as Racial Discrimination

'Racism' is not prohibited in law. The word itself does not appear in statutes as such. What does appear are references to 'race relations', 'discrimination on racial grounds', and 'discrimination on the ground of colour, race, or ethnic or national origin'. These references in the RRA 1965, the RRA 1968, and the RRA 1976 mark the semantic initiation of race-related language in statutory law in the UK. These references gesture towards anti-racism by prohibiting racial discrimination. On the face of it, racial discrimination law—as it came to be enacted in these early legislations—appears as kin to anti-racism given the obvious semantic affinities.

These affinities—between race and racial grounds, racism and racial discrimination, and anti-racism and the prohibition of racial discrimination—however raise more questions than they answer. How did race become 'racial grounds'? How did racism become 'discrimination on racial grounds'? How did anti-racism become 'race relations' and the prohibition for racial discrimination specifically? Are these cognates synonyms? If not, what is the precise relationship between them?

To answer these questions, we must return to the historical context in which the relationship between race, racism, and anti-racism, on the one hand, and racial grounds, racial discrimination, and racial discrimination law, on the other hand, came to be formed in the post-war years between 1945 and 1965.

These decades mark the tidal high point of racism. This is not necessarily because racism was in any quantitative or qualitative way worse than it was before or has been after. Rather, it is because, from a legal perspective, though racism was rife, there was a complete vacuum addressing it in law until the first race relations legislation was enacted in 1965.

The British Nationality Act 1948 had provided citizens of Commonwealth nations the right to live and work in the UK.[1] This had precipitated an increase in the numbers of non-white people from the 'new' Commonwealth especially from the Caribbean and the subcontinent (as opposed to white people from the 'old'

[1] Consider the pre-war history of immigration and the labour market in the UK in Manoj Dias-Abey, 'The Aliens Order 1920, the "Work Permit" and the Making of the National Labour Market' in Bridget Anderson (ed), *Rethinking Migration: Challenging Borders, Citizenship and Race* (Bristol University Press 2025).

Commonwealth, i.e. Australia, Canada, and New Zealand). As a government White Paper in 1965 acknowledged, this wave of 'Commonwealth immigration' had transformed the country, for the first time in its long history, into a 'multi-racial society'.[2] This rapid transformation of the country in a space of just over a decade came with economic prosperity as the new arrivals helped revive local and national economies with 'a most valuable contribution'.[3]

This transformation, however, was accompanied by racial conflict characterized by open and often violent hostility towards the Commonwealth immigrants.[4] A decade after the first arrival of HMT Empire Windrush on 22 June 1948 when the first British Caribbean citizens arrived in Tilbury, Essex, the first 'race riots' had erupted in Notting Hill, London on 29 August 1958. This was a time 'when white gangs, encouraged by fascist parties, went on the rampage in areas where New Commonwealth citizens had settled'.[5] This was not a first as race riots after the first World War, in 1919, had wrecked Black homes and businesses in Liverpool and Cardiff.[6] In fact, race-related conflict in Britain had spanned centuries, even millennia.[7] The Notting Hill race riots of 1958 only confirmed that racial conflict had not dissipated with Britain's transformation into a multiracial society.

In fact, racial conflict was ever more pronounced.[8] Statistically, Britain *was* indeed the most 'multi-racial society' it had ever been with the largest proportion of non-white population in its history. At the time of the 1961 census, the percentage of British population which was born abroad stood at an all-time high of 5 per cent.[9] The increased number of Commonwealth immigrants, however, had an inverse relationship with social harmony, cultural integration, and mutual tolerance. Incidents targeting racialized minorities were routine. Most public spaces operated a 'colour bar' denying admission to Commonwealth immigrants and Traveller Groups. Epithets like 'Keep Britain White' and 'No Blacks, No Dogs, No Irish'

2 UK Parliament, White Paper, 'Immigration from the Commonwealth' (1965) 10 [hereafter 'White Paper'].

3 ibid; Ambalavaner Sivanandan, 'Race, Class and the State: The Black Experience in Britain' (1976) 17 Race and Class 347.

4 Elliot Joseph Benn Rose et al, *Colour and Citizenship: A Report on British Race Relations* (Oxford University Press 1969).

5 Matthew Vaughan, 'Accepting the "D" Word: Discrimination in 1960s' UK Academic Discourse' (2019) 61 Race and Class 85, 87 [hereafter Vaughan, 'Accepting the "D" Word'].

6 Jackqueline Jenkinson, *Black 1919: Riots, Racism and Resistance in Imperial Britain* (Liverpool University Press 2009); Chamion Caballero and Peter J Aspinall, *Mixed Race Britain in The Twentieth Century* (Palgrave Macmillan 2018) 53.

7 Peter Fryer, *Staying Power: The History of Black People in Britain* (Pluto Press 2018); Matt Clement, *A People's History of Riots, Protest and the Law: The Sound of the Crowd* (Palgrave Macmillan 2016); Panikos Panayi, *An Immigration History of Britain Multicultural Racism Since 1800* (Routledge 2014).

8 Stephen Small and John Solomos, 'Race, Immigration and Politics in Britain: Changing Policy Agendas and Conceptual Paradigms 1940s–2000s' (2006) 47 International Journal of Comparative Sociology 243.

9 Though the 1961 census took place before the first restrictions were imposed to curb immigration from the Commonwealth in 1962, the number of British citizens born outside of the UK has only increased ever since—in 1971 it was 6.4 per cent, in 1981 it was 6.6 per cent, in 1991 it was 7.3 per cent, in 2001 it was 8.8 per cent, in 2011 it was 13.4 per cent, and in 2021 it was 18 per cent.

were common everywhere from house windows to pub doors. As Keenan Malik describes:

> Racism was vicious and visceral and woven into the fabric of society in a way that it is difficult to imagine now. Paki-bashing was the national sport ... Stabbings were common; fire bombings—these were almost routine events. If you went to the police, you were more likely to be arrested than the racist was. It was an extraordinarily difficult time.[10]

Successive governments thus explored the best responses to what was characterized as 'a race problem' which was, according to them, caused by the growing presence of non-white people in Britain, and the resulting negative attitudes of white people against them.[11] That is, the root of the problem was identified as immigration while racism was its symptom that manifested in how people treated each other.

The first response then was to curb immigration. The Commonwealth Immigrants Act 1962 imposed the first set of restrictions on immigration from the 'new' Commonwealth, especially the Caribbean, Africa, and South Asia. In 1965, employment vouchers issued to Commonwealth immigrants under the 1962 Act were reduced and a range of checks and controls imposed on the dependants of Commonwealth immigrants. The Commonwealth Immigrants Act 1968 denied non-white British citizens the right of free entry. The Immigration Act 1971 limited settlement to British passport holders born overseas only if they had a work permit and could prove that a parent or grandparent had been born in the UK. The British Nationality Act 1981 took away the automatic right of those born in the UK to be considered British citizens if one of their parents were not British or settled in the UK.

The second response was to curb racism. This was less straightforward than curbing immigration. Immigration laws had existed and regulated immigration (although far more generously) since before the spate of post-war legislation. Thus, the restrictions on entry, right to work, resettlement, and family reunification followed a pre-existing model of regulation that had preceded the first World War. But no anti-racist law had existed which regulated racism per se.

It was this search for a model for regulating racism which led to discrimination law. This model was already existing in the US and was being pursued at the UN.

[10] Taj Ali, 'To Fight Racism, the Left Should Revive Its Universalist Tradition: Interview with Kenan Malik' <https://jacobin.com/2023/07/kenan-malik-not-so-black-and-white-interview-race-class-identity-politics-universalism> (accessed 2 January 2025).

[11] White Paper (n 2); Michael Banton, *White and Coloured: The Behaviour of British people Towards Coloured Immigrants* (Alden Press 1959).

Both influenced how the UK conceived its first formal response to racism in the form of prohibition of racial discrimination.

In the first instance, an expert group led by Anthony Lester made recommendations which were considered 'the most comprehensive and strongest ... in the whole long genesis' of Britain's first race relations bill.[12] These recommendations were inspired by the US anti-discrimination model which had responded to racism through a prohibition of racial discrimination. As a result of the civil rights movement, on 2 July 1964, the US Congress had enacted Title VII of the Civil Rights Act of 1964. The Act prohibited employment discrimination on the basis of several 'grounds' including race, religion, colour, and national origin. Neither racism nor racialized groups of indigenous and Black people were mentioned in the Act. Still, the Act was deemed to be an expression of racial equality in the US.[13]

In the second instance, the UK government was inspired by the developments at the UN which had also sought to tackle racism by prohibiting racial discrimination. The UN Charter in article 1 on the purposes and principles of the UN had sought 'to achieve international cooperation ... in promoting and encouraging respect for human rights and for fundamental freedoms for all *without distinction as to race*, sex, language, or religion'.[14] Article 13(1)(b) of the UN Charter had tasked the General Assembly to initiate studies and make recommendations for this purpose. To this end, on 20 November 1963, the General Assembly had unanimously adopted the Declaration on the Elimination of All Forms of Racial Discrimination.[15] The Declaration's preamble proclaimed that '*any doctrine of racial differentiation or superiority* is scientifically false, morally condemnable, socially unjust and dangerous, and that there is no justification for *racial discrimination* either in theory or in practice'.[16] It acknowledged that 'discrimination based on race, colour or ethnic origin in certain areas of the world continues none the less to give cause for serious concern' and expressed alarm at 'the manifestations of racial discrimination ... in some areas of the world' such as in the form of 'apartheid, segregation and separation'. Article 1 thus declared that 'discrimination between human beings on the ground of race, colour or ethnic origin is an offence to human dignity'. Article 2 prohibited any 'state, institution, group or individual' from discriminating 'in matters of human rights and fundamental freedoms ... *on the ground of* race, colour or ethnic origin'.[17]

[12] Keith Hindell, 'The Genesis of the Race Relations Bill' (1965) 36 The Political Quarterly 390 [hereafter Hindell, 'The Genesis'].

[13] Kimberlé Williams Crenshaw, 'Race, Reform, and Retrenchment: Transformation and Legitimation in Antidiscrimination Law' (1988) 101 Harvard Law Review 1331, 1346ff.

[14] Charter of the United Nations (adopted 26 June 1945, entered into force 24 October 1945) 1 UNTS XVI, art 1(3) (emphasis supplied), arts 55(c) and 76(c); UN General Assembly, Resolution 217A (III), Universal Declaration of Human Rights, A/RES/217(III) (10 December 1948), art 2.

[15] United Nations General Assembly, '1904 (XVIII). United Nations Declaration on the Elimination of All Forms of Racial Discrimination' A/RES/18/1904 (20 November 1963) ('the Declaration').

[16] Emphasis supplied.

[17] Emphasis supplied.

Neither the Declaration nor, later, the International Convention on the Elimination of All Forms of Racial Discrimination, which was adopted on 21 December 1965,[18] used the word racism anywhere. Instead, they focussed on racial discrimination—a phrase the Declaration used thirteen times and the Convention used nineteen times. The Convention in article 1(1) defined racial discrimination as 'any distinction, exclusion, restriction or preference based on race, colour, descent, or national or ethnic origin which has the purpose or effect of nullifying or impairing the recognition, enjoyment or exercise, on an equal footing, of human rights and fundamental freedoms in the political, economic, social, cultural or any other field of public life'. The UN trajectory of addressing racism was thus firmly embedded in the prohibition of 'racial discrimination'—a category, which is notable, first, for being defined in relation to particular acts or instances of distinction, exclusion, restriction, or preference, and second, defined in terms of the impact on human rights and not in terms of racial disadvantage.

Thus, in both the US and the UN models of anti-racism, the broader category of racism signified by racial disadvantage was particularized to racial discrimination which was about specific instantiations or acts or omissions rather than generalized patterns of material disadvantage between racialized groups. The UK drew inspiration from these models which addressed racism as racial discrimination and enacted the first race relations legislation—RRA 1965—whose purpose, as its preamble declared, was, inter alia, to 'prohibit discrimination on racial grounds in places of public resort'. Places of public resort included hotels, restaurants, cafes, pubs, theatres, cinema, dance halls, sports grounds, swimming pools, public transport, and places maintained by local authorities or other public authorities.[19]

The rapid linking of racism with racial discrimination is curious because 'the problem', as identified in the British context, was certainly wider than what racial discrimination as a legal category captured. Racism was characterized by 'virulent discrimination, racial violence and legal measures to prevent black and Asian New Commonwealth citizens from entering Britain'.[20] This exceeded the narrow scope of 'discrimination in places of public resort' which excluded obvious sites of discrimination such as immigration, housing, and employment. The racism that characterized the post-war years in Britain was also violent and widespread and far exceeded discrete transgressions by individuals. Yet, a 'public order' framing of racism was considered unappealing and as having little political or popular

[18] International Convention on the Elimination of All Forms of Racial Discrimination (adopted 21 December 1965, entered into force 4 January 1969) 660 UNTS 195 ('the Convention').

[19] RRA 1965, s 1(2).

[20] Saima Nasar, 'Commonwealth Communities: Migration and Racial Thinking in Twentieth Century Britain' in Saul Dubow and Richard Drayton (eds), *Commonwealth History in the Twenty-First Century* (Palgrave Macmillan 2020) 116; Stuart Hall, 'The Young Englanders' in Paul Gilroy and Ruth Wilson Gilmore (eds), *Selected Writings on Race and Difference* (Duke University Press 2021); Stuart Hall et al, *Policing the Crisis: Mugging, the State, and Law and Order* (Macmillan Press 1978).

traction.[21] Even when much of racism at the time was violent, racial discrimination was defined as a civil not a criminal wrong, to be settled through conciliation between parties rather than litigation.[22] Even when much of racism at the time was widespread and ridden with racial conflict over immigration and newly arrived immigrants, racial discrimination was defined as an individual wrong rather than a collective wrong signified by the vast material gaps between racialized groups in terms of immigration, housing, health, employment, safety, and security.[23]

While specific acts denying access to places of public resort could constitute differential treatment or discrimination, as Part I of the book argued, they cannot represent drivers of racial disadvantage, at least not causally.[24] Attacking acts of racial discrimination in access to places of public resort thus does not bear any direct correspondence with attacking racism in the form of gaps in material well-being of racialized groups, even if there is perhaps a correlation between the two. Why did racial discrimination become the legal category for racism is thus a curious case of diminution for which no direct answer appears in the annals of race relations legislation whose drafting was a 'haphazard, secret and inefficient process'.[25] What appears, controversially put, is 'the smell of élite paternalism [that] has always tainted British race relations law and institutions' which sought to anticipatorily 'avoid the explosive race dynamics of the United States'[26] by adopting the very model that was favoured in the US. This model was adopted despite the campaigning of grassroots and activist organizations in the formation of the race relations legislations, which had demanded a broader and more radical model than the anti-discrimination model borrowed from the US and the UN.[27]

But with this diminution, discrimination law obtained its eternal character or 'the heart of the anti-discrimination principle',[28] that is, 'the general principle disfavouring classifications or other decisions and practices that depend on the race (or ethnic origin) of parties affected'.[29] It thus assumed an existence quite

[21] House of Commons Debates, Race Relations Bill, vol 711, cols 926–927 (3 May 1965). Though this was the initial framing of the race relations bill which was rejected, eventually, two provisions of the RRA 1965 were dedicated to creating a new offence of incitement to racial hatred and extension of the Public Order Act 1936. These provisions were deemed 'entirely separate from the anti-discrimination provisions of the race relations legislation' and later removed from the RRA 1968.

[22] House of Commons Debates, Race Relations Bill, vol 711, cols 926–1059 (3 May 1965).

[23] Sheila Patterson, *Immigration and Race Relations in Britain: 1960–1967* (Oxford University Press 1969); Gary P Freeman, *Immigrant Labour and Racial Conflict in Industrial Societies* (Princeton University Press 1979).

[24] Chapter 2 of this book.

[25] Hindell, 'The Genesis' (n 12) 405.

[26] Christian Joppke, *Immigration and the Nation-State: The United States, Germany and Great Britain* (Oxford University Press 1999) 226.

[27] Kennetta Hammond Perry, 'The Limits of Campaigning Against Racial Discrimination' in Kennetta Hammond Perry (ed), *London is the Place for Me: Black Britons, Citizenship and the Politics of Race* (Oxford University Press 2015) 187.

[28] Paul Brest, 'Foreword: In Defense of the Antidiscrimination Principle' (1976) 90 Harvard Law Review 1, 2.

[29] ibid 1; John Finnis, 'Directly Discriminatory Decisions: A Missed Opportunity' [2010] Law Quarterly Review 491, 495. Cf Fiss who favours the group disadvantaging principle which proscribes

contrasting with what was understood, even by discrimination lawyers, as racism which was 'about relationships of domination and subordination'[30] or 'ground[ed] [in] racial structure, or the material conditions that govern and maintain systems of domination and racialized social control'.[31]

Even the Race Relations Board established under the RRA 1965 had understood racial discrimination as less a matter of 'active discrimination against individuals' than the reproduction of 'situations in which equality of opportunity is consciously or unconsciously denied'.[32] Yet, in its first report, the Race Relations Board imagined racial discrimination law as:

1. A law is an unequivocal declaration of public policy.
2. A law gives support to those who do not wish to discriminate, but who feel compelled to do so by social pressure.
3. A law gives protection and redress to minority groups.
4. A law thus provides for the peaceful and orderly adjustment of grievances and the release of tensions.
5. A law reduces prejudice by discouraging the behaviour in which prejudice finds expression.[33]

This is a strikingly minimal characterization of racial discrimination law. Strangely, even the Race Relations Board did not conceive of racial discrimination law, *in principle*, as about addressing racism which manifested in significant gaps between the material conditions of racialized groups. Instead, it conceived racial discrimination law as—(i) declaratory of public policy against racism but not transformative of the actual conditions that give rise to racism; (ii) supportive but not coercive in stopping discrimination; (iii) reactive but not proactive in protecting minoritized groups; (iv) orderly in settling grievances but tolerant of structural racism that gives rise to individual grievances; and (v) discouraging of but not disabling prejudice.

Racial discrimination law, by the admission of the main body tasked with overseeing it, was thus a limited measure for addressing racism under Britain's first anti-discrimination legislation.

'aggravat[ing] the subordinate position' of racialized minorities, Owen M Fiss, 'Groups and the Equal Protection Clause' (1976) 5 Philosophy & Public Affairs 107, 157; Sunstein favours the anticaste principle which 'forbids social and legal practices from translating highly visible and morally irrelevant differences into systemic social disadvantage', Cass Sunstein, 'The Anticaste Principle' (1994) 92 Michigan Law Review 2410, 2411.

[30] Sandra Fredman, 'Combatting Racism with Human Rights: The Right to Equality' in Sandra Fredman (ed), *Discrimination and Human Rights: The Case of Racism* (Oxford University Press 2001) 10.

[31] Mark Golub, *Is Racial Equality Unconstitutional* (Oxford University Press 2018) 20.

[32] Race Relations Board, *Race Relations Legislation in Britain* (London 1973).

[33] First Report of the Race Relations Board (1967) 22.

So, while there was an understanding that racism was broader than the category of racial discrimination established in law, there was reluctance in conceiving racial discrimination law for addressing racism. The RRA 1965 reflected this reluctance by diminishing racism to racial discrimination.

The RRA 1965 though was only the first but not the last word on discrimination law. As the next section shows, over the years, successive race relations legislations extended the scope of racial discrimination law.[34] For example, racial discrimination was extended, under the RRA 1968 to housing and employment, and under the RRA 1976 to indirect discrimination. This went some way in broadening the racial discrimination that the law was targeted at. But racial discrimination, despite progressive expansion, never became racism. The fundamental diminution of racism to racial discrimination in law remains unacknowledged, unexplained, and unaddressed to date.

It is perhaps this initial but enduring chasm between racism and racial discrimination that led critical legal scholars to pour scorn on discrimination law's 'unwillingness to refer to racism ... [which] leads to the proposition of "discrimination" as an equalising discourse that brings all sufferings to the same level, and at once disconnects them from their historical origins',[35] or for racism 'to be left out of legal discourse and replaced instead with soft signifiers such as discrimination'.[36]

This diminution, along with anti-immigration legislations that punctuated race relations legislations, casts doubt on discrimination law's anti-racist credentials. The RRA 1965 was preceded by the Commonwealth Immigrants Act 1962 which effectively applied a colour bar to those immigrating from the New Commonwealth—that is, mostly those from Caribbean, African, and South Asian, as opposed to Old Commonwealth—that is, those from Australia, New Zealand, and Canada. A 1965 White Paper on Immigration reduced employment vouchers issued to Commonwealth immigrants under the 1962 Act and established checks and controls on dependants of Commonwealth immigrants. The RRA 1968 was preceded by the Commonwealth Immigrants Act 1968, which denied non-white British citizens the right of free entry, effectively denying British Asians expelled from Kenya to return to the UK. The RRA 1976 was preceded by the Immigration Act 1971 which limited settlement to British passport holders born overseas only if they had a work permit and could prove that a parent or grandparent had been born in the UK, effectively limiting settlement to white British nationals. As Robert Miles and Annie Phizacklea put it, racial discrimination law was nothing but 'sops to black interests following racist immigration legislation'.[37]

[34] For an evolution of racial discrimination law, consider Iyiola Solanke, *Making Anti-racial Discrimination Law: A Comparative History of Social Action and Anti-racial Discrimination Law* (Routledge 2009).

[35] Alana Lentin, *Racism and Anti-Racism in Europe* (Pluto Press 2004) 31.

[36] Nadine El-Enany, *Bordering Britain: Law, Race and Empire* (Manchester University Press 2020) introduction.

[37] Robert Miles and Annie Phizacklea, *Racism and Political Action in Britain* (Routledge 1979) 24.

Yet, both in the UK as elsewhere, racial discrimination law was conceptualized as an anti-racist measure—in fact, as *the* measure against racism in law, even though, as this section has shown, it truncated racism to a rather limited legal category of racial discrimination.

5.3 Anti-Racism as Racial Discrimination Law

In what way is racial discrimination law *actually* anti-racist and what kind of anti-racism does it reflect?

This section considers the quality of anti-racism—liberal, cultural, and transformative—reflected in racial discrimination law across four major legislations from 1965 to 2010.

5.3.1 Race Relations Act 1965

While racial discrimination did not address racism comprehensively, its prohibition was still deemed indispensable in opposing racism, especially 'access racism'.[38] In prohibiting racial discrimination in access to places of public resort, howsoever slimly defined, the RRA 1965 was considered 'a public proclamation against racism'[39] and 'Britain's first national policy explicitly identifying and seeking to address the social problem of racism'.[40] Racial discrimination law, as Iyiola Solanke notes, 'was envisaged as a key bridge from the colonial to the post-colonial and war to post-war periods',[41] or as Alana Lentin notes, 'a response to the anti-racist thinking in post-war years in Europe'.[42] The prohibition of racial discrimination was but a reflection of 'anti-racism as a key principle'.[43]

Before the passage of the RRA 1965, not only 'racism' but also 'discrimination' had been largely ignored in both scholarly and public discourse.[44] Matthew Vaughan's work shows 'how reluctant the powers that be and academia in Britain were to accept the D word (that is discrimination) at all in their deliberations'.[45] In

[38] Erik Bleich, *Race Politics in Britain and France* (Cambridge University Press 2003) 80.
[39] ibid 63.
[40] Kennetta Hammond Perry, *London is the Place for Me: Black Britons, Citizenship and the Politics of Race* (Oxford University Press 2015) 201.
[41] Iyiola Solanke, 'The Race Relations Act @ 50 conference: Where Were You?' (2015) 20 https://www.thebritishacademy.ac.uk/documents/729/BAR26-07-Solanke.pdf (accessed 9 December 2025).
[42] Alana Lentin, 'Racism, Anti-Racism and the Western State' in Gerard Delanty, Ruth Wodak, and Paul Jones (eds), *Identity, Belonging and Migration* (Liverpool University Press 2011) 101.
[43] Alastair Bonnett, *Anti-Racism* (Routledge 2000) 69.
[44] Simon Peplow, 'The "Linchpin for Success"? The Problematic Establishment of the 1965 Race Relations Act and its Conciliation Board' (2017) 31 Contemporary British History 430 [hereafter Peplow, 'The "Linchpin for Success"'].
[45] Vaughan, 'Accepting the "D" Word' (n 5).

the 1960s, anything like an 'antidiscrimination legislation' was 'in British terms a novelty'[46] when a waft of opinion considered discrimination as an exaggeration, an inconvenience, an aberration, and ultimately, as insignificant.[47] The RRA 1965 was thus no mean feat in prohibiting access racism that was commonplace and had gone unchallenged thus far.

The RRA 1965's 'lasting legacy was to demonstrate that there was a place for such legislation and to set a framework for future development'.[48] As Omar Khan observed: 'If one achievement of the 1965 Act was to express Government's understanding of the experiences of Britain's ethnic minorities, another was to signal to the white population that racial discrimination was clearly wrong and would not be tolerated.'[49]

It was, and remains, uncontested that the RRA 1965 had expressive value.[50] It sought to displace the banality of everyday racism by conveying that racial discrimination was wrong. In turn, it sought a cultural shift in how racialized groups related to each other and especially how Commonwealth British citizens were perceived and treated by their white counterparts, including the British government. But did it actually reflect anti-racism as a legal principle?

RRA 1965 had little to do with addressing structural racism. In fact, it reflected a commitment to cultural anti-racism, which, as Chapter 3 explained, is primarily aimed at improving the experience of racialized groups at the community level.

This is best evidenced by the administrative model of oversight preferred by the RRA 1965. The Race Relations Board was established for 'securing compliance' with and 'resolution of difficulties' arising out of the provisions of RRA 1965.[51] The Race Relations Board's primary mandate was to facilitate conciliation between parties as a means of resolving complaints of racial discrimination. According to section 2(2)(c) of the RRA 1965, it had one tool at its behest for achieving this: 'communication'.[52] The modus operandi was thus entirely dedicated to interactive dynamics—of complainants expressing what they felt was an experience of racial discrimination and for alleged perpetrators to listen to and understand

[46] John Carson, 'A Matter of Policy: The Lessons of Recent British Race Relations Legislation' (1976) 8 A Quarterly Journal Concerned with British Studies 154, 158.

[47] James Wickenden, *Colour in Britain* (Oxford University Press 1958); Ruth Glass, *Newcomers: The West Indians in London* (Allen and Unwin 1960); Michael Banton, *White and Coloured: The Behaviour of British People Towards Coloured Immigrants* (Alden Press 1959); Sheila Patterson, *Dark Strangers: A Sociological Study of the Absorption of a Recent West Indian Migrant Group in Brixton* (Tavistock 1963).

[48] Peplow, 'The "Linchpin for Success"' (n 44) 446.

[49] Omar Khan, 'How Far Have We Come? Lessons from the 1965 Race Relations Act' (8 December 2015) <https://www.equalityhumanrights.com/media-centre/blogs/how-far-have-we-come-lessons-1965-race-relations-act> (accessed 12 January 2025).

[50] Matthew D Adler, 'Expressive Theories of Law: A Skeptical Overview' (1999) 148 University of Pennsylvania Law Review 1363.

[51] RRA 1965, s 2(1).

[52] RRA 1965, s 2(2)(c); schedule 2, s 3(b).

their view, with the Race Relations Board and the local conciliation committees facilitating this exchange.

Still, the wrong of racial discrimination was defined in individual terms as committed by 'any *person*, being the proprietor or manager of or employed for the purposes of any place of public resort' and directed 'against *persons* seeking access to or facilities or services at that place'.[53] The resolution of complaints of racial discrimination veered away from any focus on adjudication of blame or responsibility of individuals and rather towards a mutual understanding of what transpired and why it may have constituted racial discrimination that needed to cease. While liberal anti-racism underlined how racial discrimination was conceived, cultural anti-racism underlined how it was meant to be addressed.

This though satisfied no one. It did not satisfy those who preferred stronger remedies for racial discrimination in the form of criminal sanctions. It also vexed liberals who preferred civil remedies in the form of court adjudication.[54] Importantly, even the Race Relations Board was dismayed with its own mandate. First, its powers did not extend to most complaints it was receiving. In the first two years of its operation, nearly 70 per cent of complaints of racial discrimination had concerned housing and employment—areas which the RRA 1965 did not cover.[55] Second, the Race Relations Board had no real coercive powers of investigation or to impose sanctions on parties. It was tasked to receive and consider complaints of racial discrimination, to make inquiries in respect of the complaints, to secure settlement between the parties, and to receive satisfactory assurance against further discrimination. If the conciliation failed, the Race Relations Board could only report to the Attorney General who had the power to bring civil proceedings. So, while, on the one hand, the Race Relations Board was overwhelmed as it had to mandatorily investigate all complaints, on the other hand, it could do little else than to 'use their best endeavours' to secure a settlement between the parties.[56]

Ultimately, no sooner than it was passed, the RRA 1965 was declared 'virtually useless',[57] 'extremely weak, ineffectual',[58] 'not just toothless, but gumless',[59] and 'truly a whimper of a law'.[60] Its detractors had received race relations legislation with a 'lack of enthusiasm' and even 'outright hostility'.[61] Its supporters

[53] RRA 1965, s 1(1) (emphasis supplied).

[54] Bob Hepple, 'Race Relations Act 1965' (1966) 29 Modern Law Review 306.

[55] Race Relations Board, Report 1966–1967, 15, 22.

[56] RRA 1965, s 2(2)(c).

[57] Colin McGlashan, 'Race Bill "Virtually Useless"', The Observer, 11 April 1965 <https://static.guim.co.uk/sys-images/Guardian/Pix/pictures/2015/12/8/1449586963946/Observer-11-April-1965-001.jpg> (accessed 27 June 2024).

[58] Peplow, 'The "Linchpin for Success"' (n 44).

[59] Institute of Race Relations, 'The Race Relations Act 1965—Blessing or Curse?' (13 November 2015) [hereafter Institute of Race Relations, 'The Race Relations Act 1965'] <https://irr.org.uk/article/the-race-relations-act-1965-blessing-or-curse/> (accessed 11 January 2025).

[60] Erik Bleich, *Race Politics in Britain and France* (Cambridge University Press 2003) 61.

[61] Anthony Lester and Geoffery Bindman, *Race and Law* (Penguin 1972) 126–127.

had exposed its inadequacies and rallied for immediate reform. It turned out, as Nadine Peppard says, that the 'class of "65" still ha[d] much to do, as did their predecessors and as will, it is clear, their successors'.[62]

In the end, it was the mounting evidence of 'substantial discrimination'[63] against racialized minorities and the noticeable inability of the RRA 1965 to deal with it that made further law reform inevitable.

5.3.2 Race Relations Act 1968

The RRA 1968 was enacted on 25 October 1968.

It did two main things. First, it extended the scope of the race relations legislation to employment, housing, service provision, and the publication or display of discriminatory advertisements or notices. Second, it reconstituted the Race Relations Board, increasing both its membership and its functions, and created a Community Relations Commission tasked to promote 'harmonious community relations' by co-ordinating local and national action to this end, and to advise the Home Secretary on any related matters. In doing these, the RRA 1968 found a renewed focus on liberal anti-racism and at the same time redoubled the existing focus on cultural anti-racism.

It was in the RRA 1968 that British discrimination law found its classical liberal framing of discrimination as 'less favourable' treatment of 'persons' 'on the ground of' named personal characteristics. With this, racial discrimination became exclusively focussed on discrete acts of individuals. Further, the extension of the material scope of racial discrimination to employment made this framing applicable to the employer–employee relationship which was soon to become discrimination law's lasting preoccupation.[64] Section 1(1) of the RRA 1968 declared that 'a *person* discriminates against another if on the ground of colour, race or ethnic or national origins he treats that other ... *less favourably* than he treats or would treat other *persons*'.[65] The act had to be based on any of the four listed race-related grounds: colour, race, ethnic origin, or national origin. The act had to result in less favourable treatment—that is, detrimental to the victim because of their race, colour, ethnic origin, or national origin. Like the RRA 1965, discrimination remained symmetrical and thus capable of being perpetrated by anyone against anyone and not necessarily against racially disadvantaged or minoritized groups.

[62] Nadine Peppard, 'The Age of Innocence: Race Relations Before 1965' (1987) 14 Journal of Ethnic and Migration Studies 45, 54.

[63] Political and Economic Planning, 'A Survey of Racial Discrimination in Employment and Other Fields in the United Kingdom' (1967) 96 International Labour Review 529.

[64] Nicholas Bamforth, 'Conceptions of Anti-Discrimination Law' (2004) 24 Oxford Journal of Legal Studies 693, 694.

[65] RRA 1968, s 1(1) (emphasis supplied).

In sum, these changes intensified the focus on interpersonal racism as the main form of racism being addressed in law. As Chapter 2 argued, interpersonal racism is not simply about individual perpetrators and victims, but about discrete acts and omissions as existing on their own and not within a network of social, cultural, political, and economic relationships between people that define structural racism. The definitional contours of racial discrimination in RRA 1968 mapped squarely onto this understanding. Though individuals still lacked direct access to courts, the liberal roots of racial discrimination law, which were only embryonic in RRA 1965, had firmly taken hold in RRA 1968.

The cultural anti-racism framing of racial discrimination law strengthened at the same time. Unlike the RRA 1965 which had said nothing about race relations explicitly despite its title, the RRA 1968 in its preamble made its purpose clear: 'to make provision with respect to relations between people of different racial origins'. The Race Relations Board established under the RRA 1965 was to continue its operations. But now it could institute civil proceedings under section 19 of the RRA 1968, refer employment related complaints to the Secretary of State for Employment and Productivity under schedule 2, and pursue matters where no complaint was made but the Race Relations Board had reason to suspect that an act of racial discrimination had taken place under schedule 3. Specifically, a Community Relations Commission was established under section 25 whose task was, inter alia, 'to encourage the establishment of, and assist others to take steps to secure the establishment of, harmonious community relations and to co-ordinate on a national basis the measures adopted for that purpose by others'.[66] In particular, the Community Relations Commission was to work with local authorities and offer advice, services, training courses, and financial assistance towards, and to organize and promote conferences on, matters connected to community relations.[67] Under section 26, the Secretary of State could conduct research 'into any matter connected with relations between people of different colour, race or ethnic or national origins'. This focus on 'community relations' was novel and a significant enhancement of the cultural anti-racism framing that was already predominant in RRA 1965 with its preference for reconciliation through communication, persuasion, settlement, and assurances. Now, cultural anti-racism appeared full-blown with the panoply of measures targeting at improving community relations between racialized groups including training courses, conferences, and other events.

Interestingly, the RRA 1968 also gestured towards transformative anti-racism by excluding from the ambit of employment discrimination acts 'done in good faith for the purpose of securing or preserving a reasonable balance of persons of different racial groups employed in the undertaking'.[68] It is arguable that this

66 RRA 1968, s 25(3)(a).
67 RRA 1968, s 25(4)–(5).
68 RRA 1968, s 8(2).

exception was rather limited and did not necessarily express either preference for or permissibility of preferential treatment or affirmative action in the form of automatic hiring or quotas.[69] Actual material disadvantage suffered by racialized minorities thus could not be corrected proactively through racial discrimination law.[70] Racial disadvantage could only be used exceptionally, as a justification for avoiding a charge of employment discrimination. Still, the racial balance exception was in *the nature of* transformative anti-racism as it acknowledged pre-existing racial disadvantage as it manifested in racial imbalance in employment settings and allowed employers to correct that imbalance. The RRA 1968 however did not mandate that racial imbalance or other racial disadvantage be necessarily targeted or overcome through racial discrimination law.

In the final analysis, the RRA 1968 was unmistakably characterized by both liberal and cultural anti-racism. Indeed, this is what Jenkins, as the Labour Home Secretary in 1966, had envisioned as British integration defined 'not as a flattening process of assimilation but as *equal opportunity* accompanied by *cultural diversity*, in an atmosphere of mutual tolerance' (emphasis in original). The RRA 1968 had delivered on both counts—though cultural anti-racism was predominant given that individuals lacked direct access to courts.

This shifted with the RRA 1976 which pivoted racial discrimination law away from cultural anti-racism and permanently towards liberal anti-racism. The next section considers this.

5.3.3 Race Relations Act 1976

The 1975 White Paper on racial discrimination had made clear that the road ahead for anti-racism in the UK was going to be paved by an equal opportunities programme targeting 'arbitrary and unfair discriminatory practices'.[71] This was a response to both the '[changed] character of race relations and in the general understanding of the issues and problems involved' and the shortcomings of the race relations legislation in dealing with this changed character.[72] The White Paper explained:

> the character of the coloured population resident in this country has changed dramatically over the decade. Ten years ago, less than a quarter of the coloured

[69] Bob Hepple, 'The British Race Relations Acts, 1965 and 1968' (1969) 19 University of Toronto Law Journal 248, 252.

[70] Chris McCrudden, Rethinking Positive Action' (1986) 15 Industrial Law Journal 219.

[71] UK Parliament, White Paper, Racial Discrimination (1975) [129].

[72] ibid [4]; Geoffrey Bindman, 'Law Enforcement or Lack of It' in Muhammad Anwar, Patrick Roach, and Ranjit Sondhi (eds), *From Legislation to Integration? Race Relations in Britain* (Palgrave 2000) 41 [hereafter Bindman, 'Law Enforcement or Lack of It'].

population had been born here ... About two out of every five of the coloured people in this country now were born here and the time is not far off when the majority of the coloured population will be British born. The Governments proposals are based on a clear recognition of the proposition that the overwhelming majority of the coloured population is here to stay, that a substantial and increasing proportion of that population belongs to this country, and that the time has come for a determined effort by Government, by industry and unions, and by ordinary men and women, to ensure fair and equal treatment for all our people, regardless of their race, colour, or national origins.

While the character of race relations had changed, racial disadvantage had only intensified, dimming the initial optimism of race relations legislations in bringing about British integration which ensured both equal opportunity and cultural diversity. The government was convinced 'as a result of its review of race relations generally and of the working of the legislation that a fuller strategy to deal with racial disadvantage will have to be deployed than has been attempted so far'.[73] Thus, it imagined that its proposals for 'a further attack on discrimination will need to be supplemented by a more comprehensive strategy for dealing with the related and at least equally important problem of disadvantage'.[74] Importantly, it thought that 'Legislation [was] capable of dealing not only with discriminatory acts but with patterns of discrimination, particularly with patterns which, because of the effects of past discrimination, may not any longer involve explicit acts of discrimination.'[75]

But the enactment of the RRA 1976 turned out to be a one-sided affair. It focussed almost exclusively on racial discrimination, leaving patterns of racial discrimination or racial disadvantage outside the purview of racial discrimination law. The RRA 1976 repealed the racial balance provision that had existed in the RRA 1968 and replaced it with softer measures for encouraging or training persons of a particular racialized group to take advantage of opportunities.[76] There was though, under section 71, established a general statutory duty of local authorities to carry out their functions 'with due regard to the need—(a) to eliminate unlawful racial discrimination; and (b) to promote equality of opportunity, and good relations, between persons of different racial groups'.[77] The duty was, quite noticeably, weak. Limited to 'due regard to the need to' eliminate unlawful discrimination

[73] UK Parliament, White Paper, Racial Discrimination (1975) [13].

[74] ibid [26].

[75] ibid [25].

[76] RRA 1976, ss 35, 37–38. Consider McColgan's discission of the weak enforcement and application of these enabling provisions, Aillen McColgan, *Discrimination Law: Text, Cases and Materials* (3rd edn, Bloomsbury 2023) 72; *R (Kaur & Shah) v London Borough of Ealing* [2008] EWHC 2062 (Admin), [23]; *Stephenson v Stockton-on-Tees Borough Council* [2005] 1 FCR 165 [28]; *R (E) v Governing Body of the Jews Free School* [2008] ELR 445 [176]; *Conwell v Newham London Borough Council* [2000] 1 WLR 1; *Lambeth London Borough Council v Commission for Racial Equality* [1990] ICR 768.

[77] RRA 1976, s 43.

and promote equality of opportunity signified no need to eliminate racism or racial disadvantage per se. Anti-racism as a legal principle—which ultimately aims to upend racial disadvantage—found little resonance in the RRA 1976 despite the hope expressed in the 1975 White Paper.

Instead, the RRA 1976 made liberal anti-racism the mainstay of racial discrimination law. It did so in two main ways. First, it broadened the definition of unlawful racial discrimination to include indirect discrimination which was, despite its reference to racial groups, ultimately about addressing individual detriment not group disadvantage. Second, it provided individuals direct access to courts for bringing claims of racial discrimination. This ushered the era of individual enforcement of racial discrimination law—which remains the hallmark of liberal anti-racism to date.

Both of these were important developments at the time. Racial discrimination, as defined by section 1 of the RRA 1976, now included not only rules prohibiting direct discrimination or less favourable treatment of persons on racial grounds but also indirect discrimination which occurred when:

> A person discriminates against another in any circumstances relevant for the purposes of any provision of this Act if—
>
> ...
>
> (b) he applies to that other a requirement or condition which he applies or would apply equally to persons not of the same racial group as that other but—
>
> (i) which is such that the proportion of persons of the same racial group as that other who can comply with it is considerably smaller than the proportion of persons not of that racial group who can comply with it; and
>
> (ii) which he cannot show to be justifiable irrespective of the colour, race, nationality or ethnic or national origins of the person to whom it is applied; and
>
> (iii) which is to the detriment of that other because he cannot comply with it.

This was indeed a leap forward in thinking about discrimination in terms of disparate impact or differential effects of neutral and generally applicable conditions, rather than treatment that was explicitly based on racial grounds. Yet, indirect racial discrimination, while admittedly broader than direct discrimination, was after all a form of interpersonal racism. It targeted individuals or collectivities on 'the demand side', that is, those 'who were usually in the position of choosing whether to engage in social and economic intercourse, e.g. employers, house owners, landladies, pub managers, etc'.[78] State's laws, policies, programmes, as well as

[78] Chris McCrudden, 'Institutional Discrimination' (1982) 2 Oxford Journal of Legal Studies 303.

governmental, political, and judicial actors were thus not its main targets, even though they were ostensibly covered by the provision.

Moreover, the final clause in the definition of indirect racial discrimination that the condition be 'to the detriment of that other because he cannot comply with it' made indirect discrimination a limited category concerned with specific, discrete, and individualized instances of detriment rather than broad-based group disadvantage that existed due to prevailing structures. No doubt, group disadvantage *was* relevant to indirect discrimination because of the requirement to show 'that the proportion of persons of the same racial group as that other who can comply with it is considerably smaller than the proportion of persons not of that racial group who can comply with it'. It was not significant on its own to show indirect discrimination. It was only a link in showing that *a requirement or condition* had led to a person's *detriment*.[79]

Importantly, this leap forward was hardly in recognition of the character of racism as much as it was a recognition that the rule prohibiting indirect discrimination was already adopted in the prior Sex Discrimination Act 1975.[80] There was in fact no considered reflection on the specific nature of indirect racial discrimination that preceded the adoption of indirect discrimination in the RRA 1976. The adoption was a strategic extension of what was already made possible for 'women's rights [which] were more popular than those of ethnic minorities'.[81]

As the following chapters show, the rule prohibiting indirect discrimination has proved to be no bulwark against racism in the absence of the principle of anti-racism. The point here is that, even at the time when indirect discrimination was adopted in the RRA 1976, it was not evident that its promise was ever to materialize.

More importantly though, despite well-known limitations,[82] the RRA 1976 placed the model of complaints-based individual justice, as opposed to proactive

[79] In fact, some recognition of the reality of racial disadvantage is required for both direct and indirect discrimination and to that extent, the explicit recognition of racial disadvantage between groups for indirect discrimination did little than making its recognition explicit. As Bob Hepple insightfully noted: 'The legal definitions of both direct and indirect discrimination depend for their effectiveness upon the recognition of collective racial disadvantage ... The traditional form of civil adjudication in Britain for the resolution of private disputes is unsuitable for this task. Lawyers are familiar with the reconstruction of occurrences between individual parties. They are unaccustomed to the processes for acquiring knowledge about the recurrent patterns of behaviour which go to make up social facts. Not surprisingly, findings as to "social facts" have been left to the 'common sense' of the courts and tribunals ... [But] very few of those judging these cases are likely to have had experience of the situations in which direct and indirect discrimination occur.' Bob Hepple, 'Have Twenty-five Years of the Race Relations Acts in Britain Been a Failure' in Bob Hepple and Erika M Szyszczak (eds), *Discrimination: The Limits of Law* (Mansell 1992) 25.

[80] Anthony Lester, 'Anti-discrimination Legislation in Great Britain' (1987) 16 New Community 21.

[81] Bob Hepple, 'The New Single Equality Act in Britain' (2010) 5 The Equal Rights Review 11, 13 [hereafter Hepple, 'The New Single Equality Act'].

[82] UK Parliament, White Paper, Racial Discrimination (1975) [36] ('complaints are random in their incidence and significance. Most victims do not complain. Many do not know that they have suffered discrimination. Others are reluctant to complain because they do not want to relive the humiliation which they have suffered, or because they have no confidence in the effectiveness of the complaints procedure and the redress which it is likely to provide for them. Some complaints are trivial; others are misconceived. Although it is necessary for the law to provide effective remedies for the individual victim,

or preventive collective justice or justice at the group level, at the heart of enforcement of racial discrimination law. As John Solomos put it:

> the role of individual complaints in the promotion of equal opportunity fitted in with the liberal notion that the main aim of policies in this field is to promote free competition between individuals. It also relied on the established emphasis in British common law on individual rather than collective dispute settlement.[83]

With the RRA 1976, justice became about an individual having the right to seek and obtain relief for the detriment they faced rather than the redressal of the general patterns of racialized group disadvantage which both served as the basis of and in turn intensified racism.[84] Enforcement of racial discrimination law thus became an event, triggered by a happening, rather than a field of law which acknowledged and redressed racism as racial disadvantage that existed here and now.

Individuals could now take their complaints directly to civil courts. Industrial tribunals were to receive most claims of racial discrimination relating to employment, while county courts were to receive those relating to education, housing, and provision of goods and service. A newly established Commission for Racial Equality which replaced the Race Relations Board and the Community Relations Commission also had the mandate for receiving complaints about instructions to discriminate and discriminatory advertising.

In the main though, the duties of the Commission for Racial Equality were '(a) to work towards the elimination of discrimination; (b) to promote equality of opportunity, and good relations, between persons of different racial groups generally; and (c) to keep under review the working of [RRA 1976]'.[85] It was also to 'give financial or other assistance to any organisation appearing to the Commission to be concerned with the promotion of equality of opportunity, and good relations,

it is also essential that the application of the law should not depend upon the making of an individual complaint.').

[83] John Solomos, 'From Equal Opportunity to Anti-Racism: Racial Inequality and the Limits of Reform' Policy Paper in Ethnic Relations, Birkbeck Public Policy Centre (1989) 8 [hereafter Solomos, 'From Equal Opportunity to Anti-Racism'].

[84] Chris McCrudden, 'International and European Norms Regarding National Legal Remedies for Racial Inequality' in Sandra Fredman (ed), *Discrimination and Human Rights: The Case of Racism* (Oxford University Press 2001) 253 ('An individual justice model generally aims to secure the reduction of discrimination by eliminating from decisions illegitimate considerations based on race ... that have harmful consequences for individuals ... This approach concentrates on cleansing the process of decision-making, and is not concerned with the general effect of decisions on grounds, except perhaps as an indication of a flawed process.'); Chris McCrudden, 'Anti-discrimination Goals and the Legal Process' in Nathan Glazer and Ken Young (eds), *Ethnic Pluralism and Public Policy* (Heinemann 1983); Chris McCrudden, 'The Commission for Racial Equality' in Robert Baldwin and Chris McCrudden (eds), *Regulation and Public Law* (Weidenfeld and Nicholson1987); Christopher McCrudden, 'British Anti-Discrimination Law: An Introduction' (1983) 2 Penn State International Law Review 65.

[85] RRA 1976, s 43.

between persons of different racial groups',[86] 'undertake or assist (financially or otherwise) the undertaking by other persons of any research, and any educational activities',[87] make an annual report of its activities,[88] issue codes of practice for guidance on matters such as elimination of discrimination in employment,[89] and conduct formal investigations.[90]

While the RRA 1976 displaced the cultural anti-racism model of reconciliation, communication, persuasion, settlement, assurances, advice, training, conferences, and events, the displacement was replaced with another model of cultural anti-racism with an expansive mandate for the Commission for Racial Equality. In a way, the Commission for Racial Equality had more powers and greater responsibilities than the Race Relations Board and the Community Relations Commission previously. In another way, although it was tasked with enforcing the legislation, it had minimal role in actually doing so directly or immediately—given that individuals had direct access to courts and tribunals. The Commission for Racial Equality could conduct research and support governmental policy on race relations but it had no mandate for conciliation or the promotion of community relations in any direct way other than by offering 'financial or other assistance'. It did have a strategic role in enforcing the law in public interest which it tried to fulfil in earnest by pursuing independent investigations and going after powerful and well-resourced entities.[91] This lasted only until the courts, including the House of Lords, became 'extremely sensitive to the exercise of coercive powers by statutory bodies'[92] and ultimately unleased their 'judicial hostility ... at the investigative powers'.[93]

The RRA 1976 ruled the roost for thirty-four years—the longest period for a single dedicated legislation on racial discrimination.

It was credited for having 'had a positive effect [as] it ... helped to curb the worst kinds of discrimination in employment and the provision of services, and ... had an invaluable impact on the general climate of opinion'.[94] But over

86 ibid, s 44(1).
87 ibid, s 45(1).
88 ibid, s 46.
89 ibid, s 47(1).
90 ibid, s 48 (1).
91 As Herman Ouseley, the chair and chief executive of the CRE from 1993 to 2000, explained: 'During my stint at the CRE, we were not afraid to use the 1976 Act in a very elastic way to support individuals in the Tribunals and courts, to challenge employers and public bodies, to undertake formal investigations fearlessly into bodies such as the MoD and generate support to fund public awareness advertising campaigns focused on the effects of racism.' Institute of Race Relations, 'The Race Relations Act 1965' (n 59).
92 Bindman, 'Law Enforcement or Lack of It' (n 72) 54.
93 ibid 41; *R v Commission for Racial Equality, Ex p Hillingdon London Borough Council* [1982] AC 779; *Commission for Racial Equality v Prestige Group Pic* [1984] ICR 473 HL; *Commission for Racial Equality v Amari Plastics* [1982] QB 1194.
94 Bhiku Parekh, *The Runnymede Trust Commission on the Future of Multi-Ethnic Britain* (Profile Books 2000) xxi [hereafter Parekh, *The Future of Multi-Ethnic Britain*].

time, evidence showed that 'patterns of inequality of access to jobs, housing, education and health ... remained fundamentally unaltered since the passing of the 1976 Act ... [including] the increase in the levels of racial attacks and harassment as linked, in part, to the limited impact of the Act in shaping public attitudes on "race" and cultural diversity'.[95] Successive reports of the Home Affairs Committee and the Commission for Racial Equality, and most importantly, the government inquiry into the Brixton riots of 1981 (Scarman report) and the government inquiry into Stephen Lawrence's murder (Macpherson report), agreed that 'the 1976 Act had failed to have a significant impact on racial discrimination in Britain'.[96]

Thus, the RRA 1976 had failed to reflect anti-racism as a legal principle and more specifically transformative anti-racism, which, as Chapter 3 argued, is about: resisting structures which produce racial disadvantage; taking disruptive, proactive, and preventive action, rather than ex-post, remedial, and incremental measures; and enabling intersectional justice. Instead, the RRA 1976 had adopted a narrow set of rules which aimed to address particular forms or manifestations of racial discrimination. The RRA 1976 had fallen short of prioritizing 'to tackle institutional racism and organisational culture',[97] including culture and religion as part of racial discrimination,[98] addressing intersectional discrimination,[99] imposing proactive duties, using plain and approachable language, reforming the individual complaints model of redressal,[100] and regulating private organizations sufficiently. In fact, not only the RRA 1976 but also discrimination law across all grounds, such as that embodied in the Sex Discrimination Act 1975, the Equal Pay Act 1970, and the Disability Discrimination Act 1995, was all 'widely criticised for being outdated, fragmented, inconsistent, inadequate and at times incomprehensible'.[101]

[95] Muhammad Anwar, Patrick Roach, and Ranjit Sondhi (eds), *From Legislation to Integration? Race Relations in Britain* (Palgrave 2000), introduction; Muhammad Anwar, 'The Impact of Legislation on British Race Relations' in Muhammad Anwar, Patrick Roach, and Ranjit Sondhi (eds), *From Legislation to Integration? Race Relations in Britain* (Palgrave 2000); David John Smith, *The Facts of Racial Disadvantage: A National Survey* (Political and Economic Planning 1976); Solomos, 'From Equal Opportunity to Anti-Racism' (n 83).

[96] Jennifer Brown, 'An Early History of British Race Relations Legislation', Briefing Paper 8360, House of Commons Library (2018) 8. Some of the shortcomings of the RRA 1976 were addressed in the Race Relations (Amendment) Act 2000 following the recommendations in the Macpherson report. The amended Act prohibited racial discrimination by public authorities in the exercise of their public functions and amended section 71 of the RRA 1976, which later because section 149 on 'public sector equality duty' which requires public authorities to have due regard to the need to promote equality of opportunity.

[97] Parekh, *The Future of Multi-Ethnic Britain* (n 94) 264.

[98] ibid 269.

[99] ibid 265.

[100] ibid 266.

[101] Bob Hepple, Mary Coussey, and Tufyal Choudhury, *Equality: A New Framework* (Hart 2000) [1.1] [hereafter Hepple, Coussey, and Choudhury, *Equality*].

5.3.4 Equality Act 2010

Near unanimous consensus had developed at the turn of the millennium that the shortcomings in racial discrimination law, and discrimination law more broadly, were best addressed through a single consolidated piece of legislation which harmonized discrimination law applicable across grounds such as race, sex, disability, and age. Interestingly and importantly, the only notable opposition to this view was expressed by the Commission for Racial Equality which argued that

> a separate Race Relations Act is useful for campaigning and education purposes as well as law enforcement. To move to a single equality statute would blur the focus on specific types of discrimination. For so long as institutional racism persists it must be tackled directly, and general concepts of equality and diversity will not have the same sharp impact.[102]

According to Hepple, Coussey, and Choudhury: 'this reservation confuse[d] a "general" concept with a unified one. The same concept of equality can be applied to each ground of discrimination without undermining specific action against particular grounds of discrimination' and that in any case, a single consolidated equality legislation was 'really aimed at the way in which an equality statute is enforced rather than the substance of the law'.[103]

Any shortcoming of the proposed single consolidated equality legislation was promptly dismissed as 'far outweighed by the inclusiveness and coordination of purpose and strategy that can be gained by a single Act'.[104] Words were spared in considering race-related issues any further during the making of the single consolidated legislation. The only mention was in the negative such as in the suggestion for the discontinuation of 'the anomalous specialist race panel' of employment tribunals[105] as it was believed that there was 'considerable support for the view that it is more important to train lay members in the judicial task than for them to become discrimination specialists'.[106] A request from the Disability Rights Task Force for retaining at least one person with disability on panels was met with a similar response: that general training in adjudication mitigated the need for expertise in specific forms of discrimination and that in any case guidance could be given 'to put aside any prejudice and stereotyped attitudes, and to deal fairly with the evidence'.[107] Given the prior merger of the Commission for Racial Equality set up

[102] ibid 24.
[103] ibid.
[104] Joanna Harrington, 'Making Sense of Equality Law: A Review of the Hepple Report' (2001) 64 Modern Law Review 757, 758.
[105] Hepple, Coussey, and Choudhury, *Equality* (n 101) 89.
[106] ibid.
[107] ibid.

under the RRA 1976 and other similar bodies to become the Equality and Human Rights Commission in the Equality Act 2006, the road ahead seemed to lead firmly away from a specialist focus on racism and towards a 'unitary and integrated perspective'.[108] The price that was paid was a further flattening and obscuring of racism in discrimination law.

Thus, despite a clear preference expressed in the 1999 Macpherson report for adoption of the concept of institutional racism in law, there was a clear move away from institutions, state, and governance as sites of racism as it was believed that discrimination law had so far placed 'too much emphasis on state regulation and too little on the responsibility of organisations and individuals to generate change'.[109] 'Modern flatter organisational structures' were considered in need of 'active participation of all stakeholders, on training and improving skills, developing wider social networks and encouraging adaptability'.[110] This was in contrast with 'calls for stronger legislation' which had included 'increased central government intervention' in the field of racial discrimination and 'a major radical programme of action to tackle the root causes of racial inequality'.[111] This was also against the grain of the last round of law reform. The 1975 White Paper on racial discrimination had 'accepted the need for a broader governmental role to tackle those "more complex situations of accumulated disadvantages and of the effects of past discrimination" '.[112] The research informing the latest round of law reform had reaffirmed this message. The government's 2005 Equalities Review (chaired by Trevor Phillips, then Chair of the Commission for Racial Equality) had undertook a 'root and branch review to investigate the causes of persistent discrimination and inequality in British society' and 'found widespread, entrenched and persistent forms of discrimination and inequality associated with the protected characteristics'.[113] The Equality and Human Rights Commission had sounded similar alarm in its report 'How Fair is Britain?'[114]—and resounded alarm in 2015, 2016, and 2018, highlighting the urgency of addressing disadvantage alongside discrimination.[115]

[108] Hepple, 'The New Single Equality Act' (n 81) 14.

[109] ibid xii.

[110] ibid xiv.

[111] John Solomos, 'Race Relations Legislation and the Political Process' in John Solomos (ed), *Race and Racism in Contemporary Britain* (Macmillan 1989) 68, 69; Solomos, 'From Equal Opportunity to Anti-Racism' (n 83) 10.

[112] Solomos, 'From Equal Opportunity to Anti-Racism' (n 83) 7.

[113] Karon Monaghan, *Monaghan on Equality Law* (2nd edn, Oxford University Press 2013) 4 [hereafter Monaghan, *Monaghan on Equality Law*].

[114] EHRC, 'How Fair is Britain? Equality, Human Rights and Good Relations in 2010: The First Triennial Review' (2010) <http://www.equalityhumanrights.com/uploaded_files/triennial_review/how_fair_is_britain_-_complete_report.pdf> (accessed 12 January 2025).

[115] EHRC, 'Is Britain Fairer?: The State of Equality and Human Rights 2018' <https://www.equalityhumanrights.com/sites/default/files/is-britain-fairer-accessible.pdf> (accessed 13 January 2025); Cabinet Office (2018), 'Race Disparity Audit' <https://assets.publishing.service.gov.uk/media/5a9ec73a40f0b64d7d48f2b7/Revised_RDA_report_March_2018.pdf> (accessed 13 January 2025); EHRC, 'Healing A Divided Britain: The Need for a Comprehensive Race Equality strategy' (2016) <https://www.equalityhumanrights.com/our-work/our-research/healing-divided-britain-need-comprehensive-race-equality-strategy-0> (accessed 13 January 2025).

As Sooben argues, it was possible that racial discrimination law was considered 'only one element within a wider strategy which also included publicity and campaigning against racism, and policies to tackle disadvantage and poverty more generally'.[116] It is indeed possible that this was meant to be the case. What is clear is that, with the turn of the new millennium and the latest round of law reform, only a rhetorical link had remained between racial discrimination law and a wider strategy to tackle racism as racial disadvantage.

The advent of the era of the single consolidated legislation thus cemented the 'racial inexplicitness'[117] that had characterized racial discrimination law in Britain for the past five decades. The era of 'race relations' legislations and its cultural, and to a very limited extent, transformative anti-racism had come to an end.

The EqA was passed on 8 April 2010.

It is now the main legislation regulating racial discrimination in Britain. What it has actually done about racism in the last fifteen years is considered in the next chapter. Here, it is useful to set out the direction of travel of the EqA, especially the particular route it chose from an anti-racist perspective.

Despite the Macpherson report, it did not adopt institutional racism as a form of racial discrimination explicitly. The broader role of the government was acknowledged in section 149 which imposed a duty on public authorities 'to exercise their functions with due regard to the need to' eliminate discrimination, advance equality of opportunity, and foster good relations between persons with different protected characteristics.[118] This duty instated an obligation to have due regard but not an obligation *to do* anything having had due regard to the need to eliminate (racial) discrimination. The reference to 'racial groups' in the previous version of such a duty was also lost.[119] The EqA did not enact positive measures for combatting racial disadvantage.[120] It did enact a provision on 'combination discrimination' which included direct discrimination based on a specified list of grounds that included race,[121] but that provision was never brought into force, and in fact remains dormant to date. In sum, the EqA did not deliver on any of the three major indicia of transformative anti-racism: of attacking drivers of racial disadvantage, intersectionally defined, and through proactive and disruptive measures rather than ex-post and incremental change.

[116] Philip N Sooben, 'The Origins of the Race Relations Act' Research Paper in Ethnic Relations No.12, Centre for Research in Ethnic Relations, September 1990, 40 [hereafter Sooben, 'The Origins of the Race Relations Act'].

[117] David L Kirp, *Doing Good by Doing Little: Race and Schooling in Britain* (University of California Press 1979).

[118] EqA, s 149(1)(c).

[119] RRA 1976, s 71.

[120] The 'positive action' provision under section 158 is limited to proportionate measures enabling or encouraging persons to overcome or minimize their disadvantage, to meet their needs, or to participate in an activity. EqA, s 159.

[121] EqA, s 14.

As argued above, none of this was even on the agenda anyway. There was little anti-racist thinking that informed the drafting and enactment of the EqA in contrast with previous law reform surrounding race relations legislations. The EqA muted the race-related focus of discrimination law that had been possible with the particularity of race relations legislation.

This was a consequence of the wider shift towards liberalism that underlined the EqA as such. This is best captured by the EqA's doubling down on individual enforcement.

Before the EqA came into force, there was yet again an exaggerated focus on individual enforcement which, it was argued, needed to become 'more effective to deal with increasingly subtle and complex nature of discrimination'.[122] Yet, neither the history of its development nor the eventual text of the single consolidated legislation indicates that any attention was paid to the subtle and complex nature of racism. There was just a general belief that 'the courts over the years since [the RRA] 1976 ha[d] made it easier for discrimination to be proved'.[123] But the reality was that the 'in the last twenty-two years [the] number remains insignificant, that is under 2000, (on average less than 100 a year)'[124] of those who had successfully claimed racial discrimination under the RRA 1976. There was growing acceptance of the fact that 'the machinery set up to implement the [RRA 1976] ha[d] not functioned effectively'.[125] The experience from the US had also shown 'an increasing awareness ... of the weakness of a system which relied almost entirely on individual complaints'.[126] Yet, instead of doing anything to reform or replace the individual justice model, the EqA made it its mainstay.

Traces of cultural anti-racism or any interest in justice for the collective or at the group level evaporated as there was no more a Race Relations Board, Community Relations Commission, or a Commission for Racial Equality. The Commission for Equality and Human Rights (EHRC) replaced all equality bodies across all grounds. This replacement was informed by the government's misguided sense of having done enough for racial equality and equality more broadly and thus requiring EHRC only as 'a symbolic edifice for equalities' or for 'high-level blue-sky waffling'.[127] Its budget was slashed, 'from £70 million in 2009/10 to £17 million in 2014/15) over a whole host of discriminations—age, disability, gender, gender realignment, sexual orientation, religion and race—the specificity of each [was] lost

[122] Hepple, Coussey, and Choudhury, *Equality* (n 101) xiv.
[123] Bindman, 'Law Enforcement or Lack of It' (n 72) 50.
[124] Muhammad Anwar, 'The Impact of Legislation on British Race Relations' in Muhammad Anwar, Patrick Roach, and Ranjit Sondhi (eds), *From Legislation to Integration? Race Relations in Britain* (Palgrave 2000).
[125] John Solomos, 'From Equal Opportunity to Anti-Racism: Racial Inequality and the Limits of Reform Policy Paper in Ethnic Relations No.17, Birkbeck Public Policy Centre, 1989, 9.
[126] Sooben, 'The Origins of the Race Relations Act' (n 116) 30.
[127] Institute of Race Relations, 'The Race Relations Act 1965' (n 59).

in the general and the fight against racism undermined'.[128] In Geoffery Bindman's view, 'consolidation means cuts and the withdrawal of necessary powers and resources. The EHRC has been decimated'.[129]

The EqA was heralded as ushering 'a period of *transformative equality*'[130] except it 'did not quite herald the revolution'[131] it was touted for. This rings true when judged against the framework of anti-racism set out in Chapter 3 and in particular the framework of anti-racism as a legal principle set out in Chapter 4. The EqA focusses almost exclusively and obsessively on liberal anti-racism, that is, specific rules regulating interpersonal racism. This rules-based 'toolbox' for addressing racial discrimination hardly scratches the surface of racism and in fact leaves structural racism intact.

As Karon Monaghan says, the EqA will 'likely to be with us for many decades and will comprise the main legal framework for addressing inequality in the public and private spheres, and to that extent will be of historic importance'.[132] The next chapter thus turns its attention to the minutia of legal doctrine developed under the EqA to understand the extent to which the EqA has managed to tackle structural racism in practice despite its liberal framing. But on the face of it, as this chapter has shown, the text of racial discrimination law across time plainly represents, as Alastair Bonnett says, a 'conservative entrenchment' of liberal anti-racism.[133]

5.4 Conclusion

This chapter began to draw the first links between anti-racism and legal doctrine in this book. It traced the development of racial discrimination law—through its first instantiation in the RRA 1965, the RRA 1968, the RRA 1976, and finally the EqA—against the framework of anti-racism presented in Chapters 3 and 4. It found two things. First, racial discrimination law *was* initially conceived as anti-racist in that it targeted 'access racism' as a form of racial discrimination. This diminution limited the racism that could be addressed as racial discrimination through law. Second, while initially, racial discrimination law began with a 'race relations' framing which put community relations and hence cultural anti-racism at its centre, it shifted towards a firmly liberal framing in later statutes. But it was

[128] ibid.
[129] Geoffery Bindman, 'Race Relations After 50 Years' in Omar Khan (ed), *How Far Have We Come? Lessons from the 1965 Race Relations Act*, Runneymede Perspectives (2015) 11.
[130] Hepple, 'The New Single Equality Act' (n 81) 13 (emphasis in original).
[131] Monaghan, *Monaghan on Equality Law* (n 113) 3.
[132] ibid 3.
[133] Alastair Bonnett, *Radicalism, Anti-Racism and Representation* (Routledge 1993) 47–48.

decidedly never transformative in nature in that neither in its initial conception nor in its subsequent operation were the three race relations legislations and later the EqA meant to disrupt structural racism. In fact, they were to leave structural racism in place in the way that they were imagined and operationalized. Racial discrimination law was thus not meant for reflecting anything like anti-racism as a legal principle.

6
Racial Discrimination under the Equality Act 2010

6.1 Introduction

The previous chapter considered how anti-racism came to be pursued in the mould of racial discrimination law in the UK. It showed the trajectory of race relations legislations from 1965 to 2010.

Since 1 October 2010, racial discrimination law has been subsumed under a general equality legislation—the Equality Act 2010 ('EqA')—which consolidated law relating to all protected characteristics, including race. The prevailing racial discrimination law in Britain[1] has thus lost the specificity it had under the explicit banner of 'race relations' in the 1965, 1968, and 1976 legislations. But substantively, the EqA, as its preamble proclaims, was meant to reform, harmonize and strengthen the law on discrimination across protected characteristics listed in Section 6.4 (age, disability, gender reassignment, marriage and civil partnership, pregnancy and maternity, race, religion or belief, sex, and sexual orientation). As an extension, it promised an advance in addressing racial discrimination law too. Has this promise materialized? It is worth considering this after the EqA has been in force for almost fifteen years. *Has* racial discrimination law under the Britain's main equality legislation addressed racism?

The chapter finds that the EqA has been ineffective against all forms of racism—interpersonal, institutional, and structural—and thus fails to be anti-racist in practice.

This conclusion is reached through a study of the doctrine of racial discrimination law under the EqA, the parameters of which are set out in Section 6.2. Section 6.3 holds up the current doctrine against the conceptual frameworks of racism and anti-racism offered in Part I of the book, especially structural racism, which has to do with attentiveness to (i) the role of the state and state-like entities in (ii) racializing and (iii) generating racial disadvantage; and transformative anti-racism—which has to do with (i) attacking drivers of racial disadvantage, (ii) intersectionally defined, and (iii) through proactive, disruptive, and broad-based measures rather

[1] The EqA applies to Great Britain, that is, England, Wales, and Scotland and does not apply in Northern Ireland.

Anti-Racism as a Legal Principle. Shreya Atrey, Oxford University Press. © Shreya Atrey 2026.
DOI: 10.1093/9780198947646.003.0009

than reactive, incremental, and piecemeal measures. The chapter identifies four substantive limitations as to the scope of the EqA which impede the redressal of structural racism and the realization of transformative anti-racism: personal, material, evidential, and remedial. In sum, these doctrinal limitations not only make the EqA ineffective against structural racism but make it act as a structural barrier to transformative anti-racism. Thus, the chapter shows that far from reflecting anti-racism as a legal principle, the doctrine under the EqA is a manifestation of structural racism itself.

6.2 The Equality Act 2010

6.2.1 The Panorama

The previous chapter discussed the history of the rules-based 'toolbox' of the EqA.[2] Before embarking on the review of legal doctrine, it is useful to recall how the EqA's rules prohibiting discrimination relate to racial discrimination in particular.

The EqA, amongst its seven preambular goals, declares its purpose as 'to reform and harmonize discrimination law and restate the greater part of the enactments relating to discrimination and harassment related to certain personal characteristics'. Race is one of the 'protected characteristics' recognized in Section 6.4 and explained in Section 6.9 as including colour, nationality, and ethnic or national origins. Race discrimination is defined as including both direct and indirect discrimination because of race under section 25(6). The language of 'racial grounds', 'racial groups', and 'racial discrimination' preferred under the Race Relations Act 1976 is thus replaced with 'race', 'persons who share a protected characteristic' and 'race discrimination' under the EqA.

Direct discrimination—defined as 'less favourable treatment because of a protected characteristic' including race—is prohibited by section 13. Indirect discrimination—defined as the application of 'a provision, criterion or practice which is discriminatory in relation to a relevant protected characteristic'—is prohibited by section 19. According to section 19(2) [read with section 9(2)-(3)[3]], a provision, criterion or practice ('PCP') is discriminatory when: (a) it applies to everyone, (b) puts persons from a racial group at a particular disadvantage as compared to others, (c) puts the claimant/victim belonging to that racial group at that disadvantage, and (d) is not a proportionate means of achieving a legitimate

[2] Chapter 5, Section 5.3.4.

[3] Section 9 of the EqA provides that: '(2) In relation to the protected characteristic of race—(a) a reference to a person who has a particular protected characteristic is a reference to a person of a particular racial group; (b) a reference to persons who share a protected characteristic is a reference to persons of the same racial group. (3) A racial group is a group of persons defined by reference to race; and a reference to a person's racial group is a reference to a racial group into which the person falls.'

aim. All four conditions need to be satisfied for indirect racial discrimination to be established.

Harassment—defined as 'unwanted conduct related to a relevant protected characteristic' which 'has the purpose or effect of' violating someone's dignity, or creating an intimidating, hostile, degrading, humiliating or offensive environment for them—is prohibited by section 26. Victimization—defined as subjecting someone to a detriment due to a protected act (such as complaining about discrimination)—is prohibited by section 27.[4]

Furthermore, Part 11 of the EqA titled 'Advancement of Equality' establishes a public sector equality duty in section 149 which obliges a public authority to 'have due regard to the need to'—(a) eliminate discrimination, harassment, victimization and any other conduct that is prohibited by the EqA; (b) advance equality of opportunity between persons who share a relevant protected characteristic and persons who do not share it; and (c) foster good relations between persons who share a relevant protected characteristic and persons who do not share it.[5]

There are a range of particular applications (exemptions and exceptions) related to race throughout the text of the EqA in relation to segregation, colour, immigration, agency work, and so on. These and other relevant text from the EqA are brought up in this chapter where relevant. Otherwise, the chapter mainly concerns the provisions concerning the prohibition of racial discrimination.

The purpose is singular: to test whether the prohibition of racial discrimination under the EqA actually addresses structural racism, which frames or scaffolds all forms of racism. As Chapter 2 argued, this means that: while it is true that direct racial discrimination depends not on the subjective state of mind but on the reliance on racial criteria, structural racism performs the background work in positing why reliance on racial criteria ('less favourable treatment . . . . because of . . . . race') is considered problematic and ultimately lawful. Similarly, while it is true that indirect racial discrimination is neutral and not based on overt racial criteria, structural racism gives meaning to the disproportionate

[4] There are also other forms of discrimination prohibited under the EqA such as combination discrimination, failure to provide reasonable adjustments, and discrimination connected to relationships that have ended. This chapter however is mainly concerned with provisions which relate to race and have been invoked by claimants before courts. For a fuller survey of the EqA, consult: Aileen McColgan, *Discrimination Law: Text, Cases and Materials* (3rd edn, Hart 2023); Bob Hepple, *Equality: The Legal Framework* (2nd edn, Hart 2014); Karon Monaghan, *Monaghan on Equality Law* (2nd edn, Oxford University Press 2013).

[5] There is also the socio-economic duty in section 1 which requires public authorities 'when making decisions of a strategic nature . . . [to] have due regard to the desirability of exercising them in a way that is designed to reduce the inequalities of outcome which result from socio-economic disadvantage'. This has been brought into force in Scotland in April 2018 and Wales in March 2021 but is still not in force in England in 2025—fifteen years after the enactment of EqA. Similarly, there is the provision on combination discrimination in section 14 which provides that 'A person (A) discriminates against another (B) if, because of a combination of two relevant protected characteristics, A treats B less favourably than A treats or would treat a person who does not share either of those characteristics.' This too has not been brought into force until now.

impact ('particular disadvantage') for it to serve as a cause of action which is presumed to be problematic.

This chapter shows the background work structural racism does in racial discrimination law, work that is rarely acknowledged, and even more rarely addressed in the arid doctrine under the EqA. An appreciation of this background work matters in understanding racial discrimination in a structural sense, which is not simply to do with individual acts of discrimination or effects of neutral acts but as arising out of structural racism. That is, racism that has to do with the totality of social, economic, political, cultural, and psychological relationships between people which are governed by how modern states and state-like corporate entities imagine and exert themselves.

6.2.2 The Parameters

The parameters of doctrine considered in this chapter are the following. This chapter analyses racial discrimination cases that have been decided under the EqA between 1 October 2010 and 9 July 2024. Racial discrimination is defined as discrimination on the basis of racial grounds listed in section 9 of the EqA, namely, race, colour, nationality, descent, and national or ethnic origin. Racial discrimination is taken to include cases based on racial grounds (alone or combined with other grounds of discrimination) and involving: (i) direct or indirect discrimination, (ii) harassment, and (iii) victimization.[6] Case law from all appellate courts adjudicating on the EqA is examined, including the Supreme Court, the Court of Appeal, the High Court, the Employment Appeal Tribunal (EAT), and, to a limited extent, the first instance decisions of the Employment Tribunal (ET).

These parameters generate a list of 235 cases classified under the tag of 'race discrimination'.[7] It is important that the list of cases and in particular the number of cases generated under the list should not be considered a definite list or as the number representing all cases of racial discrimination under the EqA in the last

[6] The discussion in this chapter and the rest of the book concerns rules prohibiting racial discrimination and does not consider case law under the public sector equality duty (EqA, s 149) which is not an action-oriented norm and is widely criticized as symbolic in its emphasis on 'the duty to have due regard' rather than to take steps to address racial discrimination actively. While suggestions have been made to improve the operation of the duty (e.g., to make it more participatory), it is also agreed that it is particularly limited in addressing structural inequality. Sandra Fredman, 'The Public Sector Equality Duty' (2011) 40 Industrial Law Journal 405; Aileen McColgan, 'Litigating the Public Sector Equality Duty: The Story So Far' (2015) 35 Oxford Journal of Legal Studies 453; Simonetta Manfredi, Lucy Vickers, and Kate Clayton-Hathway, 'The Public Sector Equality Duty: Enforcing Equality Rights Through Second-Generation Regulation' (2018) 47 Industrial Law Journal 365.

[7] The search actually returned 260 cases based on the parameters described above which Westlaw classifies as cases of 'race discrimination'. But twenty-five of these were cases under the Race Relations Act 1976 or only cited the EqA without there being a claim of racial discrimination in them. These cases are excluded from analysis.

fifteen years because the digital legal databases are not always comprehensive and the search parameters rarely return all cases relevant to the search. In the present case, an important case such as the *Independent Workers Union of Great Britain v Mayor of London*[8] which is discussed later was not captured by the search, but only manually picked up as a relevant case under the EqA. So, while more broadly, the dataset should be treated as a representative record of the racial discrimination doctrine under the EqA from 2010–2024; more precisely, the discussion and results presented in this chapter about the state of play of racial discrimination law under the EqA reflect the dataset alone.

6.2.3 The Procedure

Of the total 235 cases, 97 cases are largely procedural in nature. These cases concern either jurisdictional or admissibility issues such as: time limits, amendments and deposits for claims,[9] striking out of the claim,[10] the victim status of the claimant,[11] the identification of duty-bearers under the Act,[12] the application of the EqA to the

[8] [2020] EWCA Civ 1046.

[9] *Novak v Phones U Ltd* [2012] 9 WLUK 235; *Jooste v General Medical Council* [2012] 7 WLUK 102; *Rodrigues v Co-operative Group Ltd* [2012] 7 WLUK 495; *Lawal v Birmingham and Solihull Mental Health NHS Foundation Trust* [2013] 4 WLUK 136; *Gloucestershire Primary Care Trust v Sesay* [2013] 6 WLUK 267; *Moseka v Sheffield Teaching Hospital NHS Foundation Trust* [2014] 1 WLUK 236; *Exec Catering Ltd (ta Kaffeccinos Coffee House) v Kaczynska* [2014] 1 WLUK 823; *Fairchild v WM Morrison Supermarkets Plc* [2014] 3 WLUK 351; *Chindove v William Morrisons Supermarket Plc* [2014] 3 WLUK 752; *O'Connor v Bar Standards Board* [2014] EWHC 4324 (QB); *Torres v Cardiff and Vale University Health Board* [2015] 6 WLUK 643; *Basildon Acadamies Trust v Polius-Curran* [2015] 6 WLUK 699; *Mechkarov v Citibank NA* [2016] 2 WLUK 243; *Adams v British Telecommunications Plc* [2016] 3 WLUK 240; *Nugent v Yodel Delivery Network Ltd* [2016] 3 WLUK 748; *Malik v Oracle Corp UK Ltd* [2016] 4 WLUK 171; *O'Connor v Bar Standards Board* [2016] EWCA Civ 775; *Fairlead Maritime Ltd v Parsoya* [2016] 8 WLUK 349; *Edomobi v La Retraite RC Girls School* [2016] 11 WLUK 396; *Fanutti v University of East Anglia* [2017] 12 WLUK 279; *Patka v BBC* [2018] 4 WLUK 128; *Mirek v Graysons Automotive Services* [2018] 11 WLUK 730; *Adedeji v University Hospital Birmingham NHS Foundation* [2019] 12 WLUK 637; *Adedeji v University Hospitals Birmingham NHS Foundation* [2021] EWCA Civ 23; *Palihakkara v Robertson Bell Ltd* [2021] 4 WLUK 65; *Kumari v Greater Manchester Mental Health NHS Foundation Trust* [2022] EAT 132; *Zhang v Heliocor Ltd* [2022] EAT 152.

[10] *Timbo v Greenwich Council for Racial Equality* [2012] 10 WLUK 24; *Wright v Nipponkoa Insurance (Europe) Ltd* [2014] 9 WLUK 407; *Mechkarov v Citibank NA* [2016] 5 WLUK 200; *Warner v BAndM Europe Ltd* [2016] 7 WLUK 277; *Ukegheson v Haringey LBC* [2017] EWCA Civ 1140; *Kwele-Siakam v Co-operative Group Ltd* [2017] 7 WLUK 699; *Silape v Cambridge University Hospitals NHS Foundation Trust* [2017] 10 WLUK 600; *Nyathi v Secretary of State for Justice* [2018] 4 WLUK 589; *Sridhar v Kingston Hospital NHS Foundation Trust* [2020] 7 WLUK 613; *Bendall v Female Social Network Ltd* [2020] 8 WLUK 395; *Arvunescu v Quick Release (Automotive) Ltd* [2022] EAT 26; *Ryan v R Robertson And Son Ltd* [2021] 9 WLUK 610; *Simmonds-Plummer v Hammersmith and Fulham LBC* [2022] EAT 50; *Paczkowska v R-Com Consulting Ltd* [2022] EAT 70; *Manda v Bird and Lovibond (A Firm)* [2022] EWHC 1427; *Lasdas v Vanquis Bank Plc* [2022] EAT 198; *Arvunescu v Quick Release (Automotive) Ltd* [2022] EWCA Civ 1600.

[11] *Halawi v WDFG UK Ltd (ta World Duty Free)* [2014] EWCA Civ 1387.

[12] *Depner v General Medical Council* [2012] 6 WLUK 420; *Kulkarni v NHS Education Scotland* [2012] 10 WLUK 476.

case,[13] the adequacy of reasons and substitution of findings of fact by the tribunal/court,[14] error of fact,[15] error of law,[16] estoppel,[17] restriction on number of claims;[18] procedural irregularity or unfairness;[19] territorial jurisdiction;[20] academic nature of the dispute;[21] vexatious claims;[22] and failure to provide reasons;[23] often several of them at once.[24]

Needless to say, these are issues of process not substance of racial discrimination claims. Hence, they do not help assess how substantive law, may or may not be serving as a tool for addressing structural racism in relation to the fact situation that gave rise to the claims. But they show something important still. That law's procedure can operate as, what Bourdieu called, a 'structuring structure' and act as a structure *of* structural racism.[25] That is, legal procedure—and especially court procedure—can be a structure that makes up structural racism because it can impede the consideration of claims of racial discrimination and in doing so produce and reproduce structural racism. There are two reasons for seeing procedure in this way.

First, the number of cases dedicated to procedural issues alone, at 41.27 per cent of the total number of decided cases in the dataset, is substantial. In these cases, although the complaint concerned racial discrimination, judges were occupied not with the substance of the complaint but whether it could or should be heard or if

[13] *Uddin v General Medical Council* [2013] 2 WLUK 374; *Wittenberg v Sunset Personnel Services Ltd* [2017] 1 WLUK 628.

[14] *Koku v South London and Maudsley NHS Foundation Trust* [2013] 3 WLUK 415.

[15] *Patel v South Tyneside Council* [2013] 4 WLUK 30; *Otobor v Croydon College* [2013] 9 WLUK 114; *Hillingdon LBC v Meso* [2014] 3 WLUK 291; *Revenue and Customs Commissioners v Mabosa* [2017] 10 WLUK 676; *Mechkarov v Citibank NA* [2019] 7 WLUK 611.

[16] *Dossen v Headcount Resources Ltd (In Liquidation)* [2013] 4 WLUK 43; *Durrani v Ealing LBC* [2013] 4 WLUK 81; *Gillingham Football Club Ltd v McCammon* [2013] 9 WLUK 18; *Adeshina v St George's University Hospitals NHS Foundation Trust* [2015] 5 WLUK 18; *Ukeh v Ministry of Defence* [2015] 5 WLUK 430; *Essex CC v Jarrett* [2015] 11 WLUK 68; *Leeds and Yorkshire Housing Association Ltd v Fothergill* [2021] 1 WLUK 579.

[17] *Odu-Obi v Interserve FM Ltd* [2013] 5 WLUK 410.

[18] *Horlorku v Liverpool City Council* [2015] 5 WLUK 347; *Elijah-Jacobs v South West London and St Georges Mental Health Trust* [2015] 8 WLUK 137.

[19] *NHS Trust Development Authority (NHS TDA) v Saiger* [2017] 7 WLUK 355; *Nawaz v BG Consulting Group Ltd* [2017] 10 WLUK 560; *Jayaram v Network Rail Infrastructure Ltd* [2020] 1 WLUK 576; *Ihekwoaba v Aston Services Group Ltd* [2021] 3 WLUK 829; *Neslen v Evans* [2021] EWHC 1909 (QB); *Sami v Avellan* [2022] EAT 72.

[20] *Ravisy v Simmons and Simmons LLP* [2018] 11 WLUK 810; *Hamam v British Embassy in Cairo* [2020] EWCA Civ 73.

[21] *R (on the application of Goloshvili) v Secretary of State for the Home Department* [2019] EWHC 614 (Admin).

[22] *Attorney General v Iteshi* [2014] 3 WLUK 304; *Agbenowossi-Koffi v Donvand Ltd (ta Gullivers Travel Associates)* [2014] EWCA Civ 855; *Kenbata v Unison* [2014] 6 WLUK 800; *Kalu v Brighton and Sussex University Hospitals NHS Trust* [2019] 7 WLUK 816; *Kalu v University Hospitals Sussex NHS Foundation Trust* [2022] EAT 168.

[23] *Kenbata v Westminster City Council* [2017] 1 WLUK 185.

[24] *Ahmed v Ministry of Justice* [2015] 7 WLUK 167; *Adebowale v Isban UK Ltd* [2015] 8 WLUK 34; *Kansal v Tullett Prebon Plc* [2017] 7 WLUK 456; *Medrysa v Tower Hamlets LBC* [2021] 4 WLUK 590; *Laing v Bury and Bolton Citizens Advice* [2022] EAT 85.

[25] Pierre Bourdieu, *Outline of a Theory of Practice* (Cambridge University Press 1977) 72.

it was properly heard. Judges thus seem to be dealing with racism far less than we would think when we see them adjudicating on claims of racial discrimination. Quite apart from the central question posed in this book as to whether law embodies a principle of anti-racism, a high volume of cases dedicated to procedure show that law, very often, is actually *not* engaged in that question at all, contrary to what the presence of discrimination law or racial discrimination law projects.

Second, only 42.26 per cent claimants seem to win on procedure while 57.74 per cent lose. A proportionally high number of cases being defeated at the altar of procedure shows how difficult procedural hurdles are in actually claiming racial discrimination at courts. Procedure may be considered an impediment in engaging with racism where it actively blocks out complaints of racism. This could be through a limitation on the number of claims claimants can bring or by limiting the claim to that which directly and only concerns the claimant rather than the broader culture or environment in which racism takes place.

For example, consider the procedural requirement for a claim to be within specified time limits before courts. In the case of *Nugent v Yodel Delivery Network Ltd*,[26] the treatment of an Irish-British driver who worked with Yodel and was variously called: 'stupid Irish twat', 'stupid Irish bastard', 'thick Irish fucker', 'potato munching bastard', 'stupid Irish git', 'thick fucking Mick', 'thick Paddy', and 'thick potato munching fucker', was unequivocally considered racial harassment by the Court. But the claim was brought nearly three years out of date and after the time the harassment had stopped. The Court found no evidence on the basis of which it could have considered it just and equitable to extend time and thus concluded that it did not have jurisdiction to consider complaints of harassment related to race.[27] This was after it had already acknowledged racial harassment. Procedure thus trumped an unequivocal finding of racial harassment.

Now, procedure or process need not always be a bad thing from the perspective of the claimant. Claimants can challenge an error of law when a tribunal considers the claimant's claims in isolation rather than the totality of evidence,[28] or the length of reasons for dismissal of a claim when it is reduced to a meagre two paragraphs.[29] Process is not a trivial matter for either party and, needless to say, is important in guiding claimants, litigants, and judges alike, as a matter of justice.

But, at the same time, it cannot be ignored that from the perspective of the litigating parties, what is actually at stake is a finding on racial discrimination. Process is a step in the direction of a substantive finding on racial discrimination—whether it occurred or not. The preponderance of litigation on procedure seems to arrest a finding on racial discrimination, but in doing so, enacts structural racism

[26] [2016] 3 WLUK 748.
[27] ibid [44].
[28] *Ukeh v Ministry of Defence* [2015] 5 WLUK 430.
[29] *Revenue and Customs Commissioners v Mabosa* [2017] 10 WLUK 676.

of its own by becoming a hegemonic structure which arrests the examination of racism.

6.2.4 The Proportions

Of the total 235 cases, 138 have been decided on merits as opposed to procedure, of which only 62 have succeeded. These figures yield a success rate of 44.92 per cent. Which means that 55.08 per cent of claimants lose on merits. The overall win percentage for claimants across procedure and merits is 43.83 per cent. This indicates that claimants lose more than they win when they bring a claim of racial discrimination, whether on procedural or substantive grounds.[30]

This low overall success rate is further complicated by two things. First, I have counted claims where the claimant succeeded on *at least* one of the claims they argued—whether procedural or substantive—as a 'win' for the claimant. This does not mean that the claimant succeeded on their most important claim or a majority of their claims.[31] The 'win' may thus mean less practically for the claimant than it does statistically. Second, not all 'wins' mean a recognition of racial discrimination. In fact, some 'wins' may be more a denial than recognition of racial discrimination. For example, a successful racial discrimination challenge brought by a white claimant against positive discrimination in favour of racially disadvantaged groups is a 'win' for the claimant technically, even though the result is unfavourable to racially disadvantaged groups.[32] The already low overall success rate for those alleging racial discrimination should thus be moderated by these considerations.

Ultimately, the reality is rather sobering. To begin with, the number of people alleging racial discrimination in the UK under the EqA is rather low in contrast with studies and surveys which reveal a very high level of racial discrimination experienced by people from racially disadvantaged groups.

[30] These statistics are broadly similar to the statistics from employment tribunal for racial discrimination cases for 1990–1999 under the Race Relations Act 1976. They are also similar to the experience of the Race Relations Board in its complaints procedure under the Race Relations Act 1968. Bob Hepple, Mary Coussey, and Tufyal Choudhury, *Equality: A New Framework* (Hart 2000) 111; Report of the Community Relations Commission 1970, c 81, s 25(7); Jennifer Brown, 'An Early History of British Race Relations Legislation', Briefing Paper 8360, House of Commons Library (2018) 6 ('There were relatively few complaints lodged to the Race Relations Board and of these a small number resulted in a positive outcome for the complainant').

[31] For example, in *Nyeko v AIG Asset Management (Europe) Ltd* [2021] 10 WLUK 516 where a claimant's unfair dismissal claim failed but the claim for victimization succeeded, the case is counted as a 'win' as at least one claim of racial discrimination succeeded. Similarly, in *R (on the application of Good Law Project Ltd) v Prime Minister* [2022] EWHC 298 (Admin) while the claim for indirect racial discrimination failed, the breach of section 149 was established. Thus, arguably, what was more determinantal to the claimant was not redressed. Yet, even if relatively minor claims succeed, for the purposes of these statistics *any* success is deemed to be a 'win' for the claimant though a claimant may feel very differently about this.

[32] *Furlong v Chief Constable of Cheshire* [2019] 2 WLUK 725.

According to the 2021 Census data, out of a total population size of 59.6 million people in England and Wales, 48.7 million people (81.7%) are from white ethnic groups while 10.9 million people (18.3%) belong to Black, Asian, mixed or other ethnic groups.[33] Of these, 2.4 million people (4.0%) are from Black ethnic groups—1.5 million (2.5%) identify as Black African, and 0.6 million (1.0%) as Caribbean; 5.5 million (9.3%) are from Asian ethnic groups (Indian, Pakistani, Bangladeshi etc); 1.7 million (2.9%) have mixed ethnicity and 1.3 million (2.1%) belong to other ethnic groups such as Arab (0.6%), Gypsy or Irish Traveller (0.1%), or Roma (0.2%).

As of September 2024, 46 per cent people thought that racism was somewhat prevalent in the UK, with 34 per cent believing that there was a great deal of racism in the UK against people from a minority ethnic background.[34] A survey in 2023 found that 88 per cent of Black British population thought that they had been discriminated against at work.[35] In another study, nearly a third of people from ethnic and religious minority groups were believed to have suffered racial discrimination in education and employment and a fifth reported racial discrimination when looking for housing.[36] Disproportionately high rates of discrimination from police, public officials, and even neighbours, are reported by Black people, and Roma and Gypsy or Irish Traveller groups, in comparison with other minority ethnic groups.[37] A Guardian survey showed that people from a minority ethnic background are three times as likely to have been thrown out or denied entrance to a restaurant, bar, or club.[38] A study revealed that almost all Black British children have experienced racism at school[39] and another found that more than half Black British children live in poverty.[40]

If these studies and surveys are drawn out to scale to reflect the conditions of racialized disadvantaged groups in the UK, the number of people experiencing racism would run into hundreds of thousands and even millions.

[33] 'Ethnicity Facts and Figures' *Gov.uk* <https://www.ethnicity-facts-figures.service.gov.uk/#:~:text=82%25%20of%20people%20in%20England,group%20(2021%20Census%20data)> (accessed 10 December 2025).

[34] 'To What Extent do you Think Racism is Present in UK Society Today? (September 2019 to September 2024)' *Statista* <https://www.statista.com/statistics/1123242/opinion-on-racism-in-uk-society/> (accessed 10 December 2025).

[35] 'Black British Voices: The Findings', *University of Cambridge*, 28 September 2023 <https://www.cam.ac.uk/stories/black-british-voices-report> (accessed 10 December 2025).

[36] Nissa Finney et al (eds), *Racism and Ethnic Inequality in a Time of Crisis: Findings from the Evidence for Equality National Survey* (Policy Press 2023).

[37] ibid.

[38] Robert Booth and Aamna Mohdin, 'Revealed: The Stark Evidence of Everyday Racial Bias in Britain' *The Guardian* (2 December 2018).

[39] 'Study: Almost all Black British Children have Experienced Racism at School' (18 November 2020) *World Economic Forum* <https://www.weforum.org/stories/2020/11/racism-united-kingdom-schools-black-children-inequality/> (accessed 10 December 2025).

[40] Andrew Sparrow, 'More than Half of UK's Black Children Live in Poverty, Analysis Shows' *The Guardian* (2 June 2022).

Even going by the more optimistic numbers on the Home Office website which captures decisions made by the Employment Tribunal and the Employment Appeal Tribunals, the numbers of those alleging racial discrimination seems miniscule in comparison with those experiencing racism. For example, the number of cases which appear under the 'race discrimination' code on the Home Office website that have been decided between 2017 and 2024 is about 11,000. The number is an upper estimate as many of these cases only mention race or racial discrimination in passing and are not decided *as* claims of racial discrimination. The actual number may be much smaller and, in any case, a tiny fraction of racism that is out there.

So, while racism appears rife, racial discrimination cases do not.

What explains the low number of racial discrimination cases against the mounting evidence of racism in the UK?

A range of responses could be proffered to do with the claimants' psychological and financial burdens of litigation, awareness of rights and remedies, difficulties in reporting, past experience with courts, assessment of prospects, belief in the judicial system, and so on. Slashing of legal aid budgets and the introduction of tribunal fees between 2013 and 2017 would also have undoubtedly affected the number of claims that were made under the EqA.

Other scholarship has examined these 'external' reasons for which litigation has been and remains unattractive for claimants.[41] This book offers 'internal' reasons, to do with the doctrine of discrimination law itself, as the reason for the low uptake, an even lower rate of success for claimants, and ultimately, a rather low impact of discrimination law in addressing racism. The rest of this chapter shows the substantive limitations of doctrine in addressing racism. These limitations furnish few incentives for invoking discrimination law to challenge racism.

6.3 The Substantive Limitations

This section reveals that anti-racism is circumscribed by four substantive limitations as to the scope of the EqA—(i) personal—the ideal victim or claimant in racial discrimination cases; (ii) material—the subject of racial discrimination cases; (iii) evidential—the way in which claims of racial discrimination are proved or disproved; and (iv) remedial—the type of remedies that are awarded for claims of

[41] Gráinne de Búrca and Virginia Passalacqua, 'The Curious Absence of Race Discrimination Litigation in EU Law' (2025) Working Paper LAW 2025/15 Department of Law, European University Institute; Helen Duffy, *Strategic Human Rights Litigation: Understanding and Maximising Impact* (Hart 2021); William Twining, 'Alternative to What? Theories of Litigation, Procedure and Dispute Settlement in Anglo-American Jurisprudence: Some Neglected Classics' (1993) 56 Modern Law Review 380; Hazel Genn, 'Tribunals and Informal Justice' (1993) 56 Modern Law Review 399; Beth Van Schaack, 'With All Deliberate Speed: Civil Human Rights Litigation as a Tool for Social Change' (2004) 57 Vanderbilt Law Review 2305.

racial discrimination. This section shows how the internal workings of racial discrimination law, as it operates today, ignores structural racism in quite precise ways by ignoring (i) the role of the state and state-like entities in (ii) racializing and (iii) generating racial disadvantage. While there is no explicit embrace of anti-racism as a legal principle, there is no explicit resistance to it either. Instead, anti-racism is resisted (and structural racism is ignored) in doctrine's myriad details which together make up the structure of racial discrimination law; a structure which, as a result, ends up acting as a structure of structural racism.

6.3.1 Personal Scope

Most racial discrimination cases involve individual claimants. Their complaints do not, unless averred explicitly, concern broader institutional or structural issues questioning why things are the way they are in a particular organization or national context. These cases are paradigmatic cases of interpersonal racism where the ideal victim or claimant is an aggrieved individual who had something said or done to them by another individual.

The image in which the ideal victim or claimant of racism is cast, limits who can bring a claim of racial discrimination and ultimately, what type of claims are heard *as* claims of racial discrimination.

This is illustrated neatly by *R (on the application of Good Law Project Ltd) v Prime Minister*.[42] The case concerned a judicial review challenge to the government's appointments during the Covid-19 pandemic which were made without open competition, only to persons known to the decision makers or politicians, and for no remuneration, such as the appointment of the Chair of the NHS Test and Trace Taskforce and the Head of the National Institute for Health Protection. Section 113(3)(a) of the EqA allows, where appropriate, for discrimination complaints to be made by application for judicial review. Section 31(3) of the Senior Courts Act 1981 allows applications for judicial review when the claimant has 'sufficient interest in the matter'. The question before the Court was whether the claimants—the Good Law Project Ltd and the Runnymede Trust—had sufficient interest in the matter to challenge the appointments as indirect discrimination on the grounds of race and/or disability. The Court found that they did not for three reasons which are worth quoting in full:

> *First*, this is not a case where all members of the public are equally affected. There were individuals, directly and personally affected by the decisions under challenge, who would be capable of bringing proceedings alleging unlawful discrimination: those who were considered (or perhaps feel that they should have

[42] [2022] EWHC 298 (Admin).

been considered) for appointment to one of the posts in question but were not appointed... *Second*, the question of standing so far as it concerns the Claimants' discrimination challenge in this case, must be closely related to the statutory definition of indirect discrimination. By section 19 of the Act, indirect discrimination is defined in terms of the application by person 'A' of a 'provision, criterion or practice' to a person (referred to in the Act as 'B') in relation to a relevant protected characteristic of B's (see section 4 of the Act, including race and disability) which puts B (the person with a protected characteristic) at a particular disadvantage. The obvious person to bring legal proceedings is therefore that person B . . . *Third*, [t]he Employment Tribunal—where the relevant cause of action more appropriately exists—is far better suited than the Administrative Court to adjudicate on disputes of fact likely to be material to the outcome of any discrimination claim. It has procedures appropriate to the task. Moreover, the Employment Tribunal is a specialist tribunal.[43]

All three reasons fly in the face of an understanding of structural racism.

The first reason mistakenly deems the appointments made by the Prime Minister and the Secretary of State for Health and Social Care as matters of individual employment instead of as matters of public decision-making which impact public at large especially at a critical time like a global pandemic. The diminution of an obviously public matter is unwarranted and can only be explained in terms of a misguided assumption of racial discrimination claims of employment as necessarily being individualistic in nature. This assumption disregards a structural understanding of racism which is particularly cognizant of the way in which the state or the government wields power in public appointments. This assumption also insulates discrimination law and employment law from the logic of ordinary judicial review which is meant for scrutinizing exercise of state power.[44]

Second, the reading of section 19 is also unwarranted as the fact that the provision is worded in terms of 'A' having done something to 'B' does not automatically answer the question of standing. In particular, it disregards recognized principles of public interest standing where the matter concerns 'the public generally, or a section thereof, but no one particular individual has any more immediate interest than any other'.[45] Public interest standing exists in contrast with direct standing where the victims themselves bring a claim and associational standing where a representative group can bring a claim on behalf of the victims (such as a union bringing a claim on behalf of its members[46]). In contrast, public interest standing recognizes that some matters are indeed public in nature in that they concern the lawful exercise of public power which is essentially a democratic and a rule of law

[43] ibid [31] [32] [34].

[44] Chapter 8 of the book discusses the treatment of racial discrimination cases under common law judicial review.

[45] ibid [20] (citing Paul Craig, *Administrative Law* (9th edn, Sweet and Maxwell 2021) [25-023]).

[46] *R (Independent Workers Union of Great Britain) v Mayor of London* [2020] EWCA Civ 1046.

issue. The Parliament in enacting the provisions of the EqA could not possibly have meant to exclude public interest standing in cases of indirect racial discrimination, especially not from a claimant like the Runneymede Trust which is one of the oldest and most reputed anti-racist organizations in the country.

Third, the invocation of 'specialist' status of employment tribunals in assessing *all* claims of employment, including public appointments made during Covid-19, is a gross overestimation of the specialism of employment tribunals. In comparison to ordinary administrative courts which are naturally more versed with judicial review proceedings to review the lawfulness of the exercise of public power, it is hard to believe that an employment tribunal can be more suited to assess an issue which involved, essentially, corruption and cronyism in the government, *just* because the matter was one of appointment of an individual to a post.[47] Again, this is a diminution and deflects attention away from the essential nature of the matter which was about appointments made to *public posts* by *senior ministers* in *the government*.

The issue with a restrictive scope of standing is not simply procedural. The issue is that the personal scope of racial discrimination itself is being conceived in private and individualized terms as opposed to public and collective terms. A vastly oversized docket of employment tribunals as opposed to ordinary courts which are better placed to assess the exercise of public power as it affects people at large, confirms the strong foothold of the individualized conception of the personal scope of discrimination law, and racial discrimination law in particular. Eventually, it limits not only who can bring a claim of racial discrimination but also the kind of claims that are brought before the courts *as* cases of racial discrimination. The section below considers this.

6.3.2 Material Scope

Relatedly, a vast majority of the doctrine of racial discrimination law concerns cases which are in the nature of a person doing or saying something to another person. These are cases which are often described as 'everyday racism', that is, cases of racially discriminatory behaviour in the everyday interactions between people whether they are buying milk, taking public transport, joining a union, applying for a license or mortgage, going to cinema or school, or just doing their job. Any resultant detriment suffered because of a racially discriminatory act or omission then becomes the subject of a discrimination challenge under the EqA whose remit includes services and public functions (Part 3 of the EqA), premises (Part 4 of the EqA), work (Part 5 of the EqA), education (Part 6 of the EqA), and associations (Part 7 of the EqA).[48]

[47] *General Medical Council v Michalak* [2017] UKSC 71.

[48] The remit excludes anti-social behaviour, public nuisance, and obstruction of the highway. *Birmingham City Council v Afsar* [2019] EWHC 3217 (QB) [44] (Warby J).

Importantly, the kind of cases which seem to succeed are cases of 'bald' racism to do with racial slurs, naked bias, outright stereotyping, and prejudice such as being called 'abo',[49] 'babaji',[50] 'Paki Lover',[51] and 'lazy cheeky monkey';[52] or being told to 'Fuck off back to Poland',[53] and that 'you need to get a pool of bleach and bleach your skin so that you come back tomorrow white and the patients will be nice to you';[54] or being asked in an interview whether you can handle racism as an Asian person,[55] and being told that you would have suffered discrimination as a Latino due to your race and skin colour;[56] or being ruled out for adoption for being Sikh,[57] assessed wrongly for your immigration status and nationality,[58] mistreated for being considered as 'staring menacingly' at a white person;[59] being denied entry in a pub for being a Traveller;[60] or having your wig pulled off as a Black woman and being told that 'afro beats' was the 'music of [your] people'.[61]

There are five implications of the predominance of such cases under the EqA: (i) the predominance of 'bald' racism in the form of direct racial discrimination; (ii) the assumption of social, cultural, political, economic, psychological, and other forces as legitimating conditions of racial discrimination; (iii) the restriction on what counts as a 'racial' ground; (iv) the disregard of intersectional issues; and (v) the ignorance of the role of the state and state-like entities and institutions in racial discrimination cases.

First, such cases are often cases of direct racial discrimination or racial harassment. This is striking because, as Chapters 1 and 2 discussed, racism is observed in racial disadvantage rather than the obvious actions or omissions which use race explicitly to cause racial discrimination. So, even when racism manifests as racial disadvantage, racial discrimination law is not commonly activated to address such racism. The material scope of racial discrimination under the EqA appears to be limited to direct and often racially explicit treatment of individuals rather than the racialized disadvantage experience by racially disadvantaged groups. The exception to this trend are cases of indirect discrimination brought by Traveller groups. Though even here, it is clear that only more obvious claims, which show prima facie and inextricable connection to race, succeed.

[49] *Sharfudeen v TJ Morris Ltd (ta Home Bargains)* [2017] 3 WLUK 95.
[50] *Hossaini v EDS Recruitment Ltd (ta JAndC Recruitment)* [2019] 5 WLUK 643.
[51] *Giwa-Amu v Department for Work and Pensions* [2020] 2 WLUK 454.
[52] *Abdi v TC Facilities Management Ltd* [2022] 8 WLUK 381.
[53] *Stefanko v Maritime Hotel Ltd (In Voluntary Liquidation)* [2018] 9 WLUK 431.
[54] *Kweyama v Central and North West London NHS Foundation Trust* [2023] 10 WLUK 465.
[55] *Revenue and Customs Commissioners v Saldanha* [2017] 9 WLUK 370.
[56] *Bradbury v Sky In-Home Service Ltd* [2022] SLT (Tr) 43.
[57] *Mander v Windsor and Maidenhead RBC* [2019] 12 WLUK 79.
[58] *Sims v Lewisham LBC* [2020] 5 WLUK 517.
[59] *Akajioyi v Commissioner of the Police of the Metropolis* [2023] 9 WLUK 343.
[60] *Traveller Movement v JD Wetherspoon Plc* [2015] 5 WLUK 440.
[61] *Vial v Alsafar* [2023] 10 WLUK 454.

Smith v Secretary of State for Levelling Up Housing and Communities[62] is an apt example. The case concerned a change in the definition of 'Gypsies and Travellers' in planning policy to exclude those who had permanently ceased travelling due to disability or age. The claimant was denied planning permission to continue living on a site she had used as a Romani Gypsy with her family, including two severely disabled children, since 2011. The denial was considered to be indirect racial discrimination as it had an impact that was inextricably connected to race and ethnic identity of Travellers.[63] The Court of Appeal found that the discrimination lacked justification as the change in definition had no obvious legitimate aim. The stated aim of the change—to ensure that the planning system applies fairly to all—obviously failed to consider needs of Gypsies and Travellers who, because of their age or disability, were no longer able to travel.[64] The case thus succeeded though it is useful to note that it succeeded only in respect of the individual claimant and the Court explicitly denied making a determination about the validity of the new definition itself. The focus on the individual claimant thus appears equally strong for direct discrimination as for indirect discrimination.[65] More importantly, in both direct and indirect discrimination, the type of treatment or effect that seems to succeed under the EqA is the more obvious kind—one for which no touchstone of the meaning of racism need exist as one can 'see it and know it' as racism. As a corollary, instances of racism, which are *not* instances of 'bald' racism tend to escape scrutiny under the EqA as they seem less obvious and hence less problematic.

Secondly, and as a consequence, this affects the very conception of what is considered racial discrimination. In the way that racial discrimination has been conceived under the EqA, social, political, cultural, economic, familial, and psychological structures are not considered discriminatory in themselves. In fact, they are entirely cast off as background norms which legitimate the discrimination complained of. What is particularly interesting is that, as Chapter 2 argued, these structures of structural racism actually exist behind all cases of interpersonal and institutional racism whether they are cases of direct or indirect racial discrimination. So, even where structural racism is not itself alleged, it is possible to appreciate how structural racism 'frames' instances of racial discrimination such that they are located within the all-encompassing circumference of structural racism, as the nested Venn diagram in Chapter 2 depicted. Thus, the very cases which exemplify the normative exclusion of structural racism from the legal category of racial discrimination also exemplify the flaw in such normative exclusion given that structural racism literally makes up all racial discrimination.

62 [2022] EWCA Civ 1391.
63 ibid [62]–[66].
64 ibid [75]–[81].
65 This point is further explored in Section 6.3.3 in relation to the proof of indirect discrimination cases.

For example, in *Quality Solicitors CMHT v Tunstall*,[66] the EAT considered that remarks such as the claimant was 'Polish but very nice' or 'Polish and very nice' did not have the purpose or effect of violating the claimant's dignity or creating an intimidating, hostile, degrading, humiliating, or offensive environment. Instead, such remarks were meant to be 'introductory [and] made to a client for the purpose of encouraging the client to be given the services of a paralegal assistant.'[67] The EAT thus rejected the claimant's submission that the remark was meant to 'dominate, belittle and cause a cultural gap'[68] and 'drive a wedge'[69] between herself and the client.

From the claimant's perspective, the juxtaposition of nationality, especially Polish, and nicety, reveals a certain problematic which has only fully come to light in the UK after Brexit. This may or may not have been harassment previously, but it is today, given that bald racism is supplemented with a culture of microaggressions against people from Eastern European backgrounds.[70] But microaggressions seem to fall outside of the scope of either direct racial discrimination or racial harassment under sections 13 and 26 of the Equality Act 2010 precisely because they are considered less obvious or less obviously connected to racial grounds.[71] This exclusion leaves in place a racially charged standard of everyday interaction to circulate freely in defining the social and cultural relationships between people which are eventually impossible to unsettle. In fact, the impossibility to challenge this standard in cases like *Tunstall* reveals this dialectic between interpersonal and structural racism where individual instances feed off from and in turn feed into a wider racialized discourse that forms the baseline for relationships between people.

[66] [2014] 7 WLUK 975.

[67] ibid [31].

[68] ibid [16].

[69] ibid [31].

[70] William Shankley and James Rhodes, 'Racisms in Contemporary Britain' in Bridget Byrne et al (eds), *Ethnicity, Race and Inequality in the UK* (Policy Press 2020) 219–220; Jon Fox, 'Eastern Europeans, Brexit and Racism' (2017) *British Sociological Association* <https://www.britsoc.co.uk/about/latest-news/2017/may/eastern-europeans-brexit-and-racism/> (accessed 10 December 2025); Homa Khaleeli, 'A Frenzy of Hatred: How to Understand Post-Brexit Racism' *The Guardian* (29 June 2016); Patrick Butler, 'Politicians Fuelled Rise in Hate Crime after Brexit Vote, Says UN Body' *The Guardian* (26 August 2016).

[71] In *Bakkali v Greater Manchester Buses (South) Ltd* [2018] 5 WLUK 181, a remark that the claimant was 'still promoting IS/Daesh' was not considered harassment even though it was made against a Muslim Moroccan man who was upset and offended by the remark. Likewise, in *Tees Esk and Wear Valleys NHS Foundation Trust v Aslam* [2019] 11 WLUK 754, a comment like 'he should join ISIS' was not considered as connected to race when heard by someone from a minoritized racialized background. Also, in *Tan v Copthorne Hotels Ltd* [2018] 11 WLUK 876, being asked to act 'more Chinese' and 'not like a diva' was not considered racial harassment when similar language had been used in the past and the claimant had not objected to it. In *Tesfagiorgis v Aspinalls Club Ltd* [2021] 10 WLUK 471, a Black British woman who worked at a casino and was frequently told by patrons that they wished to be served by 'Western-looking women only' could not establish a hostile work environment claim on the basis of handful of instances.

Consider also the case of *Diop v Calibre Recruitment Ltd t/a Marriott Hotels Ltd.*[72] The claimant, a Black African Muslim man from Senegal, was passed over for work in hospitality as he refused to shave his beard. He claimed that this constituted racial discrimination either under section 13 or under section 19 of the EqA. The direct discrimination claim failed because the Tribunal found that the respondents would have treated someone who was not a Black African Muslim the same as they treated the claimant. The indirect discrimination claim too failed as the Tribunal concluded that the requirement of being clean shaven did not either put him or the group he belonged to at a particular disadvantage since they could comply with the requirement 'by being clean shaven or having a trimmed beard without offending their religious obligations.'[73]

The ethno-religious stance of the claimant not shaving his beard was seen as entirely dispensable. The question that arises is: dispensable by whom? The inarticulate work being done here is of a norm in hospitality which requires clean shaven men—a Western, Christian, white image of a server. That social and cultural structure is one that racializes the image of servers, waiters, and hosts in hospitality and hence instates a framework of disadvantage for excluding those who do not serve that image. The Court in *Diop* fails to challenge the social and cultural structure. Not because it is not possible to do so but quite the opposite—taking the structure for granted and assuming that anyone asked to comply with it must also be able to comply with their religious or cultural beliefs. That assumption though is not shared by the claimant, not proven by the respondent and for which the Court itself cited no evidence. The uncritical adoption of the social and cultural structure allowed the assumption that the requirement was accessible to all which then stopped both direct and indirect racial discrimination claims in their tracks.

Thirdly, racial discrimination is mainly that which is based strictly on racial grounds listed in section 9: race, colour, nationality, descent, and national or ethnic origin. Cases where the treatment of a victim is based on grounds such as accent, language or immigration status, often fall through the cracks of racial discrimination. One exception to this has been the recognition of caste as a prohibited ground under section 9.[74] It is arguable that caste is akin to ethnicity and hence considered an analogous ground under section 9. But a more straightforward and practical reason for its recognition is that the text of the EqA already gives a nod towards the possible recognition of caste as 'an aspect of race' under section 9(5) of the EqA.[75] Where there is no such explicit possibility, the analogy between accent, language or immigration status and racial grounds is harder to strike.

In the case of language, courts seem open to the fact that, for example, a dismissal from a job for using one's 'own language' or being a native speaker of a

[72] [2014] 3 WLUK 246.
[73] ibid [5.4].
[74] *Chandhok v Tirkey (Equality and Human Rights Commission intervening)* [2015] ICR 527.
[75] The relevant provision states that: 'Minister of the Crown may by order—(a) amend this section so as to provide for caste to be an aspect of race; (b) amend this Act so as to provide for an exception to a provision of this Act to apply, or not to apply, to caste or to apply, or not to apply, to caste in specified

certain language, could constitute direct racial discrimination.[76] Though eventually, such cases often do not succeed as courts seem to find no link in fact between, for example, an instruction not to speak in one's language and nationality.[77] In *Kelly v Covance Laboratories Ltd*,[78] the Court found that anyone could receive such an instruction, irrespective of their language, and thus the instruction did not constitute direct racial discrimination, even though no one else actually received such an instruction, other than the claimant who was from Russia and spoke in Russian. It is easier to prove direct racial discrimination when there is clear evidence that the claimant is singled out and scrutinized for their language.[79] Likewise, it is possible to prove indirect racial discrimination when a claimant is denied language interpreters in a disciplinary hearing.[80] It is much harder to prove indirect racial discrimination for language policies more broadly, which, even though they effect the claimant and those sharing the claimant's protected characteristic, are yet considered a proportionate means of achieving a legitimate aim.[81]

Courts show even greater hesitancy to see immigration status as a manifestation of nationality or race. The case of *Taiwo v Olaigbe*[82] is telling in this regard. The appellants in the case were Ms Taiwo and Ms Onu. They were both Nigerian and brought to the UK as domestic workers by their employers who were also Nigerian. Their passports were seized by their employers. They were made to work round the clock, without holiday or rest, denied minimum wage, underfed, and physically and verbally abused. There was no doubt that their circumstances gave rise to claims of unfair dismissal, unpaid wages, and a violation of the Modern Slavery Act 2010. But the specific question before the Supreme Court was whether their mistreatment based on immigration status also amounted to the statutory tort of racial discrimination on grounds of nationality under the EqA. According to the appellants, immigration status was but a function of nationality in that it was indissociable from it. Lady Hale agreed that while immigration status of a domestic worker was a function of nationality, in that their vulnerability arose out of their non-British status, still, it was dissociable from it:

> Clearly, however, there are many non-British nationals living and working here who do not share this vulnerability. No doubt, if these employers had employed British nationals to work for them in their homes, they would not have treate

circumstances.' Annapurna Waughray, 'Capturing Caste in Law: Caste Discrimination and the Equality Act 2010' (2014) 14 Human Rights Law Review 359.

76 *Atif v Dolce and Gabbana UK Ltd* [2021] 10 WLUK 604; *Atif v Dolce and Gabbana UK Ltd* [2024] EAT 47; *Kelly v Covance Laboratories Ltd* [2015] 10 WLUK 507.
77 *Kelly v Covance Laboratories Ltd* [2015] 10 WLUK 507.
78 ibid.
79 *Rogers v Barking and Dagenham LBC* [2018] 12 WLUK 813.
80 *Messeri v Royal Hospital for Neuro-Disability* [2022] 1 WLUK 205; *Logo v Payone GmbH* [2024] EAT 9.
81 *Sokolova v Humdinger Ltd* [2021] 7 WLUK 820.
82 [2016] UKSC 31.

> them so badly ... But equally, if they had employed non-British nationals who had the right to live and work here, they would not have treated them so badly. The reason why these employees were treated so badly was *their particular vulnerability* arising, at least in part, from *their particular immigration status* ... it had nothing to do with the fact that they were Nigerians. The employers too were non-nationals, but they were not vulnerable in the same way.[83]
>
> The point about this case is that the criterion in fact being adopted by these employers was not nationality but, as Mr Allen freely acknowledges, being 'a particular kind of migrant worker, her particular status making her vulnerable to abuse'.[84]

That then failed the discrimination claim since Ms Taiwo and Ms Onu's treatment was said to be because of their immigration status but not their nationality or race. This narrow view of race is susceptible to challenge. First, there does not seem to be a reason to restrict discrimination on the basis of immigration status to nationality per se. Instead, immigration status is more than nationality and indissociable from other recognized indicators of race such as colour and ethnic or national origin. The history of immigration in the UK is one which is deeply entangled with slavery, colonialism, and the Empire with marked distinctions between how (white) 'old' Commonwealth (Canadians, Australians, and New Zealanders) has been treated on the one hand and how (non-white) 'new' Commonwealth (Africans, Caribbeans, and Asians) has been treated on the other. Colour and ethnic or national origin have everything to do with how immigration status actually divides people along racial lines.[85] So, trying to fit immigration status into nationality is incorrect to begin with because it then ends up seeing immigration status as about being a British national or not, when immigration status may not be solely about the official papers (a visa or a passport) and may run along racial, colour, national and ethnic lines, often all at the same time.[86] Second, this misunderstanding feeds into the overstatement of the fact that *many non-British nationals living and working* in the UK did not face similar treatment as the appellants. Indeed, white Australians or Canadians working in the UK do not often face such treatment. Even the middle-class employers who were Nigerians in this case, did not face such treatment. But that just misses the point that immigrant status in this case was inherently bound up not only with

[83] ibid [26] (emphasis supplied).

[84] ibid [30].

[85] Ann Dummett and Adnrew Nicol, *Subjects, Citizens, Aliens and Others: Nationality and Immigration Law* (Weidenfeld and Nicolson 1990).

[86] Ali Rattansi, *Racism: A Very Short Introduction* (2nd edn, Oxford University Press 2020); Anthias and Yuval-Davis, *Racialized Boundaries: Race, Nation, Gender, Colour and Class and the Anti-Racist Struggle* (Routledge 1992).

colour and ethnic or national origin, but also with the status of a domestic worker which in turn is gendered and class-based. Thus, the comparison was not to be between British nationals and non-British nationals or the different groups of non-British nationals in the UK but specifically between domestic workers who are typically non-British, poor, Black, and women all at the same time, versus other types of migrants and workers.

There is thus a great deal of congruence between racial grounds and immigration status, given the history and context of how closely the two categories have developed in the British context. The Supreme Court in *Taiwo* ignored this history and context and instead slapped an entirely artificial understanding of the two categories onto the EqA. Other courts have also failed to distinguish themselves from this fundamental error though claims of racial discrimination based on immigration status continue to surface.[87]

Fourthly, much like in *Taiwo*, even where apparent, racial discrimination cases are restricted to racial grounds and seldom raise or address intersectional issues. For example, the case of a Black woman who had her wig pulled off was considered racial harassment with no mention of gender either by the claimant or the Court.[88] This is obviously incorrect given the vast history of discrimination faced by Black women for their hair, which is both gendered and racialized.[89] While many aspects of appearance-based discrimination are gendered and affect mainly women, many aspects of forms in which Black people wear their hair affect mainly Black people. Discrimination against Black women for their hair carries both these dimensions but also the particular combination of both which is only experienced by Black women for the diversity of their hairstyles—cornrows, dreadlocks, bantu knots, crochet braids, knotless braids, Fulani braids, afro, wigs, etc. The isolation of gender from race in cases involving Black women is thus as inappropriate as is incorrect. Where the treatment concerned is not so obviously a case of intersectional discrimination such as involving Black women's hair, the intersectional dimension against Black women is even more easily lost.[90] Either way, claims of racial discrimination are rarely decided as intersectional cases.

This can obviously be attributed to the fact that the provision on combination discrimination in the EqA (section 14) has not been brought into force until now. Claimants and courts have thus had no explicit allowance for claiming or deciding on two or more grounds of discrimination. This however has not stopped such

[87] *R (on the application of Mormoroc) v Ministry of Justice* [2017] EWCA Civ 989; *Mruke v Khan* [2018] EWCA Civ 280; *Olatinwo v Qualitycourse Ltd (ta Transline Group)* [2017] 9 WLUK 211.

[88] *Vial v Alsafar* [2023] 10 WLUK 454.

[89] Ra'Mon Jones, 'What the Hair: Employment Discrimination against Black People Based on Hairstyles' (2020) 36 Harvard Business Law Journal 27; Chanté Griffin, 'How Natural Black Hair at Work Became a Civil Rights Issue' *JSTOR Daily* (3 July 2019).

[90] *Croydon Health Services NHS Trust v George* [2016] 2 WLUK 452.

claims from appearing before courts anyway.[91] When multiple grounds are alleged as the basis of discrimination, courts jostle with assigning the treatment to one or more of the grounds on which discrimination is being claimed.[92] Though equally, there are cases where courts have been able to find for discrimination based on two grounds without segregating the grounds.[93] There is however no clear principled approach to intersectionality under the EqA.[94] This effects racial discrimination in particular, because, as Part I argued, it is based on an understanding of race and racism which are essentially intersectional categories that are infiltrated by other categories such as gender and sexism, and disability and ableism. There are thus no 'pure' cases of racial discrimination. The disregard of intersectionality in these circumstances belies the fundamental nature of racism and ultimately the realization of transformative anti-racism, which as Chapter 3 argued, is particularly concerned with intersectional justice.

Fifthly, and finally, racial discrimination cases often concern discrete instances or episodes of discrimination and exclude challenges to broader institutional norms, practices, and culture or state laws, policies, and governance. This is the case even where broader institutional and structural dimensions are implicated in the 'wrongdoing'. Except, the wrongdoing is still attributed to the individual or entity adjacent to the victim rather than where the actual source of the wrong may lie.

For example, in *Sirunyan v NCO Europe Ltd*,[95] where an employer relied on the UK Border Agency's incorrect advice that the claimant was not entitled to work in the UK when she actually was, neither the employer not the UK Border Agency were liable for nationality discrimination under the EqA. This was despite the fact that the UK Border Agency was actually wrong in its advice to the claimant's employer and the employer would have been liable to a penalty to them had they employed the claimant wrongfully. The regulation of the right to work in this manner by the UK Border Agency—the institutional norms and practices against which the employer made its decision—was however beyond challenge in this claim.[96] Furthermore, even where evidence for racial discrimination includes 'authoritative material showing that discriminatory conduct or attitudes were widespread in an institution' no doctrine of 'transferred malice' is considered to apply to the alleged discriminator.[97] Institutional norms, practices and culture are

[91] *Bahl v Law Society* [2004] EWCA Civ 1070; *Nwoke v Government Legal Service and Civil Service Commissioners* [1996] IT/43021/94; *Hewage v Grampian Health Board* [2012] UKSC 37.

[92] *Bortnik v Maria Mallaband Care Group Ltd* [2015] 3 WLUK 506.

[93] *Marangoh v Keir MG Ltd* [2015] 2 WLUK 484.

[94] Shreya Atrey, *Intersectional Discrimination* (Oxford University Press 2019) 8, 110. See generally the lack of a principled approach under the EqA Colm O'Cinneide and Kimberly Liu, 'Defining the Limits of Discrimination law in the United Kingdom: Principle and Pragmatism in Tension (2015) 15 International Journal of Discrimination and the Law 80.

[95] [2016] EWCA Civ 34.

[96] *Olatinwo v Qualitycourse Ltd (ta Transline Group)* [2017] 9 WLUK 211.

[97] *Chief Constable of Greater Manchester v Bailey* [2017] EWCA Civ 425; *Saddique v Chief Constable of Cleveland* [2015] 11 WLUK 656.

thus considered relevant but not probative because the racial discrimination is individuated to the extent that what is ultimately probative is what the discriminator does to the victim in a narrow and specific sense. That then immunizes both (i) the discriminator's actions to be considered in the context of the institutional norms, practices and culture; and (ii) the institutional norms, practices, and culture themselves to be considered as institutional racism.

Furthermore, steps taken to address institutional or structural racism may themselves be considered a form of racial discrimination under the EqA given the limited material scope of positive action under the Act. For example, section 159 allows for positive action in recruitment and promotion to enable and encourage persons who are disadvantaged by their protected characteristics to participate in an activity in which they are underrepresented. But the provision applies in an individualized sense such that there can be no general policy for treating people from racially disadvantaged groups more favourably. Also, the provision applies only to individuals who are considered 'as qualified' as others who do not belong to the underrepresented group.[98] Thus, in *Furlong v Chief Constable of Cheshire*[99] positive action taken by a police force to diversify their ranks to represent the communities they served, was found to be unlawful because after an initial round of sifting, they selected candidates from racialized minoritized groups to fill the vacancies first. This was considered a generalized rather than an individualized policy of positive action and hence disproportionate under section 159(4).

The material scope of positive action is limited in the text of the EqA itself and hence enforced in a manner that bars taking cognizance of racialized disadvantage between groups in a systematic and organized way—something that is common across a range of jurisdictions around the world.[100] The point here is not to thrown open a debate on affirmative action. The point is a narrower one, that racial discrimination—qua the limited nature of positive action under the EqA—includes even positive action which could benefit individuals from racially disadvantaged groups.

6.3.3 Evidential Scope

How racial discrimination is actually proven presents a challenge for all claims, including claims of interpersonal racism and not only institutional and structural racism.

98 EqA, s 159(4)(a).

99 [2019] 2 WLUK 725.

100 The prime examples are India and Brazil—countries far bigger than the UK—which have a much broader range of positive action, including affirmative action programmes. Cf *Z & Anor, R (on the application of) v Hackney London Borough Council & Anor (Rev 1)* [2020] UKSC 40 where positive action was deemed permissible in regard religion.

The only cases in which it is not difficult to prove racial discrimination are those where there is smoking gun evidence of 'bald' racism.[101] Such cases are rare. A vast majority of cases where judges decide on the substance of claims of racial discrimination focus mainly on facts.[102] This is especially so for first-instance decisions of the Employment Tribunal (ET) where the bulk of racial discrimination litigation is located, along with appeals to the Employment Appeal Tribunal (EAT). Relatively few cases of racial discrimination are appealed beyond the tribunal system, especially at the highest level, all the way up to the Supreme Court.[103] In comparison with appellate level cases with 'substantive' or major considerations on points of law on appeal, cases before the tribunals mainly concern dispute over primary facts and hence involve intensive fact-finding exercises. They deal with extensive evidence—written, oral, and various forms of digital evidence. As confessed by an Employment Appeal Tribunal judge himself, proceedings before the tribunal can take 'weeks to hear, with witnesses producing witness statements hundreds of pages long and being subjected to cross-examination for days on end'.[104]

[101] It is thus not sufficient to allege bald racism alone. The allegation needs to be proven and is often successful only with incontrovertible evidence that that alleged treatment did in fact take place. For example, the allegation that the claimant was called 'monkey' did not succeed as the EAT found no evidence of it in *Mathebula v Time U Ltd* [2024] EAT 89. Corollarily, claims by white claimants for racial discrimination for having been dismissed from employment or admonished for their behaviour such as for using the 'N' word (*Dell v McManus (ta Weavers Medical)* [2021] 10 WLUK 670) or for posting racist statements on their social media regarding the death of George Floyd and its aftermath (*Webb v London Underground Ltd* [2023] 1 WLUK 500) have also failed. *Hale v Brighton and Sussex University Hospitals NHS Trust* [2017] 12 WLUK 215; *Bayfield v Wunderman Thompson (UK) Ltd* [2021] 7 WLUK 578; *Palmer v AIMS Markets Ltd* [2022] 8 WLUK 382.

[102] For example, *Gomori v Tygra Ltd* [2015] 3 WLUK 796; *CP Regents Park Two Ltd v Ilyas* [2015] 6 WLUK 484; *Saddique v Chief Constable of Cleveland* [2015] 11 WLUK 656; *Kowalewska-Zietek v Lancashire Teaching Hospitals NHS Foundation Trust* [2016] 1 WLUK 394; *Cousins v Forum@ Greenwich* [2016] 2 WLUK 9; *Nikolova v M And P Enterprises London Ltd* [2016] 2 WLUK 141; *Staph v Norgren European Logistics Co Ltd* [2017] 1 WLUK 320; *Chief Constable of Kent Constabulary v Bowler* [2017] 3 WLUK 524; *Mbubaegbu v Homerton University Hospital NHS Foundation Trust* [2018] 5 WLUK 362; *Bryan v College of North West London* [2018] 7 WLUK 813; *Oladipo v Lush Retail Ltd* [2018] 8 WLUK 170; *Jesudason v Alder Hey Children's NHS Foundation Trust* [2020] EWCA Civ 73; *Hylton v Institute of Directors* [2021] 9 WLUK 159; *Atif v Dolce And Gabbana UK Ltd* [2021] 10 WLUK 604; *Tchapdeu v Unipart Group Ltd* [2022] EAT 25; *Nyeko v AIG Asset Management (Europe) Ltd* [2021] 10 WLUK 516; *Henderson v Asda Stores Ltd* [2021] 12 WLUK 632; *L v M Ltd* [2023] 1 WLUK 459; *Dadhania v SAP (UK) Ltd* [2023] 1 WLUK 458; *Jaleel v Southend University Hospital NHS Foundation Trust* [2023] EAT 10.

[103] *Taiwo v Olaigbe* [2013] 3 WLUK 77 and *Onu v Akwiwu* [2013] 5 WLUK 35 were both appealed and ultimately decided by the Supreme Court as *Taiwo v Olaigbe* and *Onu v Akwiwu* [2016] UKSC 31 (see also the Court of Appeal decision in *Taiwo v Olaigbe* [2014] EWCA Civ 279); *Essop v Home Office (UK Border Agency* [2014] 5 WLUK 580 was appealed and decided by the Supreme Court as [2017] UKSC 27 (see also the Court of Appeal decision in *Essop v Home Office (UK Border Agency)* [2015] EWCA Civ 609); *Efobi v Royal Mail Group Ltd* [2017] 8 WLUK 122 was appealed and ultimately decided by the Supreme Court as [2021] UKSC 33 (see also the Court of Appeal decision in *Efobi v Royal Mail Group Ltd* [2019] EWCA Civ 18); *R (on the application of Z) v Hackney LBC* [2019] EWHC 139 (Admin) was appealed and decided by the Supreme Court as [2020] UKSC 40 (see also the Court of Appeal decision [2019] EWCA Civ 1099); *Naeem v Secretary of State for Justice* [2014] 1 WLUK 186 was appealed at the Court of Appeal and decided as *Naeem v Secretary of State for Justice* [2015] EWCA Civ 1264; *Chief Constable of Greater Manchester v Bailey* [2015] 12 WLUK 125 was appealed at the Court of Appeal and decided as [2017] EWCA Civ 425.

[104] *Davies v Sandwell* [2013] EWCA Civ 135 [33] (Lewison LJ).

Within this lengthy and bulky litigation, two issues prove to be exceptionally thorny: comparison; and justification.

First, disputes over comparators take centre-stage in the proof of both direct and indirect racial discrimination.[105] Section 23(1) of the EqA provides that: 'on a comparison of cases for the purposes of section 13, 14, or 19 there must be no material difference between the circumstances relating to each case.' On the face of it, neither the provision on direct discrimination (sections 13[106]) nor the provision on comparison (section 23) mandate comparison to prove a claim of direct discrimination.[107] But one look at the doctrine reveals that comparison operates almost as a judicial requirement for proving discrimination.[108] This requirement is in contrast with victimization claims which do not require comparative evidence.[109] But cases of direct racial discrimination, which are not cases of 'bald' racism and lack smoking gun evidence of less favourable treatment, are frequently mired in disputes over comparators. In fact, when cases are 'not accompanied by abuse or racial slurs or anything which might give rise to an inference of deliberate and conscious race discrimination',[110] judges are quick to find that the reason for the treatment is not racial.[111] Claimants are thus better served by bringing comparative evidence which shows that others in the claimant's position were/would not have been treated as the claimant was, but for their race.

This though is hardly straightforward. Take for example the case of *Walters v Avanta Enterprise Ltd*.[112] The claimant, who was a Black Caribbean woman, had a Bounty chocolate bar thrown at her by her manager proclaiming 'I wasn't trying to say you're a coconut!'. The EAT was asked whether the use of the term 'coconut'—a slur which implies that a Black person behaved as if they were white—amounted to racial discrimination. It found that a Black person who behaved as if they were white was not a member of a group capable of falling within the scope of the EqA as the combination of being a Black person and non-stereotypical behaviour or learned characteristics (accent or manners) did not form a part of 'race' under section 9(1). It thus rejected the comparator the claimant had alluded to—a Black person *not* acting like a white person. Instead, the Court compared the treatment of the claimant—a Black person behaving as a white person, with the treatment of

[105] This is in contrast with the approach under article 14 of the ECHR wherein as Lady Hale proclaimed in *AL (Serbia) v SSHD* [2008] 1 WLR 1434 [25]: 'in only a handful of cases has the court found that the persons with whom the complainant wishes to compare himself are not in a relevantly similar or analogous position (around 4.5%)'. This is considered in the next chapter.

[106] In contrast, section 19 on indirect discrimination uses the phrase 'compared'.

[107] *Coll v Secretary of State for Justice* [2015] EWCA Civ 328 [24] (Elias LJ); *Hewage v Grampian Health Board* [2012] UKSC 37 [22] (Hope LJ).

[108] *Olalekan v Serco Ltd* [2019] 1 WLUK 320.

[109] *Woodhouse v West North West Homes Leeds Ltd* [2013] 6 WLUK 68; *Mangalore v London School of Economics and Political Science* [2013] 11 WLUK 19.

[110] *Durrant v Chief Constable of Avon and Somerset* [2014] EWHC 2922 (QB) [53].

[111] ibid.

[112] [2017] 12 WLUK 644.

a hypothetical comparator—a white person behaving as a white person. It did so, citing section 23(1), that comparators must have 'no material difference' between them but for the relevant ground under consideration.

What constitutes a 'material difference' is however not obvious. In *Walters*, the EAT assumed that both the claimant and the comparator must be 'behaving as a white person' so that there was no material difference between them but for their race for there to be racial discrimination.

This seems to be a perverse way of using comparison: one which segregates race and ethnicity from its performativity and perception. It portends that race is something objective and that accent, behaviours, manners, language, and so on, carry no racialized meaning and inform the construction of 'race' in meaningful ways.

But whether or not the claimant or a white person behaved liked a white person is surely immaterial to the fact that the claimant—a Black person—was subjected to a racial slur. The particular racial slur used in this case could not have been used against a white person at all. 'Coconut' is a racially specific slur (as racial slurs often are) and used to belittle people of colour. Its use—which was undisputed—should have been sufficient for the EAT to find that the claim had reasonable prospects of success—but the Tribunal instead went down the route of absurd comparison to find much the same.[113]

Tribunals seem to spend extraordinary energy in constructing actual or hypothetical comparators with the result that anything short of mirror comparison between the comparator and the claimant fails a racial discrimination claim because there appear material differences between the two.[114] The thing is that, there will always be material differences—because, as Part I argued, acts of racial discrimination transpire against structural racism which instates a framework of racial disadvantage in social, cultural, political, economic, and psychological relationships between people. Differences or 'material differences' qua section 23 are thus almost a given. The judicial insistence on mirror comparison which disregards material differences and isolates race and race alone, is an artificial, acontextual, and unattainable standard of proof.[115]

[113] See remarks of Hale LJ in *AL (Serbia) v SSHD* [2008] 1 WLR 1434 [27] (highlighting the 'dangers in regarding differences between two people, which are inherent in a prohibited ground and cannot or should not be changed, as meaning that the situations are not analogous'); Elias J in *Islington LBC v Ladele* [2009] LGR 30 [39] ('[A]n employee [would have] a claim for unlawful discrimination even though he would have been subject to precisely the same treatment even if there had been no discrimination, because the prohibited ground merely reinforces a decision that would have been taken for lawful reasons. In these circumstances the statutory comparator would have been treated in the same way as the claimant was treated. Therefore if a tribunal seeks to determine whether there is liability by asking whether the claimant was less favourably treated than the statutory comparator would have been, that will give the wrong answer . . .); Underhill P in *Cordell v FCO* [2012] ICR 280 [1] (reiterating that 'the reason why' refrain from *Shamoon* 'has been repeatedly emphasised since, both in this tribunal and in the Court of Appeal . . . though still too often too little heeded by tribunals').

[114] *Croydon Health Services NHS Trust v George* [2016] 2 WLUK 452; *Wandsworth LBC v CRW* [2016] 3 WLUK 206; *Olalekan v Serco Ltd* [2019] 1 WLUK 320; *Key Care Support Ltd v Johnson* [2021] 3 WLUK 795; *Martin v St Francis Xavier Sixth Form College Board of Governors* [2024] EAT 22.

[115] Aileen McColgan, 'Cracking the Comparator Problem, "Equal" Treatment and the Role of Comparisons' [2006] European Human Rights Law Review 650.

However, mirror comparison is neither necessary nor sufficient under the EqA. Instead, courts can consider all evidence as a whole[116] or holistically[117] within a shifting burden of proof framework.[118] This requires that the claimant only shows that the treatment is potentially discriminatory,[119] leaving the respondent to provide a non-racial reason for the claimant's treatment.[120] Within this rubric, mirror comparison which seeks to isolate race as *the* reason for less favourable treatment appears, as Lord Nicholls' put in *Shamoon v Chief Constable of the Royal Ulster Constabulary*,[121] 'arid and confusing'.[122]

In the case of indirect racial discrimination, comparison throws a similar challenge in respect of article 23 but also an additional challenge in respect of section 19(2)(b). First, section 23 is principally at odds with indirect racial discrimination. Section 23 requires that there be no material difference between, on the one hand, the claimant and those who share the claimant's personal characteristic, and on the other hand, those who do not share the claimant's personal characteristic. But the very idea of indirect racial discrimination acknowledges that there are fundamental differences between racialized groups which play upon how different racialized groups experience a neutral measure.[123] These differences include the pre-existing disadvantage suffered by racially disadvantaged groups as opposed to dominant racialized groups. Pre-existing racial disadvantage—which, as this book argued in Chapter 1, is part of racism—is material in nature (different levels of educational attainment, employment, income, wealth, health, security, safety, well-being, and so on) and in turn leads to differences which may be considered material when it comes to comparator groups. Courts seem to insist on finding comparator groups without any material differences between them *regardless* of this reality.[124]

Greenland v Secretary of State for Justice[125] serves as a useful illustration. It concerned fixing of a higher level of fees for retired judges who were members of the Parole Board as compared to non-judicial members of the Parole Board. The

[116] *Bham v gether NHS Foundation Trust* [2015] 8 WLUK 94.
[117] *Home Office (UK Visas and Immigration) v Kuranchie* [2017] 1 WLUK 277.
[118] EqA, ss 19, 136.
[119] *Veolia Environmental Services UK v Gumbs* [2014] 2 WLUK 214; *Alam v London Probation Trust* [2014] 12 WLUK 62; *Ahmed v Ministry of Justice* [2015] 7 WLUK 167.
[120] *Wanjau v Canary Wharf Management Ltd* [2016] 4 WLUK 5; *Staph v Norgren European Logistics Co Ltd* [2017] 1 WLUK 320; *Sharfudeen v TJ Morris Ltd (ta Home Bargains)* [2017] 3 WLUK 95; *Kumar v DHL Services Ltd* [2017] 9 WLUK 100.
[121] [2003] UKHL 11.
[122] ibid [11]; *Chief Constable of the West Yorkshire Police v Khan* [2001] 1 WLR 1947 (HL). See also discussion in Aileen McColgan, *Discrimination Law: Text Cases and Materials* (2nd edn, Hart 2005) 53.
[123] *Essop v Home Office (UK Border Agency)* [2017] UKSC 27 [24] goes some way in recognizing this. Sandra Fredman, 'Reviving Indirect Discrimination: Essop v Home Office' (2018) 8 The UK Supreme Court Yearbook 154.
[124] *R (on the application of Hottak) v Secretary of State for Foreign and Commonwealth Affairs* [2016] EWCA Civ 438.
[125] [2015] 1 WLUK 605.

claimant, who was the only Black non-judicial member claimed indirect racial discrimination as all the 36 retired judges were white. Both the ET and the EAT rejected the claim, finding material differences between retired judges and non-judicial members in terms of performance of different roles as well as the need to incentivize recruitment of retired judges. The problem with this tactless comparison is that it states rather than interrogates the obvious: that different roles have been assigned based on judicial training which itself is overwhelmingly white and elite in the UK. The tribunals thus essentially sidestepped the very issue that the material differences between the judicial and the non-judicial roles were suspect. Almost contemporaneously, the presumed differences between the roles of judicial and non-judicial members were formally abolished on 1 April 2014. The tribunals though were unable to query these differences whose legitimacy they took as a given within the framework of comparison.

Secondly, comparison seems to be mandated by section 19 itself which requires that a PCP put persons with whom the claimant shares their personal characteristic at a particular disadvantage when compared with persons with whom the claimant does not share the personal characteristic.[126] Indirect discrimination thus requires showing that (i) the claimant and (ii) the group to whom they belong are both put at 'a particular disadvantage' as opposed to (iii) the comparator group which does not share the claimant's personal characteristic. Proof in regards both the claimant's group as well as the comparator group is complicated often by the lack of available data.

Take for example the case of *Boohene v Royal Parks Ltd*.[127] The main issue in *Boohene* concerned agency work and whether Royal Parks Ltd (RPL) was responsible for indirect racial discrimination when they paid their own workers (160 in total, mainly white) the London Living Wage (LLW) but did not impose any requirement on its contractors to pay the agency workers the LLW. The claimants were sixteen agency workers (all but one being Black and minority ethnic ('BME')), employed by the contractor firm Vinci, who were responsible for 'cleaning and maintenance of toilets, landscape maintenance and horticulture, gate locking and building and maintenance repairs'.[128] The absence of data on the entire pool of contracted agency workers and their ethnic makeup was deemed fatal in establishing that those in the claimants' position had suffered particular disadvantage. Additionally, as there were obvious material differences between the comparator groups—one performing office/desk jobs related to park maintenance and another performing manual labour at parks—the Court of Appeal was unsure whether the two groups were even comparable. Thus, the claimants' challenge failed both against the section 19(2)(b) (those with whom claimant shares their

[126] EqA, s 19(2)(b).
[127] [2024] EWCA Civ 583.
[128] ibid [7].

personal characteristic being put at a disadvantage) and section 23 (barring material differences between comparators) requirements.

Again, there appears something artificial about the comparative exercise undertaken by the Court in *Boohene*. A more direct way of approaching the issue may have been to ask whether RPL's permanent workforce and Vinci's contracted workforce had anything in common. RPL's job was to maintain parks and those who actually maintained these parks were the contracted workers in a very real sense. The fact that some of these workers—such as those employed by Vinci—were overwhelmingly BME did not change the fact that they delivered RPL's main and primary job of, quite literally, maintaining the London royal parks, but did not have the same pay as RPL's permanent staff. It also should not make such difference if other contracted workers—those not employed by Vinci—were not BME.

The Court in *Boohene* seems to do two things simultaneously. It broadens the relevant group to which the claimant belonged as comprising all BME workers to establish 'more general group impact'.[129] Then, it narrows the comparator group for the purposes of section 23 by only focussing on RPL's permanent workforce. This dual move makes it harder for the claimants to show that those in their position shared their disadvantage and those who were not in their position were not disadvantaged.

If a claimant succeeds in crossing the evidentiary hurdle of comparison, they still have another hurdle to pass. Section 19(2)(d) of the EqA provides that indirect discrimination is established when the respondent cannot show that the PCP is 'a proportionate means of achieving a legitimate aim.' Thus, if the claimant succeeds in showing that they and those who share their colour, nationality, ethnicity or national origin, have been put at a particular disadvantage by a PCP which applies to everyone, the burden of proof shifts to the respondent, to show that such disadvantage may yet be justified. Respondents often succeed in showing this. This is because the test for justification—proportionality—is applied in such a way that enables the respondent to succeed, especially when the respondent is the state as the government or a public authority. This result is in diametric opposition to transformative anti-racism which challenges structural racism that is effected by the state. The application of the proportionality test which yields this result thus requires careful unravelling.

The proportionality test is set out by Lord Reed JSC in *Bank Mellat v HM Treasury (No 2)*[130] and involves a structured assessment of four things:

(1) whether the objective of the measure is sufficiently important to justify the limitation of a protected right;

[129] *NSL Ltd v Zaluski* [2024] EAT 86 [93].
[130] [2014] AC 700.

(2) whether the measure is rationally connected to the objective;
(3) whether a less intrusive measure could have been used without unacceptably compromising the achievement of the objective; and
(4) whether, balancing the severity of the measure's effects on the rights of the persons to whom it applies against the importance of the objective, to the extent that the measure will contribute to its achievement, the former outweighs the latter.[131]

It is useful to isolate how structural racism is addressed at each step—legitimate aim, suitability, necessity, and balancing.

Claimants often succeed in the first two steps, and the balance tips in favour of the respondent hereafter. Respondents, especially the state, often succeeds in the final two steps.

The exceptional cases where this does not happen is where the respondents themselves admit that they have failed to take into account or address the disproportionate impact in adopting the PCP. Where the respondents put up resistance and can show that they were aware of the disproportionate impact and took it into consideration while adopting the PCP, the proportionality test rounds up in their favour.

For example, in the case of *R (on the application of Diocese of Menevia) v Swansea CCC*,[132] the local council's amended transport policy failed to pass muster under the proportionality test when it could not show that the policy was reasonably necessary. It was clear that Black Minority Ethnic children were three times more likely to be disadvantaged than white British children as a consequence of the amended policy which restricted free transport for pupils attending faith schools. The Court found that while the policy achieved a legitimate aim, namely, promoting access to education through the medium of Welsh, it was not satisfied that the evidence established that the means the local authority chose were no more than necessary to accomplish the aim. The local authority did not have to establish that there was no other means of achieving its objectives to justify the amended policy, but it did have to demonstrate that its amended policy was reasonably necessary. In the absence of a clear appraisal that did not seem to be the case.

Likewise, in *R (on the application of TW) v Hillingdon BC (No 2)*,[133] the city council's imposition of a ten-year residence requirement for accessing social housing was found to constitute indirect racial discrimination against Irish Travellers when the council could not show that they had 'assessed the extent of

[131] ibid [74].
[132] [2015] EWHC 1436 (Admin).
[133] [2019] EWHC 157 (Admin).

the disadvantageous impact of the residence requirement on Irish Travellers and their children, in practice'.[134]

The public authority's lack of consideration and mitigation of racialized effects of its policy are thus fatal to its defence. The more self-aware the authority is, the more robust its case for justification.

Take for example the case of *R (on the application of Bapio Action Ltd) v Royal College of General Practitioners*[135] which concerned a challenge to the differential outcomes in the clinical skills assessments of the Royal College of General Practitioners and the General Medical Council. The claimant association argued that the assessments were unlawful as they constituted indirect racial discrimination against South Asian and Black Minority Ethnic (BME) doctors. There was clear evidence before the Court that there was a marked difference in the pass rate of doctors (i) who had a first degree from a UK medical school and foreign graduates, and (ii) within each of these groups between different groups of doctors based on their race. The Court agreed that the assessments put South Asians and BME doctors at a particular disadvantage in comparison with their white colleagues. The Court also agreed that the tests were in need of great improvement and that the respondents were actively exploring better means of certifying doctors.[136] However, in the final analysis, the Court found that the assessments were a proportional means of achieving a legitimate aim (patient safety) because:

> No better means of testing those skills has *yet* been devised than the Clinical Skills Assessment. The method is in common use across the civilised world ...[137]
>
> The fact that it is possible to improve on the means of achieving an aim does not mean that before improvement occurs the means are not proportionate. Section 19 does not demand perfection. What must be judged is the balance between disadvantage, aim and means at the time when the provision, criterion or practice is in place and is scrutinised.[138]

In other words, the fact that the assessments were being used and not *yet* replaced became the justification for both the necessity and balancing limbs of the proportionality test.

This is curious as necessity is necessarily tested by courts *after* a measure has been adopted vis-à-vis other measures. So other measures are obviously not *yet* adopted. The fact that other measures were not adopted or are not *yet* adopted

134 ibid [57]. Also *R (on the application of Gullu) v Hillingdon LBC* [2019] EWCA Civ 692 (although the court left open the possibility that discrimination against Kurdish refugees in relation to the ten-year residence requirement may still be justified).
135 [2014] EWHC 1416 (Admin) [hereafter *Bapio*].
136 *Kapenova v Department of Health* [2014] 4 WLUK 522.
137 *Bapio* (n 135) [42] (emphasis supplied).
138 ibid [44].

cannot itself be used as a justification for the necessity of the measure that was adopted. The proportionality test only requires other less intrusive measures to be available or possible. The Court in *Bapio* however seemed to have required other measures to be available *and* adopted—a strange counterfactual in the scheme of the proportionality test. Even more strangely, the fact that other measures were available made the Court declare that its decision had served 'a useful purpose and the Claimant ha[d] achieved, if not a legal victory, then a moral success.'[139]

Thus, legal victories seem stymied by the application of necessity and balancing limbs of the proportionality test even where the courts agree that the claimant's case of indirect racial discrimination is meritorious. Courts seem resistant to making adverse findings especially against the state—the government, public authorities, elected officials, etc.

The *right to rent case—Secretary of State for the Home Department v R (on the application of) Joint Council for the Welfare of Immigrants*[140]—brings this point into sharp relief.[141] The case involved a challenge to the provisions of the Immigration Act 2014 ('the 2014 Act') which provided for a scheme whereby landlords were tasked to carry out checks on prospective tenants to ensure that they were not irregular migrants. The scheme, as Lord Hickinbottom at the Court of Appeal described plainly, was part of the 'hostile environment' policy of the government to encourage migrants to regularize their immigration status or leave the country by imposing restrictions on accessing employment, housing, healthcare, banking, driving licences, etc, which made it difficult to continue staying without regularized status.[142] It was contended that the scheme discriminated against non-white British people and non-white migrants, by encouraging landlords to rent to those who seemed British either because they were white, had English names, or had the relevant accent.[143] In other words, landlords would simply have found it easier to rent to anyone who did not seem like a migrant.

The risk that the scheme was discriminatory was appreciated by the government from the outset.[144] The evidence before the Court was incontrovertible, that: '(i) landlords discriminated on grounds of nationality in favour of those with a British passport against those without; and (ii) in respect of those without a passport, they discriminated on grounds of race in favour of those with stereotypical ethnically British attributes (such as name, colour, and accent) against those without.'[145] The Court agreed that there was evidence of disproportionate impact and

[139] ibid [51].
[140] [2020] EWCA Civ 542 [hereafter the *right to rent* case].
[141] The following discussion on *the right to rent case* and *the minicabs case* first appeared in Shreya Atrey, 'Structural Racism and Race Discrimination' (2021) 74 Current Legal Problems 1, 23–30.
[142] ibid [3].
[143] This was a challenge under the Human Rights Act 1988, in particular, for the violation of articles 8 and 14 of the European Convention on Human Rights.
[144] *Right to Rent case* (n 140) 22.
[145] ibid 4.

the inquiry eventually centred around justification. There was little doubt that the scheme had a legitimate aim to 'support a coherent immigration system in the public interest',[146] that it was rationally connected to this aim, and that there were no other less intrusive means to further this aim. So, the question was really one of balancing.

According to Lord Hickinbottom, the scheme was justifiable on a correct application of the balancing test which gave due regard to the decision of 'democratically elected and democratically accountable national authorities in implementing social and economic policies.'[147] This meant that the scheme was owed a wider margin of appreciation such that unless the decision was 'manifestly unreasonable' it was deemed to have struck a fair balance between the infringement of non-discrimination and the public interest served.[148] The margin of appreciation and the degree of deference was meant to be reduced when the decision involved discriminatory effects on suspect grounds such as race and sex.[149] That said, in this case, the Court was of the view that the Parliament was to be afforded 'very considerable deference' because the measure concerned the aim of reducing irregular immigration and was actually successful in achieving the aim of making private accommodation unavailable to irregular migrants.[150] While the efficacy of the scheme was hard to verify empirically or even be quantified and that 'more data collection and analysis might have been done in attempt to assess it', it was agreed that 'the evidence point[ed] towards the Scheme having made *some*, and more than insignificant, contribution to that aim.'[151]

The scheme was thus allowed to stand despite the lack of clear evidence on the point that its benefits outweighed the impact on racially disadvantaged groups. In fact, at various points in the judgment, the Court reminded that *some* landlords did not discriminate, meaning that not *all* migrants or non-ethnically British persons were going to be discriminated against. But *some* discrimination was deemed acceptable. The balancing test allowed for this reductive analysis to stand without a mediating principle at work.

Yet, there *was* a mediating principle that the Court acknowledged required attaching higher standard of scrutiny to cases of discrimination involving suspect grounds such as race.[152] Nevertheless, according to the Court, extraordinary deference attached to the decisions of a democratically elected and democratically accountable representatives of the State, '*even* where discrimination is on the basis of a core attribute such as sex or race'.[153] The fact that the Parliament seems to have

146 ibid 113.
147 ibid [127].
148 ibid [134].
149 ibid [140].
150 ibid [145]–[146].
151 ibid [146].
152 ibid [173].
153 ibid [148] (emphasis supplied).

been aware of the risk of discrimination seemed to suggest to the Court that discrimination should be allowed to stand, and *if* the discriminatory impact had been *greater than that was expected by the Parliament, then* it was for the Parliament or the Secretary of State to course correct.[154] The Court simply ended the matter by stating that while 'discrimination in all its forms is, of course, abhorrent',[155] since the Parliament did not *intend* to discriminate but only *coincidentally* ended up doing so, all discrimination was justified.[156] What is more, the sheer presence of the State as the respondent in a discrimination case, seems to have hollowed out any sincere application of the justification analysis, especially at the balancing stage with little discussion of the actual discriminatory impact (both tangible and expressive) in going through the right-to-rent check as people from non-British or BME backgrounds.

Independent Workers Union of Great Britain v Mayor of London[157]—*the minicabs case*—confirms this result. The case concerned a challenge to the London Mayor's decision to remove the congestion charge exception for minicab drivers in London. Ninety-four per cent of the minicab drivers were from BME backgrounds, while 71 per cent of them lived in the most deprived areas of London earning less than an average of £23,000 per annum. The removal of the exemption cost the minicab drivers 10 per cent of their net income. In contrast, 88 per cent of drivers of hackney carriages (also known as black cabs or taxis) were white and exempted from the congestion charge.

It was conceded that the Mayor's decision disproportionately affected BME drivers: it was a neutral policy that applied not on the basis of race or ethnic origin but put BME drivers at a particular disadvantage as compared to white drivers. It was also agreed that the policy had a legitimate aim: it was aimed at reducing traffic and thereby pollution in London. The only real contention there was, was whether the policy was proportionate: whether it was suitable, necessary, and balanced.[158]

Simler LJ at the Court of Appeal found that the policy was suitable in that, Lewis J at the Court below, had carefully considered evidence which projected a 6 per cent reduction in the number of private hire vehicles which translated to 1 per cent reduction in traffic congestion as 'meaningful' and 'not insignificant'.[159] She then found that the policy was necessary and that no other less intrusive means (viz., charging operators, cap and control licensing, introducing wage protection, and/or the provision of rest areas) were available to the Mayor.[160] The Court of Appeal had one final hurdle to cross: of balancing. It was argued

154 ibid [147].
155 ibid [148].
156 ibid.
157 [2020] EWCA Civ 1046 [hereafter the *minicabs case*].
158 *Bilka-Kaufhas GmbH v Weber Von Hartz* (Case 170/84) [1984] IRLR 317; *Hardys & Hansons plc v Lax* [2005] IRLR 726, [19]–[34] (Pill LJ), [54]–[55] (Thomas LJ), [60] (Gage LJ).
159 *Minicabs case* (n 157) [41]–[43].
160 ibid [58] [62].

that the magnitude of impact especially since it was based on race and suffered by a vulnerable group, was not properly weighed up. The impact on the BAME minicab drivers was one that affected 'aspects of their personal integrity, affecting their status as citizens in London.'[161] But Simler LJ was convinced that even though the policy attracted a high level of scrutiny because it (indirectly) discriminated on the basis of race,[162] it was properly balanced since 'the stark statistical imbalance in this case [had] led both the Mayor (and Transport for London) and Lewis J to confront this concerning feature of the measure adopted, and to *scrutinise with particular care* the nature and significance of the impact on the disadvantaged groups when balancing that against the aims and objects to be achieved.'[163] In other words, it was the 'careful analysis' of the magnitude of impact that saved the policy.[164] But for those still likely to be affected by the congestion charge it just had to be accepted that 'their income would reduce or they would have to work longer hours to meet their basic costs including payment of the congestion charge'.[165]

On the face of it, there is nothing wrong with the proportionality analysis conducted in this case. But that is exactly what is troubling about this case: that racial discrimination law seems to sustain rather than address clear discriminatory impact on racially disadvantaged groups. So, even though Simler LJ described this case as 'particularly troubling', nothing in her analysis alleviates the troubling impact whereby, at best 31 per cent (35,000) and at worst 94 per cent (106,000) of BME drivers lost 10 per cent of their annual income and were relegated to being second-class workers and residents, literally, at the margins of their own city—London. It is useful to isolate what makes this impact, described as 'stark' at five different points in the Court of Appeal judgment, fall through the cracks of the proportionality analysis.

Though indirect discrimination is meant to address impact rather than the criterion of discrimination, any impact can ultimately be justified if the net gain from a policy is established. This much is uncontroversial. But the net gain from policies which address crises such as urban overgrowth, climate change or even the pandemic, can always be shown because of, perhaps, the monumental nature of the challenge the policy is trying to address. This is a very different situation than the traditional application of indirect discrimination to narrow and discrete policies of, say, a single employer. Modern States are looking at facing crises of monumental scale raising a significant challenge for discrimination law from this net gain perspective. The question for the States and for discrimination lawyers is essentially

161 ibid [76].
162 ibid [71].
163 ibid [78] (emphasis supplied).
164 ibid [79].
165 ibid.

this: who are we willing to sacrifice for net gain? Unfortunately, in a highly racialized and unequal society it will likely be racially disadvantaged groups who will be hit first and worst by most policies.[166] This is because their pre-existing disadvantage makes them disproportionately vulnerable to negative impact of a policy, which can otherwise be absorbed by those who are not so vulnerable.[167] Unless we recognize this very fact and refuse to accept net gain predicated on the dispensability of lives of racialized and minoritized people (including women, disabled persons, aged persons, sexual minorities etc) we are accepting that discrimination law will continue to sustain racial discrimination. One way to do this is to use a mediating principle, such as that developed for climate change, that any policy for adaptation and mitigation of risk not only must avoid worsening the situation of vulnerable groups but in fact must specifically cater to their needs as a matter of priority.[168] Without a mediating principle, the balancing exercise seems to plainly accept, as in the case of minicab drivers, that urban overgrowth, pollution, and climate change can be very closely, if not directly linked to, disadvantaged groups in that the risk borne by them will be the risk the State is willing to take to improve the conditions of the majority in the face of crisis. In fact, we wholly gave in to this logic during the Covid-19 pandemic which hit vulnerable groups the hardest.[169]

A mediating principle already exists; one which allows adjusting the standard of scrutiny based on the suspect-ness of the ground at stake. In the *minicabs case*, although the Court *cites* the principle that impact based on racial grounds attracted a stringent standard of scrutiny, it actually does nothing with that principle. There is no sign of the scrutiny being appropriately raised. Rather, there is every sign of extraordinary deference attached to the decision of a democratically elected representative making the policy.[170] And that is where the Court seems to not only give in to but enact structural racism consciously because the policy which had a disproportionate impact on BME drivers when enacted by the London Mayor received less scrutiny *because* of the democratic nature of election to the office of the Mayor. The two judicial principles: standard of scrutiny attached to racial discrimination and the degree of deference attached to a decision of a democratically elected representative thus seem to pull in opposite directions, with the latter

[166] Ali Rattansi, 'The Uses of Racialization: The Time-Spaces and Subject-Objects of the Raced Body' in Karim Murji and John Solomos (eds), *Racialization: Studies in Theory and Practice* (Oxford University Press 2005).

[167] Tarunabh Khaitan, *A Theory of Discrimination Law* (Oxford University Press 2015) 126.

[168] General Recommendation No 37: Gender-related Dimensions of Disaster Risk Reduction in the Context of Climate Change, UN GAOR, Committee on the Elimination of All Forms of Discrimination Against Women, 69th Sess, UN Doc CEDAW/C/GC/37 (2018) [2] [30] [64]; Shreya Atrey, 'The Inequality of Climate Change and the Difference it Makes' in Cathi Albertyn et al (eds), *Feminist Frontiers in Climate Justice* (Edward Elgar 2023).

[169] Robin Richardson, 'Racial Justice and Equalities Law: Progress, Pandemic and Potential' in Vini Lander, Kavyta Kay, and Tiffany R Holloman (eds), *Covid-19 and Racism* (Bristol University Press 2023); Afua Hirsch, 'If Coronavirus Doesn't Discriminate, How Come Black People are Bearing the Brunt?' *The Guardian* (8 May 2020); Alana Lentin, 'Coronavirus is the Ultimate Demonstration of the Real-World Impact of Racism' *The Guardian* (12 May 2020).

[170] *Minicabs case* (n 157) [72].

outweighing the former by its utter normative force. Such an overriding application of deference runs counter to the structural view of racism which sees the state, including democratically elected governments and representatives, as centrally implicated in governing the existing race relations which racialize and disadvantage people. A structural view of racism would thus warn against such an application of the principle of judicial deference, especially in reference to elected representatives, who are particularly susceptible to majoritarian impulses which exclude interests of racially disadvantaged groups; let alone allow such a principle to be one on which a case turns.

Yet, the application of the proportionality test seems to be consistently skewed towards the respondent especially when the respondent is the state (the government, elected representatives, public authorities etc). What explains this paradox of proportionality?

In the final analysis, it appears that all courts want is that 'governments must be able to govern'[171] even at the cost of structural racism which produces vast material inequality between racialized groups. This is not what the law formally mandates. The mandate is to regard racialized impact seriously and for judges to apply a commensurately heightened standard of scrutiny when applying the proportionality test.[172] There is little evidence that this is actually practised under the EqA. Racialized impact is considered entirely ignorable revealing that the understanding of racism or racial discrimination continues to be one of direct discrimination despite the existence of the legal category of indirect discrimination which is about disproportionate impact. It is not that judges think that racialized impact does not exist. Their handling of indirect racial discrimination shows that they do. The cases discussed above show how racialized impact lies at the heart of structural racism perpetrated by the state which racializes and puts in motion the cycle of racial disadvantage. It is just that the judges often do not consider such impact to be problematic within the proportionality test—defying the normative significance of indirect discrimination entirely. Judges seem to have conveyed rather clearly that racialized impact is acceptable and the government's show must go on.

6.3.4 Remedial Scope

The remedial scope of civil courts jurisdiction under the EqA includes any remedies that may be awarded in tort litigation or claims of judicial review while the employment tribunals can make declarations and recommendations, and order compensation.[173] In principal, remedies under the EqA pertain mainly to the

[171] *R v Secretary of State for Employment Ex p Seymour-Smith (No 2)* [2000] 1 WLR 435, 450 (Lord Nicholls of Birkenhead).
[172] *R (on the application of Elias) v Secretary of State for Defence* [2006] EWCA Civ 1293, [2006] 1WLR 3213.
[173] EqA, ss 119, 124.

claimant who succeeds in establishing racial discrimination. Indeed, given the individualized personal scope of racial discrimination claims and the material and evidential limitations that follow, the remedial scope is consequently narrowed in practice.

This is most obviously visible in employment cases where monetary remedies rule the roost. Independent hearings and judgments for determining the quantum of compensation show the considerable time and effort that is devoted to monetary remedies.[174] The precise amount ranges in the order of a few thousand pounds, though in some instances, the sum could be considerably higher.[175] Of particular concern to this book is the near-exclusive focus on monetary compensation as a form of remedy in racial discrimination claims, specifically, to the exclusion of broader remedies which concern remedying the very sources from which racial discrimination arises and would continue to arise beyond the case of a single individual within a particular setting.

The case of *Smith v Secretary of State for Levelling Up*[176] is a useful reminder of this. The Court held that the definition of 'Gypsies and Travellers' which excluded those who had ceased travelling due to disability, age or illness, constituted indirect racial discrimination against the claimant. But it explicitly denied making a finding about the lawfulness of the change in the definition in the 2015 policy document titled 'Planning Policy for Traveller Sites' (PPTS). Only the claimant's planning application was remitted for reconsideration, as the Court emphasized that the case was 'ultimately concerned with a challenge only to the inspector's decision [denying the claimant's application], and not to the relevant exclusion itself, or to PPTS 2015 as a whole.'[177] The Court thus did not make an order declaring PPTS unlawful under the EqA. In effect, the Court let stand a policy which would have continued to be racially discriminatory towards Gypsies and Travellers who had ceased to travel for reasons of disability, age, or illness. The remedial scope, much like the personal scope of the EqA appears decidedly individualistic.[178]

[174] *Henderson v Asda Stores Ltd* [2021] 12 WLUK 632; *Benjamin v The Markfield Project* [2022] EAT 167; *Darko v Canute Distribution Ltd* [2016] 8 WLUK 33.

[175] This was the case even in the first race relations legislations. As the government's 1975 White Paper on racial discrimination noted: 'Financial compensation is rarely an adequate remedy for the victim of the worst examples of racial discrimination, because money cannot compensate him for the indignity, humiliation and distress which he suffers from being treated as inferior on racial grounds. Nevertheless, the award of compensation ought to be able to take into account any injury to feelings as it does for other civil wrongs. The damages which can be awarded under the 1968 Act are confined to special damages and damages for loss of opportunity. The sums awarded have been very small and are reflected in the sums obtained as settlements by the Board and the conciliation committees: in 1974, the amounts ranged from £2 to £150, the median settlement being £23.50.' Home Office, White Paper on Racial Discrimination (11 September 1975).

[176] [2022] EWCA Civ 1391.

[177] ibid [139].

[178] This was the case before the EqA as well. Bob Hepple, 'Race and Law in Fortress Europe' (2004) 67 Modern Law Review 1, 12 ('Even if direct or indirect discrimination can be established, the outcome is usually compensation for an individual, not positive measures to ensure the full participation of

In other instances, however, courts have considered broader remedies for racial discrimination. Two examples are particularly instructive: *Giwa-Amu v Department for Work and Pensions*[179] and *Allay (UK) Ltd v Gehlen.*[180] In *Giwa-Amu*, the Court made an order for aggravated damages based on lengthy calculations, but also went on to make the following recommendations which were, inter alia, to direct the employer 'to read the Liability and Remedy Judgments in this case and arrange a meeting with the Claimant (if she wishes to attend such a meeting) to 'identify the failings in policies and procedures'; 'discuss the lessons that can be learnt from the Claimant's experience as recorded in these Judgments'; and 'to provide the Claimant with a written apology having reflected upon the judgments.'[181] Furthermore, the Court directed the employer to 'approach the Equality and Human Rights Commission and seek their assistance in reviewing [their] Equality Act 2010 and diversity awareness training, with a view to implementing effective training throughout the [sic] organisation' and to report back to the employment tribunal that the recommendations had been implemented in the given time frame.[182] While the Court made the order with the need to 'obviate or reduce the adverse effects of the discrimination on the Claimant',[183] it is clear that the order actually touched the institutional norms, practices, and culture that gave rise to racial discrimination against the claimant which could not have been addressed simply by compensating the claimant monetarily. In a similar vein, *Allay* found that tribunals should be actively looking for steps employers can take to avoid liability under section 109.[184] In particular, tribunals should be open to finding that the existing trainings instituted by employers are stale when instances of racial harassment are known to the employer.[185]

Now, as Chapter 3 argued, trainings, as such, represent liberal and cultural anti-racism, and are not transformative in actually changing institutional norms, practices, and culture and, in any case, do not critically examine state laws, policies, and governance within which racism is normalized. Trainings, as Chapter 3 showed, after all target individual minds and behaviour within an institution rather than the institution itself and often fail to do as much even, given their mechanical and managerial focus.

disadvantaged groups in the workforce and fair access for them to education, training, goods, facilities and services.').

[179] [2020] 2 WLUK 454 [hereafter *Giwa-Amu*].
[180] [2021] 3 WLUK 829 [hereafter *Allay*].
[181] ibid [81].
[182] ibid.
[183] ibid.
[184] The relevant part of the provision states that: 'In proceedings against A's employer (B) in respect of anything alleged to have been done by A in the course of A's employment it is a defence for B to show that B took all reasonable steps to prevent A—(a) from doing that thing, or (b) from doing anything of that description.'
[185] *Allay* (n 180) [53].

Though it is useful to remember that this discussion on trainings in remedial orders emerged from within a context where monetary remedies are the mainstay. Trainings are, after all, forward looking and proactive in not necessarily remedying the discrimination that has already taken place but preventing discrimination by intending to change individual behaviour within an organization. They can involve group work and can thus be community oriented if organized as such. They can thus reflect cultural anti-racism though as Chapter 5 argued, there is little indication of this model of anti-racism in the EqA which is perfectly synchronized with liberal anti-racism alone. However, *Giwa-Amu* and *Allay* show that remedies can go beyond the individual claimant and can in fact be broader and forward looking in instating change, though too few instances of such remedial orders exist under the EqA doctrine.

6.4 Conclusion

This chapter has shown that the EqA is a relatively minor force in combating racism despite, as the previous chapter argued, being considered *the* vehicle for addressing racism in law. The individual redressal model which establishes an individual's right to challenge acts of racial discrimination is at the heart of the EqA. A hard look at how the model has transpired in practice reveals a fundamental incompatibility between racial discrimination law and anti-racism. In particular, the doctrine of racial discrimination law gives a short shrift to the drivers of structural racism as they are wielded by the state.

Writing in 2000, Anthony Lester had lamented the lack of a 'comprehensive, consistent, effective, and user-friendly' anti-discrimination legislation one which had the 'benefit of a constitutional framework guaranteeing the equal protection of the law and equal access to justice' and one which took a 'inclusive, pro-active, non-adversarial approach, which avoids unnecessary bureaucratic requirements, while ensuring that the law is effectively enforced'.[186] The EqA was supposed to respond to these woes. Except, as Chapter 5 argued, the EqA only entrenched a model of liberal anti-racism which relied almost exclusively on a rules-based framework centred around individual enforcement as the cornerstone of discrimination law. Chapter 6 has confirmed that this model has been ineffective against racism, especially structural racism, and does not reflect anti-racism as a legal principle.

[186] Bob Hepple, Mary Coussey, and Tufyal Choudhury, *Equality: A New Framework* (Hart 2000) foreword.

7
Racial Discrimination under the Human Rights Act 1998

7.1 Introduction

Having considered how racism is addressed under the Equality Act 2010 ('EqA'), this chapter turns to consider how the UK courts have addressed racism under the Human Rights Act 1998 ('HRA'), the legislation which partially incorporates the European Convention on Human Rights ('ECHR' or 'the Convention') into UK law. Of particular relevance is the prohibition of discrimination in article 14 of the Convention which provides that:

> The enjoyment of the rights and freedoms set forth in this Convention shall be secured without discrimination on any ground such as sex, race, colour, language, religion, political or other opinion, national or social origin, association with a national minority, property, birth or other status.

Article 14 is the only relevant provision in the ECHR which speaks of racial grounds such as race, colour, language, national or social origin, association with a national minority, birth or other status, and may thus be considered the cornerstone of anti-racism in the Convention. Like elsewhere in law, the context in which racial grounds are mentioned is the rule prohibiting discrimination. Article 14 thus reinforces the pre-eminence of the rule prohibiting racial discrimination in addressing racism.

Given that the HRA gives effect to article 14 and in turn the prohibition of racial discrimination in the UK, it is only legitimate to ask whether it reflects a legal principle of anti-racism. That is, how does it fare in addressing racism, especially structural racism and in effecting transformative anti-racism. It is also pertinent to ask whether it fares any different from the EqA considered in the previous chapter.

To recall, Part I of this book defined structural racism as the complex totality of forces which bring about racialized outcomes in a society. Transformative anti-racism aims to overhaul the entirety of these complex forces. Both have three salient features. Structural racism has to do with how (i) the state and state-like entities (ii) racialize (iii) to instate racial disadvantage. Transformative anti-racism (i) opposes the state and state-like entities which bring about structural

Anti-Racism as a Legal Principle. Shreya Atrey, Oxford University Press. © Shreya Atrey 2026.
DOI: 10.1093/9780198947646.003.0010

racism to enact (ii) broad-based change and (iii) intersectional racial justice. The legal principle of anti-racism embodies both these tripartite understandings in that it is geared towards addressing structural racism and enacting transformative change.

Article 14 fills a crucial gap in the landscape of discrimination law which the EqA leaves open. This gap is in scrutinizing the state itself—its institutions such as public bodies and courts, structures such as law and policy, and everyday governmentality. Although the EqA does apply to the state and in particular public authorities, in practice, the previous chapter showed that it is ineffective in responding to structural racism that is effected by the state.

In contrast, the HRA is essentially about scrutinizing the state as it gives effect to human rights obligations of the UK as a State Party to the ECHR. It does not concern relationships between private individuals. Instead, the HRA was introduced as part of the Labour government's pledge to 'modernise', 'decentralise', 'open up', and 'reform' British politics, government, and the Parliament.[1]

Section 6(1) of the HRA provides that 'it is unlawful for a public authority to act in a way which is incompatible with a Convention right' where 'public authority' according to article 6(3) includes '(a) a court or tribunal, and (b) any person certain of whose functions are functions of a public nature, but does not include either House of Parliament or a person exercising functions in connection with proceedings in Parliament'. Section 6 thus throws open most public action to scrutiny at the highest level. Furthermore, subordinate legislation enacted by the government can be struck down for non-compliance with the HRA. Primary legislation enacted by the Parliament cannot be struck down, but a 'declaration of incompatibility' can be issued when a provision of a primary legislation is incompatible with a Convention right.[2]

The HRA has had 'the effect of opening a wide range of public decision-making, including in the form of legislation, to judicial scrutiny'[3] and in turn opening 'the possibility of legal challenge at the macro, rather than the micro, level'.[4] Consequently, article 14 too is considered 'more fluid'[5] than 'the sometimes rigid framework of anti-discrimination statutes'[6] such as the EqA. For example,

[1] 'Rights Brought Home', The Human Rights Bill presented to Parliament by the Secretary of State for the Home Department, By command of Her Majesty (October 1997).

[2] HRA, s 4. Aileen Kavanagh considers this power of courts to be a form of 'constitutional review' as opposed to ordinary 'judicial review' of acts of public authorities. Aileen Kavanagh, *Constitutional Review under the UK Human Rights Act* (Cambridge University Press 2009) 5–6.

[3] Karon Monaghan, *Monaghan on Equality Law* (2nd edn, OUP 2013) 12 [hereafter Monaghan, *Monaghan on Equality*].

[4] Aileen McColgan KC and Eddie Bruce-Jones, 'Race' in Aileen McColgan KC, *Discrimination Law: Text, Cases and Materials* (Hart 2023) 416.

[5] ibid 24.

[6] Aileen McColgan, *Discrimination, Equality and the Law* (Hart 2014) 1.

discrimination which cannot be challenged under the EqA, say, because the EqA does not apply extraterritorially, can be challenged under the HRA.[7] Likewise, decisions such as the rejection of an asylum application on grounds of being an asylum seeker or a refugee, which cannot be challenged under the EqA, can be challenged under the HRA.[8]

Article 14 is 'an important tool in addressing inequality, particularly in the context of public law, but the provision has its limits'.[9] These limits become apparent when tested against structural racism. In practice, article 14 case law reveals substantive limitations as to the personal, material, and evidential scope of racial discrimination claims which resist addressing structural racism. Within each remit—personal, material, and evidential—the chapter reveals further doctrinal hurdles which limit the UK courts' ability to address structural racism.

Given these limitations, the chapter shows that while article 14 allows for a broad range of public action to be challenged on the basis of both enumerated grounds as well as 'other status', in practice, broad-based challenges especially those based on 'other status' rarely succeed in addressing structural racism. At the same time, cases where the claimants do occasionally succeed prove instructive in observing how structural racism can indeed be addressed doctrinally. In this latter set of cases we see anti-racism as a legal principle emerge and make a difference, especially to the quality of judicial reasoning.

The chapter follows a similar scheme as the previous chapter. Section 7.2 provides a brief overview of article 14 as it applies to racial discrimination cases, introduces the parameters of case law considered in this chapter, describes the procedural limitations that apply, and finally reveals the rate of success in claiming racial discrimination under article 14. Section 7.3 examines three substantive limitations as to the personal, material, and evidential scope of article 14 case law.[10] Section 7.4 identifies the patterns which subvert these limitations in six seminal successful cases under the HRA. Section 7.5 concludes by reminding that while the HRA doctrine does not often address structural racism, the occasional successes confirm its transformative anti-racist potential especially in contrast with the EqA.

[7] *Al-Jedda v United Kingdom* [2011] ECHR 1092; *Al-Skeini v United Kingdom* [2011] ECHR 1093.

[8] For example, *Devaseelan v Secretary of State for the Home Department* [2002] UKIAT 702.

[9] Monaghan, *Monaghan on Equality* (n 3) 8.

[10] Unlike the previous chapter no limitations as to remedial scope are considered as they are less pertinent in the context of article 14. The remedial scope of article 14 is governed by the HRA which provides for declarative orders as to the compatibility of a provision in primary or subordinate legislation or a measure taken by a public authority with the Convention rights. This no doubt limits the courts' ability to enact transformative anti-racism via remedial orders broader than declarations of incompatibility. Although important, the case law is still governed by this hard limitation and thus does not generate substantive discussion on what broader remedies can or should be.

7.2 Human Rights Act 1998

7.2.1 The Panorama

Although article 14 prohibits racial discrimination in a similar way as direct and indirect racial discrimination is prohibited in section 25(6) of the EqA, there are two peculiarities which frame the judicial approach under the HRA.

First, the most obvious of these differences is the parasitic/accessory/adjectival nature of article 14 in that it is concerned with 'the mode of enjoyment of the other substantive rights guaranteed by the ECHR'.[11] This means that racial discrimination can be claimed only when another Convention right is engaged, namely, right to life (article 2), prohibition of torture (article 3), prohibition of slavery and forced labour (article 4), right to liberty and security (article 5), right to a fair trial (article 6), no punishment without law (article 7), right to respect for private and family life (article 8), freedom of thought, conscience and religion (article 9), freedom of expression (article 10), freedom of assembly and association (article 11), right to marry (article 12), and right to an effective remedy (article 13). This does not mean that article 14 is engaged only upon the proof of violation of another Convention right. Crucially, the matter only needs to fall within the ambit of another Convention right for article 14 to be engaged.[12]

Second, both direct and indirect racial discrimination can be justified under article 14. This is obviously different from the EqA where direct racial discrimination cannot be justified. But under the ECHR:

> the principle of equality of treatment is violated if the distinction has no objective and reasonable justification. The existence of such a justification must be assessed in relation to the aim and effects of the measure under consideration, regard being had to the principles which normally prevail in democratic societies. A difference of treatment in the exercise of a right laid down in the Convention must not only pursue a legitimate aim: Article 14 is likewise violated when it is clearly established that there is no reasonable relationship of proportionality between the means employed and the aim sought to be realised.[13]

As set out by Baroness Hale in *R (on the application of DA and others) v Secretary of State for Work and Pensions*,[14] courts ask the following questions in sequence to assess a violation of article 14:

[11] *Strbac v Secretary of State for the Home Department* [2005] EWCA Civ 848 [44] (Laws LJ).
[12] *Belgian Linguistic Case (No 2)* (1968) 1 EHRR 252.
[13] ibid [10].
[14] [2019] UKSC 21 [136]; *R (S) v Chief Constable of the South Yorkshire Police* [2004] UKHL 39 [42].

(i) Does the subject matter of the complaint fall within the ambit of one of the substantive Convention rights?
(ii) Does the ground upon which the complainants have been treated differently from others constitute a status?
(iii) Have they been treated differently from other people not sharing that status who are similarly situated or, alternatively, have they been treated in the same way as other people not sharing that status whose situation is relevantly different from theirs?
(iv) Does that difference or similarity in treatment have an objective and reasonable justification, in other words, does it pursue a legitimate aim and do the means employed bear a reasonable relationship of proportionality to the aims sought to be realised?

Section 7.3 below shows the particular ways in which the recognition of structural racism is thwarted at each stage of the article 14 analysis.

7.2.2 The Parameters

This chapter analyses racial discrimination cases that have been decided under the HRA between 2 October 2000–9 July 2024. Cases of racial discrimination include claims based on racial grounds, including both enumerated grounds (race, language, colour, ethnicity, national/social origin, association with a national minority, and birth) and 'other status' (such as nationality and immigration status).

These parameters generate 149 cases which concern discrimination based on racial grounds (as defined above).[15] While the analysis presented in this chapter reflects the main takeaways from this dataset, it is useful to note that not all cases within this dataset deal with racial discrimination substantively as not all cases, not even those on racial grounds, are necessarily cases of racism. This is important to appreciate and is neatly demonstrated by one of the earliest cases on article 14: *Nasser v United Bank of Kuwait (Security for Costs)*.[16] The case concerned the question whether the right to order costs of an appeal wrongly discriminated against residents of those countries outside of the scope of the Brussels Convention and the Lugano Convention in breach of article 14. The question was answered in the negative on a discussion of the courts' powers to order costs rather than any link of residence or nationality-based discrimination to racism.

[15] The searches were run on Westlaw and LexisNexis. Just as the previous chapter, it is important to stress here too, that the list of cases and in particular the number of cases generated under the list should not be considered a definite list or number representing all cases of racial discrimination under the HRA in the last twenty-five years because the digital legal databases are not always comprehensive and the search parameters do not always return all cases relevant to the search.

[16] [2002] 1 WLR 1868.

This approach avoids treating all claims based on apparently racial grounds as necessarily giving rise to racial discrimination or racism.[17] Conversely, the approach also matters in cases which are *not* based on apparently racial grounds but may yet constitute racism. As explained below, great sensitivity to context is required to detect how non-racial grounds can be racialized to yield racism. This chapter shows that courts seldom appreciate how racialization works. In fact, a vast majority of article 14 case law shows little appreciation of how the state racializes to instate racial disadvantage, and thus, enact structural racism.

7.2.3 The Procedure

In contrast with what we saw in the previous chapter, where over 40 per cent of the cases were dedicated to procedure under the EqA, claims which invoke article 14 under the HRA are mostly decided on merits. This does not necessarily mean that article 14 claims (specifically) are decided on merits. For example, in 24 out of the 149 cases (16.10 per cent) in the dataset, the claim based on article 14 was not decided.

This happens for a range of reasons. For example, where a claimant alleges a breach of both the EqA and the HRA, for the sake of expediency and to avoid duplication, courts often decide first under the former, and decline to consider the article 14 claim especially when the claim under the EqA has already succeeded.[18] Thus, when other grounds of judicial review succeed in a claim, article 14 claim may be bypassed.[19]

Article 14 claims may also be sidelined when they are not pleaded specifically.[20] Article 14 claims thus need to be argued substantively and substantially by the claimants and not just 'relegated to a footnote in the Claimants' skeleton argument ... and [left] unmentioned in [the] oral submissions'.[21]

Even when specifically argued, article 14 claims may fall away based on the court's view of the dispute. For example, *R (Ghai) v Newcastle City Council (Hitchin*

[17] *R (Carson) v Secretary of State for Work and Pensions* [2005] UKHL 37 (appealed from *R (Carson) v Secretary of State for Work and Pensions* [2003] EWCA Civ 797; *R (Carson) v Secretary of State for Work and Pensions* [2002] EWHC 978 (Admin).

[18] *R (Moore) v Secretary of State for Communities and Local Government (Equality and Human Rights Commission Intervening)* [2015] EWHC 44 (Admin); *R (Diocese of Menevia) v Swansea City Council* [2015] EWHC 1436 (Admin); *Elegbede v Nexen Petroleum UK Ltd* [2011] EWCA Civ 718. This was also the case preceding the EqA and under the Race Relations Act 1976; *Sheena Ramalingum v Secretary of State for the Home Department* [2009] EWHC 453 (Admin).

[19] *R (W (A Child)) v Secretary of State for the Home Department (Project 17 Intervening)* [2020] EWHC 1299 (Admin).

[20] *R (Z) v Hackney London Borough Council* [2020] UKSC 40; *R (Patel) v Secretary of State for the Home Department* [2015] EWCA Civ 645 (appealed from *R (Patel) v Secretary of State for the Home Department* [2014] EWHC 501 (Admin)).

[21] *R (A) v Secretary of State for the Home Department* [2022] EWHC 360 (Admin) [5].

Ramgharia Gurdwara and Alice Barker Welfare and Wildlife Trust Intervening)[22] concerned a challenge to the local authority's refusal to allow open funeral fires for Hindus as discrimination on the basis of religion and/or ethnic origin. The Court of Appeal found that the claimant's wishes to be cremated could be accommodated within the existing regulations on cremations and thus declined to consider the discrimination issue.

Likewise, though a claim may involve article 14 and in particular racial discrimination, the legal dispute may lie elsewhere. For example, *Benkharbouche v Embassy of the Republic of Sudan*[23] concerned complaints of racial discrimination in employment in relation to harassment, payment of wages, worktime regulations, unfair dismissal (etc) of workers at embassies. The embassies were believed to have immunity from such claims. The Supreme Court held that the application of immunity in this context was unjustifiable as it infringed access to justice, irrespective of whether the conduct was discriminatory.[24] The case was thus decided on the law of immunities rather than racial discrimination and could ostensibly be seen as a befitting anti-racist outcome in immunities law rather than racial discrimination law.[25]

Finally, article 14 claims could be prematurely decided and dismissed as a matter of procedure rather than merits. *R (Francis) v Secretary of State for Justice*[26] is an apt example of this. It concerned a challenge to refusal of home detention for a claimant who was liable to be deported as she was not a British citizen on grounds that the refusal constituted discrimination on the basis of nationality. The claimant argued that she should have been allowed to amend the claim to plead her article 14 argument. The Court refused permission to amend the claim as it found that she was treated differently not because she was Jamaican but because of her immigration status. Neither race nor nationality were considered 'causally relevant' to the article 14 argument.[27]

7.2.4 The Proportions

Similar to the finding in the previous chapter on the EqA, the number of cases in which racial discrimination is being claimed under the HRA is minuscule as compared to the racism out there. In fact, many of the cases in the dataset relate to the

[22] [2010] EWCA Civ 59 (appealed from *R (Ghai) v Newcastle City Council (Hitchin Ramgharia Gurdwara and Alice Barker Welfare and Wildlife Trust Intervening)* [2009] EWHC 978 (Admin)).
[23] [2017] UKSC 62 (appealed from *Benkharbouche v Embassy of the Republic of Sudan* [2015] EWCA Civ 33 and *Benkharbouche v of the Republic of Sudan* [2013] 10 WLUK 168).
[24] ibid [77].
[25] Thank you to Hayley Hooper for pointing this out.
[26] [2012] EWCA Civ 1200 (appealed from *R (Francis) v Secretary of State for Justice* [2011] EWHC 1271 (Admin)); *R (Serrano) v Secretary of State for Justice* [2012] EWHC 3216 (Admin).
[27] ibid [41].

same matter. A third of the 149 cases are appealed to a higher court at least once, and several go up until the Supreme Court. The success rate for the claimants alleging racial discrimination under article 14 is only 20.80 per cent. This means that only one in five claimants succeeds in their claim of racial discrimination under the HRA. This is half the success rate under the EqA—which itself is less than half the racial discrimination claims brought under the EqA. It would be fair to say that, while the HRA enables challenging structural racism, such claims are occasional and succeed only occasionally.

7.3 The Substantive Limitations

7.3.1 Personal Scope

While the HRA is broader than the EqA as disputes necessarily concern challenges against public authorities as opposed to private individuals and entities, its personal scope is similar to the EqA as disputes often concern the effects on particular individuals rather than the broad-based effects of structures in the form of challenges to primary or subordinate legislation. In order to challenge the acts of public authorities under section 6, section 7 of the HRA requires that:

> a person who claims that a public authority has acted (or proposes to act) in a way which is made unlawful by section 6(1) may—(a) bring proceedings against the authority under this Act in the appropriate court or tribunal, or (b) rely on the Convention right or rights concerned in any legal proceedings, *but only if he is (or would be) a victim of the unlawful act.*

Challenges to acts of public authorities under the HRA thus cannot be hypothetical and must involve a victim who is or would be a victim of the unlawful act committed by the public authority. Challenges cannot be broad-based—concerning anyone who *could* or *may* be affected by the acts of the public authority, and must necessarily involve an actual or potential victim. This means that pre-emptive challenges, though permissible in theory, need to be imminent or inevitable in reality.

This avoids courts adjudicating on fictional as opposed to actual disputes. This in turn avoids disrupting the work of public authorities and allows governments to run efficiently without being stymied by overly broad and presumptive challenges.

But this stymies challenges to structural racism—which are not about discrete acts of public authorities directed at or experienced by particular individuals—but about 'structures' per se—that is, how state law, policy, and practice racialize (instil a racial order or hierarchy) to instate racial disadvantage. The victim requirement in section 7 draws attention away from the everyday practice or governmentality, that is, how things are ordinarily done, and instead zooms in on particular instances of exercise of power and their effect on specific individuals, reversing the causal sequence of racism, where structural racism lies at the root of all individual instances and not vice versa. Ultimately, with a narrowly construed victim requirement, courts often end up missing the wood for the trees in racial discrimination cases.

Two examples are in order to appreciate this.

Mac Giolla Catháin v The Northern Ireland Court Service[28] concerned a challenge to the prohibition of court proceedings in Irish language under the Administration of Justice (Language) Act (Ireland) 1737. As the claimant in this case could speak in English he was not considered a victim under section 7 of the HRA. In any case, the Court held that even if he were considered a victim under section 7, the discrimination in this case between English and non-English speakers was justified as it was 'manifestly necessary and proportionate in a democratic society':[29]

> In a jurisdiction where English is the language of the overwhelming majority of the population the requirement that court documents initiating proceedings be in English as the working language of the court is a practical necessity in the interests of fairness. Where a party or witness cannot speak English he must, of course, be entitled to give his evidence in the language he speaks subject to translation. Otherwise his right to access to the court would be illusory. That, however, does not prevent English being the working language of the court or make it incompatible with Article 14 to require English, the language of the vast bulk of the community, to be the working language of the court.[30]

There is of course background to this: the suppression of the Irish language, first during the 700 years of British colonization of Ireland, and then since the division of the Republic of Ireland and Northern Ireland in 1921. Against this background, legal instruments such as the Administration of Justice (Language) Act (Ireland) 1737 operated as structures of colonial dominance and racialized supremacy of the British, and the English language in particular. These structures instated a framework which legitimized and contributed to the continued marginalization, disuse, and underdevelopment of the Irish language. Language, in this case, thus served to racialize and racially disadvantage Irish people. The diminution of a legal challenge to discrimination based on language to a matter of individual justice and administrative convenience misses the point of the challenge entirely.

[28] [2010] NICA 24 (appealed from *Mac Giolla Catháin v The Northern Ireland Court Service* [2009] NIQB 66).
[29] ibid [8].
[30] ibid [8].

The point here is not to litigate whether courts can or should see cases like these as cases of structural racism. The point is that they don't. That the personal scope of the victim requirement prevents courts from seeing cases of structural racism as such.

Likewise, the case of *O'Connor v Bar Standards Board*[31] shows that structural racism may go unseen *even* where alleged, as cases are often delimited to the cause of the particular victim who is before the court.

In *O'Connor*, the claimant, a Black woman barrister, had challenged the disciplinary proceedings pursued by the Bar Standards Board ('BSB') as discriminatory on the grounds of race. Writing for the Supreme Court, Lord Lloyd-Jones first considered it 'necessary to establish whether the complaint is directed at the conduct of the BSB in bringing and pursuing the prosecution against this appellant or, more generally, at alleged systemic discrimination against BME barristers'.[32] Given that the claim was pleaded in 'very general terms which are vague and unclear',[33] he concluded that 'the appellant's challenge is to the conduct of the BSB in bringing and pursuing disciplinary proceedings against her, not to an alleged state of affairs in which BME lawyers were more likely to be the subject of such proceedings'.[34] The claimant though *had* challenged the alleged state of affairs. But it was precisely that broader claim that the Court rendered general, vague, and unclear. The very qualities of breadth and scale which define institutional, systemic, or structural racism also seemed to have made such racism unintelligible to the Court.

Finally, it is useful to remember that victim status is not a requirement for challenging laws and policies as such (instead of the operation of those laws and policies in individual instances under section 6) and the HRA allows the courts, in case of incompatibility with Convention rights, to strike down subordinate legislation and issue a declaration of incompatibility in case of primary legislation (under section 4). Yet, as confirmed by the Supreme Court in the seminal case of *R (Bibi) v Secretary of State for the Home Department*,[35] making a case against a law or policy is a 'difficult task'.[36] The case concerned a challenge to Immigration Rules of 2010 which had imposed a requirement for settlement of foreign spouses or partners of British citizens to pass a test of English language competence. Since the greatest numbers of foreign spouses or partners were drawn from India, Pakistan, and Bangladesh the Rule was challenged as constituting direct racial discrimination on the basis of nationality and indirect racial discrimination on the basis of race and ethnicity. The Court declined to conduct a separate analysis under article 14

[31] [2017] UKSC 78 (appealed from *O'Connor v Bar Standards Board* [2016] EWCA Civ 775 and *O'Connor v Bar Standards Board* [2014] EWHC 4324 (QB)) [hereafter *O'Connor*].
[32] ibid [15].
[33] ibid [16].
[34] ibid [21].
[35] [2015] UKSC 68.
[36] ibid [2].

and dismissed the challenge under article 8. In an oft-quoted passage, Lady Hale explained:

> It may well be possible to show that the application of the Rule in an individual case is incompatible with the Convention rights of a British partner ... It is much harder to show that the Rule itself is inevitably unlawful, whether under the Human Rights Act 1998 or at common law... the fact that it might be possible to argue that the operation of the Rule was a disproportionate infringement of an individual's article 8 rights did not render the Rule itself disproportionate.[37]

Thus, the Rule was not struck down as invalid as it was not 'an unjustified interference with article 8 rights in *all* cases'.[38] The high bar for showing that a law or policy operates as discriminatory in *all* cases, or in absolute totality, belies the nature of both indirect discrimination as well as structural racism where the emphasis is on the disproportionate impact on racially minoritized groups rather than on disproportionate impact on *everyone* from racially minoritized groups. There is in fact no significance of the latter in appreciating any form of discrimination under article 14. To use the logic that in *some* cases a racially discriminatory rule will *not* operate as discriminatory is to use statistics to deny the fundamental understanding in discrimination law that members of social groups suffer disadvantage *as* members of social groups. The logic treats the meaning of *discrimination* triflingly and in turn the reality of racial disadvantage suffered as a consequence of structural racism. The logic though appears ingrained in article 14 case law.[39]

7.3.2 Material Scope

There are three things to consider as to the material scope of article 14: (i) the implication of ambit; (ii) the meaning of racial grounds; and (iii) the determination of analogous situations (these correspond to the first three steps of the article 14 analysis set out above).[40]

First, given the parasitic/accessory/adjectival nature of article 14, claims of racial discrimination under article 14 must be tethered to other Convention rights.

[37] ibid.
[38] ibid [60].
[39] *R (Joint Council for the Welfare of Immigrants) v Secretary of State for the Home Department (Residential Landlords Association, EHRC and Liberty Intervening)* [2020] EWCA Civ 542 (appealed from *R (Joint Council for the Welfare of Immigrants) v Secretary of State for the Home Department (Residential Landlords Association, EHRC and Liberty Intervening)* [2019] EWHC 452 (Admin)); *Christian Institute v Lord Advocate* 2016 SLT 805; *Roberts v Commissioner of Police of the Metropolis* [2014] EWCA Civ 69.
[40] *R (DA) v Secretary of State for Work and Pensions (Shelter Children's Legal Services intervening)* [2019] 1 WLR.

This has the implication of limiting the material scope of racial discrimination such that not all kinds of racialized outcomes can be challenged under article 14.

R (European Roma Rights Centre) v Immigration Officer, Prague Airport[41] is an apt example of this limitation. The case concerned a challenge to the agreement between the UK and the Czech Republic, whereby British immigration officers posted at the Prague airport could 'pre-clear' all passengers before they boarded flights to the UK. Leave to enter was denied to those who stated that they were intending to claim asylum in the UK. The question on appeal before the House of Lords was whether the procedure adopted at the Prague airport (i) unlawfully discriminated against Roma people on racial grounds under the Race Relations Act 1976 and (ii) was contrary to the UK's obligations under the Refugee Convention 1951 and customary international law, including provisions of the ECHR. The House of Lords answered in the affirmative to the first question but not the second. No Convention right was considered to be at stake under the second question. Thus, no article 14 argument was considered in relation to racial discrimination even though the impugned procedure was held as constituting racial discrimination under the Race Relations Act 1976. Article 14 was thus deemed 'a weak provision'[42] to sustain a challenge under the ECHR.

Similarly, in *R (Watkins-Singh) v Governing Body of Aberdare Girls' High School*,[43] a 14-year-old Sikh school girl was placed in isolation for wearing a 'kara' around her wrist. According to the Court, while the isolation constituted indirect discrimination on the basis of race and religion under the Race Relations Act 1976, it did not engage any Convention right and hence did not fall foul of article 14.[44]

So, racial discrimination cases *do* need to fall within the ambit of another Convention right for article 14 to be triggered. Even when they do, that Convention right must be said to apply to the claimant in the case, as some rights are not available to everyone, such as, article 6 which is limited to British nationals in the context of extradition proceedings.[45]

What does this mean for anti-racism? Given that racism and in particular structural racism in this book are both defined in terms of racial disadvantage or material conditions of racialized groups, the parasitic nature of article 14 appears

[41] [2004] UKHL 55 (appealed from *(European Roma Rights Centre) v Immigration Officer, Prague Airport* [2003] EWCA Civ 666; *European Roma Rights Centre and 6 Others v The Immigration Officer at Prague Airport, The Secretary of State for the Home Department* [2002] EWHC 1989 (Admin)).

[42] ibid [43].

[43] [2008] EWHC 1865.

[44] *R (Couronne) v Crawley Borough Council* [2007] EWCA Civ 1086 (appealed from *R (Couronne) v Crawley Borough Council* [2006] EWHC 1514 (Admin)) (where a challenge to the 'habitual residence rule' which excluded Chagonnisan British citizens from jobseekers allowance and homelessness assistance was deemed not to engage article 8, for the purposes of claiming indirect racial discrimination based on ethnic or national origins).

[45] *Adgari v Penitentiary Judge of the Metropolitan Court, Hungary* [2014] EWHC 3433 (Admin); *Bestfort Developments LLP v Ras Al Khaimah Investment Authority* [2016] EWCA Civ 1099 (appealed from *Bestfort Developments LLP v Ras Al Khaimah Investment Authority* [2015] EWHC 3197 (Ch)).

sound. It tethers discrimination to other interests and thus makes discrimination a material concern beyond simply a status or identitarian concern.[46] That said, article 14 is perhaps too strongly tethered to (some) *other* rights—which are limited to those enumerated in the Convention and exclude a range of socio-economic rights and other entitlements such as equal pay or access to basic goods and services, unless guaranteed by the state. Even a broad reading of article 14 may not permit *all* material conditions to be challenged under the Convention. Further, as Section 7.3.3 below shows, even when different material conditions and interests are challenged on a broad reading of the Convention rights, these challenges do not often succeed as the level of scrutiny they attract is lower as compared with interests squarely protected under civil-political rights.[47]

The next two points about the material scope of article 14 are related. Secondly, whether an enumerated or unenumerated ground constitutes a relevant status for the purpose of article 14 often proves tricky for racial discrimination claims. This is because of two interrelated reasons that: (i) claims are rarely argued on explicitly racial grounds such as race, colour, or ethnicity; and (ii) courts often fail to appreciate how grounds such as nationality or immigration status inexplicitly racialize and in turn instate racial disadvantage. Thirdly, even if a ground constitutes a status, the claimant must be able to point to another individual or group in a 'materially analogous situation'[48] to be able to challenge discrimination on its basis. This also proves to be tricky for direct and indirect racial discrimination, and even more so, for racial discrimination which may be considered as discrimination based on 'other status'. I elaborate on these below.

The dataset reveals that claims under article 14 are rarely being brought on racial grounds explicitly. Thus, cases based on race, colour, or ethnicity, such as *O'Connor*,[49] are uncommon. This is not surprising for direct racial discrimination. The Parliament does not often enact primary or secondary legislation based explicitly on racial grounds such as those enumerated in article 14. Public authorities also do not normally use racial grounds bluntly in their decision-making. But that does not mean that laws, policies, and practices of the state do not have disparate impact on racialized groups. Surprisingly, few claims under the HRA

[46] *R (MD) v Secretary of State for the Home Department* [2022] EWCA Civ 336 [90] (appealed from *R (MD) v Secretary of State for the Home Department* [2021] EWHC 1370 (Admin)) ('The admitted difference in treatment as between asylum-seekers and non-asylum-seekers is purely nominal. As a matter of substance, the Claimants, and others in group 2, received the same sums of money from the Secretary of State in respect of the needs of their dependent children as those in groups 1 and 3.').

[47] Bob Hepple, 'Race and Law in Fortress Europe' (2004) 67 Modern Law Review 1, 4 (describing article 14 as 'incapable of redressing collective racial disadvantage' as it does not 'provide for the enforcement of positive social, economic and cultural obligations'); Merris Amos, 'The Second Division in Human Rights Adjudication: Social Rights Claims under the Human Rights Act 1998' (2015) 15 Human Rights Law Review 549; Aaron Baker, 'The Enjoyment of Rights and Freedoms: A New Conception of the "Ambit" under Article 14 ECHR' (2006) 69 Modern Law Review 679.

[48] *R (The 3Million Ltd) v The Minister for the Cabinet Office* [2021] EWHC 245 (Admin) [113].

[49] *O'Connor* (n 31).

seem to be testing this. Instead, what seems to be more common a strategy is to claim direct discrimination based on 'other status'. This has the effect that cases of direct discrimination based on other status, unlike cases of indirect racial discrimination, are not tested for their racialized impact and are instead treated as their own thing with no connection to racial discrimination. That some of these other statuses like nationality, immigration status, or refugee status act as proxies for racial grounds and hence racialize certain groups, and end up disadvantaging them, escapes examination completely. Further, some difference in treatment may not even qualify as discrimination based on other status and may thus fail to be examined as well.[50]

The most common example of inexplicit racial discrimination is that which is based on immigration status—which is either assessed as direct discrimination based on 'other status' and not as indirect racial discrimination; or not considered a status for the purposes of article 14 at all.

For instance, in *R (HC) v Secretary of State for Work and Pensions*,[51] the claimant and her children were denied mainstream welfare benefits as she was an Algerian national and had overstayed her visitor visa before marrying her estranged British husband. She claimed nationality discrimination under article 14. The Supreme Court held that article 14 did not apply as the relevant 'status' here was the claimant's immigration status or her status as a carer for her children but not her nationality. As discrimination against third-country nationals was an accepted part of EU law, the denial of welfare benefits to third-country nationals, such as the claimant, was considered beyond challenge.[52]

Similarly, in *R (Badmus) v Secretary of State for the Home Department*,[53] the Claimants sought judicial review of the Secretary of State's decision to pay £1 per hour to immigration detainees for all work (cleaning, catering, etc) at removal centres authorized under the Immigration and Asylum Act 1999. They argued inter alia that the difference between the paid work regimes at the removal centres versus the prisons constituted unjustified discrimination on grounds of their status as immigration detainees. Their claim failed as the Court held that there was no relevant comparison to be made between immigration detainees and prisoners.

[50] *R (Carson) v Secretary of State for Work and Pensions* [2005] UKHL 37 (appealed from *R (Carson) v Secretary of State for Work and Pensions* [2003] EWCA Civ 797; *R (Carson) v Secretary of State for Work and Pensions* [2002] EWHC 978 (Admin)).

[51] [2017] UKSC 73 (appealed from *R (HC) v Secretary of State for Work and Pensions* [2015] EWCA Civ 49 and *R(HC) v Secretary of State for Work and Pensions* [2013] EWHC 3874 (Admin)).

[52] *R (BXS) v Secretary of State for the Home Department* [2014] EWHC 737(Admin); *Johnson v Secretary of State for the Home Department* [2020] EWCA Civ 1032 (appealed from *Johnson v Secretary of State for the Home Department* [2019] UKUT 126); *R (SHU) v Secretary of State for Health and Social Care* [2019] EWHC 3569 (Admin); *R (EOG) v Secretary of State for the Home Department* [2020] EWHC 3310 (Admin).

[53] [2020] EWCA Civ 657 (appealed from *R (Badmus) v Secretary of State for the Home Department* [2019] EWHC 758 (Admin)).

The reasoning in *HC* and *Badmus* immunizes immigration status from discrimination challenges because the difference between the claimant's position on the basis of their immigration status and that of others is considered 'so obvious that they cannot be regarded as "analogous"'.[54] This reasoning shields immigration status from being tested for discrimination. In particular, it shields immigration status for being tested for racialization or the possibility that it can be used to (re) produce racial order and hierarchy. A vast range of difference in treatment based on immigration status—whether as immigration detainees, refugees, asylum seekers, migrant workers, irregular migrants, etc—all fail not because they do not racialize or instate racial disadvantage, but because they are seldom tested for their racialized impact.[55] Even in those rare cases where discrimination based on immigration status is successfully established under article 14, no link with racial grounds is made.[56]

In contrast, an unenumerated ground such as nationality has been considered on par with racial grounds and attracts a high level of scrutiny.[57] However, that too has not had courts check for nationality's connection with racial grounds or racial discrimination as such. In fact, courts have specifically struck down the contention that the difference in pay, conditions of work, pension entitlements (etc) between Gurkha soldiers and white British soldiers constituted discrimination on grounds of race as opposed to nationality.[58] This is at the same time as courts, in similar cases involving Gurkha soldiers, have found racial discrimination based on ethnicity or national origin under the Race Relations Act 1976.[59]

[54] *Carson v Secretary of State for Work and Pensions* [2006] 1 AC 173 [3] (Lord Nicholls).

[55] *ST (A Child) v Secretary of State for the Home Department* [2021] EWHC 1085 (Admin); *R (Secretary of State for the Home Department) v First Tier Tribunal (Social Entitlement Chamber)* [2021] EWHC 1690 (Admin); *R (BK) v Secretary of State for Work and Pensions* [2023] EWHC 378 (KB); *Allister v Secretary of State for Northern Ireland* [2022] NICA 15 (appealed from *Allister v Secretary of State for Northern Ireland* [2021] NIQB 64); *R (DK) v The Commissioners for Her Majesty's Revenue and Customs* [2021] EWHC 1845 (Admin); *R (King) v Secretary of State for Education* [2021] EWHC 2509 (Admin); *R (SWP) v Secretary of State for the Home Department* [2023] EWCA Civ 439 (appealed from *R (SWP) v Secretary of State for the Home Department* [2022] EWHC 2067 (Admin)); *R (Detention Action) v Secretary of State for the Home Department (Equality Human Rights Commission Intervening* [2014] EWHC 2245 (Admin); *R (Johnson) v Secretary of State for the Home Department* [2014] EWHC 2386 (Admin); *R (FA (Sudan) v Secretary of State for the Home Department* [2021] EWCA Civ 59 (appealed from *R (FA (Sudan) v Secretary of State for the Home Department* [2018] EWHC 3475 (Admin)); *R (Goloshvili) v Secretary of State for the Home Department* [2019] EWHC 614 (Admin); *R (YA) v Secretary of State for the Home Department* [2013] EWHC 3229 (Admin).

[56] *R (SM) v Lord Chancellor (Bail for Immigration Detainees Intervening)* [2021] EWHC 418 (Admin).

[57] *A & ors v Secretary of State for the Home Department* [2004] UKHL 56 (appealed from *A & ors v Secretary of State for the Home Department* [2002] EWCA Civ 1502); *A v Secretary of State for the Home Department* [2002] ACD 98); *R (Al-Rawi) v Secretary of State for Foreign and Commonwealth Affairs* [2006] EWCA Civ 1279 (appealed from *R (Al-Rawi) v Secretary of State for Foreign and Commonwealth Affairs* [2006] EWHC 972 (Admin)).

[58] *R (Purja & ors) v Ministry of Defence* [2003] EWCA Civ 1345 (appealed from *R (Purja & ors) v Ministry of Defence* [2003] EWHC 445 (Admin)); *R (British Gurkha Welfare Society) v Ministry of Defence* [2010] EWCA Civ 1098 (appealed from *R (British Gurkha Welfare Society) v Ministry of Defence* [2010] EWHC 3 (Admin)).

[59] *Secretary of State for Defence v Mrs Diana Elias* [2006] EWCA Civ 1293.

Similarly, in *R (Al-Rawi) v Secretary of State for Foreign and Commonwealth Affairs*,[60] the Court found that the Secretary of State's refusal to make a formal request for the removal of claimants held in Guantanamo Bay was based on their legal status as non-nationals rather than their nationality or race. Since the difference in legal status of nationals and non-nationals was recognized in international law, it was considered justified under article 14. No connection with race, ethnicity, or religion was made even though it was well known that the detainees at Guantanamo Bay were all overwhelmingly Muslim men, like the claimants in *Al-Rawi*.[61]

Likewise, in cases which have been brought by victims of the Windrush scandal for having been denied leave to remain, leave to enter, citizenship or passports, courts have examined discrimination on the basis of status as a Windrush victim.[62] They have made no connection with race despite knowing that 'the Windrush generation shar[es] the protected characteristic of race ("national origin, ethnicity, nationality, and colour; the majority are black")'.[63] Even though courts have acknowledged that 'the status relied upon, Windrush victim, is linked to race'[64] neither the claimants nor the courts have made any more of it. This directly affects the level of scrutiny applied to a case as 'the connection with race tempers the substantial degree of weight that the Court would otherwise accord to the decision-maker'.[65] The treatment of Irish Catholics too seems to evade any analysis of discrimination based on race, ethnicity, or religion.[66]

Courts have been open to recognizing a range of grounds as 'other status' such as residence,[67] status as a British national with non-British children,[68] status as a

[60] [2006] EWCA Civ 1279 (appealed from *R (Al-Rawi) v Secretary of State for Foreign and Commonwealth Affairs* [2006] EWHC 972 (Admin)).

[61] Amnesty International, 'Guantánamo Bay: Over 20 Years of Injustice' (1 April 2025) <https://www.amnesty.org.uk/guantanamo-bay-human-rights> (accessed 21 April 2025).

[62] *R (Howard) v Secretary of State for the Home Department* [2021] EWHC 1023 (Admin); *Mahabir v Secretary of State for the Home Department* [2021] EWHC 1177 (Admin); *R (Vanriel) v Secretary of State for the Home Department* [2021] EWHC 3415 (Admin).

[63] Wendy Williams, 'Windrush Lessons Learned Review' (Independent Review, March 2020) at 24 <https://assets.publishing.service.gov.uk/media/5e74984fd3bf7f4684279faa/6.5577_HO_Windrush_Lessons_Learned_Review_WEB_v2.pdf> (accessed 21 April 2025); *R (Trevor Donald) v Secretary of State for the Home Department* [2024] EWHC 1492 (Admin) [hereafter *Trevor Donald*].

[64] *Trevor Donald*, ibid [248] [249].

[65] ibid [248].

[66] *Lancaster v The Police Service of Northern Ireland* [2023] NICA 63 (appealed from *Lancaster v The Police Service of Northern Ireland* [2023] NIKB 12); *Dillon v Secretary of State for Northern Ireland (Northern Ireland Human Rights Commission, Equality Commission for Northern Ireland, Wave Trauma Centre and Amnesty International Intervening)* [2024] NIKB 11.

[67] *R (Carson) v Secretary of State for Work and Pensions* [2005] UKHL 37 (appealed from *R (Carson) v Secretary of State for Work and Pensions* [2003] EWCA Civ 797; *R (Carson) v Secretary of State for Work and Pensions* [2002] EWHC 978 (Admin)).

[68] *R (Morris) v Westminster City Council (No.3)* [2004] EWHC 2191 (Admin); *R (Morris) v Westminster City Council (No.2)* [2004] EWHC 1199 (Admin); *R (Morris) v Westminster City Council (No.1)* [2003] EWHC 2266 (Admin).

recent migrant,[69] refugee status,[70] asylum seeker,[71] and status as a victim of trafficking.[72] But whether the court allows actually claiming on these bases in a particular case depends on the claimant being able to point to a comparator group in an analogous situation. The presence of a comparator in an analogous situation thus appears to be critical not only in establishing difference in treatment or discrimination. It appears critical in establishing the availability of a ground as a status for staking a claim under article 14 itself. This is why the second and third limbs of the article 14 analysis (grounds as status and analogous situation test) are related and often stand or fall together.

The result is that article 14 case law is much more open to reading in new grounds or statuses given that the list of grounds in the provision is meant to be open-ended. But these newer grounds are considered independent of racial grounds which are enumerated in article 14 including race, colour, language, religion, national or social origin, association with a national minority, and birth. They are thus not tested for racialization or the possibility that they are being used to instate a racial order or hierarchy and in turn to advantage some racialized groups at the expense of others. Thus, structural racism appears to go untested against an approach which limits racial discrimination to claims brought explicitly on racial grounds. Such cases are few and far between. Ultimately, neither claims based explicitly on racial grounds, nor claims based on 'other status' as proxies of racial grounds, seem to be represented in the case law, giving the impression that racial discrimination has almost ceased.

7.3.3 Evidential Scope

If a claimant succeeds in establishing that they are a victim, that their claim falls within the ambit of another Convention right, and that their treatment or impact is based on a racial ground and can be compared to another in a materially analogous situation, the inquiry under article 14 turns to the final step: to assess whether the discriminatory measure could yet be justified as proportionate. This

[69] *Esfandiari v Secretary of State for Work and Pensions* [2006] EWCA Civ 282.
[70] *B (Eritrea) v Secretary of State for Work and Pensions* [2015] EWCA Civ 141 (appealed from *B (Eritrea) v Secretary of State for Work and Pensions* [2013] UKUT 433 (AAC)); *R (Bashir) v Secretary of State for the Home Department* [2017] EWCA Civ 397 (appealed from *R (Bashir) v Secretary of State for the Home Department* [2016] EWHC 954 (Admin)); *R (SG) v Secretary of State for the Home Department (Equality and Human Rights Commission Intervening)* [2016] EWHC 2639 (Admin).
[71] *AL (Serbia) v Secretary of State for the Home Department* [2008] UKHL 42 (appealed from *AL (Serbia) v Secretary of State for the Home Department* [2006] EWCA Civ 1619).
[72] *R (Tirkey) v Director of Legal Aid Casework* [2017] EWHC 3403 (Admin); *R (JP) v Secretary of State for the Home Department* [2019] EWHC 3346 (Admin).

step, as set out by the Supreme Court in *Bank Mellat (Appellant) v Her Majesty's Treasury*,[73]

> depends on an exacting analysis of the factual case advanced in defence of the measure, in order to determine (i) whether its objective is sufficiently important to justify the limitation of a fundamental right; (ii) whether it is rationally connected to the objective; (iii) whether a less intrusive measure could have been used; and (iv) whether, having regard to these matters and to the severity of the consequences, a fair balance has been struck between the rights of the individual and the interests of the community.[74]

As Lord Sumption rightly noted in *Bank Mellat*, the four steps in the proportionality test are 'logically separate ... [though] in practice they inevitably overlap because the same facts are likely to be relevant to more than one of them'.[75] Analysis across the four steps of the proportionality test is thus often indistinguishable.

If the claimant succeeds in the steps preceding the determination of proportionality, it is here at proportionality analysis that their claim often fails. There are several paths to failure in the application of the proportionality test, but they differ from critiques of proportionality that have been mounted in other contexts to do with the intensity of review, deference, subjectivity, incommensurability, etc.[76] It is thus useful to isolate what is distinct in the failure of racial discrimination cases and the resulting failure in addressing structural racism.

First, although the proportionality test is meant to test whether racial discrimination is justified, sometimes it is applied in vacuum without regard to the racial discrimination at hand. In fact, proportionality analysis sometimes trumps any analysis of racial discrimination, or the prior determination of whether there was any difference in treatment or differential impact based on racial grounds or other status. In this application of the proportionality test, there appears to be no normative significance of rights generally or the prohibition of racial discrimination specifically.[77]

Take for example the case of *R (Mahoney) v Secretary of State for Communities and Local Government*.[78] The question before the Court was whether section 33(2)

[73] [2013] UKSC 38.
[74] ibid [20] (Lord Sumption).
[75] ibid.
[76] Julian Rivers, 'Proportionality and Variable Intensity of Review' (2006) 65 Cambridge Law Journal 174; Stavros Tsakyrakis, 'Proportionality: An Assault on Human Rights?' (2009) 7 International Journal of Constitutional Law 468; Tom Hickman, 'Problems for Proportionality' [2010] New Zealand Law Review 303; Cora Chan, 'Proportionality and Invariable Baseline Intensity of Review' (2013) 33 Legal Studies 1; Timothy Endicott, 'Proportionality and Incommensurability' in Grant Huscroft et al (eds), *Proportionality and the Rule of Law* (CUP 2014); Cora Chan, *Deference in Human Rights Adjudication* (OUP 2024).
[77] George Letsas, 'Rescuing Proportionality' in Rowan Cruft (ed), *Philosophical Foundations of Human Rights* (OUP 2015) 340 ('the best reconstruction of what courts actually do under the heading of proportionality must begin with normative assumptions about the nature of rights').
[78] [2015] EWHC 589 (Admin).

of the Land Compensation Act 1973, which precludes the making of a home loss payment to a caravan dweller unless no suitable alternative site is available to him on reasonable terms, was incompatible with article 14 on grounds of ethnicity. The Court was categorical that this was not a claim of direct discrimination based on race or ethnicity.[79] It made no mention of indirect discrimination either. It simply went on to uphold the provision based on reasoning which engaged with a motley of justificatory arguments, none of which seemed to engage with the disproportionate impact suffered by the claimants as Irish Travellers. Racial discrimination experienced by Irish Travellers, though explicitly alleged by the claimant and apparently rejected by the Court, was actually not examined. The discussion seemed to have leaped to justification from the very outset.

R (Wilson) v Wychavon District Council[80] had followed a similar course in the case of indirect racial discrimination. The case involved a challenge to section 183(4) of the Town and Country Planning Act 1990 wherein a dwelling was protected from a 'stop notice' issued by the land authority to prevent environmental damage while the same protection was not available to dwellings such as caravans. The claimant, a Romani Gypsy, was a caravan dweller and challenged the stop notice issued against her for unjustifiably discriminating on the grounds of her ethnicity. The challenge failed. The Court accepted that the regime disproportionately affected Gypsies and Travellers, but it held that the regime was justified given that it was aimed at preventing environmental degradation and harm. From the very outset, the Court bought into the assumption that caravans caused environmental harm—itself a racialized assumption—which paid no heed to a lifestyle choice which was central to Traveller life and identity. The Court held that the examination of a less intrusive option was not necessitated and abandoned the proportionality analysis even before it embarked on it with its wholesale adoption of government's justification based on environmental harm.

Second, the proportionality test is passed over for another test—for the impugned measure to be justified if it is not 'manifestly without reasonable foundation'. On the face of it, the test appears to be a low bar for the respondent to pass as compared to the four-step analysis of legitimacy, suitability, necessity, and balancing in the proportionality test. Courts still seem to prefer the application of this test in cases involving social or economic policy or questions of essentially political nature.[81] Though there is an argument that it is apt mainly in the context of welfare

[79] ibid [78].

[80] [2007] EWCA Civ 52 (appealed from *R (Wilson) v Wychavon District Council* [2005] EWHC 2970 (Admin)).

[81] *R (HC) v Secretary of State for Work and Pensions* [2017] UKSC 73 [32] (citing *R (MA) v Secretary of State for Work and Pensions (Equality and Human Rights Commission intervening)* [2016] 1 WLR 4550 [32] (Lord Toulson)) ('the allocation of limited public funds in the social security and welfare context is pre-eminently a matter for national authorities, subject only to the requirement that their decisions should not be 'manifestly without reasonable foundation'); *R (Joint Council for the Welfare of Immigrants) v Secretary of State for the Home Department (Residential Landlords Association, EHRC and Liberty Intervening)* [2020] EWCA Civ 542 [125]–[130].

benefits cases.[82] But quite aside from the particular context in which this test is applied, what is problematic about its use is its fundamental incompatibility with the prohibition of racial discrimination. It is a particular misfit for claims of racial discrimination, and in particular structural racism, which is not detected in any obvious unreasonableness on the part of the state but rather in the considered ways in which the state governs including by instating a racial order and racial disadvantage in turn. It is in the quotidian exercise of state power that structural racism is enacted rather than in any manifestly unreasonable exercise of power. The test should thus not trump the application of a substantive standard of review expected in cases of racial discrimination, such as the proportionality test.[83] This, however, does not seem to be the case.

Take for example the case of *R (Public Law Project) v Secretary of State for Justice*.[84] The case concerned a challenge to the Legal Aid, Sentencing and Punishment of Offenders Act 2012 (Amendment of Schedule 1) Order 2014 which restricted access to legal aid on the basis of residence, on grounds that this unjustifiably discriminated against foreigners who required legal aid. The challenge failed. The Court held that whether state funding of legal expenses in civil matters should be limited to those living in the UK was essentially a political question. It held that the appropriate test to apply to assess whether there was a breach of article 14 was whether the residence requirement was manifestly without reasonable foundation. The Court found that this was not the case.

Similarly, in *R (Kebede) v Secretary of State for Business, Innovation and Skills*[85] the article 14 challenge failed with the application of the manifestly without reasonable foundation test. The claimants had discretionary leave to remain after having been abandoned by their father who brought them to the UK. They had since completed their education in the UK and had no prospects of leaving the UK having secured university places. They would have completed over ten years in the UK by the time their discretionary leave to remain expired. They were still not considered as settled in the UK for the purposes of student loan. The Court found that that their treatment did not constitute discrimination on the basis of immigration status as the impugned measure was 'not manifestly without reasonable justification' as it was justified by 'first the need to husband scarce resources and secondly to spend the money available on those who one could be sure were entitled to remain to benefit the economy'.[86]

[82] *Humphreys v Revenue and Customs* [2012] 1 WLR 1545; *R (JS) v Secretary of State for Work and Pensions (Child Poverty Action Group intervening)* [2015] 1 WLR 1449; *Adiatu v Her Majesty's Treasury* [2020] EWHC 1554 (Admin).

[83] On proportionality as a substantive standard of review: Mark Elliott, 'The HRA 1998 and the Standard of Substantive Review' (2002) 7 Judicial Review 97.

[84] [2015] EWCA Civ 1193 (appealed from *R (Public Law Project) v Secretary of State for Justice* [2014] EWHC 2365 (Admin)); *Stach v Department for Communities* [2020] NICA 4 (appealed from *Stach v Department for Communities* [2018] NIQB 93).

[85] [2013] EWHC 2396 (Admin).

[86] ibid [31].

Third, courts, especially at the appellate level, often do not conduct an independent justification analysis under the proportionality test. Instead, they assess whether the court below had applied the proportionality test correctly. This assessment is based on an inarticulate standard of review which is decidedly light touch.

Take for example the case of *R (Connors) v Secretary of State for Communities and Local Government*.[87] The Court of Appeal held that the determination of statutory appeals in cases of planning permission filed by Gypsies and Travellers could be made by the Secretary of State. It did not independently consider the potential breach of article 14 even though the case involved Traveller groups. Instead, it relied on the judgment of the Court below and the determination made by the Secretary of State in respect of the two claimants and found that determination incontrovertible.[88]

Fourth, racial discrimination cases succeed under the proportionality test when there is little evidence that the government considered the discriminatory impact of the impugned law, policy, or practice and/or does not advance an extensive case for justification. Conversely, when the government *has* considered the discriminatory impact while adopting the impugned measure and/or makes a case justifying it, proportionality analysis often fails. This sets the bar too low for the government which cannot justify negligent racism but can defend any inadvertent racism.

For instance, in *R (Winder) v Sandwell Metropolitan Borough Council (The Equality and Human Rights Commission Intervening)*,[89] a challenge to the local council's Council Tax Reduction Scheme, which applied the tax reduction to those who had lived in the borough for at least two years, was deemed discriminatory against non-British nationals because the council had evaded 'any assessment of the looked-for beneficial effects of the measure on the one hand, or of the unwanted adverse effects on the other'.[90]

Similarly, in *R (MM (Lebanon)) v Secretary of State for the Home Department*,[91] the article 14 challenge—to income thresholds for foreign spouses to immigrate to the UK to join their British partners—failed because of the Secretary of State's awareness of the possibility of indirect discrimination against different groups

[87] [2017] EWCA Civ 1850 (appealed from *R (Connors) v Secretary of State for Communities and Local Government* [2014] EWHC 2358 (Admin)) (The Court of Appeal held that determination of statutory appeals in cases of planning permission filed by Gypsies and Travellers can be made by the Secretary of State. It did not independently consider the potential breach of article 14 especially since it involved the grounds of race or ethnicity. Instead, it wholly relied on the judgment of the Court below and the determination made by the Secretary of State in case of the two claimants and found their reasons incontrovertible).

[88] *Roberts v Commissioner of Police of the Metropolis* [2015] UKSC 79 (where the Supreme Court did not reopen the discussion on whether the suspicionless stop and search power discriminated against Black people as it had been considered by courts below).

[89] [2014] EWHC 2617 (Admin).

[90] ibid [90].

[91] [2017] UKSC 10 (appealed from *R (MM (Lebanon)) v Secretary of State for the Home Department* [2014] EWCA Civ 985 and *R (MM (Lebanon)) v Secretary of State for the Home Department* [2013] EWHC 1900 (Admin)).

including migrants from Asia and Africa and refugees.[92] The fact that the government had 'taken into account'[93] the possibility of differential impact based on race, ethnic, cultural and national origins, gender, and refugee status assailed the article 14 challenge.

In fact, cases of indirect racial discrimination in the context of immigration policy fail more easily with *any* evidence that shows that the state has applied its mind to the discriminatory law, policy, or measure at hand.[94] If the state can show that it was aware of the potential discriminatory impact on 'different national, ethnic, racial or sexual groups',[95] its case for justification succeeds across all stages of the proportionality analysis.[96] There appears to be no requirement to act to redress or minimize such differential impact despite the proportionality analysis—especially its final two steps of necessity and balancing—built to do just that.

In cases of *ab ante* challenges to law or policy, all that the government needs is to show that it is 'capable' of not operating in a discriminatory manner.[97] This means that justification is often dependent not on the quality or substance of the government's case for justification but the *possibility* of such a case. In *ex ante* challenges, the sheer *existence* of the state's justificatory case assails the claimant's case. Thus, in *R (Trevor Donald) v Secretary of State for the Home Department*,[98] the article 14 challenge to the Home Secretary's inadequate implementation of certain recommendations from the Windrush Lessons Learnt Report concerning meaningful engagement and consultation with members of the Windrush community succeeded in part because the Home Secretary had given 'very limited evidence'[99] of the basis for her decision.[100]

Fifth, and finally, even though in principle racial grounds are meant to attract a high level of scrutiny, racial discrimination claims often fail due to the application of too low a standard of scrutiny. The application of the proportionality test is thus overly deferential to the respondent, the state. This is commonly the case when

[92] *R (MM (Lebanon)) v Secretary of State for the Home Department* [2014] EWCA Civ 985 [156].

[93] ibid.

[94] In contrast, bright line rules in the context of public safety, for instance, are more thoroughly examined for racial discrimination under the proportionality test. *Gulshan v Lord Chancellor* [2023] EWCA Civ 306 (where the challenge by a Sikh person to the prohibition of bringing in a *kirpan* of 8 inches into the courtroom as constituting indirect racial discrimination failed as there was no absolute ban and the claimant could have carried a kirpan of 6 inches or below into the courtroom).

[95] *R (MM (Lebanon)) v Secretary of State for the Home Department* [2014] EWCA Civ 985 [156].

[96] *R (Clift, Hindawi & anor) v Secretary of State for the Home Department* [2006] UKHL 54 (appealed from *R (Hindawi & anor) v Secretary of State for the Home Department* [2004] EWCA Civ 1309; *R (Hindawi & anor) v Secretary of State for the Home Department* [2004] EWHC 78 (Admin)).

[97] *R (Joint Council for the Welfare of Immigrants) v Secretary of State for the Home Department (Residential Landlords Association, EHRC and Liberty Intervening)* [2020] EWCA Civ 542 [119] (appealed from *R (Joint Council for the Welfare of Immigrants) v Secretary of State for the Home Department (Residential Landlords Association, EHRC and Liberty Intervening)* [2019] EWHC 452 (Admin)).

[98] [2024] EWHC 1492 (Admin).

[99] ibid [291].

[100] ibid [238].

discrimination is alleged on grounds such as immigration status or residence,[101] but surprisingly, is also often the case when other racial grounds like ethnicity or nationality are involved.

Take for example the case of *R (LR (Afghanistan) v Secretary of State for the Home Department*[102] where the claimant, an Afghan national living in Ukraine prior to the 2022 Russian invasion, challenged the refusal of his application to join his brother in the UK under the Ukrainian Family Scheme and the Homes for Ukraine Sponsorship Scheme. The schemes were open only to Ukrainian nationals. The claimant argued that in being excluded from the schemes he was discriminated against on the basis of nationality. The Court found that the exclusion constituted direct racial discrimination because (i) the matter fell within the ambit of article 8 as it affected the claimant's private life; (ii) the claimant was in an analogous situation to a Ukrainian national ordinarily resident in Ukraine and with family in the UK; (iii) there was 'no dispute between the parties' that difference between the claimant and Ukrainian nationals who qualified under the schemes was based on 'race or nationality'.[103] But it concluded that discrimination in this case was justifiable. Relying on the European Court of Human Rights' decision in *Biao v Denmark*, the Court determined that it must apply 'stricter standard of review'[104] in examining the state's justification for the schemes:

> It might be thought that cases involving immigration policy ought to be treated in the same way as those involving social and economic policy given that they involve matters that are quintessentially governmental, and will necessarily impact on social and economic matters. Accordingly, it might be thought that cogent justification is required for differential treatment on grounds of race or nationality in the immigration context. Nevertheless… 'compelling or very weighty reasons' were required to justify differential treatment on the grounds of nationality.[105]

Even applying this stricter standard of review, the Court accepted the panoply of reasons advanced by the state for the bright line distinction made in the schemes to do with risk of abuse, position of third-country nationals, administrative convenience, efficient use of resources and the existence of a bespoke Afghan scheme, to find that the schemes had a legitimate aim and were rationally connected to those aims. Ultimately, though, it found that no less intrusive measure was available 'without unacceptably compromising the achievement of the objective'.[106] It

[101] *R (Peiris) v First Tier Tribunal* [2023] EWCA Civ 1527 (appealed from *R (Peiris) v First Tier Tribunal* [2022] UKUT 91 (AAC)).
[102] [2024] UKUT 236 (IAC).
[103] ibid [40].
[104] ibid [48].
[105] ibid [45].
[106] ibid [58].

appears that the sheer range of considered reasons provided by the government sustained its case for justification in the context of immigration policy.

The Court's complete deference to the government's bright line immigration policies in the context of article 14 is even more evident in *R (AAA (Syria)) v Secretary of State for the Home Department*[107] which concerned an article 14 challenge by six asylum seekers to the application of the government's scheme to send asylum seekers to Rwanda if they had made a 'dangerous journey' to arrive in the UK. The question before the High Court was whether the Secretary of State's decisions were discriminatory on the grounds of nationality and/or status as an asylum seeker in breach of article 14. It answered that question in the negative and although the scheme was eventually found to be unlawful by the Supreme Court, the article 14 issue was never re-examined.[108] The High Court's decision on article 14 is thus critical for our purposes. The decision essentially reproduced the government's case for justification as its own justification analysis. There appears no independent judicial reasoning on the discrimination issue or why offshore processing may actually be racist.[109] There appears little understanding of the nature of the case as indirect racial discrimination based on race or nationality. There does appear a very high level of deference accorded to the government as the decision maker justifying the impugned discrimination.

To summarize, five paths lead to the failure of racial discrimination claims at the final step of justification when: (i) no justification analysis is conducted; (ii) manifestly without reasonable foundation test is applied, often beyond cases with far-reaching economic implications involving social and economic policy; (iii) no independent proportionality assessment is made; (iv) the government shows that it was aware of the discriminatory impact of the impugned measure; and (v) undue deference is accorded to the state in the application of the proportionality test.

These five paths to failure at the altar of justification are common. Less common are claims which succeed. The next section assesses how these are avoided in rare claims that succeed.

7.4 Structural Racism and the HRA

As the introduction to this chapter mentioned, there is a very good reason for considering how anti-racism fares in the HRA. It is to do with the possibility of scrutinizing the state itself—its law, policy, and practice as wielded by the Parliament, the government, courts, public authorities, public institutions, and

[107] [2022] EWHC 3230 (Admin).
[108] [2023] UKSC 42; [2023] EWCA Civ 745.
[109] Shreya Atrey, 'Why Offshore Processing of Asylum Applications is Actually Racist', Verfassungsblog: On Matters Constitutional (23 October 2024) <https://verfassungsblog.de/why-offshore-processing-of-asylum-applications-is-actually-racist/> (accessed 21 April 2025).

anyone exercising public power, under the HRA. This scrutiny of the limits of state power in enacting structural racism is made possible through the prohibition of discrimination on a number of racial grounds enumerated in article 14 of the ECHR, and also, 'other status'. Article 14 thus opens the doors to scrutinizing states and their role in governing processes of racialization—that is, how racial order and hierarchy are instated on the basis of racial or other grounds. Furthermore, article 14's focus on discrimination enables a recognition of racial disadvantage suffered by one group as opposed to another whether as a matter of difference in treatment or as a matter of disproportionate impact. In this way, all three elements of structural racism to do with how (i) the state and state-like entities (ii) racialize (iii) to instate racial disadvantage, can, in principle, be addressed via article 14. There appears no textual or conceptual bar to addressing structural racism through article 14.

However, as the previous section showed, case law has been unable to recognize structural racism in practice. Which is why it is imperative to study the few examples in case law that *have* been able to do so. This section is dedicated to these examples. The purpose is to isolate the particular conceptual and doctrinal moves which enable the recognition and redressal of structural racism. While this does not entail the naming of or use of the label 'structural racism' or even 'racism', it does entail an appreciation of the three elements of structural racism within the article 14 analysis, and in rarer instances still, even a nod towards the three elements of transformative anti-racism. In sum, the judicial reasoning in these cases shows a clear application of anti-racism as a legal principle.

The strongest example is the *Belmarsh case*: *A v Secretary of State for the Home Department*.[110]

The case concerned a challenge to the validity of section 23 of the Anti-Terrorism, Crime and Security Act 2001 which allowed the indefinite detention of foreign nationals who were suspected of international terrorism but not British nationals who were suspected of international terrorism. The claimants, who were all foreign nationals, argued that section 23 discriminated against them as non-UK nationals in breach of article 14 of the ECHR.

The House of Lords agreed with the claimants by a majority of 8–1. It is useful to consider how the Court responded to each of the aspects of the discrimination inquiry: victim status, ambit, racial grounds, analogous situation, and justification.

First, in respect of victim status, there was no requirement before the Court for the claimants to prove that they were victims. As Lady Hale helpfully reminded, this case was 'not a challenge to the individual decisions to detain [the claimants] ... [but] a challenge to the validity of the law under which the detainees are detained'.[111] While in other cases, broad-based challenges are either delimited to

[110] [2004] UKHL 56 (appealed from *A v Secretary of State for the Home Department* [2002] EWCA Civ 1502; *A v Secretary of State for the Home Department* [2002] ACD 98).

[111] ibid [220] (Hale LJ).

an individual claimant's case or entirely sidelined, the broad-based challenge to the legislative provision in this case was duly acknowledged and reviewed.

Second, in respect of ambit, the Court was convinced that the matter engaged the right to liberty guaranteed in article 5 and hence triggered article 14.[112] Nothing turned on this point.

Third, in respect of racial grounds, the majority held that there was 'no doubt' that the claimants had been discriminated against on the basis of their nationality or immigration status because section 23 had treated the problem of international terrorism as 'an immigration problem'.[113] Although nationality or immigration status were not enumerated grounds under article 14, Lord Bingham observed that: (i) nationality had been considered a ground akin to race by the ECtHR which had required very weighty reasons for nationality discrimination to be justified;[114] (ii) nationality was a forbidden ground under the Race Relations Act 1976;[115] and (iii) it was accepted by the Attorney General that in any case immigration status was covered under 'other status'.[116] Lord Hope too alluded that discrimination in this case could be considered as one based on national origins.[117] Either way, there was no jostling with grounds. The majority was open to seeing discrimination in this case as based on one or more of the enumerated or unenumerated grounds in article 14.

Fourth, whatever be the ground (nationality, immigration status, or national origins), the majority was clear that that ground distinguished between claimants and home-grown international terrorists.[118] The majority was unequivocal that the threat of international terrorism was a matter of security not immigration and hence existed irrespective of nationality, immigration status, or national origins of the international terrorists.[119] The Court thus confirmed that there *was* difference in treatment based on grounds which treated people in analogous situation differentially.[120]

Fifth, and finally, the question was whether such discrimination could be justified. In Lord Bingham's lead judgment, he cited a range of materials in international law especially from the UN Human Rights Committee and the UN Committee on the Elimination of Racial Discrimination to establish the impermissibility of discrimination based on nationality and immigration status. In contrast, he found no authority in international law which suggested otherwise. Instead of going through the four stages of the proportionality test, he reasoned, on the basis of these

112 ibid [51] (Bingham LJ).
113 ibid [51] (Bingham LJ), [134] (Hope LJ).
114 ibid [49] (Bingham LJ).
115 ibid.
116 ibid.
117 ibid [136] [138] [139] (Hope LJ).
118 ibid [54] (Bingham LJ).
119 ibid [161] (Rodger LJ).
120 ibid [54] (Bingham LJ).

materials, that the discrimination in the present case was unjustifiable. Likewise, in Lord Nicholls' judgment, he noted the absence of any 'satisfactory' or 'persuasive' explanation from the government justifying the difference in treatment between home-grown and foreign terrorists.[121] In Lord Hope's judgment, the fact that it was well known that the threat of international terrorism existed from home-grown terrorists in greater numbers than it did from foreigners made the detention of the latter class unjustifiable.[122] Lord Scott's seems to have applied the test of proportionality as irrationality.[123] In Lady Hale's judgment, no sooner than she embarked on the application of the first stage of the proportionality test to find a legitimate aim for the impugned provision, did she remark that: 'If the situation really is so serious, and the threat so severe, that people may be detained indefinitely without trial, what possible legitimate aim could be served by only having power to lock up some of the people who present that threat?'[124] Ultimately, none of the eight judgments for the majority conducted proportionality assessment going over each of the four stages individually. But all found that the impugned provision was disproportionate. The justification analysis was thus much more discursive than the discrete and sequential framework of the proportionality test.

Importantly, the analysis struck a delicate balance between deferring to the Parliament and discharging its own judicial function under the HRA. As Lord Nicholls noted, while counterterrorism was firmly a domain of the elected government, courts too were charged by the Parliament 'with a particular responsibility'. This responsibility was to ensure that 'legislation and ministerial decisions do not overlook the human rights of persons adversely affected'.[125] He continued:

> For their part, when carrying out their assigned task the courts will accord to Parliament and ministers, as the primary decision-makers, an appropriate degree of latitude. The latitude will vary according to the subject matter under consideration, the importance of the human right in question, and the extent of the encroachment upon that right. The courts will intervene *only* when it is apparent that, in balancing the various considerations involved, the primary decision-maker must have given *insufficient weight to the human rights factor*.[126]

In the present case, that the Parliament could not be accorded 'the substantial latitude normally to be given to decisions on national security' was the reason that the matter had *not* been treated as one of security and had 'not prompted a similar negation of the right to personal liberty in the case of nationals who pose a similar

[121] ibid [78] (Bingham LJ).
[122] ibid [138] (Hope LJ).
[123] ibid [159] (Scott LJ).
[124] ibid [236] (Hale LJ).
[125] ibid [80] (Nicholls LJ).
[126] ibid (emphasis supplied).

security risk.'[127] In treating the problem of national security as a problem of immigration, the Parliament was considered to have lacked any objective or reasonable relationship with proportionality to merit a discrete analysis of legitimate aim, suitability, necessity, and balancing.

No other example in case law matches the stridency of the House of Lords in *A v Secretary of State for the Home Department* in dealing with, what was essentially, a claim of structural racism.

A v Secretary of State for the Home Department, the *Belmarsh* case, is a case of structural racism because it is about how (i) the state, by enacting a provision like section 23 of the Anti-Terrorism, Crime and Security Act 2001, (ii) can racialize by instating a racial order where foreigners resident in the UK, who have links with terrorist organizations, are considered inherently suspect and more dangerous as compared to home-grown British terrorists, and thus in turn (iii) instate a framework of racial disadvantage by depriving them of their liberty by indefinitely imprisoning them without charges. The Court paid due regard to each of the elements of structural racism in its reasoning. First, it showed acute awareness of the limits of state power in the context of discrimination. In Lord Hope's strong words: 'A state is not permitted to discriminate against an unpopular minority for the good of the majority.'[128] Likewise, in Lord Scott's words:

> If those who are suspected terrorists include some non–Muslims as well as Muslims, it would, in my opinion, be irrational and discriminatory to restrict the application of the measures to Muslims even though the bulk of those suspected are likely to profess to be Muslims. Some might well not be professed Muslims. Similarly, it would be irrational and discriminatory to restrict the application of the measures to men although the bulk of those suspected are likely to be male. Some might well be women. Similarly, in my opinion, it is irrational and discriminatory to restrict the application of the measures to suspected terrorists who have no right of residence in this country. Some suspected terrorists may well be home–grown.[129]

This line of reasoning does not deal with race or racism bluntly. Conventional 'racial' grounds such as race, colour or ethnicity are not at stake in the *Belmarsh* case. There is also no obvious racialized minority at hand—such as Traveller groups or Black and Minority Ethnic people. The facts do not resemble the kind of 'obvious' racial discrimination claims that, as the previous chapter showed, are commonly alleged under the EqA. Consequently, the reasoning of the Court also

[127] ibid [83] (Nicholls LJ).
[128] ibid [136] (Hope LJ).
[129] ibid [158] (Scott LJ).

does not trade in blunt tropes, even though it does seem to hint at Islamophobia indirectly.

Instead, the reasoning in *Belmarsh* demonstrates a clear appreciation for a principle against the state's role in instating hierarchies which appear racialized in that they mark out or classify a group of people based on certain characteristics as inherently inferior and hence liable to be disadvantaged. This appreciation is substantive and engages with the essence of the three elements of structural racism within the elements of article 14 analysis (victim status, ambit, grounds, analogous situation, and justification).

The majority's reasoning in *Belmarsh* also shows engagement with other elements of transformative anti-racism beyond the opposition of the state and its role in enacting structural racism. The Court's insistence of the fact that the government could not simply replace the claimant's group with another unpopular group on the basis of their religion or gender to address the discrimination at hand shows its openness to broad-based structural change (of the constitution no less) and intersectional justice (which extends racial justice to all and not just racialized minorities). As expressed by Lord Hoffman: 'the power of detention is at present confined to foreigners and I would not like to give the impression that all that was necessary was to extend the power to United Kingdom citizens as well ... such a power in any form is not compatible with our constitution.'[130] *A v Secretary of State for the Home Department* is thus an exemplar of transformative anti-racism in (i) opposing the state for bringing about structural racism and enacting (ii) broad-based constitutional change and (iii) intersectional justice; and ultimately an exemplar of the application of anti-racism as a legal principle in human rights adjudication.

It is important to observe that the majority did not stray from the established doctrinal path but rather integrated the application of the principle *with* the doctrine. To remind, as recounted above, three lines of reasoning assisted the majority in taking a principled approach to addressing structural racism.

First, the Court helpfully remembered that it could review the primary legislation—as is permissible under the HRA—and hence issued a declaration of incompatibility when it found that its provision in section 23 contravened article 14. As shown in Section 7.2, it has not always done so and in fact when faced with claims by individual victims has confined itself to declarations about the contravention with their rights particularly. Broad-based claims against the state, even when permitted, are rarely treated as in *A v Secretary of State for the Home Department.*

Second, the Court did not overindulge in the determination of the precise ground of discrimination at stake. Instead, it focussed on determining what possible grounds such as nationality, immigration status, and national origin

[130] ibid [97] (Hoffmann LJ).

did: instate a hierarchy or order which disadvantaged non-nationals as opposed to nationals. That is essentially a focus on the *process of racialization* and the *nature of discrimination* it results in. This shifted the discrimination analysis away from the mechanistic technicality of grounds and towards the causal and empirical reality of racial discrimination. This non-mechanistic approach to grounds has been adopted with approval by the Supreme Court, most recently by Lady Black as she cautioned against 'spending too much time on an analysis of whether the proposed status has an independent existence, as opposed to considering the situation as a whole'.[131]

Third, the Court pursued the justification analysis contextually and engaged with the substance of the government's defence without being caught up in the scheme of the proportionality analysis as the defence seemed to contradict that scheme anyway. Importantly, it showed appropriate deference to the Parliament but did not abdicate its own judicial functions under the HRA. Deference thus did not precipitate into abandonment of judicial review.

For these reasons, both conceptually and doctrinally, the *Belmarsh* case stands out from an anti-racist perspective. It was not a slam dunk case. It was, at the time, as the justices themselves noted, the 'most important' case they had encountered during their tenure on the bench.[132] It was a highly political case which dealt with the government's reaction to 9/11 attacks in the US. It was a non-obvious case of racial discrimination based not on race, colour or ethnicity but instead on nationality, immigration status, and national origin. Yet, the House of Lords was unencumbered. It achieved in this important and a rather hard case, what courts since have been unable to in quotidian cases.[133]

Five other notable successes show similar lines of reasoning through which structural racism is successfully challenged. It is useful to note them briefly.

R (on the application of Tigere) v Secretary of State for Business, Innovation and Skills[134] concerned a challenge to the requirement that a person be settled in the UK in order to qualify for a student loan to fund their higher education. The claimant had failed to meet the requirement as her mother had failed to take steps to regularize their status after having overstayed their visas. The claimant had no knowledge of this. She had lived in the UK since the age of six and had done very well at school and obtained three A levels to be offered a place in several universities. She was denied student loan in the absence of settled status in the

[131] *R (Stott) v Secretary of State for Justice* [2018] UKSC 59 [75] (per Lady Black); *R (on the application of Tigere) v Secretary of State for Business, Innovation and Skills* [2015] UKSC 57; *R (A) the Criminal Injuries Compensation Authority* [2021] 1 WLR; *R (SC, CB and 8 children) v SSWP* [2021] UKSC 2671.

[132] *A v Secretary of State for the Home Department* (n 110) [86] (Hoffmann LJ), [219] (Hale LJ).

[133] Initial hope that the House of Lords' decision in *Belmarsh* had wider implications for equality and democracy has not materialized. Sandra Fredman 'From Deference to Democracy: The Role of Equality under the Human Rights Act 1998' (2006) 122 Law Quarterly Review 53; David Feldman, 'The Human Rights Act 1998 and Constitutional Principles' (2018) 19 Legal Studies 165.

[134] [2015] UKSC 57.

country. The Supreme Court found that she had been unlawfully discriminated against under article 14 by a majority of 3–2. In Lady Hale's lead judgment, she explained that the claimant's complaint was not the 'denial of access to a student loan'. Her 'real complaint' was that 'some people get student loans and others do not, in short of discrimination'.[135] Lady Hale noted that immigration status was considered a status under article 14 and swiftly proceeded to the issue of justification.[136] Addressing the 'debate before us as to the approach which we should take to scrutinising a governmental decision in this area',[137] she categorically rejected that the relevant approach to justification was the test of 'manifestly without reasonable foundation'.[138] According to her, while the test was appropriate in cases relating to property rights, education was 'rather different'.[139] That said, she acknowledged that the case concerned 'the distribution of finite resources at some cost to the taxpayer, and the court must treat the judgments of the Secretary of State, as primary decision-maker, with appropriate respect. That respect is, of course, heightened where there is evidence that the decision maker has addressed his mind to the particular issue'.[140] But in this case there was 'no evidence that the Secretary of State addressed his mind to the educational rights of students with [limited or discretionary leave to remain in the UK] when making these regulations'.[141] With that in mind, Lady Hale applied the fourfold *Bank Mellat* test for proportionality sequentially to find that while the regulations (i) had a legitimate aim (serving settled students who had a greater chance of contributing to the economy), (ii) they were not rationally connected to the aim (they excluded those who were likely to stay in and contributed to the UK economy), (iii) were not necessary (they excluded a rather small number of students on grounds of administrative convenience); and (iv) did not strike a fair balance between those who were excluded and the rest of the community (they deprived the students of higher education and cost the community a productive workforce). The regulations were thus deemed to have unjustifiably discriminated against the claimant. However, the Court did not quash the regulations as such because it reasoned that 'there must be cases in which it is not incompatible with the Convention rights'.[142] The claim only succeeded in respect of the claimant and no more broadly.

More recently, *R (Naeem) v Secretary of State for Education*[143] has shown that a broader victory *is* possible in facts similar to *Tigere*. The case concerned a challenge to the Secretary of State for Education's (Student Support) Regulations 2011

[135] ibid [25] (Hale LJ), [51] (Hughes LJ).
[136] ibid [26] (Hale LJ), [52] (Hughes LJ).
[137] ibid [27] (Hale LJ).
[138] ibid [32] (Hale LJ).
[139] ibid [28] (Hale LJ).
[140] ibid [32] (Hale LJ).
[141] ibid.
[142] ibid [49] (Hale LJ).
[143] [2022] EWHC 15 (Admin).

which required a student to be 'settled in the United Kingdom' on the first day of the first academic year to be eligible for student finance. The claimant had failed to obtain student finance as he had not obtained settled status by the first day of the first academic year of his course. The claimant could not apply for settled status under the priority route which was suspended due to the Covid-19 pandemic, but which may have resulted in him obtaining the settled status within days instead of months. Although he did obtain settled status shortly thereafter, the failure to achieve settled status on the first day of the first term of the first academic year meant that he was not entitled to student finance for the entire course. As Foster LJ identified, 'the central areas of dispute between the parties were as to whether it was possible to discern "other status" into which the Claimant and Interested Party fell, and if so whether differential treatment could be justified'.[144] Following the claimant's suggestion to adopt a 'broad, non-mechanistic approach'[145] to grounds like in *Tigere*, which the Court agreed was correct by virtue of 'the recent developments in understanding of how Article 14 operates to right public law wrongs',[146] the Court adopted a 'broad', 'more generous', 'uncomplicated', and less 'technical' approach to grounds.[147] Instead, it focussed on the difference in treatment between those who had settled status by the cut-off date and those, like the claimant, who were just as entitled to settled status but had failed to achieve it formally by the said date due to the suspension of the priority route. The Court found it unlikely that those in the claimant's position would emigrate and thus concluded that they were as valuable to the UK as those who had achieved Indefinite Leave to Remain by the cut-off date. The difference between the two classes was thus deemed unjustifiable. While no discrete and sequential analysis under the proportionality test was undertaken, the main consideration that the Court took into account was the fact that the defendant—the Secretary of State for Education—had not addressed the discrimination against the claimant and another interested party in the case. It thus concluded that there was no risk 'of treading inappropriately into an area of legislative discretion ... by requiring the Defendant to mitigate the effects of the discriminatory treatment under the secondary legislation of the Regulations'.[148] The defendant was ordered to do so retrospectively, not only in respect of the claimant but also over two thousand others who may have been similarly impacted.

Challenges to the state's approach to immigration have succeeded not only in the context of terrorism (*A v Secretary of State for the Home Department*) and education (*Tigere* and *Naeem*) but also in contexts such as domestic violence, modern slavery, and social welfare.

[144] ibid [53].
[145] ibid [54].
[146] ibid.
[147] ibid [68] [72] [75].
[148] ibid [97].

In *R (AM) v Secretary of State for the Home Department*,[149] the exclusion of survivors of severe domestic violence culminating in Transnational Marriage Abandonment ('TMA') from obtaining Domestic Violence Indefinite Leave to Remain ('DVILR') was successfully challenged under article 14. Even though the claimant in the case had been issued indefinite leave to remain subsequently, the issue was not considered academic and hence adjudicated upon given its 'wider significance'.[150] And even though no other case had made it before the Court, according to Lady Lieven, 'this merely illustrates why it is important that the legal issues raised in this case are determined'.[151] She predicted that the exclusion impacted 'considerably more' number of women than known by the government.[152] The determination of the issue was also compelled by the 'the level of detriment' at stake.[153] The Court thus determined that (i) the present case fell within the ambit of article 8; (ii) being in a foreign country for the purposes of obtaining DVILR constituted a relevant status for the purposes of article 14; (iii) the position of those with this status was similar to those in an analogous situation such as a dependant spouse who was abandoned in the UK who could obtain a DVILR; (iv) the difference in treatment lacked an objective and reasonable justification and hence was disproportionate as the defendant—the Secretary of State for the Home Department—had 'not put forward any evidence as to her justification for not making any provision for victims of TMA'.[154] Given that challenges to immigration rules often failed, Lady Lieven appreciated that this was 'the unusual case where the Defendant has failed to meet the requirements of Article 14',[155] essentially because the Secretary of State for the Home Department had all but conceded the case.[156]

[149] [2022] EWHC 2591 (Admin).
[150] ibid [36].
[151] ibid [44].
[152] ibid [41] [45].
[153] ibid [42].
[154] ibid [65].
[155] ibid [71].
[156] *R (Baiai) v Secretary of State for the Home Department* [2008] UKHL 53 (appealed from [2006] EWHC 823 (Admin)) succeeded on similar grounds (the decision was appealed on grounds other than article 14). The Claimants had brought a judicial review challenge to the new regime that limited the rights of those subject to immigration control to enter into a civil marriage under sections 19–25 of the Asylum and Immigration (Treatment of Claimants, etc) Act 2004, together with the Immigration (Procedure for Marriage) Regulations 2005 and the Nationality Directorate's instructions. The regime change had sought to prevent sham marriages and required that marriages involving a party subject to immigration control could not take place without a Certificate of Approval from the Secretary of State, which cost £135 to apply for per individual applicant. The Claimants challenged the regime on the ground that it, inter alia, constituted unfair discrimination against applicants subject to immigration control on the grounds of nationality contrary to article 14. The Court agreed on the basis that although the government had a legitimate aim in mind (of preventing sham marriages), the aim was not connected to the measures as the government had arbitrarily failed to take into account factors that could be relevant to considering whether a proposed marriage was a sham. A declaration of incompatibility was issued.

Likewise, in *XY v Secretary of State for the Home Department*,[157] the claimant successfully challenged the 'secret policy'[158] of the Secretary of State to make but not serve decisions in cases where confirmed victims of modern slavery were seeking asylum on the grounds of a fear of re-trafficking, as unlawful discrimination under article 14. The Court held that the present case: (i) fell within the ambit of articles 4 and 8 of the Convention; (ii) involved a modern slavery victim seeking asylum which constituted a relevant status for the purposes of article 14; (iii) concerned the position of those with this status who were in an analogous position to those who were victims of modern slavery but did not require leave to remain in the country; and (iv) that since 'the difference in treatment arose directly from the operation of the unlawful policy' under article 8, it was 'plainly' disproportionate under article 14.[159]

In *R (BCD) v Birmingham Children's Trust*,[160] the claimant successfully challenged the difference in accessing welfare benefits between British born children and foreign-born children, each cared for by a foreign carer who had leave to remain in the UK but was subject to 'No Recourse to Public Funds' ('NRPF') condition. The Court acknowledged that while the case raised political issues, it also raised 'important legal issues about how local authorities should meet the needs of children in families ineligible for welfare benefits—as the Home Office terms it in immigration leave conditions: "No Recourse to Public Funds" ('NRPF').'[161] The Court held that the present case: (i) fell within the ambit of article 8 of the Convention; (ii) involved the status of either nationality or immigration status or national origin taken alone or in combination;[162] (iii) concerned difference in treatment between groups defined by each of the possible statuses in the analogous situation of having their essential living needs met; (iv) required 'weightier reasons' for justification but found them 'conspicuously lacking' across all four stages of the proportionality test (legitimate aim, suitability, necessity and balancing).[163] Two decades before, a similar result had followed in *R (Morris) v Westminster City Council*[164] where the Court had found section 185(4) of the Housing Act 1996 to be incompatible with article 14 as it denied priority for accommodation on grounds that a non-British child was subject to immigration control while her

[157] [2024] EWHC 81 (Admin).
[158] ibid [58] [65].
[159] ibid [103].
[160] [2023] EWHC 137 (Admin).
[161] ibid [1].
[162] ibid [137] [139].
[163] ibid [194.3].
[164] *R (Morris) v Westminster City Council (No.3)* [2004] EWHC 2191 (Admin); *R (Gabaj) v First Secretary of State* (Administrative Court; unreported; 28 March 2006) (*Gabaj* involved the claimant's pregnant wife, rather than the claimant's child, as the person from abroad. Following *Morris*, the government agreed to extend the declaration of incompatibility in respect of section 185(4) of the Housing Act 1996 to this context. Schedule 15 to the Housing and Regeneration Act 2008 amended section 185(4) in response to the declaration of incompatibility).

British mother was not. While the defendant's policy was struck down in *BCD*, a declaration of incompatibility was issued in *Morris*.

Now, none of these cases may be said to involve 'classical' racial discrimination—overtly based on the grounds of race, colour or ethnicity. Yet, racial grounds for the purposes of racial discrimination are wide in law and include grounds such as national origins and nationality; and as this book has argued, should also include any ground which ends up *racializing* such as religion, language, immigration status, etc. It is in the latter sense that cases concerning immigration status or immigration rules fall under the broad category of racial discrimination and may be considered as cases of structural racism when they involve state law, policy, or practice which has the effect of racializing (considering some as innately or inherently belonging to a particular group) and disadvantaging some as opposed to others. As Section 7.3 of this chapter showed, while most of immigration-related challenges under article 14 fail, this section has shown that they can and do succeed.

The particular conceptual and doctrinal cues that emerge in the six successes can be summed up as follows. Courts can recognize and redress structural racism, substantively, when they: (i) show openness to broad-based challenges to law, policy, and practice going beyond an individual's experience of discrimination; (ii) consider the ambit of interests protected under article 14 as well as other Convention rights widely; (iii) take a broad and non-mechanistic approach to enumerated and unenumerated grounds as statuses relevant for the purposes of article 14; (iv) adopt a contextual approach to comparison of analogous situations; (v) do not apply the manifestly without reasonable foundation test; (vi) require weighty reasons for justification and hence apply a searching standard of scrutiny, and consequently a commensurate level of deference to the state.

7.5 Conclusion

The extraordinary success of the *Belmarsh* case demonstrates the important work anti-racism as a legal principle can do in guiding judicial reasoning. Other occasional successes, albeit in cases far less politically flammable but no less materially consequential, such as *Tigere*, *Naeem*, *AM*, *Baiai*, *XY*, *BCD* and *Morris*, further confirm the relevance of the principle in addressing structural racism through article 14.

No explicit adoption of the principle of anti-racism or labelling of a discrimination case as a case of structural racism has been necessary. The anti-racism practised in these cases has resisted structural racism substantively rather than rhetorically, incidentally, symbolically, or superficially. More importantly, anti-racism here seems to be a considered resistance to each of the three elements of structural racism *in* the doctrine. It is thus dispersed and embedded in the crevices of doctrine rather than present as a headline.

But these are, to emphasize, occasional successes. The success rate for claimants of racial discrimination under article 14 is only 20.80 per cent, nearly half the success rate for racial discrimination claims under the EqA. Thus, it does seem to be relatively harder to succeed under the HRA. The HRA is indeed conceptually and textually open to all three elements of structural racism involving (i) the scrutiny of state and state-like entities (ii) in enacting processes of racialization and thereby (iii) instating racial disadvantage. But often, doctrinally, (i) the scrutiny of the state attracts a low standard of scrutiny, especially in the application of the proportionality test; (ii) racialization is not easily appreciated when not based on explicitly racial grounds, and that is seldom the case; and (iii) racial disadvantage, especially material disadvantage, is often ignored in the scheme of the ECHR which predominantly protects civil-political rights. In addition, the chapter revealed a range of other doctrinal hurdles specific to article 14 which come in the way of addressing structural racism. Often it is not a single doctrinal hurdle but the effect of the application of doctrine as such that obscures structural racism in a case. It is understandable then that claims of racial discrimination remain sparse in the HRA case law. Seemingly self-evident cases of structural racism, such as the application of stop-and-search policies or hostile environment policies, which have a disproportionate impact on Black and minority ethnic people in the UK have thus either not been explicitly challenged or examined as cases of racial discrimination under article 14.[165]

Nevertheless, on balance, the HRA does seem to be a much better fit for challenging the state than the EqA is. Since it does not concern relationships between private individuals, it avoids the focus on interpersonal racism as the mainstay of discrimination law. So, even occasional successes under the HRA concern relevant cases of structural racism. They are thus more meaningful for transformative anti-racism given their primary focus on protecting people against excesses of state power. Common law judicial review shares this focus. The next chapter turns to consider how far common law fares in addressing structural racism.

[165] *R (Gillan (FC)) v Commissioner of Police for the Metropolis* [2006] UKHL 12; *Roberts v Commissioner of Police of the Metropolis* [2015] UKSC 79.

8

Racial Discrimination at Common Law

8.1 Introduction

Part I of this book erected a broad canvas for understanding racism and anti-racism in structural terms. In Part II, Chapters 6 and 7 showed the gulf between addressing structural as opposed to individualized forms of racial discrimination under the Equality Act 2010 and the Human Rights Act 1998. This chapter now turns to the body of common law to assess how structural racism is addressed therein. It shows three things. First, that claims of racial discrimination under common law are not uncommon. These claims show a commitment to the prohibition of racial discrimination even though no general principle of equality exists under common law. Secondly, however, there is a lack of consistency in how claims of racial discrimination at common law are treated. Racial discrimination under common law is often curiously subsumed by, merged with, or ignored vis-à-vis statutory law. Thus, finally, although the context of these claims—of judicial review proceedings against the state—seems to naturally fit the mould of structural racism sketched in Part I better than the context of statutory law considered in Chapters 5, 6, and 7, common law as a site remains marginal in enacting anti-racism in the UK.

8.2 Equality at Common Law

Before considering the trajectory of claims of racial discrimination, it is important to set out the general background of the broader principle of equality or equal treatment at common law. The legal status of the principle of equality has occupied British public law for decades.[1] Given the primordial significance of equality as a

[1] TRS Allan, *Law, Liberty, and Justice: The Legal Foundations of British Constitutionalism* (Clarendon Press, 1993) ch 7; Jeffery Jowell, 'Is Equality a Constitutional Principle' (1994) 7 Current Legal Problems 1 [hereafter Jowell, 'Is Equality a Constitutional Principle']; Aileen McColgan, 'Discrimination Law and the Human Rights Act 1998' in Tom Campbell, Keith Ewing, and Adam Tomkins (eds), *Sceptical Approaches to Human Rights* (Oxford University Press 2001) [hereafter McColgan, 'Discrimination Law and the Human Rights Act 1998']; Colm O'Cinneide, 'Fumbling Towards Coherence: The Slow Evolution of Equality and Anti-discrimination Law in Britain' (2006) 57 Northern Ireland Legal Quarterly 57 [hereafter O'Cinneide, 'Fumbling Towards Coherence']; Christopher McCrudden, 'Equality and Non-Discrimination' in David Feldman (ed), *English Public Law* (2nd edn, Oxford University Press 2009); Colm O'Cinneide, 'Equality: A Constitutional Principle?' (2011) UKCLA Blog <https://ukconstitutionallaw.org/2011/09/14/colm-ocinneide-equality-a-constitutional-principle/> (accessed 12 June 2023); Colm O'Cinneide, 'Equality: A Core Common Law Principle, or "Mere"

Anti-Racism as a Legal Principle. Shreya Atrey, Oxford University Press. © Shreya Atrey 2026.
DOI: 10.1093/9780198947646.003.0011

feature of rule of law and democracy,[2] the interest in its status and application at common law is only justified. For our purposes, if there were a general principle of equality that existed at common law, there would perforce be a recognition of equality or equal treatment on racial grounds. But as this section shows, despite great efforts spearheaded by Jeffrey Jowell for the recognition of a general principle of equality,[3] the fate of such a principle is, for the time being, sealed by the Supreme Court decision in *R (on the application of Gallaher Group Ltd and others) v The Competition and Markets Authority*.[4]

Jowell made an impassioned case for equality as a constitutional principle in his 1994 Dennis Lloyd Memorial Lecture.[5] He argued for 'a *principle* to limit governmental power ... a conception of equality that requires government not to treat people unequally without justification [and to] not discriminate'.[6] While Jowell admitted that equality cases under common law were adjudicated mainly as a matter of *Wednesbury* unreasonableness, he argued that '[u]nderneath the *Wednesbury* camouflage, however, a principle of equality can be discerned'[7] and even where the principle of equality was not mentioned, it was 'surely applied'[8] so that there was 'no doubt that equality is used as a test of official action in our law'.[9] He thus asked: 'is it wise for it to be explicitly articulated and declared—to be elevated to the status of lion under the throne, and not just a well-disguised rabbit to be hauled occasionally out of the *Wednesbury* hat?'[10] Answering in the affirmative, Jowell concluded that equality deserved recognition as a self-standing principle of judicial review given its overwhelming importance in a democracy.[11]

Five years later, the Privy Council in the Mauritian case of *Matadeen v Pointer*,[12] citing Jowell, agreed that there was '[no] doubt that such a principle [of equality] is one of the building blocks of democracy and necessarily permeates any democratic constitution'[13] but disagreed that 'a general justiciable principle of equality'[14] existed at common law. *Matadeen* concerned a constitutional challenge to regulations

Rationality?' in Mark Elliott and Kirsty Hughes (eds), *Common Law Constitutional Rights* (Bloomsbury 2020) [hereafter O'Cinneide, 'Equality: A Core Common Law Principle, or "Mere" Rationality?'].

2 Albert Venn Dicey, *Introduction to the Study of the Law of the Constitution* (1st edn 1915, Liberty Fund edn 1982); Jeffrey Jowell, 'The Rule of Law: Rhetoric or Universal Principle?' (2012) 20 Asia Pacific Law Review 3; *Ghaidan v Godin-Mendoza* [2004] UKHL 30 [132] (Baroness Hale).
3 Jowell, 'Is Equality a Constitutional Principle' (n 1).
4 [2018] UKSC 2 [hereafter *Gallaher*].
5 Jowell, 'Is Equality a Constitutional Principle' (n 1).
6 ibid 7 (emphasis in original).
7 ibid 11.
8 ibid.
9 ibid 14.
10 ibid.
11 ibid 18.
12 [1999] 1 AC 98 [hereafter *Matadeen*].
13 ibid [8].
14 ibid [12].

which changed how students who took an optional 'Oriental language' (Hindi, Urdu, Tamil, Telegu, Marathi, Mandarin Chinese, and Arabic) fared against those who only took the four compulsory subjects (English, Mathematics, French, and Environmental Studies) in obtaining the 'Certificate of Primary Education' ('certification'). The certification determined who got admission in the top schools of Mauritius. The effect of the new regulations was that students who took an 'Oriental language' were ranked on their marks in English, Mathematics, and the best two out of the other three papers while students with only the four compulsory subjects were entirely ranked on those subjects. The question before the Privy Council was whether the difference in treatment arising out of this change was unconstitutional. The Constitution of Mauritius provided that:

> Section 3. It is hereby recognised and declared that in Mauritius there have existed and shall continue to exist without discrimination by reason of race, place of origin, political opinions, colour, creed or sex, but subject to respect for the rights and freedoms of others and for the public interest, each and all of the following human rights and fundamental freedoms—
>
> (a) the right of the individual to life, liberty, security of the person and the protection of the law;
> (b) freedom of conscience, of expression, of assembly and association and freedom to establish schools; and
> (c) the right of the individual to protection for the privacy of his home and other property and from deprivation of property without compensation ...
>
> Section 16 (1) ... no law shall make any provision that is discriminatory either of itself or in its effect.
>
> (3) In this section, 'discriminatory' means affording different treatment to different persons attributable wholly or mainly to their respective descriptions by race, caste, place of origin, political opinions, colour, creed or sex whereby persons of one such description are subjected to disabilities or restrictions to which persons of another such description are not made subject or are accorded privileges or advantages that are not accorded to persons of another such description.

Lord Hoffmann found that section 16—although it clearly prohibited racial discrimination—was not involved since the difference in treatment was neither based on an enumerated ground such as race, nor could the provision be extended to grounds not enumerated therein. More importantly, section 3 was also not invoked since—although it did refer to non-discrimination by reason of, inter alia, race—neither did the case involve any of the specific justiciable rights mentioned in the provision, nor did section 3 enshrine a general justiciable principle of equality under which distinctions like the present one could be challenged.[15] Thus, while he agreed that section 3 did express the general principle of equality which is important in a democracy and thus frequently invoked by courts in judicial review as a matter of reasonableness or rationality review, it did not express an independent principle for courts to adjudicate on. According to him: '[t]he fact that equality of treatment is a general principle of rational behaviour does not entail that it should necessarily be a justiciable principle—that it should always be the judges who have the last word on whether the principle has been observed.'[16]

Although *Matadeen* concerned a specific constitutional context (Mauritian), the case came to be regarded as sounding the death knell for the recognition of a general principle of equality at common law.[17] Indeed, *Matadeen* was directly relied upon by the Supreme Court in *Gallaher* to hold that: 'the domestic law of this country does not recognise equal treatment as a distinct principle of administrative law'[18] and that '[t]he common law principle of equality is usually no more than a particular application of the ordinary requirement of rationality imposed on public authorities.'[19]

Gallaher though is an unusual case. Its facts concerned the revocation of an assurance offered by the Office of Fair Trading which was made in error. The claimant had argued that such revocation was a breach of the public law duty of equal treatment. Arguably, the facts did not quite fit the mould of equal treatment. There seemed to be a mismatch between the contention that the public authority was obliged to follow through on its erroneous decision and the ground chosen for making that contention: equal treatment. The Supreme Court found that no such ground actually existed at common law to be making this contention.

As Hayley Hooper argues, *Gallaher* may be correct in its finding that UK public law excludes an independent ground of judicial review like equality or equal treatment. But the finding is acontextual because it was made in the context of *Gallaher* which was 'a straightforward rationality case'[20] and not a case of equal treatment. *Matadeen*, which *was* a case of equal treatment, had already established that equal treatment was not an independent principle either under the Mauritian constitution or under common law. *Gallaher* only confirmed what was already plain, that 'common law has historically lacked a well-developed equality dimension.'[21]

[15] ibid [16].
[16] ibid [9].
[17] Cf O'Cinneide, 'Fumbling Towards Coherence' (n 1).
[18] *Matadeen* (n 12) [24] (Lord Carnwath).
[19] *Matadeen* (n 12) [50] (Lord Sumption).
[20] Hayley J Hooper, 'From Early Resolution to Conceptual Confusion: *R (on the application of Gallaher Group Ltd) v Competition and Markets Authority*' [2019] Public Law 460, 466.
[21] O'Cinneide, 'Equality: A Core Common Law Principle, or "Mere" Rationality?' (n 1) 177.

8.3 Racial Discrimination at Common Law

The rejection of a general principle of equality at common law could be seen, inter alia, as implying the rejection of a principle of prohibition of racial discrimination or a principle of anti-racism. This section argues that this is not the case. In fact, anti-racism, and in particular the prohibition of racial discrimination, is treated distinctly from equality and often with great significance. But given that it is nestled within the traditional grounds of review—especially *Wednesbury* unreasonableness—it remains obscure and, as a consequence, overshadowed in practice by statutory law.

8.3.1 Early Developments

One of the strongest early expressions of the prohibition of racial discrimination at common law appears in *Oppenheimer v Cattermole*.[22] The case concerned the question whether UK courts could recognize a decree passed by the Nazi government which stripped Jewish persons of their citizenship when they emigrated from Germany. The consequence of such recognition would have been the deprivation of benefit of a double taxation treaty between the UK and Germany. In the words of Lord Cross:

> if the decree had simply provided that all Germans who had left Germany since Hitler's advent to power with the intention of making their homes elsewhere should cease to be German nationals it may be that our courts would have had to recognise it even though many of those concerned were not in truth voluntary emigrants but had been driven from their native land. But the 1941 decree did not deprive all 'émigrés' of their status as German nationals. It only deprived Jewish émigrés of their citizenship ... what we are concerned with here is legislation which takes away without compensation from a section of the citizen body *singled out on racial grounds* all their property on which the state passing the legislation can lay its hands and, in addition, deprives them of their citizenship. To my mind a law of this sort constitutes so grave an infringement of human rights that the courts of this country ought to refuse to recognise it as a law at all.[23]

Similarly, Lord Hodson was unequivocal: 'The courts of this country are not in my opinion obliged to shut their eyes to the shocking nature of such legislation as the 1941 decree if and when it falls for consideration.'[24] The 'shocking nature' of the

22 [1976] AC 249 [hereafter *Oppenheimer*].
23 ibid 277 (emphasis supplied).
24 ibid 265.

law was not that it deprived some or even all émigrés of their German citizenship, but that it specifically 'singled out' Jewish people 'on racial grounds'.[25] In other words, it was not *any* distinction or a breach of the general principle of equality which led the UK courts to disregard the decree. It was racial discrimination in particular which the Court found shocking.

This distinction between the general principle of equality or equal treatment on the one hand and the prohibition of racial discrimination on the other hand has been crucial yet overlooked in common law jurisprudence. In *Matadeen*, Lord Hoffmann had relied on this distinction in deciding whether the impugned regulations were constitutional:

> It is perhaps a tribute to the scheme ... that it has not at any stage been claimed by its opponents in these proceedings that it discriminates unfairly on racial grounds; that it gives an advantage to children from families which speak an Oriental language as their mother tongue. Indeed, it can be said that no objection is made to the principle of introducing an optional Oriental language subject into the syllabus of the CPE. The complaint is about timing. It is said that to make the change on less than a year's notice was unfair to those children who had, for one reason or another, not studied an Oriental language from the beginning of their primary schooling. Thus the allegation is of discrimination, not on grounds of race, or place of origin, or home language, but simply between those children who had studied an Oriental language at school and those who had not.[26]

The challenge in *Matadeen* failed because this 'simple' distinction between those who had and had not studied an Oriental language was not one that was unconstitutional under section 3 of the Constitution of Mauritius for two reasons: first, no general justiciable principle of equality existed in section 3; and secondly, the distinction was not made on racial grounds. Had the distinction been made on racial grounds, Lord Hoffmann's remarks leave little doubt that the distinction would have been unconstitutional not because it breached the general principle of equality but specifically the prohibition of racial discrimination under section 16 of the Mauritian Constitution. Yet, the blow to the recognition of a general principle of equality delivered by the *Matadeen* court has overshadowed the recognition of the embargo on racial discrimination both under the written constitution of Mauritius and perhaps even under common law. Lord Hoffmann's passages in *Matadeen* can be mistaken for rejecting the principle of equality at common law wholesale, despite their categorical rejection of racial discrimination.

But *Oppenheimer* and *Matadeen* are essentially about discrimination which occurred outside the UK. Writing in 1972, Anthony Lester and Geoffrey Bindman

[25] ibid 277.
[26] *Matadeen* (n 12) [3].

had foreseen this trend.[27] According to them, common law had mainly dealt with 'discriminatory status existing under *foreign* law' rather than 'racial discrimination committed *in this country*'.[28] Their sense was that common law judicial review in the UK had been devoid of 'a coherent, egalitarian philosophy', marked by 'ethical aimlessness' which was 'especially striking in the relationship between racial discrimination and the Common Law ... the English Bench hav[ing] displayed a marked insensitivity to the manifestations of racial discrimination'.[29]

For example, in the 1944 case of *Constantine v Imperial Hotels*,[30] Birkett J had found against an innkeeper who had refused to accommodate a well-known West-Indian cricketer on the grounds of his race. Despite a favourable judgment, it was not obvious on the face of the record that the case was decided on the ground of prohibition of racial discrimination rather than simply the breach of an innkeeper's duty under common law.

Ambiguity persisted in late r cases such as *Scala Ballroom (Wolverhampton) Ltd v Ratcliffe*[31] which concerned a challenge to a musician's union barring its members from performing for a ballroom which excluded patrons of colour. The ballroom sought to obtain an injunction against the union. The Court denied the injunction, holding that a union barring members from performing for a venue was 'lawful protection of their members' interests and livelihood'.[32] Yet, the Court held that the ballroom could retain the colour bar in its own business interest. The Court thus prevented the union from effectively enforcing a prohibition of racial discrimination against the ballroom, adopting, in the final analysis, a laissez-faire understanding of anti-racism in the context of private relationships and contracts: that those who wanted to not discriminate could well do so but there was no duty under common law for authorities or service providers to follow suit. In the absence of a statute prohibiting private individuals from discrimination (before 1965 when the first race relations statute was enacted), common law was 'essentially passive' in combating racial discrimination in the UK.[33]

This passivity is also visible in the judicial treatment of racial discrimination outside the UK when it has concerned the conduct of private actors. Consider, for example, *R v Lewisham LBC ex p Shell UK*[34] which involved a judicial review challenge to a policy adopted by the Lewisham Borough Council boycotting all Shell products. The Council represented over 18 per cent Black people in the borough

[27] Anthony Lester and Geoffrey Bindman, *Race and Law* (Penguin 1972) [hereafter Lester and Bindman, *Race and Law*].

[28] ibid 24 (emphasis in original).

[29] ibid 70; Anthony Lester, 'English Judges as Lawmakers' [1993] Public Law 269; Anthony Lester, 'Discrimination: What Can Lawyers Learn from History' [1994] Public Law 224.

[30] [1944] KB 69.

[31] [1958] 3 All ER 220.

[32] [1958] 1 WLK at 72.

[33] Lester and Bindman, *Race and Law* (n 27) 53–57.

[34] [1990] Pens LR 241 (1987).

of Lewisham and had over time taken steps to show opposition to apartheid in South Africa to promote good race relations and to show its anti-racist commitment.[35] The boycott of Shell and its products was adopted as the company traded in South Africa. Shell argued that the policy was ultra vires because it was based on irrelevant considerations or purpose, or in the alternative, was unreasonable in the *Wednesbury* sense.[36] The Court held that:

> having regard to the fact that this is a multi-racial borough, the Council was entitled to decide on the basis of its own experience and perception that it was in the interests of good race relations that trading with a particular company should cease because of its links with apartheid... the Council's decision not to continue to trade with Shell UK, unless in effect it was obliged to do so, could not be successfully attacked as being unreasonable in a Wednesbury sense.[37]

On the one hand, the Court was clear that a policy to pursue good race relations and anti-racism could be achieved by a boycott such as the present one, and that it was reasonable to do so. On the other hand, the policy was found to be ultra vires because despite this reasonable purpose, it was mixed-up with another 'extraneous and impermissible purpose': of having Shell cease trading in South Africa.[38] Shell itself had done nothing unlawful in the UK. The ultimate purpose was thus found to be tainted, making the policy unlawful.[39]

Ex p Shell did two things. First, it relegated the promotion of good race relations and anti-racism to norms of lesser importance than the freedom of private companies to run their businesses. It showed that under common law (and apart from the positive duty that existed then under section 71 of the Race Relations Act 1976), the promotion of good race relations and anti-racism, although reasonable on their own, eventually had to give way to private interests. Second, it established that indifference, or even support, for racial discrimination abroad was not per se against UK law.

Similarly, *Wheeler v Leicester CC*[40] concerned a judicial review challenge to a decision of a city council refusing the use of a sports ground to a football club, unless it condemned the English team's proposal to send a team to apartheid South Africa. The Court of Appeal held that the council which had a population of about 25 per cent Asian, African, and Caribbean origins could consider 'that good relations between persons of different racial groups were encouraged by their taking a firm

[35] ibid [9]–[10].
[36] ibid [45] [48].
[37] ibid [69].
[38] ibid [70] [72].
[39] ibid [71].
[40] [1985] AC 1054.

stand on relations with South Africa'.[41] However, the House of Lords found that although the council were entitled to take into account the need to promote good race relations in allowing use of a sports ground, the manner in which the decision was taken was unfair. As Lord Templeman put it: 'A private individual or a private organisation cannot be obliged to display zeal in the pursuit of an object sought by a public authority and cannot be obliged to publish views dictated by a public authority.'[42] In effect, the council's decision to punish a club for not doing as it would have liked the club to do (to condemn the team's decision to tour South Africa) was considered to infringe on individual freedoms to an extent considered unfair. As Lord Roskill noted:

> Persuasion, even powerful persuasion, is always a permissible way of seeking to obtain an objective. But in a field where other views can equally legitimately be held, persuasion, however powerful, must not be allowed to cross that line where it moves into the field of illegitimate pressure coupled with the threat of sanctions.[43]

The pursuit of anti-racism thus had only persuasive value when it came to judging the reasonableness of the actions of public authorities. Since *Wheeler* is, as Lord Carnwath notes, 'one of the very few at the highest level where pure *Wednesbury* has been used directly as a ground of decision,'[44] it stands as one of the clearest examples of the slight weight attached to anti-racism in judging unreasonableness 'in the Wednesbury sense'.[45]

This shows three things. First, when anti-racism comes into conflict with established constitutional rights such as freedom of contract or freedom of speech, the former gives way to the latter. Secondly, the pursuit of anti-racism outside the UK, though deemed permissible, is actually limited. Thirdly and most importantly, common law has taken a strange shape where public authorities may pursue or even be bound by anti-racism, but they cannot compel private actors to abide by it lest they impinge on individual freedoms. This demarcation effectively undermines the structural view of racial discrimination which connects racial discrimination enacted at the very top by the state with how individuals and private actors behave. The inability to conceive common law as steering public authorities to in turn steer private actors thus draws an artificial wedge in the understanding of racism or racial discrimination which undermines what anti-racism should be about.

[41] ibid 1058.
[42] ibid 1080.
[43] ibid 1078.
[44] Lord Carnwath, 'From Judicial Outrage to Sliding Scales – Where Next for Wednesbury?' ALBA Annual Lecture (12 November 2013) <https://www.supremecourt.uk/docs/speech-131112-lord-carnwath.pdf> (accessed 19 June 2023).
[45] ibid 1078 (Lord Roskill).

8.3.2 Recent Strides

So, what has changed since Lester and Bindman wrote their seminal text in 1972? There is some evidence that decisions like *Oppenheimer* and *Matadeen* have had sway in the context of the exercise of state power and how it is judged when it may constitute racial discrimination 'in this country'.[46] A series of cases brought in the early noughties concerning entitlement of non-white soldiers who served in the British army during the second world war shows this development prominently.

Gurung v Ministry of Defence[47] was the first and the most emphatic in the series of developments. The case concerned an application for judicial review by a group of octogenarian Nepalese nationals who were recruited for the Gurkha rifle brigades. They served in the British contingent against the Japanese in the second world war and were captured and released at the end of the war. They were excluded from the scheme of ex gratia payment of compensation to former prisoners of war announced by the British government in November 2000. There were about 650 such soldiers who were excluded. The assumption was that, post-independence, these soldiers were now the responsibility of the sovereign states of India, Pakistan, Nepal, and so on and the scheme was mainly for European members of the British army who had served in the second world war.[48]

The exclusion of Nepalese soldiers from ex gratia compensation was challenged on two grounds: 'first, on the basis that the Defendant's decision to deny compensation is "irrational" as infringing common law principles of equality of treatment, and secondly, on the basis that the decision infringes the Claimants' rights under Articles 14 and 8 of the European Convention on Human Rights'.[49] In both instances, the main question before the Court was whether the exclusion of Gurkha soldiers was based on race and thus irrational or in contravention of the rights under the European Convention on Human Rights (ECHR). Mr Justice McCombe explained the nature of the common law challenge thus:

> What we are concerned with are questions of alleged irrationality in the decision making process and I find myself convinced that, at the present day, if a decision-maker is considering the application of a distinction of this kind, originally deriving from 19th century United Kingdom and Colonial legislation, he or she will be concerned with whether the criteria thrown up by such legislation were for <u>practical</u> purposes racial in nature.[50]

46 Lester and Bindman, *Race and Law* (n 27) 24.
47 [2002] EWHC 2463 (Admin) [hereafter *Gurung*].
48 ibid [10].
49 ibid [3].
50 ibid [28] (emphasis in original).

He found that the exclusion of Gurkha soldiers, indeed, 'was racial in nature'[51] and that a decision maker in the year 2000 could not rationally rely on colonial legislation which drew a distinction between European and non-European soldiers for apportioning benefits.[52] Though Mr Justice McCombe also saw the principle of equal treatment favourably as part of the common law tradition, his decision yet rested on what was argued before the Court in particular: that racial distinctions, de jure or de facto, are irrational.[53] In particular, in his view, *Wednesbury* unreasonableness or irrationality could accommodate both the conceptual view of discrimination based on racial grounds and the contextual and historical view of racial discrimination to be judged in light of colonialism.

Gurung however is an outlier. Succeeding common law cases involving racial discrimination cite *Gurung* for the principle of prohibition of racial discrimination as part of rationality review but do not find for racial discrimination in fact. More importantly, the full thrust of *Gurung's* reasoning has not been reckoned with in later case law.

Gurung was followed by *The Association of British Civilian Internees Far Eastern Region v Secretary of State for Defence*,[54] which concerned the situation of people who were British subjects at the time of their internment and who had permanently settled in the UK after the second world war. They were refused a £10,000 payment by the Secretary of State for Defence because neither they nor any of their parents or grandparents was born in the UK. The Court agreed that the refusal could not be rationally based on race, but it could yet be based on 'close links' with the UK at the time of internment.[55] The birth criterion was seen as giving effect to 'close links' as a rational basis of distinction.

The question that the Court in *Abcifer* did not ask was whether anyone other than those ethnically white-British could have had 'close links' with the UK in the sense of having been born or having parents or grandparents who were born in the UK at the time of the second world war. *Abcifer* did not follow *Gurung*'s lead of a contextual and historical analysis of apparently neutral distinctions which were not racial on the face of it but operated to racialize people in the context of colonization. The Court thus ended up ignoring the direct correspondence between the birth criterion and race, which a later court in *Secretary of State for Defence v Mrs Diana Elias*[56] found 'surprising' given that 'a race discrimination challenge had succeeded [*Gurung*] in an earlier application for judicial review of a scheme to compensate military prisoners of war, who had suffered at the hands of the Japanese in the Second World War'[57]. In fact, even the Secretary of State later

51 ibid [19].
52 ibid [53] [54].
53 ibid [59].
54 [2003] EWCA Civ 473 [hereafter *Abcifer*].
55 ibid [42] [46].
56 [2006] EWCA Civ 1293 [hereafter *Elias*].
57 ibid [28].

conceded that the birth link criterion was indirectly discriminatory and contrary to the Race Relations Act 1976.[58] The Court in *Elias* rightly saw *Abcifer* as 'argued and therefore decided on more conventional judicial review lines'[59] given that race discrimination was not argued explicitly as part of rationality review.

The *Elias* court chose a different path for itself, in what Lord Justice Mummery called, 'no ordinary race discrimination case'.[60] The facts were similar to other challenges to ex gratia compensation schemes set up by the Secretary of State for Defence in the early 2000s. The claimant, Mrs Diana Elias, was an octogenarian who took great pride in being a British subject. She was born in Hong Kong and was interned during Japanese occupation between 1941 and 1945. As the Court noted: 'She was interned because she was a British civilian, as evidenced by her registration with the British High Commission and by the inclusion of her name and the names of her parents and siblings in a list handed to the Japanese by the British authorities.'[61] Yet, she was ineligible for compensation of £10,000 because neither she nor her parents or grandparents were born in the UK. Mrs Elias was deeply aggrieved and found it 'offensive to be told that she is not "British enough" to be compensated, although she was "British enough" to be interned'.[62] The Court held that her exclusion constituted indirect discrimination under the Race Relations Act 1976 because:

> The birth link criteria take an apparently neutral form, which applies or would apply equally to all applicants for payments under the Compensation Scheme. It is the application of the neutrally worded criteria which produces the disparate adverse impact and puts persons of the same national origins at a particular disadvantage when compared with other persons.[63]

Such adverse impact on those of non-UK national origin could not be justified since the Secretary of State had not discharged their burden for showing that they had had due regard to the potentially discriminatory effects of the birth link criteria.[64] This finding, unlike *Gurung*, was made in the context of the Race Relations Act 1976 and not under common law since *Elias* was argued as such. Nevertheless, judges in *Elias* noted the 'constitutional' dimensions of the case and did not seem to limit the finding of racial discrimination to the statutory context.[65]

Thus, courts since *Gurung* seem to have reiterated the importance of the prohibition of racial discrimination but their iterations seem to be obiter and largely

58 ibid [23] [28].
59 ibid.
60 ibid [1].
61 ibid [4].
62 ibid [6].
63 ibid [115].
64 ibid [131]–[133].
65 ibid [268] (Arden LJ), [49] [76] (Mummery LJ).

rhetorical. What is clear is that despite *Gurung*, common law appears to resist a strong or unambiguous commitment to anti-racism.

8.4 The Discomfiture with Common Law

The significance of the trajectory of cases considered in the previous section lies in the fact that succeeding case law has come to accept the 'common ground' that racial discrimination is contrary to both the common law and statutory law.[66] Yet, claims of racial discrimination at common law are rarely argued on their own like in *Gurung*, or even when invoked alongside statutory law like in *Elias*, they are largely overlooked. Though examples of either kind are sparse, this section collates them and shows that from the little attention common law claims do receive, it is difficult to discern a unified approach to racial discrimination.[67] It explores two approaches to judicial review which show the marked discomfiture in applying common law when it comes to racial discrimination.

8.4.1 Common Law as Indistinct from Statutory Law

On the one hand is the approach which equates common law with statutory law. For example, in *R v Birmingham City Council ex p Darshan Kaur*,[68] it was held that a consultative process was not characterized by racial discrimination at common law when interpreters were provided only in some languages such as Punjabi, Hindi, and Urdu, while those who spoke other languages were not catered for. This was the approach taken by Lord Woolf in *R v Governors of Small Heath School ex p Birmingham City Council*[69] under statutory law, but Lord Farquharson in *Darshan Kaur* 'could see no reason why at common law the approach should be any different'.[70] The remark seems to equate the law on racial discrimination under statutory law with common law but without a clear explanation, the remark seems to be no more than an obiter.

A later decision in *Annis Mangera v Ministry of Defence*[71] confirms that equating common law with statutory protections serves to limit the ambit of the former

[66] *R (Mohammed) v Secretary of State for Defence* (2007) 104(20) LSG 32 [10] (Latha LJ) [hereafter *Mohammed*].

[67] This is perhaps true of common law in general in any area given its very nature. Rules of common law are not obvious and discernible only with deductive reasoning with some effort and often without consensus. The application of rules of common law is consequently, relatively sparse in comparison with statutory law. The treatment of racial discrimination is no different within common law jurisprudence.

[68] [1990] 7 WLUK 11.

[69] [1989] IRLR 173.

[70] The Times Law Report (11 July 1990) at p 37.

[71] [2003] EWCA Civ 80.

rather than to expand common law or to strengthen the prohibition of racial discrimination at common law that was set out in *Gurung*. The appellant in *Mangera* served in the army for over ten years but alleged that he was never offered red meat in that period and that this constituted racial discrimination under the Race Relations Act 1976. Section 75(9) of the Race Relations Act 1976 provided that complaints in relation to service in forces should be brought to a Defence Council and not an Employment Tribunal, or first made to an officer and only then can the Employment Tribunal be approached. Mr Mangera neither went before the Defence Council nor did he present his complaint to an officer. The question before the Court of Appeal was whether the requirement to make a prior complaint under the Race Relations Act 1976 was compliant with article 6 of the ECHR which guaranteed access to courts. Lord Justice Buxton found that it was and held that:

> The offence of discrimination there created however is not and cannot be a common law tort ... That is because there is no general right in our law not to be discriminated against. That right, important though it is, is enforced only in particular situations, of which employment is one.[72]

Mangera confirmed that the Race Relations Act 1976 did no more in either common law or in human rights law under the Human Rights Act 1998 to create a self-standing right against non-discrimination or specifically one in relation to racial discrimination. In other words, according to the *Mangera* court, neither was there a constitutional prohibition of racial discrimination under common law nor had the statutory prohibitions of racial discrimination had a constitutionalizing effect. This has largely been the position since the advent of the Human Rights Act 1998 and confirms McColgan's observation that:

> judicial attitudes towards the discrimination legislation have at times been little short of obstructive, particular hostility being reserved for legislative attempts to eradicate race discrimination. There have been many judicial utterances as to the importance of non-discrimination, but the common law has afforded scant protection to it.[73]

Claims under common law and convention rights have thus been merged to perilous effect. Take for example, *R (on the application of Bibi) v Secretary of State for the Home Department*[74] which concerned an immigration rule requiring foreign spouses to pass a test in English before moving to the UK. The rule was challenged as contrary to articles 8 and 14 of the ECHR and as 'irrational and therefore

[72] ibid [24].
[73] McColgan, 'Discrimination Law and the Human Rights Act 1998' (n 1) 241.
[74] [2015] UKSC 68.

unlawful on common law principles'.[75] Lady Hale's judgment dealt with the article 8 contention on its own but, without preamble or explanation, merged the contention on article 14 with rationality review in the following way:

> [D]irect discrimination, even on grounds of nationality, is capable of justification under article 14. In the context of immigration, nationality is not a particularly 'suspect' classification. The appellants complain that the exemptions are irrational. Canadians, for example, are exempt, even though there are many Franco-phone Canadians for whom English is not the first language and some for whom it is not even a second language. Nigerians, on the other hand, are not exempt even though English is the medium of instruction in all Nigerian secondary and most Nigerian primary schools. The Anglo-phone Caribbean countries are exempt, even though their success rate in the LUK test for ILR is only average.[76]
>
> [I]n the context of a language requirement, being a national of an Anglo-phone country is a reasonable proxy for a sufficient familiarity with the English language to be able to begin to integrate with the local community immediately on arrival. This is a context in which a bright line rule makes sense.[77]

The effect of this merger was twofold. First, 'irrationality' as a ground of judicial review mysteriously became the standard of review for justifying direct discrimination based on nationality under article 14. Secondly, the claim of discrimination based on race or ethnicity, which was a claim of indirect not direct discrimination, was entirely ignored. Thus, nothing was said either about the common law challenge or about indirect discrimination based on race or ethnicity. No other individual opinion in *Bibi* queried this approach. Lord Hodge simply agreed with Lady Hale's approach which dismissed the article 14 challenge in the same breath as the common law challenge.[78] Lord Neuberger too agreed with the article 14 analysis but made no mention of the common law challenge.[79] The claim ultimately failed.

Common law claims are also clubbed with challenges under the Equality Act 2010. For example, *R (Hottak) v Foreign Secretary*[80] challenged the difference in a British scheme of assistance applicable to locally employed Afghan staff as compared to those governed by the scheme in Iraq, both under the Equality Act 2010 and the 'common law prohibition of discrimination'.[81] The Divisional Court summarily dismissed the claim as a claim of *Wednesbury* unreasonableness where no unreasonableness could be detected when the two schemes were distinguishable

75 ibid [2].
76 ibid [57].
77 ibid [58].
78 ibid [75].
79 ibid [99].
80 [2016] 1 WLR.
81 ibid [84].

given that: 'The security considerations were different; the ability to investigate threats was different; the possibility of differentiating between an intimidation policy and ex gratia benefits to reflect service arose only in Afghanistan. The two schemes were developed to reflect the circumstances prevailing at different time in different countries.'[82] The Court of Appeal agreed.[83] While the Court had considered the claim of direct discrimination under the Equality Act 2010 to be based on the ground of race, the claim under common law was seen as simply one of irrationality and not one based on racial discrimination in the *Gurung* sense, that is, one that is 'racial in nature'. No explanation for this variance was offered in the judgment.

8.4.2 Common Law as Too Distinct from Statutory Law

On the other hand is the approach which draws a sharp line between common law and statutory law. For example, in *R (on the application of Limbu et al) v Secretary of State for the Home Department*,[84] the Court insisted that a common law claim for discrimination had to be examined as a matter of the common law principle of equal treatment which in turn was part of rationality review, even if the claim based on convention rights did not apply. According to Mr Justice Blake:

> Even if Article 14 was not engaged, the common law principle of equal treatment certainly would be. Moreover, for the reasons explained by McCombe J in *Gurung*, that I gratefully adopt, the common law principle is an important instrument whereby it can be determined whether a discretionary public law decision is rational ... the common law and Convention principle essentially walk hand in hand together, although the common law principle has to be applied through the public law doctrine of rationality. Thus even if Article 14 was not in play the court *should* enquire: "Was it open to a reasonable [Secretary of State for the Home Department] properly directing herself to conclude that the differences in treatment between Gurkhas and other non UK nationals was justified by reasons of differences of distinction in their situation so as not to infringe the common law principle of equality?"[85]

Mr Justice Blake's view appreciates the distinction between common law and convention rights and accords appropriate weight to the authority of *Gurung* not only to the extent that it necessitates rationality review but also requires rationality

[82] ibid [85].
[83] ibid [86].
[84] [2008] EWHC 2261 (Admin).
[85] ibid [50] (emphasis in original).

review in light of relevant historical and contextual background.[86] However, the racial discrimination challenge in *Limbu* was confined to the Race Relations Act 1976 and was summarily dismissed as discrimination therein was seen as one based on nationality not race and in any case authorized by immigration law.[87] Thus, the contextual and historical analysis under rationality review which identified Gurkha soldiers' historic debt to the UK had little to do (at least explicitly) with racial discrimination. So, even though that part of the challenge succeeded, it was purely on grounds of irrationality and not because the irrational distinction was 'racial in nature'[88]. No connection between racial discrimination under Convention rights or the Race Relations Act 1976 and the ground of irrationality seems to have been made.

In yet other cases, there is no link made between statutory and common law challenges with the effect that the latter is entirely ignored. Thus, in *Saleh Mohammad Turani v Secretary of State for the Home Department*,[89] Simler LJ made no link between the claim of indirect racial discrimination and the claim of irrationality under common law alleged against a scheme which excluded Palestinian refugees for consideration for asylum.[90] The claim of racial discrimination was subsumed by statutory law entirely.

Similarly, the common law cause of action may be mentioned but never examined. For example, *R (on the application of Coughlan) v Minister for the Cabinet Office*[91] concerned a judicial review challenge to proposed changes to secondary legislation governing local elections and in particular the requirement for voters to produce specified identification documents. The appellant argued that the requirement served 'to disenfranchise the poor and vulnerable who already struggle to have their voices heard'.[92] Five intervenors made written submissions in the case. Operation Black Vote, Runnymede Trust, and Voice4Change England argued that the requirement presented 'a significant barrier to democratic participation for ethnic minority communities by deterring or preventing those who are entitled to vote from voting'.[93] LGBT Foundation and Stonewall raised similar concerns on behalf of the lesbian, gay, bisexual, and transgender community. The legal question considered though was not whether the requirement was discriminatory but whether it was ultra vires section 10(2)(a) of the Representation of the People Act 2000. The Supreme Court found that the requirement was well within the powers of the parent legislation especially the phrase 'how voting at the elections is to take

86 ibid [15].
87 ibid [44].
88 *Gurung* (n 47).
89 [2021] EWCA Civ 348.
90 Affirmed in *R (on the application of Marouf) v Secretary of State for the Home Department* [2023] UKSC 23 [17].
91 [2022] UKSC 11.
92 ibid [2].
93 ibid (scare quotes removed).

place'.[94] The challenge was thus dismissed without any discussion of racial discrimination or other forms of discrimination.

The current state of the prohibition of racial discrimination at common law can be summed up thus. First, *qua Gurung*, there is evidence that the prohibition of racial discrimination has meaning of its own which is distinct from the general principle of equality. The prohibition of racial discrimination is considered to attack distinctions which 'single out' people on racial grounds, thus making the distinction particularly 'shocking',[95] 'unfair',[96] or 'offensive'[97] or which are 'for practical purposes racial in nature' when viewed, for example, in the context of a colonial legislation.[98] The prohibition seems on all fours with anti-racism as a legal principle as understood in Chapter 4. Yet, secondly, like equality or equal treatment, the prohibition of racial discrimination is not a self-standing ground of review and is invoked largely within the ground of *Wednesbury* unreasonableness or rationality review. That though has not helped it being addressed evenly across case law. There is considerable variance in the attention devoted to a common law claim based on racial discrimination—often such a claim is curiously merged with, entirely subsumed within, or bluntly ignored by, claims of racial discrimination under statutory law. As a result, no consistent application of a prohibition of racial discrimination at common law can be discerned, but more importantly, the thrust of early decisions such as *Oppenheimer*, *Gurung*, and *Elias* in giving effect to a principle of anti-racism in racial discrimination seems to have been entirely lost.

8.5 Structural Racism and Common Law

The interest in what happens to common law in 'an age of statutes'[99] is an old one.[100] But it is worth reflecting why common law is of relevance to *this* book. In *Race and Law*, the first and till date the only comprehensive text in discrimination law on race, racism, and racial discrimination in the UK, Lester and Bindman had begun their foray dedicating the first chapter of the book to common law.[101] Having examined the rather tardy pace of development of common law on racial discrimination, they had dedicated the rest of the book for making a case for a

94 Representation of the People Act 2000, s 10(2)(a).
95 *Oppenheimer* (n 22) 265.
96 *Matadeen* (n 12) [3].
97 *Elias* (n 56) [6].
98 *Gurung* (n 47) [29].
99 Guido Calabresi, *A Common Law for the Age of the Statutes* (Harvard University Press 1982).
100 Roscoe Pound, 'Law and Legislation' (1908) 21 Harvard Law Review 383; HR Hahlo and LCB Gower, 'Here Lies the Common Law: Rest in Peace' (1967) 30(3) Modern Law Review 241; JF Burrows, 'The Interrelation Between Common Law and Statute' (1976) 3 Otago Law Review 583; PS Atiyah, 'Common Law and Statute Law' (1985) 48 Modern Law Review 1; Peter L Strauss, 'The Common Law and Statutes' (1999) 70 University of Colorado Law Review 225.
101 Lester and Bindman, *Race and Law* (n 27).

shift towards statutory law. The tide of development of the law in the area has since firmly turned towards statutory law. Discussions of common law are thus rare, and where they do exist, relatively brief.[102] This is understandable since, as this chapter confirms, common law's contribution to addressing racial discrimination has been confirmedly minor. In contrast, the pace of development of statutory law has been rapid and has surpassed common law substantively in terms of developing wide-ranging case law on the meaning of racial discrimination, the scope of racial grounds, the test for racial discrimination, the range of appropriate remedies, etc.[103]

But common law, as Allan Hutchinson argues, is thoroughly organic, 'a perpetual work-in-progress—evanescent, dynamic, messy, productive, tantalizing, and bottom up'.[104] It thus has not remained still while statutory law on racial discrimination was developing. It deserves examination as it stands today and not only at the time Lester and Bindman wrote, that is, before statutory law on the subject emerged. In fact, it is common law's constantly evolving relationship with statutory law which gives us both a reason for worry and hope in the context of anti-racism. As argued in this chapter, the current state of common law on racial discrimination is worrisome for its unresolved but unquestionably inferior relationship to statutory law. Yet there is good reason for considering common law and its relationship with statutory law seriously on normative grounds for there is hope in what it can yield in addressing structural racism, alongside statutory law.

As a general matter, in a country such as the UK where there is no single document in the form of a written constitution, it is often common law which embodies principles of constitutional importance developed over a considerable period of time. Common law provides the necessary dynamism where 'legislation, even when fleshed out by detailed subordinate legislation, simply cannot anticipate and provide for the great variety of cases which are likely to arise'.[105] At the same time, though open to change and being revised by the judges, common law principles cannot be 'repealed' in the same way as a statute which can be withdrawn by the government of the day. Common law thus serves as a backstop to majoritarian politics. Consequently, it is of particular significance to anti-majoritarian issues such as anti-racism which concerns interests of racialized minorities.

More specifically though, common law can be especially relevant in addressing structural racism. To recall, structural racism, as discussed in Part I of this book, has three principal features in terms of who enacts it, how it comes about, and what it does. First, it is ideated and effected primarily by the state at the highest level: the Parliament, the government or the executive, and the judiciary, rather

[102] McColgan, 'Discrimination Law and the Human Rights Act 1998' (n 1); O'Cinneide, 'Equality: A Core Common Law Principle, or "Mere" Rationality?' (n 1).
[103] Chapters 6 and 7 of this book.
[104] Allan C Hutchinson, *Evolution and the Common Law* (Cambridge University Press 2005).
[105] PS Atiyah, 'Common Law and Statute Law' (1985) 48 Modern Law Review 1, 5.

than private actors whether individuals or corporations. Second, it comes about through racialization which is the process of assigning racial meaning to different groups based on ethnicity, colour, national origin, nationality, language, etc. Third, it puts in place a framework of disadvantage for certain racialized groups to the advantage of others, a framework which can in turn be adopted and deployed by everyone whom the state governs.

Although public authorities can be challenged under statutory law, as we saw in Chapter 6, the Equality Act 2010 is mostly invoked and effective against private bodies as employers, service providers, etc. The possibility of challenging state action is greatly stymied under the Equality Act 2010 given how the sheer force of both legislative will and executive power has trumped any evidence of racial discrimination in recent case law.[106] The Equality Act 2010 has thus developed as a truly liberal model of discrimination which is perpetrated by individual actors against individual victims.

Likewise, the Human Rights Act 1988 can be engaged against public authorities.[107] But as we saw in Chapter 7, extraordinary weight is attached to the power of public authorities such that any proportionality analysis under the Human Rights Act 1998 necessarily fails. This is despite particularly high level of scrutiny attached to race as a 'suspect' ground of discrimination.[108] Further, not all cases of racial discrimination are challenged under the Human Rights Act 1998 as article 14 of the ECHR is only triggered when the matter falls within the ambit of another Convention right.

In contrast, common law judicial review is chiefly about the lawfulness of state action.[109] Although judicial review cannot strike down primary legislation in the UK, doctrines such as ultra vires, for example, are fundamental in checking excesses of executive power. In fact, as David Jenkins argues, given that ultra vires review is 'an original creation of the court ... [it] could conceivably stand as a common-law restraint upon parliamentary authority'.[110] Common law judicial review thus seems to act as an independent check on exercise of state power.[111]

Structural racism which is ideated and effected by the state can be addressed through common law judicial review because it puts the government in the dock. In particular, common law judicial review can be a useful site for challenging structural racism in matters which fall through the cracks of article 14 of the ECHR

[106] Chapter 6 of this book.

[107] Human Rights Act 1998, s 6.

[108] *Abdulaziz, Cabales and Balkandali v The United Kingdom* (1985) 7 EHRR 471.

[109] Timothy Endicott, *Administrative Law* (2nd edn, Oxford University Press 2011) 303 ('the core rationale for judicial review: that is, to promote responsible government by holding it unlawful for a public authority to act in a way that judges can identify as arbitrary').

[110] David Jenkins, 'From Unwritten to Written: Transformation in the British Common-Law Constitution' (2003) 36 Vanderbilt Journal of Transnational Law 863, 901.

[111] ibid 903 ('Common-law review should allow courts to feel more confident in scrutinizing secondary or even primary legislation against higher legal principles, even if Parliament still claims the theoretical authority to override judicial determination.').

if they do not fall within the ambit of another Convention right. Judicial review under common law can thus accomplish the first step in addressing structural racism by shifting the focus away from private agents and instead towards state action.

Gurung—where the common law prohibition of racial discrimination was most clearly stated and applied—is a good example of a case which was well-served by common law judicial review. To recall, *Gurung* concerned the exercise of non-statutory power by the Secretary of State for Defence for enacting discretionary compensation schemes. The exclusion of Gurkha soldiers from the scheme on racial grounds is arguably not something within the ambit of a convention right to invoke the protection of article 14 of the ECHR. The matter may be amenable for review under the Equality Act 2010 in principle; and indeed, a similar compensation scheme in *Elias* was successfully challenged under the Race Relations Act 1976. But given the practical limits explored in Chapter 6 to how the jurisprudence under the Equality Act 2010 has developed over time—to do with the focus on individual victims and perpetrators and a lack of a structural view of discrimination and the role of the state in it—Equality Act 2010 may provide little relief today.

But common law—especially the ground of irrationality—proved to be malleable enough to include interpretation akin to a principle of anti-racism in *Gurung*. First, as the Court put it, irrationality as a ground of review was open to asking whether a distinction 'originally deriving from 19th century United Kingdom and Colonial legislation ... [was] for practical purposes racial in nature'.[112] The reasoning allows the concepts of both coloniality and racialization to be accounted for. That is, the way irrationality review is carried out in *Gurung*, it shows awareness of both the context in which the review must take place (of colonization and its implications on how people were racialized) and to draw from that context the implications in the current context (whether importing a distinction between British and non-British soldiers from a colonial era legislation could racialize groups today). This then accords with the second feature of structural racism which concerns finding whether a distinction racializes or singles out people into racial groups in any way. Second, this approach seems principled because unlike adjudication of individual claims of discrimination brought under the Equality Act 2010, adjudication under common law expresses not only what was the right course of decision-making in the individual case, but also the normative dimension of what the right course of decision-making should be. As noted above, the prohibition of racial discrimination was thus duly recognized in later cases challenging similar compensation schemes enacted by the Secretary of State for Defence, as part of rationality review.[113]

112 *Gurung* (n 47) [28] (emphasis in original).
113 *Elias* (n 56) [268] (Arden LJ), [49] [76] (Mummery LJ); *Mohammed* (n 66).

Yet, the seeds sown in *Gurung* do not seem to have materialized and in fact remain aspirational in tapping into the potential of common law judicial review in taming state power. The aim of this chapter has been to show, *per* cases like *Oppenheimer*, *Gurung* et al—where common law can make a difference—in cases which (i) do not concern matters of human rights, and (ii) are to do with exercise of non-statutory power whose limits have traditionally been set by common law. Though judges have only done so rarely, a clear principle of anti-racism *can* be applied judicially as part of conventional judicial review grounds such as irrationality.

8.6 Conclusion

> Does it matter that the status of the equality principle within the common law is less than satisfactory? …The answer to this is 'yes'. There are grounds to be concerned about the current sub-optimal state of the common law.[114]

Colm O'Cinneide's remarks can be imported into the present context. Does it matter that the status of the prohibition of racial discrimination at common law is less than satisfactory? The answer to this, like for the broader question about the principle of equality, is 'yes'. As this chapter has shown, the interest in the status of prohibition of racial discrimination is independent of the status of the principle of equality given that racial discrimination at common law has often been treated distinctly from equal treatment generally. But despite early signs of a clear prohibition of racial discrimination developing at common law, the current state of jurisprudence of such a prohibition is sub-optimal. This is a matter of concern because it undermines the radical possibility of addressing structural racism and applying a principle of anti-racism via common law judicial review, especially where statutory law is inapplicable or ineffective. This is also important because structural racism finds an appropriate, more natural, fit with common law judicial review than statutory law which is not primarily concerned with structural discrimination to do with the state itself and has rather, as Chapters 6 and 7 showed, been limited to challenging actions of private actors as employers or service providers, or when it comes to the state, it is too lenient. As things stand however, common law appears to be doing much too little about anti-racism in the UK.

114 O'Cinneide, 'Equality: A Core Common Law Principle, or "Mere" Rationality?' (n 1) 191.

9
Racial Discrimination in Comparative Law

9.1 Introduction

'Racial discrimination is a topic rarely broached by comparative law scholars.'[1]

Tanya Katerí Hernández is right. It is hard to come by comparative work on racial discrimination law. The exceptions, that are out there, limit the work to two countries or to a specific issue such as affirmative action.[2] The vast differences in the intricacies of race and racism across contexts often make jurisdictional comparisons either laborious or worthless.

Jurisdictional and contextual specificities, however, need not arrest considered comparative reflection on legal doctrine. In fact, a self-conscious appreciation of the specificities can contribute to understanding the role of legal doctrine in pursuing anti-racism.

Chapter 9 turns to comparative law with this aim. It explores how jurisdictions beyond the UK respond to structural racism, and whether they exceed liberal and cultural anti-racism and put into effect anti-racism as a legal principle in a transformative sense.

The interest in looking beyond the UK and towards comparative law is simple. As the previous chapter showed, there is no constitutional principle of equality in the UK. The copious doctrine we have considered so far in the book is thus statutory. The natural question that arises then is whether 'a constitutional conception'[3] of equality can make a difference to the pursuit of anti-racism? In particular, do constitutions which embrace equality also embrace anti-racism as a legal principle?

The chapter answers this question in the affirmative. Constitutions *do* embrace anti-racism and in particular transformative anti-racism. They do not do so explicitly with the use of the term anti-racism. But their constitutional text and the normative frameworks informing the text, together, can signal a strong and unequivocal commitment to anti-racism. The commitment does not, by itself,

[1] Tanya Katerí Hernández, 'Racial Discrimination' in Laura Carlson et al (eds), *Comparative Discrimination Law* (Brill 2019) 1.

[2] Elaine Kennedy-Dubourdieu (ed), *Race and Inequality: World Perspectives on Affirmative Action* (Routledge 2006); Anne-Marie Mooney Cotter, *Race Matters: An International Legal Analysis of Race Discrimination* (Routledge 2006); Zoya Hasan et al (eds), *The Empire of Disgust: Prejudice, Discrimination, and Policy in India and the US* (OUP 2018).

[3] Nicholas Bamforth, 'Conceptions of Anti-Discrimination Law' (2004) 24 Oxford Journal of Legal Studies 693, 696–701.

Anti-Racism as a Legal Principle. Shreya Atrey, Oxford University Press. © Shreya Atrey 2026.
DOI: 10.1093/9780198947646.003.0012

effect transformative anti-racism, which, as Chapters 3 and 4 argued, is an action-oriented norm. Transformative anti-racism is activated by (i) opposing the state and state-like entities in enacting structural racism; (ii) through broad-based and urgent as opposed to piecemeal and incremental measures; (iii) to further intersectional justice. Transformative anti-racism in law can thus only be gauged appropriately by studying how law—constitutional, statutory, regulatory, common, comparative, or international—is actually *interpreted and applied*, not *imagined* or *stated*. The complete answer ultimately lies in constitutional doctrine, not constitutional text or spirit.

The chapter isolates four dimensions of legal doctrine considered in this book—personal, material, evidential, and remedial. It shows how each jurisdiction expands the scope of their constitutional law across these dimensions when responding to structural racism, in contrast with the British statutory and common law. The expansive scope of comparative doctrine enables the pursuit of transformative anti-racism. The chapter thus furnishes a basis for the UK to consider: first, adopting anti-racism as a legal principle; and second, developing coherent and consistent doctrine which gives effect to this principle in a transformative sense.

Two reasons justify the choice of jurisdictions in this chapter.

First, each of the jurisdictions—Canada, India, and South Africa—were part of the Empire and connected to the UK as their erstwhile colonizer and metropole. Race was critical in colonization in that it served a key function of both dividing colonized populations and also dividing the colonized and the colonizer.[4] In this way, race became a category of difference and ultimately hierarchy which justified the rule of the colonizer (deemed racially superior) over the colonized (deemed racially inferior).[5] This trajectory of difference *to* hierarchy *to* oppression is essentially the sequence of racialization *to* race *to* racism explained in Part I of this book. Decolonization thus entails the reversal of this logic, that is, anti-racism. Each of the jurisdictions has had to engage with anti-racism in imagining their postcolonial democracies. In the main, they have done this through their constitutions. For this reason, their constitutional law provides important lessons for *all* postcolonial democracies, including, mutatis mutandis, the UK.

Second, each of the four jurisdictions presents a unique postcolonial anti-racist illustration. The central case of race and the resulting racism in each of these jurisdictions is different: indigeneity (Canada), caste (India), and colour (South Africa).[6] It is the unique contexts pertaining to Indigenous peoples, Dalits, and

[4] Enakshi Dua, Narda Razack, and Jody Nyasha Warner, 'Race, Racism, and Empire: Reflections on Canada' (2005) 32 Social Justice 1.

[5] Partha Chatterjee, *The Nation and its Fragments* (Princeton University Press 1993) 19, 33; Tayyab Mahmud, 'Colonialism and Modern Constructions of Race: A Preliminary Inquiry' (1999) 53 University of Miami Law Review 1219, 1224–1228.

[6] These are, needless to say, not the only instantiations of issues of race and racism in these countries, and other kinds of racism exist as much, for example, anti-Black racism in Canada, Islamophobia in

Black people in these jurisdictions that animate the discussion in this chapter. Of course, there are commonalities between these jurisdictions too, given that these are all common law countries where English is one of the main languages of law.

It is nigh impossible to capture the full range of issues around race, racism, and anti-racism in comparative constitutional law. So, unlike the rest of this book, this chapter is *not* a root and branch review of these issues in constitutional law. Instead, it is a whistle-stop tour of constitutional responses to structural racism in Canadian, Indian, and South African constitutional law. The purpose is simply to gauge what difference a constitutional prohibition of racial discrimination makes in giving effect to anti-racism as a legal principle.[7] With this aim in mind, only illustrative apex courts' jurisprudence is considered. Much reliance is placed on what experts in these jurisdictions have said on the topic. The main interest is to draw lessons for the UK both from the primary and secondary literatures in comparative constitutional law.

9.2 Canada

The three sections below examine Canada's constitutional commitment to substantive equality (Section 9.2.1), its application in cases concerning discrimination against Indigenous peoples (Section 9.2.2), and finally, the doctrinal reasons for the limited evidence of transformative anti-racism in action despite lingering possibilities in Canadian constitutional law (Section 9.2.3).

9.2.1 Substantive equality

The Canadian Charter of Rights and Freedoms[8] ('Charter') was enacted as part of the Canadian Constitution in 1982. Section 15 of the Charter, titled 'equality rights' came into force three years later on 17 April 1985, and provides that:

(1) Every individual is equal before and under the law and has the right to the equal protection and equal benefit of the law without discrimination and, in

India, xenophobia in South Africa. The chapter cannot do justice to the full range of racial issues that arise in each jurisdiction and instead focusses on racism that has animated constitutionalism in each.

[7] This chapter mainly considers constitutional law as it has developed under the constitutional guarantees of equality and non-discrimination (except in the case of South Africa where constitutional anti-racism is considered more broadly in Section 9.4.3). But statutory anti-discrimination legislation too may be considered to have quasi-constitutional status, though this chapter does not consider statutory law in Canada, India, and South Africa. *O'Malley v Simpsons-Sears* [1985] 2 SCR 536, 547.

[8] Part I of the Constitution Act, 1982 (Canada).

particular, without discrimination based on race, national or ethnic origin, colour, religion, sex, age or mental or physical disability.

(2) Subsection (1) does not preclude any law, program or activity that has as its object the amelioration of conditions of disadvantaged individuals or groups including those that are disadvantaged because of race, national or ethnic origin, colour, religion, sex, age or mental or physical disability.

There was 'unanimous agreement'[9] that section 15 guaranteed substantive equality.[10] In particular, it was meant to exceed the earlier, more formal, equality jurisprudence under the Canadian Bill of Rights 1970.[11] In fact, much of the pre-Charter jurisprudence on 'race and ethnicity issues … included both active discrimination and passive tolerance of inequality'.[12] There was acute awareness that the Canadian legal system had 'played a principal and dominant role in creating and preserving racial discrimination'[13] and thus was 'profoundly implicated in Canada's racist history'.[14] Section 15 of the Charter was imagined as a break from this racist past as a 'socially progressive'[15] provision to counter 'systemic racism' in Canada.[16]

Indeed, section 15 *is* one of the early progressive constitutional guarantees of equality and non-discrimination in the world. First, it is extremely broad in its formulation, guaranteeing to everyone equality *before* and *under* the law, the right to the *equal protection* and *equal benefit* of the law without *discrimination*, and also the allowance for measures for the *amelioration of conditions of disadvantaged individuals or groups*. Second, section 15 is not limited to grounds enumerated therein including race, national or ethnic origin, colour, religion, sex, age, or mental or physical disability. Third, section 15 does not distinguish between direct and indirect forms of discrimination and thus lays down a common foundation

[9] David Harris, 'Equality, Equality Rights and Discrimination under the Charter of Rights and Freedoms' (1987) 21 University of British Columbia Law Review 389, 411.

[10] WS Tarnopolsky, 'The Equality Rights in the Canadian Charter of Rights and Freedoms' (1983) 61 Canadian Bar Review 242; Marc Gold, 'A Principled Approach to Equality Rights: A Preliminary Inquiry' (1982) 4 Supreme Court Law Review 131; Anne Bayefsky, 'Defining Equality Rights' in Anne Bayefsky and Mary Eberts (eds), *Equality Rights and the Canadian Charter of Rights and Freedoms* (Carswell 1985); Lynn Smith, 'A New Paradigm for Equality Rights' in Lynn Smith et al (eds), *Righting the Balance: Canada's New Equality Rights* (Canadian Human Rights Reporter 1986).

[11] Consider Wilson J's remarks in *Singh v Minister of Employment and Immigration* [1985] 1 SCR 177.

[12] Beverley McLachlin, 'Racism and the Law: The Canadian Experience' (2002) 1 Journal of Law and Equality 7, 14; James W St G Walker, *"Race," Rights and the Law in the Supreme Court of Canada* (Osgoode Society for Canadian Legal History and Wilfred Laurier University Press 1997).

[13] Constance Backhouse, *Colour-Coded: A Legal History of Racism in Canada, 1900–1950* (Osgoode Society for Canadian Legal History and University of Toronto Press 1999) 17.

[14] ibid 15; Benjamin Berger, 'Race and Canadian Legal History' (2000) 38 Osgoode Hall Law Journal 519.

[15] Richard Sigurdson, 'The Left-Legal Critique of the Charter: A Critical Assessment' (1993) 13 Windsor Yearbook of Access to Justice 117.

[16] Colleen Sheppard, 'Challenging Systemic Racism in Canada' in Elaine Kennedy-Dubourdieu (ed), *Race and Equality* (Routledge 2006).

for both,[17] and indeed all forms of discrimination, such as harassment and denial of reasonable accommodation, to be interpreted as part of the prohibition on discrimination.

Yet, section 15 is also limited in at least the following two ways. First, it is an individual right. It did not reimagine equality in collective terms—which was critical for Indigenous peoples.[18] Second, section 15 does not reimagine equality in intersectional terms—which was critical for Indigenous women and indeed all women of colour.[19]

On balance, however, these shortcomings were in principle capable of being addressed in what section 15 *did* provide.[20] The first ever section 15 ruling of the Supreme Court of Canada ('SCC') confirmed section 15's potential. In *Andrews v Law Society of British Columbia*,[21] the SCC extended section 15(1) to 'citizenship' as an analogous ground, to protect non-citizens resident in Canada from discrimination. This was done, in appreciation of the fact that 'discrimination on the basis of nationality has from early times been an inseparable companion of discrimination on the basis of race and national or ethnic origin, which are listed in s. 15'.[22] Still, *Andrews* was a claim brought by a white Oxford-educated man on the basis of his membership in the 'disadvantaged group' of non-citizens. It was not a case concerning racially disadvantaged groups. The real test of section 15's potential thus is not *Andrews* but cases concerning racially disadvantaged groups, especially Indigenous peoples. It is here that the SCC's record falters.

9.2.2 Discrimination against Indigenous Peoples

Cases concerning Indigenous peoples have had a mixed reception at the SCC.

Warning signs appeared early in the case of *Native Women's Association of Canada v Canada*.[23] The case was brought by the Native Women's Association of Canada (NWAC) on behalf of Aboriginal women. NWAC challenged the denial of equal funding and rights of participation in constitutional discussions when funding was awarded only to, what NWAC called, 'male-dominated'[24]

[17] Indirect discrimination was first recognized under section 15 in *O'Malley v Simpson Sears Ltd* [1985] 2 SCR 536; the common foundation of direct and indirect discrimination was later confirmed in *Fraser v Canada (Attorney General)* [2020] 3 SCR 113 [hereafter *Fraser*].

[18] Mary Ellen Turpel, 'Aboriginal Peoples and the Canadian Charter: Interpretive Monopolies, Cultural Differences' in Anthony J Connolly (ed), *Indigenous Rights* (Routledge 2009).

[19] Diana Majury, 'The Charter, Equality Rights, and Women: Equivocation and Celebration' (2002) 40 Osgoode Hall Law Journal 297.

[20] Ian B McKenna, 'Legal Protection Against Racial Discrimination in Canada' (1994) 20 Journal of Ethnic and Migration Studies 415.

[21] [1989] 1 SCR 143.

[22] ibid 195 (La Forest J).

[23] [1994] 3 SCR 627.

[24] ibid 637, 650.

groups: Assembly of First Nations (AFN), the Native Council of Canada (NCC), the Métis Council of Canada (MCC), and the Inuit Tapirisat of Canada (ITC). While funding was not allocated to NWAC, a portion of the total of 10 million dollars distributed to the four groups was earmarked for women's issues. NWAC received 130,000 dollars from AFN and NCC, and eventually, also received 300,00 dollars from the federal government directly. NWAC argued that their exclusion from direct funding and participation in constitutional matters violated the equality of Aboriginal women under section 15(1) of the Charter. In particular, they feared the undermining of their pro-Charter view of Aboriginal self-government by the male-dominated anti-Charter Aboriginal groups. The SCC did not examine the section 15(1) claim and, on the basis of its examination of other Charter rights, concluded that there was no violation of section 15(1) in this case. Its reasoning in respect of other Charter rights—sections 2(b) and 28 on freedom of expression—was that:

> it cannot be said that every time the Government of Canada chooses to fund or consult a certain group, thereby providing a platform upon which to convey certain views, that the Government is also required to fund a group purporting to represent the opposite point of view. Otherwise, the implications of this proposition would be untenable. For example, if the Government chooses to fund a women's organization to study the issue of abortion to assist in drafting proposed legislation, can it be argued that the Government is bound by the Constitution to provide equal funding to a group purporting to represent the rights of fathers?[25]

This formal interpretation of equality rested on the SCC's view that there was 'no evidence' before it that the funded groups were indeed male-dominated and excluded Aboriginal women.[26] According to the Court, there was nothing before it to substantiate a distinct reality of Aboriginal women as opposed to Aboriginal men and in turn the organizations led by each group. The Court did not take judicial notice of the pre-existing intersectional disadvantage suffered by Aboriginal women not only on the basis of Aboriginality and coloniality (a disadvantage they shared with Aboriginal men) but also gender (a disadvantage they suffered *at the hands of* Aboriginal men and others including the state).[27] In ignoring this, the SCC ignored the structural nature of discrimination resulted by the exclusion from state funding which was colonial, racial *and* gendered—all at the same time.

From a doctrinal perspective, three main problems emerge in *NWAC*. First, the SCC lacked a structural perspective of the material scope of section 15(1). Second,

[25] ibid 656.
[26] ibid 657–658.
[27] Kerri A Froc, 'Multidimensionality and the Matrix: Identifying Charter Violations in Cases of Complex Subordination' (2010) 25(1) Canadian Journal of Law and Society 21.

the SCC demanded proof that the four funded groups be shown to be male-dominated while being closed off to any sociological, economic, cultural, or political analysis from a historical and contextual perspective. Third, given the finding that there was no violation of section 15(1), no redistributive (funding) or expressive (declaration) remedies followed for Aboriginal women. Thus, the SCC's material, evidential, and remedial scope of section 15(1) foreclosed an appreciation of structural racism in the form of intersectional gendered racism. This was despite the fact that the enlarged personal scope of section 15(1) allows not only individuals but also organizations like NWAC to challenge the state.

Another delimitation to the material scope of racial discrimination followed in *Lovelace v Ontario*.[28] The case concerned the distribution of funds from first nations casinos to communities registered as bands under the Indian Act. Two of the excluded Aboriginal communities challenged their exclusion from the fund as constituting racial discrimination under section 15(1). The challenge was unanimously rejected on the basis that the excluded communities could not show that they suffered disadvantage under section 15(1). The case was decided not under section 15(2) of the Charter which especially allows for programmes such as the present fund whose object is the amelioration of conditions of disadvantaged individuals or groups.[29] Section 15(2) was thus rendered a mere 'interpretive aid'[30] to section 15(1)—stripping it off its transformative potential in allowing positive measures addressing pre-existing disadvantage associated with grounds such as race, national or ethnic origin, and colour.[31]

Corbiere v Canada (Minister of Indian and Northern Affairs)[32] was the first major victory for Aboriginal rights under section 15(1). The case concerned the requirement under section 77(1) of the Indian Act which required band members to be 'ordinarily resident' on the reserve in order to vote in band elections. The SCC found that the requirement violated section 15(1) of the Charter on the basis of a new analogous ground of 'Aboriginality-residence'.[33]

The lead judgment was delivered by McLachlin and Bastarache JJ. They explained that the rationale behind the recognition of the 'embedded'[34] ground of 'Aboriginality-residence' was based on the appreciation of the 'profound decisions

[28] [2000] 1 SCR 950 [hereafter *Lovelace*].

[29] This was because of the decision in *Law v Canada (Minister of Employment and Immigration)* [1999] 1 SCR 497 which had read in the ameliorative nature of programmes as one of several 'contextual' factors in the adjudication of section 15(1). The SCC in *Lovelace* followed *Law* and applied section 15(1) in adjudging the impugned ameliorative programme despite the explicit words in section 15(2) allowing 'law, program or activity that has as its object the amelioration of conditions of disadvantaged individuals or groups'.

[30] *Lovelace* (n 28) [106].

[31] Michael H Morris and Joseph K Cheng, 'Lovelace and Law Revisited: The Substantive Equality Promise of Kapp' (2009) 47 The Supreme Court Law Review 281, 296.

[32] [1999] 2 SCR 203.

[33] ibid [6] (McLachlin and Bastarache JJ).

[34] ibid [15].

Aboriginal band members make to live on or off their reserves' given the 'unique and complex' reality of their situation.[35] It was this appreciation which ultimately led to the finding that the disenfranchisement was discriminatory because it denied full participation in band governance and stereotyped off-reserve band members as disinterested in their cultural identity.[36] The 'message' this conveyed was that off-reserve band members were not as deserving as band members who lived on their reserves.[37] The SCC deemed this message a violation of dignity, and ultimately, a denial of substantive equality under section 15(1).[38] But the violation of dignity was a conclusion and not a touchstone for infringement of section 15(1). The touchstone was one of material 'detriment'[39] which was the denial of 'political rights in question [that] are related to the race of the individuals affected, and to their cultural identity'.[40]

The SCC thus expanded the material scope of racial discrimination in *Corbiere* by appreciating the racialization at work in a status like off-reserve band residence. It recognized off-reserve band members as a '"discrete and insular minority" defined by race and place of residence'.[41] It even recognized that it was Aboriginal women who suffered 'double disadvantage on the basis of both sex and race'.[42] The disenfranchisement affected them in particular given the colonial and patriarchal history of being divested of their status and rights. It also applied a test of material detriment in finding for discrimination. Importantly, the Court admitted historical and contemporary sociological evidence in appreciating this detriment and did not demand claimants to prove their case acontextually or ahistorically. Its justification analysis was also brief and led by the fact that given that the detriment was not minimal (but a complete disenfranchisement), it could not be justified.[43] Finally, its remedy was expansive and, in respect of the constitutional invalidity of the impugned provision as such and unlike the courts below, not restricted to the claimants in this case.[44] The SCC thus struck out the words 'and is ordinarily resident on the reserve' from section 77(1) of the Indian Act.[45]

Ten years later, in *R v Kapp*,[46] the SCC rejected a racial discrimination challenge by non-Aboriginal commercial fishers against the exclusive communal fishing license granted to Aboriginals. The majority found that the communal license was

35 ibid.
36 ibid [18].
37 ibid.
38 ibid.
39 ibid [19].
40 ibid.
41 ibid [62] [71] (L'Heureux-Dubé J).
42 ibid [72] (L'Heureux-Dubé J).
43 ibid [21].
44 ibid [22].
45 ibid [22].
46 [2008] SCC 41.

protected under section 15(2) as it had the object to ameliorate the conditions of disadvantaged groups.[47]

In Bastarache J's concurring opinion, he agreed that the challenge failed, but on different grounds. According to him, the applicable Charter provision was not section 15 but section 25 which provides that the Charter 'shall not be construed so as to abrogate or derogate from any aboriginal, treaty or other rights or freedoms that pertain to the aboriginal peoples of Canada'. He explained that section 25 served 'the purpose of protecting the rights of aboriginal peoples where the application of the *Charter* protections for individuals would diminish the distinctive, collective and cultural identity of an aboriginal group'.[48] Its 'real effect'[49] was thus to protect collective native rights and freedoms by excluding individual rights challenges under section 15.[50] In assigning primacy to section 25, Bastarache J essentially avoided the absurdity of determining whether the protection of Aboriginal rights and interests constituted racial discrimination against non-Aboriginal people. Such a determination would have been against both the legislative history and plain text of section 25.[51]

The majority in *Kapp* was less sure. First, it questioned, without deciding, whether a communal fishing license was indeed protected under section 25.[52] Second, it raised, again without deciding, the question of whether section 25 was an absolute bar to all racial discrimination claims under section 15 as opposed to an interpretive provision which informed the determination of Charter rights.[53] The majority declined to rule on the basis of section 25 given the complexity of these issues.[54]

While the majority could not avoid framing *Kapp* as a case of reverse-racism against non-Aboriginal people, Bastarache J did. As a consequence, he avoided enacting structural racism by framing the state's grant of a communal fishing license as racializing non-Aboriginal people and disadvantaging them to the advantage of Aboriginal people.[55] The majority however ended up *first* enacting structural racism and *only then* refuting it.

Ultimately, the decision in *Corbiere* may be the only bright spot in the SCC's racial discrimination jurisprudence under section 15. Much like *Kapp*, later cases

47 ibid [58] (McLachlin CJ and Abella J).
48 ibid [89] (Bastarache J).
49 ibid [80] (Bastarache J).
50 ibid.
51 ibid [84]–[96] (Bastarache J).
52 ibid [63] (McLachlin CJ and Abella J).
53 ibid [64] (McLachlin CJ and Abella J).
54 ibid [65] (McLachlin CJ and Abella J).
55 This could also have been avoided, as Sonia Lawence argues, by not having the section 15 claim pass the differentiation stage and by not framing this case as a case of racial discrimination at all and instead as a case based on indigeneity or band membership. Sonia Lawrence, '"The Admittedly Unattainable Ideal": Adverse Impact and Race Under Section 15' in Law Society of Upper Canada, *Special Lectures 2017: Canada at 150—The Charter and the Constitution* (Irwin Law 2017) 549.

concerning Aboriginal peoples have been less than satisfactory in addressing structural racism from a material, evidential, and remedial perspective.

Ermineskin Indian Band v Canada[56] held that the state's failure to invest wisely under the Indian Act on behalf of the band members of Ermineskin Nation and the Samson Nation, which led to losses of millions of dollars, did not constitute discrimination under section 15(1). The SCC, unlike the courts below, was lax about the personal scope of section 15(1) and in particular the standing of the band members bringing claims on behalf of the band itself rather than its individual members.[57] But it was strict about the proof it required from the band members in establishing a prima facie case of discrimination. Even though the SCC found that there was difference in returns for investments for band members versus non-band members, it found that the difference was not based on a stereotype or prejudice and hence was not discriminatory. It reasoned so because the band members had historically resisted greater control of their investments and were thus assumed to have foregone the opportunity to make a claim that the state's lack of investment led to their material disadvantage.[58] The evidence of actual material disadvantage suffered by band members was thus cast aside.

Kahkewistahaw First Nation v Taypotat[59] also cast aside evidence of actual material disadvantage, deeming it too broad and unspecific to demonstrate the discriminatory effects of the impugned law. The case concerned a statutory amendment which instated a grade 12 educational requirement for electoral eligibility of Chief and Councillors at the Sahkewistahaw First Nation in Saskatchewan. The amendment was challenged under section 15(1) as discriminating against 'older community members who live on reserve'[60] such as the 76 years old Louis Taypotat who had served as the Chief for almost three decades but only had grade 10 education. Although, writing for the unanimous court, Abella J admitted that 'intuition may well lead us to the conclusion that the provision has some disparate impact', the evidence before the Court was deemed insufficient to have established a prima facie case of discrimination.[61] In particular, the SCC lacked disaggregated age-related data on educational attainment of Aboriginal people living on reserve as compared to non-Aboriginal and Aboriginal people living off reserve. The SCC did not take into account historical, social, economic, and cultural context as evidence of the qualitative nature of intersectional discrimination in this case defined by Aboriginal status, age, and educational attainment.[62] In an uncharacteristically brief judgment, the SCC dismissed the case as evidentiarily lacking.

[56] [2009] SCC 9.
[57] ibid [187].
[58] ibid [196]–[202].
[59] [2015] SCC 30.
[60] ibid [14].
[61] ibid [34].
[62] Jonnette Watson Hamilton and Jennifer Koshan, 'Kahkewistahaw First Nation v Taypotat: An Arbitrary Approach to Discrimination' (2016) 76 The Supreme Court Law Review 243.

R v Kokopenace[63] had relevant statistical evidence of structural racism in Canada's jury system where Aboriginal jurors were 'drastically underrepresented'[64] in a district. That is, the Court had on evidence the out-of-date jury roll, which included people it ought not to, excluded four First Nations reserves in the district entirely; and serious problems in delivering jury notices to on-reserve residents.[65] Despite clear and overwhelming evidence of race-based under-representation, the majority found no violation of section 15(1). It reasoned that section 15(1) guaranteed equal or fair opportunity in jury selection but not equality of results in jury composition. McLachlin CJ and Cromwell J dissented. They found for the claimant in respect of their right to jury trial under section 11 but did not 'find it necessary to address the equality rights issue' under section 15 of the Charter.[66] Thus, even for the minority, the disproportionate racialized impact of exclusion from juries on Aboriginal peoples signalled a violation of a different right (the right to jury trial) than the prohibition of racial discrimination.

Ewert v Canada[67] also found a violation on grounds other than racial discrimination. The majority found against the use of psychological and actuarial risk assessment tools for Indigenous offenders. It held that correctional policies, programmes, and practices 'must respect cultural differences and be responsive to the needs of Indigenous peoples'.[68] As in this case they were not, the majority asked for the tools to be better researched for application to Indigenous offenders. But it did not find a Charter violation under section 15(1). In fact, the majority noted that while there was an 'established [sic] risk that the impugned tools are less accurate when applied to Indigenous inmates than when they are applied to non-Indigenous inmates', it could not be concluded that 'the impugned tools do in fact overestimate the risk posed by Indigenous inmates or lead to harsher conditions of incarceration or to the denial of rehabilitative opportunities because of such an overestimation'.[69]

R v Sharma[70] too found against a claim of racial discrimination on grounds that the claimant had not provided sufficient evidence to demonstrate that the impugned statutory provisions on limited access to conditional sentences had a disproportionate impact on Indigenous offenders, especially Indigenous women.[71] In her dissent, Karakatsanis J found a violation of the Charter including under

[63] *R v Kokopenace* [2015] SCC 28.
[64] ibid [191] (Cromwell J, dissent).
[65] ibid [191] (Cromwell J, dissent).
[66] ibid [201] (Cromwell J, dissent).
[67] [2018] SCC 30 [79] [91]. The Court unanimously held that the state's risk assessment tools for inmates are not discriminatory because, while they risked inaccuracy when applied to Indigenous inmates, no such inaccuracy was proven at first instance.
[68] ibid [6] (Wagner J).
[69] ibid [79] (Wagner J).
[70] [2022] SCC 39 [hereafter *Sharma*].
[71] Where sentences are served in the community rather than in the prison for certain non-serious offences.

section 15(1) on the basis that the overincarceration of Aboriginal offenders reinforced, perpetuated, and exacerbated the historical disadvantage of Indigenous peoples.[72] The difference between the majority and the minority was how each understood the evidential requirements of racial discrimination claims. The majority framed 'causation … [as the] central issue' and thus demanded evidence of adverse impact flowing directly from the impugned provision.[73] The minority instead took judicial notice of the historical, social, cultural, political, and economic context within which the overincarceration of Aboriginal peoples existed, and located the impugned provision within the evidence of this overarching structure.

Finally, *Dickson v Vuntut Gwitchin First Nation*[74] found against a claim of discrimination based on non-resident status in a self-governing Indigenous community. At the heart of the challenge was an election rule of a self-governing First Nation in the Yukon which provided that the elected Chief and Councillors reside on the settlement land of the First Nation. Here, unlike in *Kapp*, majority *applied* section 25 to shield the application of section 15(1) in assessing the residency requirement. But *Kapp* was a case of racial discrimination brought by non-Indigenous claimants. *Dickson* involved a claimant, Cindy Dickson, who was an Indigenous woman who lived off reserve due to her childcare responsibilities as a single mother. Yet, much like in *NWAC v Canada*, the SCC failed to consider the case from a colonial, gendered, and racialized perspective simultaneously to appreciate the nature of structural discrimination at stake in excluding women like Cindy Dickson from band governance. Instead, it prioritized the collective right of Indigenous peoples to maintain their Indigenous difference under section 25 over the equality rights of non-resident Indigenous women. There was little appreciation of the dangers in elevating section 25 in cases (unlike *Kapp*) concerning competing interests of members *within* a single self-governing First Nation intra-se and not the competing interests of non-Aboriginal and Aboriginal people inter-se. Consequently, there was little appreciation of the differing and competing interests of Indigenous men and women (especially single mothers) living both on and off reserve. It was without this appreciation that the Court went on to declare the incompatibility of Cindy Dickson's rights as an Indigenous woman, with the collective right of the self-governing First Nation to maintain their Indigenous difference.

[72] *Sharma* (n 70) [118] [231] [236] (Karakatsanis J, dissent) ('Tracing the lineage of intergenerational trauma makes clear that our criminal justice system is a significant and ongoing source of discrimination against Indigenous peoples. The fact that the challenged provisions did not create the problem is irrelevant … To blame overrepresentation solely on the pre-existing disadvantages suffered by Indigenous peoples is to ignore the plain reality that incarcerating people is an exercise of state power. And since the state is deeply implicated in the incarceration of Indigenous women through the criminal justice system, it has a constitutional obligation under s. 15(1) of the Charter to ensure that its laws do not operate to reinforce, perpetuate, or exacerbate conditions of inequality').

[73] ibid [42] (Brown and Rowe JJ).

[74] [2024] SCC 10 [hereafter *Dickson*].

9.2.3 Anti-Racist in Theory, not Practice

There is open acknowledgement of 'systemic racism' in Canada, no less by the Canadian Human Rights Commission itself,[75] a concept which is understood in much the same way as structural racism is understood in this book. The acknowledgement is even accompanied by access to justice under section 15 whose personal scope remains wide and hospitable for claims challenging broad-based state law, policy, or practice.[76] Even the remedial scope of section 15 is meant to give effect to substantive equality.[77] These normative possibilities though do not seem to guarantee success for claims of structural racism.

Ultimately, in almost five decades of the SCC's jurisprudence on racial discrimination under section 15, only one successful example of anti-racism can be found: *Corbiere*. That is, only *Corbiere* attacked (i) state-led drivers of racial disadvantage (disenfranchisement in the Indian Act) in an (ii) intersectional (recognizing 'Aboriginality-residence' as a ground) and (iii) broad-based way (striking down the legislative provision rather than limiting the invalidity of the legislative provision to the claimants and their Band alone).

Yet, as the discussion above showed, indigenous rights cases continue to appear frequently before the SCC. They are rarely appreciated *as* cases *of* structural racism, although they *are*—per the framework of structural racism suggested in this book—about how (i) the state (ii) racializes to (iii) instate racial disadvantage.

[75] Canadian Human Rights Commission, 'Discussion Paper on Systemic Racism' (23 October 2023) ('Systemic racism is deeply entrenched in Canadian society. It is in our written and unwritten policies, our laws, public practices, beliefs, and systems which "produce, condone, and perpetuate widespread, unfair treatment and oppression" of racialized people'); *Canadian National Railway Co v Canada* (Canadian Human Rights Commission) [1987] 1 SCR 1114, 1139 ('Systemic discrimination ... is discrimination that results from the simple operation of established procedures'); Joshua Sealy-Harrington, 'The Charter of Whites: Systemic Racism and Critical Race Equality in Canada' (2024) 39 Windsor Yearbook of Access to Justice 544, 545 ('systemic racism—refers to how intergenerational legacies and ongoing practices of oppression and dispossession translate into contemporary societal inequality'); Canadian Race Relations Foundations, 'Glossary of Terms' ('The Canadian Race Relations Foundation defines systemic racism as 'an interlocking and reciprocal relationship between the individual, institutional and structural levels, which function as a system of racism. These various levels of racism operate together in a lockstep model and function together as a whole system'); Colleen Sheppard, Tamara Thermitus, and Derek J Jones, 'Understanding How Racism becomes Systemic', The Globe and Mail (24 July 2020) ('Race-based discrimination may be understood as systemic when it goes beyond isolated individual wrongdoing to encompass broader patterns of racial inequality').

[76] Though *Sharma* limited the personal scope, especially by limiting intervenor's role: 'We note here, in passing, our serious concern with interveners supplementing the record at the appellate level ... Interveners must, however, accept the record as defined by the parties in first instance ... Interveners creating a new evidentiary record at the appellate level undermines the trial process. That is not how our system of justice, including constitutional adjudication, is designed to work.' *Sharma* (n 70) [75] (Brown and Rowe JJ) (emphasis in original).

[77] Though *Sharma* limited the remedial scope of the Charter in insisting that 's. 15(1) does not impose a general, positive obligation on the state to remedy social inequalities or enact remedial legislation'; 'when the state does legislate to address inequality, it can do so incrementally' and that 'incrementalism is deeply grounded in Charter jurisprudence'. *Sharma* (n 70) [63] [64] [65] (Brown and Rowe JJ) (emphasis in original).

Cases of Islamophobia, anti-Black racism, and xenophobia do not even appear before the SCC even though there are growing concerns around their unabated rise.[78]

Two main doctrinal limitations can be identified as stifling the redressal of structural racism in Canadian constitutional law under section 15.

First, in one sense, the material scope of claims of racial discrimination is broad in that grounds such as citizenship and Aboriginality-residence have been recognized as analogous grounds of discrimination, relatively easily by the SCC. This has involved awareness of how processes of racialization generate racial categories. But, in another sense, the material scope of claims of racial discrimination is narrow in that the meaning of racial discrimination based on these racially analogous grounds is underdeveloped. How processes of racialization create racial categories to instate *racial disadvantage* is often sidelined, despite all the rhetoric that follows in section 15 cases. This happens because of two things in particular. First, the SCC pays scant attention to intersectional discrimination despite its avowing to it.[79] It has only once, that too very recently, found for intersectional discrimination.[80] Second, the SCC pays scant attention to the racialized postcolonial context of racial discrimination claims, again, despite its avowing to it.[81] The absence of a clear and capacious accounts of racial discrimination, structural discrimination, and intersectional discrimination, thus, confirms the 'chronic mis-alignment between the Court's high rhetoric and a stream of underwhelming results'.[82]

[78] As shown by Doudou Diene, the United Nations Special Rapporteur on contemporary forms of racism, racial discrimination, xenophobia and related intolerance, in their report based on the mission to Canada in 2003, E/CN.4/2004/18/Add.2 (2004); Catherine Dauvergne, 'How the Charter Has Failed Non-citizens in Canada: Reviewing Thirty Years of Supreme Court of Canada Jurisprudence' (2013) 58 McGill Law Journal 663; Delores V Mullings, Anthony Morgan, and Heather Kere Quelleng, 'Canada the Great White North where Anti-Black Racism Thrives: Kicking Down the Doors and Exposing the Realities' (2016) 53 Phylon 20, 21 ('challenge Canada's reputation of having comprehensive human rights policies that address systemic racism and further expose not only the insidiousness of Canadian anti-black racism, but the racialized rhetoric of community blaming that policy-makers often adopt and endorse when African Canadians' rights are obliterated resulting in their re-victimization and death'); Joshua Sealy-Harrington, 'The Charter of Whites: Systemic Racism and Critical Race Equality in Canada' (2024) 39 Windsor Yearbook of Access to Justice 544, 546 ('the Supreme Court has barely considered racial discrimination claims. Race is, thus, first listed yet last enforced—a constitutional token to a promise of racial equality left not only with little success but with little attempt'); Jenny Godley, 'Everyday Discrimination in Canada' (2018) 43 Canadian Journal of Sociology 111, 112 ('Internationally, Canada has a reputation as a multicultural haven, where social inequality is low, difference is welcomed, and government programmes work to create a more egalitarian society' and at the same time there is 'a long history of questioning the idealistic view of Canadian society as egalitarian by providing evidence of ongoing structural inequalities').

[79] Fuller discussion of the reception of claims of intersectional discrimination at the SCC can be found in Shreya Atrey, *Intersectional Discrimination* (OUP 2019) [hereafter Atrey, *Intersectional Discrimination*].

[80] *Quebec (Attorney General) v Kanyinda* [2026] SCC 7.

[81] Though the contextual factors in *Law v Canada (Minister of Employment and Immigration)* [1999] 1 SCR 497 require as much. For example, in *Sharma* the SCC majority barred historical and contextual group-related evidence in the first step of the discrimination analysis. *Sharma* (n 70) [71]–[76] (Brown and Rowe JJ) (emphasis in original).

[82] Carissima Mathen, 'Equality Before the Charter: Reflections on Fraser v Canada' [2022] The Supreme Court Law Review: Osgoode's Annual Constitutional Cases Conference 104; Diana Majury,

Second, and most importantly, the reason for this substantively stunted scope is perhaps the stilted evidential standards for section 15 claims. While there is an onerous standard of proof imposed on claimants of racial discrimination to establish a prima facie case of infringement, there is an undemanding standard of justification imposed on the state. What is required of the claimant is hardly commensurate with what is required of the state. In *Sharma*, the majority insisted that there was a 'causation requirement' under section 15(1) 'between the impugned law or state action and the disproportionate impact'[83] and thus insisted that the claimant '*did* have to demonstrate a causal connection'.[84] *Sharma* essentially guts the proof of structural racism before courts. This is because, as Part I of this book argued, structural racism cannot be understood in terms of immediate causes. Instead, it is understood in terms of the overall scaffolding or background conditions which act upon discrete state laws, policies, and practices to (re)produce racialized disadvantage. An evidential requirement for the most proximate cause essentially misses how structural racism works. This, coupled with the disturbing tendency of the SCC to *not* take judicial notice of Canada's racial and colonial past and its continuing legacy today, makes proof of structural racism hopeless.

In this landscape, *Corbiere* emerges as the sole beacon of anti-racism.[85] *Corbiere* must thus be continued to be reiterated and reaffirmed as demonstrating not just the possibility but the actuality of addressing structural racism through constitutional adjudication. It alone keeps alive the possibility that 'racial-justice advocacy under section 15 of the Charter is doctrinally viable and, thus, should be contemplated in the toolkit of social-change strategies in Canada'.[86]

'Equality and Discrimination According to the Supreme Court of Canada' (1991) 4 Canadian Journal of Women and the Law 407; Margot Young, 'Unequal to the Task: 'Kapp'ing the Substantive Potential of Section 15' (2010) 50 Supreme Court Law Review 183; Jennifer Koshan and Jonnette Watson Hamilton, 'Meaningless Mantra: Substantive Equality after Withler' (2011) 16 Review of Constitutional Studies 31; Patricia Hughes, 'Supreme Court of Canada Equality Jurisprudence and "Everyday Life"' (2012) 58 Supreme Court Law Review 245; Diana Majury, 'Equality and Discrimination According to the Supreme Court of Canada' (1991) 4 Canadian Journal of Women and the Law 407.

[83] *Sharma* (n 70) [45] (Brown and Rowe JJ).

[84] *Sharma* (n 70) [73] (Brown and Rowe JJ) (emphasis in original).

[85] There are of course dissenting opinions in cases considered in this section which too must be added to this hopeful list. Most recently the dissent in Sharma found that the overrepresentation of Indigenous peoples in Canada's prisons was 'a present-day product of this country's colonial past' and 'a striking sign of the discrimination that Indigenous peoples experience in "all parts of the criminal justice system"'. The dissent also focussed its analysis on Indigenous women, using the claimant's own intersectional disadvantage as a single poor Indigenous woman with a young child, whose history of coloniality, poverty, and sexism vividly illustrated the vast material disadvantages suffered by her and those in her intersectional position. It cited a wide range of both official (governmental) as well as scholarly research in support of historical and contemporary nature of discrimination. *Sharma* (n 70) [114] [120]–[121] (Karakatsanis J, dissent).

[86] Joshua Sealy-Harrington, 'The Charter of Whites: Systemic Racism and Critical Race Equality in Canada' (2024) 39 Windsor Yearbook of Access to Justice 544, 546 (develops six doctrinal principles from Canadian equality law which align with critical race theory and point towards the enduring possibility of the SCC recognizing systemic or structural racism: (1) broad understanding of race, racial discrimination, and racial equality, (2) contextual analysis of race and racism as embedded in social, political, cultural and economic milieu, (3) ideological openness to the existence of racism (as opposed

9.3 India

The three sections below examine India's constitutional commitment to anti-casteism (Section 9.3.1), the realization of this commitment through constitutional affirmative action or 'reservations' (Section 9.3.2) and the constitutional guarantee of non-discrimination (Section 9.3.3), and finally, the recent retrenchment of this commitment alongside occasional revival, ultimately revealing a schizophrenic doctrine of transformative anti-racism in India (Section 9.3.4).

9.3.1 Anti-Casteism

The Constitution of India came into force in 1950. The word 'race' appears over a dozen times in the text of the constitution. What appears tenfold more are the words 'caste' and 'tribe', especially as 'Scheduled Castes' (SCs) and 'Schedule Tribes' (STs). While caste refers to stratification under the Hindu caste-system, tribes specifically refer to the *Adivasis* or the aboriginal or indigenous peoples in India.[87] Caste and tribe are general, sociological, terms for historically relevant personal characteristics, whereas SCs and STs are legally recognized caste and tribal groups under articles 341 and 342 of the Constitution. The list of such groups is lengthy with over a thousand SCs and over seven hundred STs listed in the constitution.[88] More recently, categories such as 'Other Backward Classes' (OBCs) and 'Economically Weaker Sections' (EWSs) have been added to the constitution.

The main purpose of the constitutional recognition of these groups is to provide not just protection from discrimination in a negative sense but also affirmative action or 'reservations' in a positive sense.[89] Thus, much like the Canadian counterpart, the Indian constitutional design exceeds the negative prohibition of racial discrimination and guarantees substantive equality through positive action in the form of reservations or quotas.

to denial of racism or colour blindness), (4) comparative outlook to equality (as opposed to equality as sameness), (5) systemic (the enduring intergenerational nature of racism), and (6) the positive character of equality in not only recognizing but disrupting inequality. Sealy-Harrington developed these doctrinal principles in light of the SCC's decision in *Fraser* (n 17). Their activation is now dimmed (though not extinguished) after *Sharma* (n 70) and *Dickson* (n 74)).

[87] Sudha Pai, *Dalit Assertion* (OUP 2013); Ramchandra Guha, 'Adivasis, Naxalites and Indian Democracy' (2007) 42 Economic and Political Weekly 3305.

[88] First identified in the Constitution (Scheduled Castes) Order 1950 and the Constitution (Scheduled Tribes) Order 1950.

[89] Marc Galanter, *Competing Equalities: Law and the Backwards Classes in India* (OUP 1991) 361; Vinay Sitapati, 'Reservations' in Sujit Choudhry, Madhav Khosla and Pratap Bhanu Mehta (eds), *The Oxford Handbook of The Indian Constitution* (OUP 2016) 720.

In fact, Indian constitutionalism is imagined as much more, as ushering in 'social revolution'[90] or 'social transformation'[91] to 'offset ... entrenched and cumulative nature of group inequalities'.[92] In particular, the 'equality code' of the constitution enshrined in articles 14–18 of the Constitution reflects a strong anti-caste vision of India's transformation.[93] Indeed, this was the vision imagined by the constitution's foremost creator, Bhimrao Ramji Ambedkar, who was Dalit himself.[94]

While article 14 guarantees to everyone 'equality before the law or the equal protection of the laws'; article 15(1) prohibits discrimination against citizens 'on grounds only of religion, race, caste, sex, place of birth or any of them'. Article 15(2) prohibits spatial and social segregation.[95] Article 15(3) allows the state to make special provisions for women and children. The Constitution (First Amendment) Act 1951 added clause (4) to article 15 which permits the state to make 'any special provision for the advancement of any socially and educationally backward classes of citizens or for the Scheduled Castes and the Scheduled Tribes'.[96] Likewise, the Constitution (Ninety-third Amendment) Act 2005 added clause (5) to article 15 which permits the state to make 'any special provision, by law, for the advancement of any socially and educationally backward classes of citizens or for the Scheduled Castes or the Scheduled Tribes [sic] [for] their admission to educational institutions including private educational institutions'.[97] The Constitution (One Hundred and Third Amendment) Act 2019 added a final clause (6) to article 15 which permits the state to make 'any special provision for the advancement of any economically weaker sections of citizens' *other than* SCs, STs and OBCs.[98] Similarly, article

[90] Glanville Austin, *The Indian Constitution: Cornerstone of a Nation* (OUP 1966) xxi.

[91] *Indian Young Lawyers Association v State of Kerala* (2019) 11 SCC 1 [3] (Chandrachud J). For a discussion on this, consult Gautam Bhatia, *The Transformative Constitution: A Radical Biography in Nine Acts* (Harper Collins 2019) [hereafter Bhatia, *The Transformative Constitution*].

[92] Marc Galanter, *Law and Society in Modern India* (OUP 1989) 185.

[93] Bhatia, *The Transformative Constitution* (n 91).

[94] BR Ambedkar, *Annihilation of Caste* (Verso 2014).

[95] Article 15(2) provides that 'No citizen shall, on grounds only of religion, race, caste, sex, place of birth or any of them, be subject to any disability, liability, restriction or condition with regard to— a) access to shops, public restaurants, hotels and places of public entertainment; or (b) the use of wells, tanks, bathing ghats, roads and places of public resort maintained wholly or partly out of State funds or dedicated to the use of the general public.'

[96] Article 15(4) provides that 'Nothing in this article or in clause (2) of article 29 shall prevent the State from making any special provision for the advancement of any socially and educationally backward classes of citizens or for the Scheduled Castes and the Scheduled Tribes.'

[97] Article 15(5) provides that 'Nothing in this article or in sub-clause (g) of clause (1) of article 19 shall prevent the State from making any special provision, by law, for the advancement of any socially and educationally backward classes of citizens or for the Scheduled Castes or the Scheduled Tribes in so far as such special provisions relate to their admission to educational institutions including private educational institutions, whether aided or unaided by the State, other than the minority educational institutions referred to in clause (1) of article 30.'

[98] Article 15(6) provides that 'Nothing in this article or sub-clause (g) of clause (1) of article 19 or clause (2) of article 29 shall prevent the State from making,—economically weaker sections of citizens other than the classes mentioned in clauses (4) and (5); and (b) any special provision for the advancement of any economically weaker sections of citizens other than the classes mentioned in clauses (4) and (5) in so far as such special provisions relate to their admission to educational institutions

16(1)–(2) guarantee to citizens equality of opportunity in employment and prohibit discrimination 'on grounds only of religion, race, caste, sex, descent, place of birth, residence or any of them'; while article 16(4)–(6) allow the state to make provisions for reservation in employment for SCs, STs, OBCs, and EWCs. The penultimate provision of the equality code, article 17, abolishes 'untouchability' and makes it a criminal offence.[99] Finally, article 18 abolishes titles, except military and academic titles, and prohibits acceptance of titles, awards, and office of profit or trust from foreign states.

The bulk of the equality code is thus dedicated to actively addressing discrimination against socially, educationally, and economically disadvantaged groups—collectively and colloquially referred to as *Bahujan*, a term which includes *Dalits* (SCs), *Adivasis* (STs), and OBCs. *Bahujan* comprise not a numerical minority, but the majority of India's total population (about 52 per cent).[100] Thus, special provisions or reservations—as the main tool in the equality code and its anti-caste vision—too concern the majority of the country and consequently dominate the equality jurisprudence under the constitution.[101]

While this section cannot capture the entire breadth of reservation jurisprudence in India, it is worth reflecting on its broad contours from the anti-racist perspective set out in this book. The arc of development bends towards a progressively expansive view of reservations to give effect to the anti-caste vision of the constitution, specifically by addressing the material inequality of *Bahujans*.[102] There are though developments which contradict this progressive view. The sections below capture how Indian constitutional jurisprudence, though firmly anti-caste in its text and spirit, is more ambiguous in practice.

9.3.2 Reservations

The spate of constitutional amendments providing for reservations was spurred by an early rejection of caste-based reservations in educational institutions

including private educational institutions, whether aided or unaided by the State, other than the minority educational institutions referred to in clause (1) of article 30, which in the case of reservation would be in addition to the existing reservations and subject to a maximum of ten per cent of the total seats in each category.'

[99] Article 17 provides that '"Untouchability" is abolished and its practice in any form is forbidden. The enforcement of any disability arising out of "Untouchability" shall be an offence punishable in accordance with law.'

[100] According to the 2021 census.

[101] Tarunabh Khaitan, 'Transcending Reservations: A Paradigm Shift in the Debate on Equality' (2008) 43 Economic and Political Weekly 8.

[102] Cf Lance Brennan, John McDonald, and Ralph Shlomowitz, 'Caste, Inequality and the Nation-state: The Impact of Reservation Policies in India, c. 1950–2000' (2006) 29 Journal of South Asian Studies 117; Ishita Banerjee-Dube, 'Caste, Constitution, Court, Equality: The Social Justice Imbroglio in Contemporary India' (2025) 19 Studies in Social Science 1.

introduced in the then-Madras Presidency by the Communal Government Order of 1927.[103] The Supreme Court had found that the impugned order violated article 15(1) of the constitution, which prohibits discrimination based on caste. This paved the way for the very first amendment to the constitution, which added article 15(4), allowing the state to make special provisions for the advancement of socially and educationally backward classes, including SCs and STs.

However, even with the newly minted constitutional amendment, the Supreme Court was quick to clarify that the permissibility of special provisions was not to be interpreted as the permissibility of discrimination under article 15(1).[104] For example, special provisions such as those exempting Dalits and Muslims from paying additional charges for a police force which were paid by other caste and religious groups were deemed impermissible because they contravened article 15(1) which prohibits discrimination on grounds of caste and religion.

Equally, the exclusion of Dalit Muslims and Dalit Christians (i.e. Dalits who converted to other religions) from the list of SCs included in the constitution, as per the Constitution (Scheduled Castes) Order of 1950,[105] was deemed constitutional.[106] The Court placed a high burden of proof on the claimants to show that they continued to suffer caste discrimination despite conversion to Christianity. Caste is thus imagined as an intersectional category but asymmetrically, and as applicable to Hindu caste groups and not to Christian and Muslim caste groups. This is despite evidence that caste cuts across religions in India.[107]

These clarifications led to a series of seminal cases which reinforced that special provisions under the constitution do not and should not contravene article 15(1). This meant four things. First, as per the text of the constitution, special provisions are for 'socially and educationally backward classes', 'Scheduled Castes', or 'Scheduled Tribes'. These groups could be identified by caste or other factors which contribute to their social and educational backwardness.[108] No 'rigid formula' is devised but relevant factors can include occupation, poverty, place of residence, etc.[109] Second, that constitutional amendments allowing special provisions are considered not an exception to article 15(1) but a fundamental aspect of it.[110] They are meant to advance substantive equality by actively guaranteeing

[103] *State of Madras v Champakam Dorairajan* AIR 1951 SC 226.
[104] *State of Rajasthan v Thakur Pratap Singh* AIR 1960 SC 1208.
[105] The Order specifies that no person who practices a religion other than Hinduism shall be considered a member of a Scheduled Caste.
[106] *Soosai v Union of India* (1985) Supp SCC 590.
[107] Anthony Jeremiah, 'Caste and Christianity in India' in Kenneth R Ross et al (eds), *Christianity in South and Central Asia* (Edinburgh University Press 2019); Imtiaz Ahmad, 'Is There Caste Among Muslims in India?' (2015) 68 The Eastern Anthropologist 1.
[108] *MR Balaji v State of Mysore* AIR 1963 SC 649; *R Chitralekha v State of Mysore* AIR 1964 SC 1823.
[109] *Indra Sawhney v Union of India* 1992 Supp (3) SCC 217 [44] [45] [Pandian J].
[110] *State of Kerala v NM Thomas* (1976) 2 SCC 310; *Indra Sawhney v Union of India* 1992 Supp (3) SCC 217 [799] [859] (Jeevan Reddy J), [44] [45] (Pandian J).

'equality of opportunity',[111] 'proportionate equality',[112] 'redistributive justice',[113] or 'complete economic and social freedom'.[114] Third, and consequently, reservations need not pass the American standard of 'strict scrutiny' to be considered constitutional.[115] That is, they are deemed permissible and not a contravention of equality/non-discrimination to be subjected to a very high standard of scrutiny. Fourth, however, this does not mean that reservations permit 'reverse discrimination'.[116] They are subject to some limitations such as the capping of reservations at 50 per cent,[117] bar on 'carrying forward' unfilled reserved seats to another year,[118] and the exclusion of 'creamy layer' or the economically well-off sections of socially and educationally backward classes from reservation.[119]

In clarifying the scope of reservations, constitutional jurisprudence centred reservations around the goal of addressing material inequality of *Bahujans*.[120] Yet, growing political and ideological opposition to constitutional reservations for *Bahujans* has weakened the focus on material inequality as the mainstay of reservations and in turn the anti-caste vision of the constitution. The constitutional amendments enabling reservations for 'economically weaker sections' (EWS) *to the exclusion of Bahujans* are an obvious example of this weakening. These amendments were upheld as constitutionally valid by the Supreme Court in *Janhit v Union of India*.[121] The reasoning of the Court, discussed below, is revealing in its rejection of the anti-caste framing of reservations—undoing the consensus around reservations being the mainstay of anti-casteism in the constitution.

Janhit concerned a challenge to the validity of the Constitution (One Hundred and Third Amendment) Act 2019.[122] The amendment added new clauses to articles 15 and 16 of the constitution enabling the state to provide up to 10 per cent reserved spots to 'economically weaker sections' (EWS) in education and employment. The amendment was challenged, inter alia, on grounds that: (i) reservations based solely on economic criterion were impermissible under the constitution; (ii) and in any case, the exclusion of creamy layer among the socially and educationally backward classes (SCs, STs and OBCs) from reservations for EWS was discriminatory.

111 *State of Kerala v NM Thomas* (1976) 2 SCC 310 [27] (Ray CJ).
112 ibid [53] (Matthew J).
113 ibid [117] (Krishna Iyer J).
114 ibid [158] (Fazal Ali J).
115 *Ashoka Kumar Thakur v Union of India* (2008) 6 SCC 1.
116 *M Nagaraj v Union of India* (2006) 8 SCC 212.
117 *MR Balaji v State of Mysore* AIR 1963 SC 649.
118 *T Devadasan v Union of India* AIR 1964 SC 179.
119 *Indra Sawhney v Union of India* (1992) Supp (3) SCC 217; *Indra Sawhney v Union of India* (2000) 1 SCC 168.
120 Sukhadeo Thorat, 'Why Reservation is Necessary' <https://www.india-seminar.com/2005/549/549%20sukhadeo%20thorat.htm> (accessed 12 August 2025).
121 (2000) 1 SCC 168 [hereafter *Janhit*].
122 The Supreme Court of India has the power to review all law, including constitutional amendments, under articles 32 and 136 of the Constitution.

A majority of the Supreme Court rejected the petitioners' argument that caste comprised of social, educational, political, as well as, economic disadvantage, and thus could not be isolated from economic status.[123] It upheld the government's argument that economic status alone, to the exclusion of caste, could be the basis of affirmative action, something that was not originally mandated in the text of the constitution.

The majority thus viewed caste and economic status as mutually exclusive categories. Consequently, it viewed reservations based on caste and reservations based on economic status as mutually exclusive too: casteism could be addressed through reservations based on caste while classism could be addressed by reservations based on economic status.

This was despite the overwhelming statistical evidence that low caste status and low economic status coincided in reality and that those belonging to the lowest caste groups *were* the most economically poor section in the country.[124] In excluding the economically weakest section which was also the lowest caste (Dalits) from reservations meant for economically weaker sections, the majority of the Supreme Court enacted casteism of its own in addition to the casteism of the constitutional amendment.

The 103rd constitutional amendment and *Janhit* have dealt a serious blow to reservations by minimizing their anti-caste potential. This anti-caste potential was for addressing material inequality of Dalits first and foremost.[125] It was also meant to exceed the context of reservations and achieve transformation of the Indian society as such. Anti-casteism has, however, not only been limited *within* but also *to* the context of reservations. The latter is explored below.

9.3.3 Beyond Reservations

Beyond reservations, constitutional challenges to caste discrimination are not common.[126] Instead, most litigation is concentrated at the statutory level. This is because the statutes create both civil rights and remedies—through their articulation of specific rights and entitlements (including in the form of offences) as well as access to ordinary courts and a range of remedies. For example, the Untouchability (Offences) Act 1955 was amended and renamed in 1976 as the Protection of

[123] *Janhit* (n 121) [7.6] [10.2].

[124] ibid [101] (Bhat J, dissenting). Ashwini Deshpande and Rajesh Ramachandran, 'The 10% quota: Is Caste still an Indicator of Backwardness?' (2019) 54 Economic & Political Weekly 27.

[125] This argument is made in Shreya Atrey, 'The Grounds of Affirmative Action' (2025) 47 Human Rights Quarterly 189.

[126] In fact, more broadly, most equality jurisprudence under the constitution, until recently, has been about reservations, with the consequence that the guarantee of equality and non-discrimination is relatively underdeveloped aside of the context of constitutionally mandated affirmative action. Tarunabh Khaitan, 'The Architecture of Discrimination Law' in Vidhu Verma (ed), *Unequal Worlds: Discrimination and Social Inequality in Modern India* (OUP 2015).

Civil Rights Act 1955. Paradigmatic cases of untouchability, such as denial of access to wells—a matter specifically mentioned both in articles 15(2) and 17 of the Constitution—are thus prosecuted and punished under the Protection of Civil Rights Act 1955 rather than the constitution.[127] Similarly, criminal prosecutions are pursued under the Scheduled Castes and Scheduled Tribes (Prevention of Atrocities) Act of 1989 even though enforcement gaps remain glaring.[128]

Recent case law such as *Patan Jamal Vali v State of Andhra Pradesh*[129] presents a striking example of transformative anti-casteism in statutory law.[130] The case concerned the rape of blind Dalit girl from a family of manual workers in a village in the state of Andhra Pradesh. The Supreme Court applied an intersectional lens to analyse the nature of sexual assault based on gender, caste, and disability.[131] Importantly, it held that: 'Intersectionality merely urges us to have "an open-textured legal approach that would examine underlying structures of inequality". This requires us to analyse law in its social and economic context allowing us to formulate questions of equality as that of "power and powerlessness".'[132] Applying this lens, the Supreme Court held that a conviction under the Scheduled Castes and Scheduled Tribes (Prevention of Atrocities) Act of 1989 'can be sustained as long as caste identity is one of the grounds for the occurrence of the offence' and not necessarily the 'only' ground involved in the offence.[133] Further, even where prosecution cannot not lead evidence on the point that the offence is committed *on grounds of* caste, the Supreme Court was clear that when the victim is Dalit, their caste cannot be 'extraneous to the sentencing process for an offence'.[134]

Patan Jamal does not refer to the constitution's anti-caste mandate. It is plainly a case under statutory law and does not concern the constitution's equality code or the constitutional prohibition of discrimination. Yet, its anti-caste perspective is clearly giving effect to the constitution's anti-caste mandate.

[127] *State of Karnataka v Appa Balu Ingale* (1995) Supp (4) SCC 469.

[128] *National Campaign on Dalit Human Rights v Union of India* AIR 2017 SC 132; *Hariram Bhambhi v Satyanarayan* (2021) INSC 701.

[129] (2021) INSC 272 [hereafter *Patan Jamal*].

[130] *Safai Karamchari Andolan v Union of India* (2016) 1 SCC 463 and *Dr Balram Singh v Union of India* (2014) 11 SCC 224 enforcing anti-casteism under the Employment of Manual Scavengers and Construction of Dry Latrines (Prohibition) Act 1993 and the Prohibition of Employment as Manual Scavengers and their Rehabilitation Act 2013.

[131] *Patan Jamal* (n 129) [12] ('the experiences of assault are different in the case of a woman who belongs to a Scheduled Caste community and has a disability because the assault is a result of the interlocking of different relationships of power at play. When the identity of a woman intersects with, inter alia, her caste, class, religion, disability and sexual orientation, she may face violence and discrimination due to two or more grounds. Transwomen may face violence on account of their heterodox gender identity. In such a situation, it becomes imperative to use an intersectional lens to evaluate how multiple sources of oppression operate cumulatively to produce a specific experience of subordination for a blind Scheduled Caste woman.')

[132] ibid [17] (reference omitted).

[133] ibid [55].

[134] ibid [72].

It is surprising then that judges at times fail to do this for constitutional law. Importantly, when the constitution is invoked to challenge casteism, the results are not necessarily favourable. *Rajbala v State of Haryana*[135] is a good illustration of the absence of anti-casteism in constitutional adjudication beyond reservations.

Rajbala concerned a constitutional challenge to the Haryana Panchayati Raj (Amendment) Act 2015 which imposed (i) a minimum educational qualification of matriculation and (ii) the requirement to have a functional toilet at home, as criteria of eligibility for candidature for the village 'panchayats' or local self-governing bodies. These requirements were argued as having the effect of disqualifying over 50 per cent of those eligible to stand for panchayat elections and especially poor people, women, and Dalits. For example, in Haryana, only 59 per cent of Dalit men and 32 per cent of Dalit women were educated, which meant that, 41 per cent Dalit men and 68 per cent Dalit women were rendered ineligible for panchayats.[136] Writing for the Court, Chelameswar J found the requirements to be consistent with the right to equality guaranteed under article 14 of the constitution which provides that 'the State shall not deny to any person equality before the law or the equal protection of the laws within the territory of India'. He found that 'it is only education which gives a human being the power to discriminate between right and wrong, good and bad' and hence concluded that the 'prescription of an educational qualification is not irrelevant for better administration of the Panchayats'.[137] This was the extent of the Supreme Court's non-discrimination analysis. There was no consideration of caste and gender discrimination under article 15(1) of the Constitution which provides that: 'The State shall not discriminate against any citizen on grounds only of religion, race, caste, sex, place of birth or any of them.' There was no consideration of poverty or class discrimination either.

Ultimately, Chelameswar J treated the impact of the impugned classification with trifling importance, choosing to focus instead on the benefits of education and its tenuous link with governance. He thus ignored that the lack of education and toilets were often a consequence of poverty, gender, and caste and not a matter of will or choice. Equally, he ignored that the impugned legislation, by disqualifying poor, women, and Dalits, exacerbated not only their political marginalization but also their material deprivation of resources or income, of education, and of basic amenities such as toilets.[138]

Shri Krishna Singh v Mathura Ahir[139] is another example of the absence of anti-casteism in constitutional rights adjudication. Here, the practice of excluding Dalits from priesthood as a 'mahant' in a 'math' or temple was deemed constitutionally

[135] (2016) 1 SCC 463.
[136] ibid [80] [82].
[137] ibid [85].
[138] This discussion can be found in Shreya Atrey, 'The Intersectional Case of Poverty in Discrimination Law' (2018) 18 Human Rights Law Review 411, 419–420.
[139] (1981) 3 SCC 689.

valid. Likewise, in *Adi Saiva Sivachariyargal Nala Sangam v State of Tamil Nadu*,[140] the Supreme Court declined to subject the appointment of certain temple priests ('Archakas') to the constitutional anti-caste mandate. Instead, the Supreme Court upheld the religious rights of temples constructed as per 'Agamas' to restrict the appointment of Archakas to particular religious denominations. In other words, caste discrimination was justified as a matter of religious freedom and not caught by the constitution's anti-caste mandate.

The problem is not limited to the disapplication of the constitution's anti-caste mandate. The problem lies also in its misapplication, specifically overextension to contexts beyond caste. Chandrachud J's opinion in the *Sabrimala* case—*Indian Young Lawyers Association v State of Kerala*[141]—is a cautionary tale against the overextension of the constitution's anti-caste mandate to gender.

In *Sabrimala*, the majority of the Supreme Court lifted the ban on women of reproductive age from entering the famed Sabrimala temple. The ban was based on the belief that menstruating women could lure the deity worshipped at Sabrimala. While three of the four judges in the majority considered the ban as a matter of women's right to religion under article 26 of the Constitution, Chandrachud J considered it a discrimination issue. In particular, he considered it a matter of article 17 which prohibited 'untouchability' in all forms. Chandrachud J went through the drafting history of the provision and found that the provision, although it concerned the caste-system, was broad enough to encompass any exclusionary practice. In particular, Chandrachud J extended 'the notion of "purity and pollution"' that underlies article 17 from caste-based untouchability to gender-based restrictions related to menstruation.

Menstruation though is not the only context in which women's bodies, like Dalit bodies, are deemed impure and polluted.[142] Views on impurity of women's vaginas that seek to justify the practice of female genital mutilation (FGM), or impurity of hair which seek to justify practices pertaining to sacrifice of hair, and of pregnant and post-partem bodies on which a range of religious and cultural exclusions apply, are all gendered. Seeing all of these exclusionary views and practices based on them as now simply about untouchability does away with the caste link of untouchability as much as it does away with what may be specific to gendered aspects of discrimination.[143] It treats not only Dalit men and upper-caste women who suffer caste-based and gender discrimination respectively interchangeably,

[140] (2016) 2 SCC 725.

[141] (2019) 11 SCC 1 [hereafter *Sabrimala*].

[142] This discussion can be found in Shreya Atrey, 'Feminist Constitutionalism: Mapping a Discourse in Contestation' (2022) 20 International Journal of Constitutional Law 611, 639–640.

[143] In Malhotra J's dissent, she insisted that: 'All forms of exclusion would not [be] tantamount to untouchability. Article 17 pertains to untouchability based on caste prejudice. Literally or historically, untouchability was never understood to apply to women as a class.' *Sabrimala* (n 141) [14.2] (Malhotra J, dissenting).

but also treats those defined at the intersection of caste and gender, viz. Dalit women, triflingly. Equating gender discrimination with untouchability does little to explain the specific position of Dalit women. For Dalit women, untouchability is equally pronounced as for Dalit men, being barred from, say, temples generally; but disconcertingly, also specifically, being admitted to temples as *devdasis*, or temple prostitutes, made available for sexual service to upper-caste men, in the name of god. The intersectional position of Dalit women and their complicated experience of untouchability throws the caste–gender analogy in doubt. In drawing a simplistic analogy between caste and gender, Chandrachud J erased the specificity of both casteism as well as gendered casteism in *Sabrimala*.

9.3.4 Transformative Anti-Casteism in the Making

Where in Indian constitutional jurisprudence do we see anti-casteism practised then?

In *Sukanya Shanta v Union of India*,[144] the petitioner, a journalist, challenged caste-based discrimination in Indian prisons in relation to division of labour, segregation in barracks, designation of certain tribes as 'habitual offenders', etc.[145] This time, writing for the Supreme Court as the Chief Justice of India, Chandrachud CJ began with a reminder of the anti-caste mandate of the constitution which prohibits caste discrimination and requires 'sustained effort, dedication, and the willingness to confront and challenge societal norms'.[146] He confirmed that the anti-caste mandate of the constitution is imagined as an 'ongoing struggle to dismantle caste-based discrimination'[147] and thus reaffirmed the need for continuity of efforts to eliminate both de jure and de facto caste discrimination.[148]

The Supreme Court recalled the long history of caste discrimination in colonial prisons,[149] along with the prohibition of caste discrimination in the postcolonial constitution,[150] to impose a high burden of justification on the state to show that caste-based discrimination in prisons could be sustained.[151] It found that, in fact, no such justification, whether based on correction, rehabilitation, discipline, etc, could exist as caste-based segregation was 'rights-effacing and inherently discriminatory' and hence had 'no place under the Indian Constitution'.[152] It concluded

144 2024 INSC 753 [hereafter *Sukanya Shanta*].
145 Sukanya Shantha, 'From Segregation to Labour, Manu's Caste Law Governs the Indian Prison System' (3 October 2024) The Wire <https://thewire.in/caste/india-prisons-caste-labour-segregation> (accessed 28 July 2025).
146 *Sukanya Shanta* (n 144) [5]–[24].
147 ibid [24].
148 ibid [228].
149 ibid [151]–[160].
150 ibid [164].
151 ibid [165]–[166].
152 ibid [167].

that caste-based provisions in prisons were directly discriminatory where they 'discriminate against marginalized castes and act to the advantage of certain castes [b]y assigning cleaning and sweeping work to the marginalized castes, while allowing the high castes to do cooking'.[153] Likewise, the provisions were indirectly discriminatory where they used 'broad terms which act to the disadvantage of the marginalized castes. Phrases such as "menial" jobs to be performed by castes "accustomed to perform such duties" may appear to be ostensibly neutral, but refer to marginalized communities, given the history of systemic discrimination against them ... These provisions disproportionately harm marginalized castes, perpetuate caste-based labour divisions and reinforce social hierarchies'.[154] The impugned provisions were thus declared unconstitutional, inter alia, under article 15(1) of the constitution and also under article 17 which prohibits untouchability.

Sukanya Shanta is significant because its facts represent not only a central case of structural racism but also because the judgment is an exemplar of transformative anti-racism.

The Supreme Court classified *Sukanya Shanta* as 'an instance of institutional systemic discrimination'.[155] In classifying *Sukanya Shanta* as such, the Supreme Court reminded that when 'the State itself' discriminates on the basis of caste it is 'discrimination of the highest form'.[156] Relying on its previous decisions in *Joseph Shine v Union of India*[157] and *Nitisha v Union of India*[158] which had articulated a clear view on structural discrimination, the Supreme Court was able to articulate a clear view on casteism as a structural issue:

> hierarchical view of social status plays into the caste-based division of labour and morality that has long been entrenched in Indian society. While those from higher castes or classes were perceived as refined and deserving of more lenient treatment (even within the colonial criminal justice system), those from lower castes or marginalized communities were viewed as having a natural tendency

[153] ibid [171].
[154] ibid [172].
[155] ibid [230].
[156] ibid [35].
[157] (2019) 3 SCC 39 ('provision of law must not be viewed as operating in isolation from the social, political, historical and cultural contexts in which it operates').
[158] (2021) 15 SCC 125 ('A particular discriminatory practice or provision might often be insufficient to expose the entire gamut of discrimination that a particular structure may perpetuate. Exclusive reliance on tools of direct or indirect discrimination may also not effectively account for patterns arising out of multiple axles of discrimination. Therefore, a systemic view of discrimination, in perceiving discriminatory disadvantage as a continuum, would account for not just unjust action but also inaction. Structures, in the form of organizations or otherwise, would be probed for the systems or cultures they produce that influence day-today interaction and decisionmaking. The duty of constitutional courts, when confronted with such a scheme of things, would not just be to strike down the discriminatory practices and compensate for the harm hitherto arising out of them; but also structure adequate reliefs and remedies that facilitate social redistribution by providing for positive entitlements that aim to negate the scope of future harm').

towards criminality or immorality. This was not only an injustice but also reinforced existing *power structures*, ensuring that marginalized groups were trapped in cycles of poverty and discrimination, unable to transcend the stigmatization they faced.[159]

In addition, the Supreme Court formulated an extensive range of remedies. It directed the impugned provisions to be declared unconstitutional and the prison manuals/rules to be revised. It also declared taking 'suo moto cognisance of the discrimination inside prisons on any ground such as caste, gender, disability, and [listing] the case from now onwards as In Re: Discrimination Inside Prisons in India'.[160] It mandated the states and the central government to file compliance reports on the judgment and also directed the relevant authorities to conduct 'regular inspections to identify whether caste-based discrimination or similar discriminatory practices, as highlighted in this judgment, are still taking place inside prisons'.[161] These forward-looking continuing administrative remedies clearly go beyond the interpretation and declaration of constitutional law but towards its monitoring and enforcement of the constitution's anti-caste mandate.

In sum, *Sukanya Shanta* did four things to pursue transformative anti-racism doctrinally. First, it enlarged the personal scope of racial discrimination claims by allowing a journalist to bring a claim and then taking suo moto cognizance of all such claims in the future. Second, it enlarged the material scope of racial discrimination to include structural racism (casteism) by appreciating the state's role in racializing and instating racial disadvantage. Third, it enlarged the evidential scope of racial discrimination by drawing on a range of testimonial, documentary, historical, sociological, official, and other evidence. Fourth, it enlarged the remedial scope of racial discrimination to include broad-based remedies.[162]

[159] *Sukanya Shanta* (n 144) [184] (emphasis supplied).
[160] ibid 147.
[161] Ibid.
[162] Under statutory law, the expansion of personal, material, evidential, and remedial scope of law to enforce anti-casteism can be observed in *Amanatullah Khan v The Commissioner of Police, Delhi* (2024) INSC 383 [14] [16] ('Having partially addressed the grievance of the appellant, we now, in exercise of our suo motu powers, propose to expand the scope of these proceedings so that the police authorities in other States and Union Territories may also consider the desirability of ensuring that no mechanical entries in History Sheet are made of innocent individuals, simply because they happen to hail from the socially, economically and educationally disadvantaged backgrounds, along with those belonging to Backward Communities, Scheduled Castes & Scheduled Tribes. While we are not sure about the degree of their authenticity, but there are some studies available in the public domain that reveal a pattern of an unfair, prejudicial and atrocious mindset. It is alleged that the Police Diaries are maintained selectively of individuals belonging to Vimukta Jatis, based solely on caste-bias, a somewhat similar manner as happened in colonial times ... We must bear in mind that these preconceived notions often render them 'invisible victims' due to prevailing stereotypes associated with their communities, which may often impede their right to live a life with self-respect ... It seems that a periodic audit mechanism overseen by a senior police officer, as directed for the NCT of Delhi, will serve as a critical tool to review and scrutinize the entries made, so as to ascertain that these are devoid of any biases or discriminatory

All that said, much like Canadian constitutional law, Indian constitutional law too seems to have too few examples actually *doing* transformative anti-racism or anti-casteism to unequivocally reflect anti-racism as a legal principle. This is despite the constitutions' text and spirit instating such a principle, especially in the constitutional guarantees prohibiting racial and caste discrimination and a range of other enabling provisions for Indigenous peoples and *Bahujans*. Just as *Corbiere* was the only genuine example of transformative anti-racism under article 15 of the Canadian Charter, *Sukanya Shanta* is the only genuine example of transformative anti-casteism under article 15 of the Indian constitution.

However, unlike Canadian constitutional law, Indian constitutional law's resistance to anti-casteism cannot be pinned down to uniform doctrinal patterns. Indian constitutional jurisprudence on caste discrimination both within and beyond reservations, can, depending on the composition of the bench and its proclivities, be broad or narrow in terms of its personal, material, evidential, and remedial scope. In this landscape, successful cases often appear fortuitously rather than consciously in appreciation of precedent or principle.[163] There is an unpredictability to the Indian Supreme Court's doctrine which even the clearest constitutional mandate for anti-casteism cannot seem to counter.

9.4 South Africa

The three sections below capture South Africa's constitutional commitment to three values—non-racialism, transformation, and decolonization—and the extent to which they reflect a principle of anti-racism (Section 9.4.1), and the treatment of claims of racial discrimination (Section 9.4.2) and other constitutional claims (Section 9.4.3) in light of this principle. The discussion shows that much like Canada and India, South Africa too recognizes anti-racism as a legal principle. But the principle does not seem to be applied consistently across racial discrimination claims. Other than rare instances such as *Mahlangu v Minister of Labour*,[164] the jurisprudence on racial discrimination under section 9 of the South African constitution is poor in responding to structural racism and ultimately in giving effect to anti-racism. Remarkably, however, the principle is applied with greater consistency and effect in other constitutional claims. The discussion unravels the interpretive work done by anti-racism as a legal principle

practices. Through the effective implementation of audits, we can secure the elimination of such deprecated practices').

[163] Gautam Bhatia and Shreya Atrey, '70 Years of Gender Jurisprudence in India' in Wen-Chen Chang et al (eds), *Gender, Sexuality and Constitutionalism in Asia* (Hart 2023) 265.

[164] [2020] ZACC 24 [hereafter *Mahlangu*].

in these other claims. Ultimately, the discussion confirms the doctrinal limitations which plague racial discrimination law in terms of its personal, material, evidential, and remedial scope. But the discussion also reveals the possibilities that exist and are realized outside of the context of racial discrimination law in constitutional law generally.

9.4.1 Non-Racialism, Transformation, and Decolonization

9.4.1.1 Non-Racialism

Chapter 1 of the South African Constitution 1996 lists 'founding values' and in section 1 declares that:

> The Republic of South Africa is one, sovereign, democratic state founded on the following values: (a) Human dignity, the achievement of *equality* and the advancement of human rights and freedoms. (b) *Non-racialism* and non-sexism. (c) Supremacy of the constitution and the rule of law. (d) Universal adult suffrage, a national common voters roll, regular elections and a multi-party system of democratic government, to ensure accountability, responsiveness and openness.[165]

Non-racialism, alongside dignity, equality, human rights, and non-sexism, is not simply a foundational constitutional value but a 'state policy as well as a constitutional principle'.[166] As we have seen so far, while references to race and racial discrimination are common in law, references to racism and anti-racism are less common. Non-racialism is thus unique and captures something distinct about post-apartheid South Africa and its constitution.

Non-racialism can be traced back to the African National Congress (ANC) and its politics of strategic engagement and coalition building wherein non-racialism was conceived as a way of 'being together'.[167] The ANC imagined the post-apartheid non-racial democratic state as belonging to everyone who lived in it, irrespective of race. That is, South Africa was imagined as a multiracial 'rainbow' nation (as opposed to both the white apartheid nation as well as a post-apartheid Black African nation) where racial diversity is accepted and appreciated rather than denied and disadvantaged. Thus, while non-racialism rejects

[165] Emphasis supplied.

[166] Neeshan Balton, 'Becoming a 21st Century Non-Racialist in South Africa' (2016) Short Paper Series on Race and Identity (ASRI) <https://asri.org.za/race-identity/> (accessed 6 September 2025).

[167] Shula Marks, 'The Tradition of Non-Racism in South Africa', Eleanor Rathbone Memorial Lecture (Liverpool University Press 1994) 19–20.

the biological construction of race, it is not blind to the social construct of race and can be distinguished from the colourblind constitutionalism of the United States.[168]

Yet, non-racialism is also not anti-racism. Its preference for a multiracial South Africa is on all fours with Chapter 3's account of cultural anti-racism which responds to racism by trying to change how people express and experience their racial identities rather than by addressing the vast material gaps between racialized groups. Non-racialism, like cultural anti-racism, thus does not recognize or respond to structural racism and leaves intact the reality of material deprivation of Black people in South Africa.[169] Non-racialism thus stops well short of transformative anti-racism and its 'opposition to the capitalist structures for the perpetuation of which the ideology and theory of "race" exist'.[170]

9.4.1.2 Transformation

Even if non-racialism does not chime with transformative anti-racism, the South African constitution itself, and as a whole, is considered transformative, in the specific sense that it is aimed at 'social redistributive justice'[171] or 'redistribution of power and resources'.[172] Though transformative constitutionalism is

[168] Deborah Posel, 'Whither "Non-Racialism": The "New" South Africa Turns Twenty-One' (2015) 38 Ethnic and Racial Studies 2167, 2169 ('the meaning of non-racialism as it was used in South Africa's transition to democracy, was never post-racial. It was not a Utopian project looking to a future in which race would be erased. It was, rather, a fundamentally more pragmatic, if also principled, engagement with the realities of the present—a critical tool, in fact, in stabilizing a precarious transition and performing the conditions of an emergent and fragile national collective').

[169] Joel M Modiri, 'Towards a "(Post-)Apartheid" Critical Race Jurisprudence: "Divining our Racial Themes"' (2012) 27 South African Public Law 231, 256 [hereafter Modiri, 'Towards a "(Post-) Apartheid" Critical Race Jurisprudence'] ('While South Africa, through its Constitution and the establishment of a liberal democratic multicultural political order, has seemingly rejected white supremacy as a "normative vision", this rejection has not been tethered to a transformative social commitment to eradicate the substantive conditions of Black suffering and racial subordination. Because South Africa was, for over 350 years, organised expressly around white supremacist principles, it cannot simply cease to be white supremacist through a formal declaration of racial equality and non-racialism.'); Nikolay Zakharov et al (eds), *Futures of Anti-Racism Paradoxes of Deracialisation in Brazil, South Africa, Sweden, and the UK* (Palgrave 2022) 22 [hereafter Zakharov et al (eds), *Futures of Anti-Racism*] ('The politics of non-racialism contained in rainbowism has failed in South Africa because of continuing white supremacy and Black disadvantage.').

[170] Robin M Petersen, 'Discourses of Difference and Sameness in South Africa: Race, Racism and Non-Racialism' in James R Cochrane and Bastienne Klein (eds), *Sameness and Difference: Problems and Potentials in South African Civil Society* (Council for Research in Values and Philosophy 2000); Raymond Suttner, 'Understanding Non-racialism as an Emancipatory Concept in South Africa' (2012) 59 Theoria: A Journal of Social and Political Theory 22; Greg Ruiters, 'Non-Racialism: The New Form of Racial Inequality in a Neo-Apartheid South Africa' (2020) 56 Journal of Asian and African Studies 889.

[171] Dikgang Moseneke, 'The Fourth Braam Fischer Memorial Lecture: Transformative Adjudication' (2002) 18 South African Journal on Human Rights 309, 318.

[172] Catherine Albertyn and Beth Goldblatt, 'Facing the Challenge of Transformation: Difficulties in the Development of an Indigenous Jurisprudence of Equality' (1998) 14 South African Journal on Human Rights 248, 249.

all-encompassing,[173] at its heart, transformation is about redistributive justice to address the vast material gaps between white and Black South Africans.

It is also 'widely acknowledged that the South African Constitution incorporates the *ubuntu* value system; an African philosophical system of community, caring, and restorative and redistributive justice'.[174] As Yvonne Mgkoro explains, ubuntu signifies 'a philosophy of life, which in its most fundamental sense represents personhood, humanity, humaneness and morality; a metaphor which describes group solidarity where such group solidarity is central to the survival of communities with a scarcity of resources'.[175] *Ubuntu* 'permeates the Constitution generally and more particularly... the entrenched fundamental human rights'.[176]

Likewise, equality is considered fundamental to the constitution as a value, as a principle and as a right.[177] In fact, transformative constitutionalism includes not only a formal declaration of equality but also a commitment to substantive equality which includes intersectionality.[178] Section 9 of the constitution embodies this expansive vision of equality and provides that:

(1) Everyone is equal before the law and has the right to equal protection and benefit of the law.
(2) Equality includes the full and equal enjoyment of all rights and freedoms. To promote the achievement of equality, legislative and other measures designed to protect or advance persons, or categories of persons, disadvantaged by unfair discrimination may be taken.
(3) The state may not unfairly discriminate directly or indirectly against anyone on one or more grounds, including race, gender, sex, pregnancy, marital status, ethnic or social origin, colour, sexual orientation, age, disability, religion, conscience, belief, culture, language and birth.
(4) No person may unfairly discriminate directly or indirectly against anyone on one or more grounds in terms of subsection (3). National legislation must be enacted to prevent or prohibit unfair discrimination.
(5) Discrimination on one or more of the grounds listed in subsection (3) is unfair unless it is established that the discrimination is fair.

[173] Karl Klare, 'Legal Culture and Transformative Constitutionalism' (1998) 14 South African Journal on Human Rights 146, 150 [hereafter Klare, 'Legal Culture'] ('long-term project of constitutional enactment, interpretation, and enforcement committed... to transforming a country's political and social institutions and power relationships in a democratic participatory and egalitarian direction').

[174] Christopher G Thomas, 'Ubuntu: The Missing Link in the Rights Discourse in Post-Apartheid Transformation in South Africa' (2008) 3 International Journal of African Renaissance Studies 39, 53–54.

[175] Yvonne Mokgoro, 'Ubuntu and the Law in South Africa' (1998) 4 Buffalo Human Rights Law Review 15.

[176] *S v Makwanyane* [1995] ZACC 3 [237] (Madala J).

[177] Hugh Corder, 'Towards a South African Constitution' (1994) 57 Modern Law Review 491, 511.

[178] Klare, 'Legal Culture' (n 173) 194.

Five things stand out in the text of section 9. First, section 9(3) contains a much longer list of grounds than is found in the Canadian Charter or the Indian constitution. It thus includes a longer list of racial grounds too—race, ethnic or social origin, colour, culture, language, and birth—and in any case that list is open-ended and allows for the recognition of analogous grounds. Second, section 9(3) prohibits discrimination on 'one or more grounds' and thus also prohibits intersectional discrimination. Third, section 9(4) recognizes that not only the state but also 'no person' may unfairly discriminate against another and thus prohibits discrimination both vertically and horizontally. Fourth, discrimination on listed grounds is *presumed* to be unfair under section 9(5). Fifth, only unfair discrimination is prohibited, leaving open the possibility of affirmative action under section 9(2). These characteristics enable the recognition of structural racism as a form of racial discrimination by *the state or state-like entities* which *racializes* based on a range of racial grounds to instate *racial disadvantage*. Further, the recognition of intersectionality and affirmative action furthers transformative anti-racism in not only *redressing structural racism* but doing so on *an intersectional basis* and through *broad-based proactive measures*. Section 9 on the right to equality and non-discrimination may thus rightly be considered as embodying a principle of transformative anti-racism.

In a similar vein, dignity is both recognized as a value in section 1 of the constitution and a right under section 10 of the constitution. It is considered a 'lodestar' of the constitution.[179] The inclusion of socio-economic rights,[180] the accommodation for customary law,[181] and the importance of international law in interpreting the constitution[182] are also aspects which make the South African constitution 'transformative'. These aspects are collectively meant to enable South Africa's transition from a colonial, racist, apartheid state to a new order which is its anti-thesis.

Given South Africa's commitment to transformation, it is safe to say that the constitution's anti-racist mandate cannot be limited to the value of non-racialism which is simply about multiracialism. Instead, the right to equality and non-discrimination may be rightly interpreted to embrace a principle of anti-racism. In fact, a fuller and more accurate account of the constitution's anti-racist mandate would include its entire transformative agenda which in turn includes a commitment to redistributive justice and the replacement of oppressive structures with emancipatory ones. Anti-racism should thus be considered as underlying not only the right to equality and non-discrimination but transformative constitutionalism as a whole.

[179] Laurie Ackermann, *Human Dignity: Lodestar for Equality in South Africa* (Juta 2012).
[180] The Constitution of the Republic of South Africa 1996, ss 22–31.
[181] The Constitution of the Republic of South Africa 1996, ss 39(2)–(3), 211, 212.
[182] The Constitution of the Republic of South Africa 1996, ss 39(1)(b), 233.

9.4.1.3 Decolonization

The text and spirit of the South African constitution signal an unequivocal commitment to transformation. As argued above, this commitment goes beyond non-racialism and even the right to equality and non-discrimination. It embodies the whole range of values, principles, and rights entailed in the constitution. It includes, in particular, a commitment to redistributive justice for advancing the material well-being of Black people. It is plainly reflected in provisions such as section 25(5) of the constitution which provides that: 'the state must take reasonable legislative and other measures, within its available resources, to foster conditions which enable citizens to gain access to land on an equitable basis.' After all, as Makau Mutua reminds us, 'the struggle against apartheid was not waged so that blacks can boast of abstract political rights. It was waged so that blacks could have equal access to economic resources.'[183]

However, redistributive justice has failed to materialize in the first thirty years of the new constitutional order.[184] South Africa, today, is the most unequal country in the world.[185] Race is the single biggest determinant of inequality in terms of income, wealth, health outcomes, employment rates, and educational attainment.[186]

The root cause of this racial inequality is obviously historical—the forced dispossession of Black people's land by white people during colonialism and apartheid. The constitution, despite its commitment to transformation, has failed to resolve the land question—the return of and reparation for the land stolen from Black people. Quite simply, the constitution 'offered black people the right and not the means to own land'.[187] Racial inequality has thus remained 'a disturbing constant' in both apartheid and post-apartheid state.[188] No wonder, public protests against state failures have generated a 'spectre of angry and disillusioned people holding up the Constitution and asking whether this is what the struggle was all about'.[189]

As Zackie Achmat, former Treatment Action Campaign leader, says, the failure to resolve the land question and to share wealth and resources, especially

[183] Makau W Mutua, 'Hope and Despair for a New South Africa: The Limits of a Rights Discourse' (1997) 10 Harvard Human Rights Journal 63, 89.

[184] Kevin Durrheim and Amy Jo Murray, 'The Haunting Quality of Racism' (2021) 62 Psychology in Society 46, 54 ('The post-apartheid state—like the post-colonial world—continues to be defined by deepening inequality, racial exclusions and Whiteness.').

[185] The World Inequality Database <https://wid.world/world/#sptinc_p90p100_z/US;FR;DE;CN;GB;WO/last/eu/k/p/yearly/s/false/25.030500000000004/80/curve/false/country> (accessed 5 September 2025).

[186] The World Bank, 'Inequality in Southern Africa: An Assessment of the Southern African Customs Union', Country Brief: South Africa <https://documents1.worldbank.org/curated/en/099125003072240961/pdf/P1649270b73f1f0b5093fb0e644d33bc6f1.pdf> (accessed 5 September 2025).

[187] Mabogo More, 'Fanon and the Land Question in (Post-)apartheid South Africa' in Nigel C Gibson (ed), *Living Fanon: Global Perspectives* (Palgrave Macmillan 2011) 173–187.

[188] T Alexander Aleinikoff, 'The Constitution in Context: The Continuing Significance of Racism' (1992) 63 University of Colorado Law Review 325, 326.

[189] Christof Heyns and Daine Brand, 'Introduction to Socio-economic Rights in the South African Constitution' (1998) 2 Law, Democracy and Development 153, 154.

land, is one of 'the most dangerous forms of racism in this country'.[190] The post-apartheid constitution and its 'master frame' of transformation are thus legitimately critiqued for having contributed to, or at the very least, for being complicit in, 'neo-apartheid' in contemporary South African society.[191] Demands for a new decolonial constitutional order 'in which the back of White supremacy has been broken by the thoroughgoing material undoing of colonialism'[192] continue to grow.[193]

Whether or not these demands should come to pass cannot be mooted here. What is critical for our purposes is the centrality of anti-racism in both the current 'transformative' constitutional order and the demands for a new 'decolonial' constitutional order. As Jonathan Jansen reminds us: 'It is only through anti-racism that we can engage with the 'de' of deracialization and decolonization. That is, where 'de' means to remove, to negate, to reverse the intensity of, to change something to its opposite. 'De' is active in its reversals, in doing the opposite of.'[194] In a similar vein, Part I of the book argued that anti-racism is only entailed in the active reversal of structural racism through disruptive, broad-based, and intersectional change. This framing of anti-racism coincides with the idea of transformation as much as it coincides with decolonization and its emphasis on 'replacing of a systemic plague of conditions … a fundamental paradigm shift in social redress that affects all lives in South Africa in order to achieve real independence and freedom'.[195] Normatively, anti-racism appears to be a part of all radical imaginaries which seek to dismantle and replace structures which generate racial disadvantage and poverty.

So, whether one chooses a constitutionalism of transformation or decolonization, anti-racism, as a legal principle, will be central either way. In any case, what is

[190] Yolisa Tswanya, 'Activists Cry Racism Over "Toxic" Housing Quote' <http://www.iol.co.za/news/south-africa/western-cape/activists-cry-racism-over-toxic-housing-quote-2027442> (accessed 5 September 2025).

[191] Tshepo Madlingozi, 'Social Justice in a Time of Neo-apartheid Constitutionalism: Critiquing the Anti-black Economy of Recognition, Incorporation and Distribution' (2017) 28 Stellenbosch Law Review 123.

[192] Kevin Durrheim and Amy Jo Murray, 'The Haunting Quality of Racism' (2021) 62 Psychology in Society 46.

[193] Heinz Klug, 'Challenging Constitutionalism in Post-Apartheid South Africa' (2016) 2 Constitutional Studies 41; Modiri, 'Towards a "(Post-)Apartheid" Critical Race Jurisprudence' (n 169); Nigel C Gibson 'What Happened to the Promised Land: A Fanonian Perspective of Post-apartheid South Africa' (2011) 44 Antipode 51; Mogobe B Ramose, 'In Memoriam: Sovereignty and the "New" South Africa' (2007) 16 Griffith Law Review 310; Mogobe B Ramose, 'Philosophy and Economic Independence in Africa' (2006) 25 Politea 3; Mahmood Mamdani, 'When does Reconciliation Turn into a Denial of Justice?' (Sam Nolutshungu Memorial Series No 1, HSRC Publishers 1998).

[194] Zakharov et al (eds), *Futures of Anti-Racism* (n 169) 50 (quotation from interview); ibid 65–66 (quoting Zethu Matebeni: 'in South Africa deracialization is not yet something that we are engaging with … It's not deracialization but anti-racism that is important'); ibid 67 ('Decolonization focused on what it is to be South African / who can be African allied with anti-racism and profound socio-economic, psychological, cultural and political change is the current motor for social justice transformation and much needed racial equality').

[195] Patrick Tariq Mellet, *The Lie of 1652: A Decolonised History of Land* (Tafelberg 2020) 313.

clear is that the present South African constitution already reflects this principle. The next two sections explore how the principle manifests in guiding not only the interpretation of the prohibition of racial discrimination under section 9 (Section 9.4.2) but also the constitution as a whole (Section 9.4.3).

9.4.2 Racial Discrimination

Anti-racism is most directly linked to the prohibition of racial discrimination under section 9(3) of the South African constitution. In particular, the three elements of transformative anti-racism—(i) resistance to structural racism, (ii) call for broad-based change, and (iii) commitment to intersectional justice—can inform how section 9(3) is interpreted and applied. The South African Constitutional Court's jurisprudence on racial discrimination shows perpetual embrace of transformative anti-racism in principle, but only occasional application in practice. Ultimately, even a strong and unequivocal commitment to transformative anti-racism in the South African constitution does not seem to translate automatically into constitutional doctrine. It is important to understand this gap between the principle and its practice.

The early case of *City Council of Pretoria v Walker*[196] brings this gap into sharp relief. The case concerned a white claimant from a predominantly white affluent suburb in Pretoria who complained of racial discrimination by the city council that had continued differential billing for water and electricity by treating residents of Black townships more favourably. The differential pricing for white and Black neighbourhoods was a legacy of apartheid. The slow pace of phasing out differential pricing was a result of the same legacy. The city council was having to manage the vast economic disparity between the neighbourhoods while trying to impose uniform pricing. It thus continued to charge Black neighbourhoods (which had historically not had meters) a lower flat rate while charging white neighbourhoods a higher consumption-based metered rate, until meters could be installed everywhere to ensure uniform pricing.

According to Langa DP, the discrimination inquiry in this case hinged on 'the interplay between the discriminatory measure and the person or group affected by it'.[197] According to Sachs J, 'the less vulnerable the group, the less the likelihood of unfairness. It follows that the place of a complainant in the structures of advantage and disadvantage will always be one of the central elements in the determination

[196] [1998] ZACC 1 [hereafter *Walker*].
[197] ibid [45] (Langa DP).

of how fair or unfair the challenged discrimination is.'[198] This played out in the following way in *Walker*:

> The respondent belongs to a group that has not been disadvantaged by the racial policies and practices of the past. In an economic sense, his group is neither disadvantaged nor vulnerable, having been benefited rather than adversely affected by discrimination in the past ... The fact of the matter is that the discriminatory practices of the past were designed to and did benefit the white community whilst inflicting disadvantage on the black community ... Courts should however always be astute to distinguish between genuine attempts to promote and protect equality on the one hand and actions calculated to protect pockets of privilege at a price which amounts to the perpetuation of inequality and disadvantage to others on the other.[199]

Despite noting that there was 'no evidence that the respondent has been adversely affected in any material way'[200] and that differential pricing and enforcement 'did not impact adversely on the respondent in any material way',[201] Langa DP, writing for the majority, found that the discrimination was indeed unfair because it invaded the respondent's dignity by treating him as less deserving of equal concern, respect, and consideration as a white man as compared to Black people.[202] Sachs J disagreed and for the lack of any material loss to the claimant[203] found that there was no discrimination,[204] and certainly no unfair discrimination in the present case:

> I find it jurisprudentially incongruous to regard the complainant as a victim of unfair discrimination ... He was disturbed in no way in his enjoyment of residence in a neighbourhood which had been made affluent by state-enforced advantage in the past. The group with which he identified himself continued to get the benefit of regular municipal services at all material times. He was not called upon to do any more than to pay what he owed for services he had always received. He was not being singled out or targeted in any way, neither because of his race nor even because he lived in a comfortable neighbourhood. In my view, although treated differently, he was not discriminated against in any manner whatsoever; alternatively, if the council's conduct can correctly be classed as discriminatory against him, it was by no means unfair.[205]

198 ibid [123] (Sachs J, partly dissenting); *President of the Republic of South Africa v Hugo* [1997] ZACC 4 [112] (O'Regan J).
199 *Walker* (n 196) [47] [48] (Langa DP).
200 ibid [65] (Langa DP).
201 ibid [68] (Langa DP).
202 ibid [79]–[81].
203 ibid [110] (Sachs J, partly dissenting).
204 ibid [105] (Sachs J, partly dissenting).
205 ibid [103] (Sachs J, partly dissenting).

Although both Langa DP and Sachs J championed the principle of anti-racism—by taking into account the history of structural racism (apartheid) and the constitutional commitment to transform it—their application of the principle to interpret the right to equality and non-discrimination could not be more different. For the majority, anti-racism did not mean transformation of the material conditions of inequality between historically disadvantaged group (Black people) and historically advantaged group (white people). In any case, for the majority, anti-racism could not undo the otherwise haphazard approach of the city council. For the sole dissenter, anti-racism was nothing but the transformation of material inequality between racialized groups. The city council's approach to redressing such material inequality, even if haphazard, had to be considered reasonable as against the history of racialized poverty in South Africa.

Ultimately, the anti-racism applied by the South African Constitutional Court in *Walker* seems to disregard racism—understood in Chapter 1 in terms of the material conditions of racial disadvantage. The Court seems to understand the other elements of structural racism rather well. That is, given the history of apartheid, the Constitutional Court appreciates that (i) the state through its laws, policies, and practices (ii) can racialize by instating racial ordering and hierarchy. It also seems to understand that such racialization has material consequences such as the concentration of racialized poverty amongst Black people in South Africa. But this understanding is consigned to history; with material consequences of racism *today* treated trivially. Almost thirty years after the post-apartheid constitutional order was instated, the amnesia of material conditions of disadvantage of Black people in present day South Africa remains the main source of discontent with the Constitutional Court's doctrine.[206]

Decided in 1998, the same year as *Walker, Premier, Province of Mpumalanga v Executive Committee of the Association of Governing Bodies of State Aided Schools: Eastern Transvaal*[207] reinforced the Constitutional Court's amnesia of material conditions of racial disadvantage. The case involved a challenge to the termination of government bursaries for needy students in state-aided schools. The termination had affected mainly white students as the bursaries were paid mainly to white students. The termination was not in dispute as there was 'no doubt that this system could not continue for long under the new constitutional dispensation'.[208] The dispute concerned only the manner of termination and whether the termination without reasonable notice breached any legitimate expectation of state schools receiving the bursaries.[209]

206 Consider references in (n 169).
207 [1998] ZACC 20.
208 ibid [37] (O'Regan J).
209 ibid [2] (O'Regan J).

In the very first paragraph of the judgment, O'Regan J recalled the importance of the principle to 'eradicate patterns of racial discrimination and to address the consequences of past discrimination which persist in our society' but then placed procedural fairness at the same level insisting that 'both principles are based on fairness' and thus 'both need to be honoured'.[210] She dismissed as 'too sweeping' the argument that 'because the bursaries were discriminatory in effect, their existence was unconstitutional, and that any means employed to terminate them could not be subject to constitutional challenge'.[211] Only the following words were spared addressing this argument:

> A harmonious balance needs to be found between the urgent need to eradicate unfair discrimination on the one hand, and the obligation to act fairly, on the other. There is no doubt that, in the process of transition upon which we have embarked, we need to remain committed to the goal of equality, but that goal must be pursued in a manner consistent with the other constitutional requirements, including procedural fairness, enshrined in section 24 of the interim Constitution.[212]

The defect in this reasoning is plain: that it puts procedural fairness before anti-racism without justification. The reasoning does not consider or explain how the same constitutional order which made grant of bursaries on a racialized basis illegal also granted procedural rights for the retraction of those illegal bursaries. That O'Regan J found no incongruity in this, again, exposes the Constitutional Court's amnesia of the material reality of racism.[213]

Occasionally, this amnesia lifts and the Constitutional Court takes material conditions of Black people seriously. The decision in *Moseneke v Master of High Court*[214] was one such occasion. The case concerned a challenge to the constitutionality of the Black Administration Act 1927 under which estates of Black deceased persons who died intestate were administered by magistrates—not by the Master of the High Court as for others. A unanimous court summarily found that the impugned provisions were 'so manifestly discriminatory that there can be no doubt as to their unconstitutionality'.[215] 'The real problem in this case', as Sachs J noted, was 'to devise an order that is just and equitable in all the circumstances'.[216] He explained:

[210] ibid [1] (O'Regan J).
[211] ibid [44] (O'Regan J).
[212] ibid.
[213] *DVB Behuising (Pty) Limited v North West Provincial Government* [2000] ZACC 2; *Bel Porto School Governing Body v Premier of the Western Cape Province* [2002] ZACC 2; *Mazibuko v City of Johannesburg* [2009] ZACC 28.
[214] [2000] ZACC 27.
[215] ibid [19] [22] (Sachs J).
[216] ibid [25] (Sachs J).

> To keep a manifestly racist law on the statute books is to maintain discrimination; to abolish it with immediate effect without making practical alternative arrangements is to provoke confusion and risk injustice. Such a dilemma is inherent in transition. The Black Administration Act, as its very name indicates, both reminds us of South Africa's shameful and disgraceful past and continues to make invidious and wounding distinctions on grounds of race. It survives, however, because it has become encrusted with processes of great practical, day-to-day importance to a large number of people.[217]

The Court thus devised a remedy which allowed Black people to 'require the Master to administer the deceased estate as provided for in the Administration of Estates Act, or else opt for the cheaper and more accessible process under the control of the local magistrate, as regulated by the Black Administration Act'.[218] The Court was, though, made aware by the amici of the likely negative impact of this order on Black women but expressed that there was 'not enough material before [it], however, to justify in this matter an investigation into what are complex questions thrown up by the intersection of race, gender, culture and class'.[219]

Unlike *Walker* and *Mpumalanga*, the Court in *Moseneke* showed awareness of the material impact of thrusting a more expensive system of estate management on Black people. But its inability to probe further than race and into gendered racism which affected Black women reveals the limitations of this momentary awareness. It appears that if not racial disadvantage, then another element of transformative anti-racism: intersectionality, seems to be forgotten in constitutional adjudication.

This intersectional awareness also lacked in *Bhe v Magistrate, Khayelitsha*.[220] The case challenged the rule of male primogeniture, according to which only males related to the deceased qualified for intestate succession under customary law. The rule was found to be discriminatory because it excluded: (a) widows from inheriting from their late husbands; (b) daughters from inheriting from their parents; (c) younger sons from inheriting from their parents; and (d) extra-marital children from inheriting from their fathers. The Court was thus fully aware of the gendered nature of the exclusion of the rule of male primogeniture but showed little awareness of the patterns of racialized poverty that intersected with it and affected not any women but Black women in particular.[221]

The material and intersectional amnesia lifted only recently, in 2020, in *Mahlangu v Minister of Labour*.[222] The Constitutional Court in *Mahlangu* held

217 ibid.
218 ibid [27] (Sachs J).
219 ibid [30] (Sachs J).
220 [2004] ZACC 17.
221 Atrey, *Intersectional Discrimination* (n 79) 122–123; Catherine Albertyn and Sandra Fredman, 'Equality Beyond Dignity: Multi- dimensional Equality and Justice Langa's Judgments' (2015) Acta Juridica 430, 446–447.
222 *Mahlangu* (n 164).

that the exclusion of domestic workers from compensation for workplace injury was unconstitutional and violated, inter alia, the constitutional protection against discrimination because it constituted indirect intersectional discrimination against Black women domestic workers on the basis of their social status, gender, race, and class.[223]

While the main judgment (penned by Victor AJ) as well as the two separate opinions all agreed on the unconstitutionality of the exclusion, it was Mhlantla J's opinion which made the historical intersectional discrimination suffered by Black women the mainstay of her judgment. As she declared at the outset, she wrote the concurring opinion 'to underscore the historical significance of this matter coupled with its intersectional nature'.[224] In analysing whether the impugned exclusion constituted unfair discrimination under the South African constitution, Mhlantla J preferred the excavation of the root causes of such discrimination which originated from the 'grinding together of the tectonic plates of racism, sexism, and social class'.[225] She thus traced back the discrimination in domestic work as a relic of white settler colonialism and the slavery, servitude, subordination, and oppression which accompanied it.[226] Taking note of the evidence before the Court, she found that these conditions had not really changed in post-apartheid South Africa and that domestic workers had remained 'severely exploited, undermined, and devalued as a result of their lived experiences at the intersecting axes of discrimination'.[227] It was the appreciation of the structural nature of discrimination suffered by domestic workers that drove Mhlantla J's determination of unfair discrimination. Furthermore, it was explicitly the fact that this case concerned both 'intersectional discrimination' and 'systemic discrimination' that Victor AJ's main judgment in *Mahlangu* provided a retrospective remedy for 'breaking the cycle of poverty' suffered by Black women.[228] A structural view of discrimination thus fed directly into fashioning a retrospective remedy—something far from the norm in cases with significant monetary implications.[229]

Yet, *Mahlangu* is quite an outlier within the Constitutional Court jurisprudence.[230] The tendency to reduce intersectional claims to a single ground continues.[231] Furthermore, between race and gender, it appears that it is easier to

[223] ibid [18].
[224] ibid [184] (Mhlantla J, concurring).
[225] ibid [187] (Mhlantla J, concurring).
[226] ibid [188] (Mhlantla J, concurring).
[227] ibid [195] (Mhlantla J, concurring).
[228] *Mahlangu* (n 164) [128] (Victor AJ).
[229] Shreya Atrey, 'Beyond Discrimination: Mahlangu and the Use of Intersectionality as a General Theory of Constitutional Interpretation' (2021) 21 International Journal of Discrimination Law 168.
[230] *King NO v De Jager* [2021] ZACC 4. Cf *Women's Legal Centre Trust v President of the Republic of South Africa* [2022] ZACC 23; *Centre for Child Law v T S* [2023] ZACC 22; *VJV v Minister of Social Development* [2023] ZACC 21.
[231] For example, Rogers J, writing for a unanimous court in *EB (born S) v ER (born B); KG v Minister of Home Affairs* [2023] ZACC 32 [145] said that: 'I am doubtful whether race, religion, culture or marital status are implicated as direct or indirect grounds of discrimination in these other cases. Although, for

establish a claim of gender as opposed to racial discrimination.[232] That is, cases of racial discrimination find it harder to succeed, unless they are obvious cases of racism such as those involving racist hate speech.[233] Cases which are not explicitly based on racial grounds, but for example, citizenship, are not even examined for racial discrimination.[234] As the next section shows, the prohibition of racial discrimination under section 9(3) of the constitution is not invoked in cases which seem to be about structural racism. Claims of racial discrimination thus do not populate the Court's otherwise prolific jurisprudence. This is strange considering the extremity of racialized disadvantage and poverty in South Africa.

Before moving on to consider how anti-racism fares beyond section 9(3), it is useful to briefly consider how it fares under section 9(2).

Section 9(2) permits affirmative action which is deemed 'crucial to the eradication of the legacy of cemented racism and sexism, which typified the apartheid social, economic, political and legal edifice'.[235] In fact, affirmative action is considered 'an integral part of a bill of rights and not simply a marginal, subsidiary measure to eliminate certain aspects of inequality'.[236]

Even though section 9(2) permits affirmative action, the jurisprudence on section 9(2) has often been read as limiting the transformative potential of the provision. In the very first case under section 9(2), *Minister of Finance v Van Heerden*,[237] the Constitutional Court subjected section 9(2) to a vague and deferential standard

example, the spouses in BAA marriages would be black persons, the lawmaker's reason for granting them the redistribution remedy and withholding it from new ANC marriages was not the race of the spouses but the absence or availability of the accrual regime. Many black persons are spouses in new ANC marriages. If there is indirect discrimination, it is that black wives in new ANC marriages are disproportionately prejudiced as against black husbands by the absence of the redistribution remedy. This is indirect discrimination on the basis of gender rather than race.' *Duncanmec (Pty) Limited v Gaylard NO* [2018] ZACC 29. Cf *Sithole v Sithole* [2021] ZACC 7.

232 ibid.

233 *Rustenburg Platinum Mine v SAEWA obo Bester* [2018] ZACC 13; *South African Revenue Service v Commission for Conciliation, Mediation and Arbitration* [2016] ZACC 38.

234 *Rafoneke v Minister of Justice and Correctional Services and Others (Makombe Intervening)* [2022] ZACC 29 [hereafter *Rafoneke*] (The Constitutional Court upheld the validity of the provisions of the Legal Practice Act 28 of 2014 which bars foreigners from being admitted and authorized as non-practising legal practitioners in South Africa on the basis that it did not constitute unfair citizenship discrimination. It did not test the claim for xenoracism in light of the applicants and the amici's arguments that the impugned provisions fed into an already charged xenophobic environment in South Africa where non-citizens and non-permanent residents are being targeted as dangerous, unreliable or opportunistic). On 'Afrophobia' in South Africa: David Everatt, 'Xenophobia, State and Society in South Africa, 2008–2010' (2011) 38 South African Journal of Political Studies 7; Mamokhosi Choane et al, 'An Analysis of the Causes, Effects and Ramifications of Xenophobia in South Africa' (2011) 3 Insight on Africa 129; Hussein Solomon and Hitomi Kosaka, 'Xenophobia in South Africa: Reflections, Narratives and Recommendations' (2013) 2 Southern African Peace and Security Studies 5.

235 Penelope E Andrews, 'Affirmative Action in South Africa: Transformation or Tokenism?' (1999) 15 Law in Context 80, 83 [hereafter Andrews, 'Affirmative Action in South Africa: Transformation or Tokenism?'].

236 Albie Sachs and André Astrow, 'Post-Apartheid South Africa: A Constitutional Framework' (1989) 6 World Policy Journal 589, 599–600.

237 [2004] ZACC 3.

of review. This approach was muddled further in the second case under section 9(2), *South African Police Service v Solidarity obo Barnard*,[238] where four separate opinions offered different standards of review ranging from mere rationality to full-blown proportionality.[239] In both cases, the challenges to affirmative action policies brought by white claimants failed. The outcomes were thus favourable to Black South Africans. But the Constitutional Court in both cases was clear that affirmative action has its limits and could not be applied rigidly to favour Black people over white people. The cautionary stance of the Constitutional Court has had an impact on affirmative action policies which have been less proactive and ultimately ineffective in addressing the most significant of South Africa's problems: extreme material inequality of wealth and resources.[240]

Even a clear mandate for constitutional affirmative action seems to fail in arresting the exponential rise of material inequality between racialized groups in South Africa. After all, constitutions are not self-activating.[241] Constitutional mandates—for transformation, affirmative action, non-racialism, or substantive equality—ultimately need activating by the state, as in the legislature, the government, and the judiciary. In the case of section 9(2), much like section 9(3), it is not constitutional text but judicial doctrine which has contributed to truncate transformative anti-racism.

In the final analysis, the result in South Africa is the same as the result in Canada and India. That even a commitment to transformative anti-racism in the constitution does not, of its own, further transformative anti-racism. The furtherance of transformative anti-racism in law must happen via doctrine. Doctrine in case law however is not furthering but truncating transformative anti-racism by limiting the scope of racial discrimination.

In the case of South Africa, the personal and remedial scope of racial discrimination is not limited by doctrine and is in fact as broad as can be. This is due to section 38 of the constitution which allows not only individual claims of victims but also class action and public interest litigation.[242] The Constitutional Court has further confirmed that:

[238] [2014] ZACC 23.

[239] Chris McConnachie, 'Affirmative Action and Intensity of Review: South African Police Service v Solidarity Obo Barnard - Affirmative Action' (2015) 7 Constitutional Court Review 163; Catherine Albertyn, 'Adjudicating Affirmative Action within a Normative Framework of Substantive Equality and the Employment Equity Act - An Opportunity Missed - South African Police Service v. Solidarity OBO Barnard' (2015) 132 South African Law Journal 711.

[240] Andrews, 'Affirmative Action in South Africa: Transformation or Tokenism?' (n 235).

[241] Catherine Albertyn, '(In)equality and the South African Constitution' (2019) 36 Development Southern Africa 751.

[242] The Constitution of the Republic of South Africa 1996, s 38 provides that: 'Anyone listed in this section has the right to approach a competent court, alleging that a right in the Bill of Rights has been infringed or threatened, and the court may grant appropriate relief, including a declaration of rights. The persons who may approach a court are—

(a) anyone acting in their own interest;

(b) anyone acting on behalf of another person who cannot act in their own name;

> Our constitutional provisions on standing could properly be characterised as an open invitation and encouragement to natural and corporate citizens to vigilantly guard against and resist violations of the Constitution, by testing compliance with fundamental rights. These provisions are self-evidently designed to ease, smoothen and in a way fuel insistence on the fulfilment of constitutional obligations and the rigorous observance of rights, in view of our shameful past. The language is more inviting, progressive and understandably permissive. Additionally, fundamental rights do not necessarily have to be infringed on before litigation is initiated. It is enough that they be threatened. Resource constraints or any other cause of the inability to litigate personally or as a group does not necessarily amount to an unliftable embargo on the litigation vessel. It is permissible for others to litigate on behalf of those enmeshed in any situation of incapacitation or disadvantage. This approach to standing is consistent with the constitutional mandate our higher courts have to uphold the supreme law of the land and 'ensure that constitutional rights enjoy the full measure of protection to which they are entitled'.[243]

The remedial scope of the Constitutional Court's powers generally and in relation to racial discrimination particularly are also broad—given that the Constitutional Court is the final authority on all law in the country.[244] The Constitutional Court has used its powers creatively to issue structural interdicts, suspended orders, retrospective orders, and general guidelines, often going beyond the strictures of an individual case to address the wider structures or root causes which sustain the constitutional violations. A case like *Mahlangu* may be an outlier in respect of its treatment of a claim of indirect intersectional discrimination but is not much of an outlier in respect of its detailed consideration of a retrospective remedy concerning not just the victim before the Court but the entire group of Black women domestic workers and their families who may have been affected by the impugned provision. *Moseneke* had done much the same in respect of a suspended order.

That leaves the material and evidential scope of racial discrimination claims and it is here that the problem lies. There is no doubt that the South African constitutional jurisprudence recognizes the concept of structural racism and in particular the role of the state and state-like entities in racialization and eventually in instating a framework of racial disadvantage. However, the understanding of

(c) anyone acting as a member of, or in the interest of, a group or class of persons;
(d) anyone acting in the public interest; and
(e) an association acting in the interest of its members.'

[243] *AfriForum v University of the Free State* [2017] ZACC 48 [24] (Mogoeng CJ) (citing *Ferreira v Levin NO*; *Vryenhoek v Powell NO* [1995] ZACC 13 [165]). The Constitution of the Republic of South Africa 1996, ss 2, 167, 168, and 172.

[244] The Constitution of the Republic of South Africa 1996, s 167(5).

racialization and racial disadvantage is unduly limited. That is, the material scope of racial discrimination—in particular what is considered 'racial' and 'discrimination'—is unduly limited in section 9(3) claims. Thus, cases such as *Rafoneke* are not tested for racial harms as they are assumed to be on non-racial grounds such as citizenship, nationality, or residential status.[245] Likewise, claims like *Walker* and *Mpumalanga* show that material disadvantage has been sidelined in understanding racial discrimination from the very beginning of the post-apartheid constitutional order. While *Mahlangu* did consider intersectional discrimination, other cases preceding it (*Moseneke, Bhe*) and those succeeding it (*EB (born S) v ER (born B); KG v Minister of Home Affairs*[246]) did not.

Similarly, the evidential scope of racial discrimination seems overly deferential. This is the case for section 9(3) claims but more so for section 9(2) claims where the standard of review is unclear and ultimately too weak to support robust affirmative action programmes. The transformative possibilities of affirmative action are thus judicially diluted with a weak standard of review.

These doctrinal patterns belie an awareness of structural racism—especially how processes of racialization lead to material harm for racially marginalized groups. A sincere application of the principle of transformative anti-racism should prevent these in interpreting and enforcing the constitutional prohibition on racial discrimination. Mhlantla J's opinion in *Mahlangu* is one such clear example of a sincere application of anti-racism as a legal principle.

9.4.3 Beyond Racial Discrimination

The reason why this book has focussed on racial discrimination is that racism has been addressed in law predominantly through the prohibition of discrimination on racial grounds. This is true for the UK as argued in Chapters 5–8, for Canada and India as shown in this chapter, and even for international law as will be seen in the next chapter. But in the case of South Africa, anti-racism seems to go beyond racial discrimination law. In fact, anti-racism seems to be invoked more liberally and arguably more transformatively outside of claims of racial discrimination under the constitution. What work does anti-racism do in constitutional cases generally?

It is useful to trace the trajectory of application of anti-racism as a legal principle in constitutional cases to answer this question.

One of the first cases before the Constitutional Court—*State v Makwanyane*[247]—concerned a challenge to death penalty under the interim constitution. It was argued that the death penalty was unconstitutional because it was arbitrary such that

[245] *Rafoneke* (n 234).
[246] [2023] ZACC 32.
[247] [1995] ZACC 3 [hereafter *Makwanyane*].

race and poverty, amongst other factors, contributed to its uneven application. As noted in the amicus brief of Lawyers for Human Rights, Centre for Applied Legal Studies and the Society for the Abolition of the Death Penalty in South Africa, the overwhelming majority of those sentenced to death were in fact poor and Black people. The Court recognized that 'race and class' were 'factors that run deep in our society and cannot simply be brushed aside as no longer being relevant'.[248] The racialized impact of the death penalty was thus deemed unjustifiable especially as against the 'new order' established by the interim constitution.[249] In one of the oft-quoted passages from the judgment, Mahomed J, explained:

> The South African Constitution is different: it retains from the past only what is defensible and represents a decisive break from, and a ringing rejection of, that part of the past which is disgracefully racist, authoritarian, insular, and repressive and a vigorous identification of and commitment to a democratic, universalistic, caring and aspirationally egalitarian ethos, expressly articulated in the Constitution ... The past institutionalized and legitimized racism. The Constitution expresses in its preamble the need for a 'new order ... in which there is equality between ... people of all races' ... The past was redolent with statutes which assaulted the human dignity of persons on the grounds of race and colour alone; section 10 constitutionally protects that dignity. The past accepted, permitted, perpetuated and institutionalized pervasive and manifestly unfair discrimination against women and persons of colour; the preamble, section 8 [on the right to equality and non-discrimination] and the postamble seek to articulate an ethos which not only rejects its rationale but unmistakenly recognizes the clear justification for the reversal of the accumulated legacy of such discrimination.[250]

There was no dedicated analysis of racial discrimination under the constitutional right to equality and non-discrimination in *Makwanyane*. Yet, the history of structural racism in the past and the present commitment to undo it in the new constitutional order informed the Court's analysis of the breach of the right to life and dignity and the ultimate finding of unconstitutionality.

Soon after, in *Brink v Kitshoff*,[251] the Constitutional Court considered the constitutional validity of a statutory provision which discriminated against married women by depriving them, in some circumstances, of certain benefits of life insurance policies of their husbands. The case was thus about discrimination on the basis of gender and marital status. Even so, as O'Regan J noted, since this was 'the first case in which the court has been directly concerned' with the then interim

[248] ibid 34–35 (Chaskalson P).
[249] The Interim Constitution of the Republic of South Africa 1994, pmbl.
[250] *Makwanyane* (n 247) [262] (Mahomed J).
[251] [1996] ZACC 9.

constitution's section on equality and non-discrimination 'some consideration of the approach to that section [was] appropriate'.[252] She thus began by affirming that equality has 'a very special place in the South African constitution'[253] and is 'a recurring theme in the Constitution'[254] where the Constitution itself is 'an emphatic renunciation of our past in which inequality was systematically entrenched'.[255] History was thus deemed 'of particular relevance to the concept of equality'.[256] This history, as O'Regan J reminded was one of:

> apartheid, in law and in fact, [which] systematically discriminated against black people in all aspects of social life. Black people were prevented from becoming owners of property or even residing in areas classified as 'white', which constituted nearly 90% of the landmass of South Africa; senior jobs and access to established schools and universities were denied to them; civic amenities, including transport systems, public parks, libraries and many shops were also closed to black people. Instead, separate and inferior facilities were provided. The deep scars of this appalling programme are still visible in our society. *It is in the light of that history and the enduring legacy that it bequeathed that the equality clause needs to be interpreted.*[257]

In this history, even though 'the most visible and most vicious pattern of discrimination has been racial, other systematic motifs of discrimination were and are inscribed on our social fabric'.[258] Thus, according to O'Regan J:

> Although in our society, discrimination on grounds of sex has not been as visible, nor as widely condemned, as discrimination on grounds of race, it has nevertheless resulted in deep patterns of disadvantage. These patterns of disadvantage are particularly acute in the case of black women, as race and gender discrimination overlap. That all such discrimination needs to be eradicated from our society is a key message of the Constitution.[259]

With this, the history of structural racism (state sanctioned apartheid based on race), and the constitutional commitment to overcome it, became the interpretive guide to equality under the South African constitution. *This* is a principle of anti-racism—where the recognition of the history of structural racism and a concomitant commitment to address it in the present—serves as a guide for interpreting

[252] ibid [32] (O'Regan J).
[253] ibid [33] (O'Regan J).
[254] ibid.
[255] ibid.
[256] ibid [40] (O'Regan J).
[257] ibid (emphasis supplied).
[258] ibid [41] (O'Regan J).
[259] ibid [44] (O'Regan J).

formal rules and norms such as the right to equality and non-discrimination. Importantly, such a principle is not reserved for application to the context of race or racism but is of general applicability, such as in the context of *Brink* which was a case brought by a white woman on the basis of gender and marital status.[260] Applying this interpretive principle to the present case, the Court found that the impugned legislative provisions which disadvantaged married women but not married men constituted unfair discrimination under the South African constitution.

This interpretive function of the principle of anti-racism though cannot overrule express words or read absences into constitutional or statutory text. In a case decided shortly after *Brink*, in *De Plessis v De Clerk*,[261] the Constitutional Court declined to apply constitutional rights horizontally, that is, between private individuals on grounds that the effect of such an application would 'be to allow the ethos and pathology of racism effectively to sustain a new life, subverting the gains which the Constitution seeks carefully to consolidate'.[262] Kriegler J, in his dissent on horizontality (with which Didcott J concurred), disagreed, on his reading of the Constitution which promised 'a radical break with the "untold and injustice" of the past'.[263] He was clear: 'No one familiar with the stark reality of South Africa and the power relationships in its society can believe that protection of the individual only against the state can possibly bring those benefits'.[264] Similarly, in his dissent on the question of horizontality, Madala J too was clear that:

> The extent of the oppressive measures in South Africa was not confined to government/individual relations but equally to individual/individual relations. In its effort to create a new order, our Constitution must have been intended to address these oppressive and undemocratic practices at all levels. In my view our Constitution starts at the lowest level and attempts to reach the furthest in its endeavours to *restructure the dynamics in a previously racist society*.[265]

The nuances of the debate on horizontal application of constitutional rights are beyond the scope of this book. What is notable here though is the pivot on which the horizontality debate was settled in *De Plessis*—anti-racism—and in particular its influence on the right to equality and non-discrimination as the animating

[260] *S v Lawrence; S v Negal; S v Solberg* [1997] ZACC 11, which concerned the constitutionality validity of limitations on the sale of liquor. For one of the judges, Sachs J, the limitations were justifiable despite their impact on non-Christians because the limitations had to be judged in light of 'a context of a legacy of institutionalised religious favouritism that is far less pronounced and pervasive than, say, the systematic racism and sexism'. ibid [172] (Sachs J).

[261] [1996] ZACC 10.

[262] ibid [75] (Mahomed DP), [108] (Ackermann J).

[263] ibid [145] (Kriegler J, partly dissenting).

[264] ibid [145] (Kriegler J, partly dissenting).

[265] ibid [163] (Madala J, partly dissenting) (emphasis supplied).

feature of the constitution (alongside dignity and freedom). For the majority, anti-racism as a constitutional principle was important but did not allow reading in what was not obvious in the constitutional text: the horizontal application of constitutional rights. For the minority, anti-racism as a constitutional principle guided the interpretation of the constitutional text such that horizontality was rendered inescapable. For neither was anti-racism dispensable. Even though the case had nothing to do with racism per se.

The spate of cases on the right to education in the language of one's choice reveal an even stronger application of the principle of anti-racism. These cases concern section 29(2) of the Constitution which provides that:

> Everyone has the right to receive education in the official language or languages of their choice in public educational institutions where that education is reasonably practicable. In order to ensure the effective access to, and implementation of, this right, the state must consider all reasonable educational alternatives, including single medium institutions, taking into account—
> (a) equity;
> (b) practicability; and
> (c) the need to redress the results of past racially discriminatory laws and practices.

According to this provision, the state, including the judiciary, is required to apply the principle of anti-racism and in particular 'the need to redress the results of past racially discriminatory laws and practices' in implementing section 29(2). It is useful to consider four landmark cases in which this requirement is given effect—*Mpumalanga Department of Education v Hoërskool Ermelo*;[266] *AfriForum v University of the Free State*;[267] *Gelyke Kanse v Chairperson of the Senate of the University of Stellenbosch*;[268] and *Chairperson of the Council of UNISA v AfriForum NPC*.[269]

In 2009, the Constitutional Court in *Hoërskool Ermelo* considered the validity of change in language policy at a predominantly white school from exclusively Afrikaans to parallel instruction in both English and Afrikaans. As the Court reminded at the very outset, the case arose 'in the context of continuing deep inequality in our educational system, a painful legacy of our apartheid history'.[270] The change was brought about in this context as a response to the long history of exclusion of Black learners who did not speak Afrikaans. The Court held that the

[266] [2009] ZACC 32 [hereafter *Hoërskool Ermelo*].
[267] [2017] ZACC 48 [hereafter *AfriForum*].
[268] [2019] ZACC 38 [hereafter *Gelyke Kanse*].
[269] [2021] ZACC 32 [hereafter *UNISA*].
[270] *Hoërskool Ermelo* (n 266) [2].

change was consistent with the requirements of the constitution and in particular the considerations in section 29(2) of equity, practicability, and the need to ameliorate past racial injustice. Of particular relevance here was the need to ameliorate past racial injustice which continued into the present. Education, as the 'engine of any society',[271] was to attend to this need. Change in the language of instruction from Afrikaans to English was in turn critical to this mission as Afrikaans had been the source of racial division and disadvantage. The change was thus deemed constitutionally consistent and indeed necessitated. The Court issued an order in the form of a structural interdict or a supervisory order for the school to reconsider its language policy in light of the change and for the Head of the Department to report back on the likely demand and the responses to it for English or parallel language education.[272]

In 2017, the Constitutional Court in *AfriForum* was asked to consider whether the University of Free State's policy phasing out Afrikaans as a medium of instruction was consistent with section 29(2) of the Constitution. Mogoeng CJ opened the majority judgment with the following words: 'Whenever we seek to resolve disputes that have the potential to divide our people along racial lines or exacerbate pre-existing divisions, a proper context would always be essential.'[273] The context entailed the centrality of Afrikaans in white settler colonialism and apartheid where the language operated as 'a virtual synonym to "racism and racially based practices".'[274] It was against this context that the universities were moving away from Afrikaans and towards English as the medium of instruction 'to advance a constitutional-inspired transformational agenda'.[275] As Mogoeng CJ explained, the aim was 'to deracialise classes, foster unity and reconciliation and to defuse observable racial tensions'.[276] The other two section 29(2) requirements of equity and practicability had to be interpreted in light of this aim and 'the need to cure the ills of our shameful apartheid past ... [to] not post a threat to racial harmony or inadvertently nurture racial supremacy'.[277] In fact, as Mogoeng CJ explained, even if a language policy was practical and not constrained by resources and made instruction in mother tongue equally and freely accessible to all, it would still have to be judged against anti-racism.[278] In the present case, Mogoeng CJ found that the impugned policy had 'become necessary' as racially segregated lectures had 'poisoned' race relations.[279] The use of Afrikaans as a sole or a parallel language of

[271] ibid [2].
[272] ibid [106].
[273] *AfriForum* (n 267) [1] (Mogoeng CJ).
[274] ibid [5] (Mogoeng CJ) (reference omitted).
[275] ibid [7] (Mogoeng CJ).
[276] ibid.
[277] ibid [53] (Mogoeng CJ).
[278] ibid [54] (Mogoeng CJ).
[279] ibid [62] (Mogoeng CJ).

instruction (with English) would have perpetuated segregation and racism.[280] The Constitutional Court thus upheld the phasing out of Afrikaans.

In 2019, the Constitutional Court in *Gelyke Kanse* considered a challenge to the University of Stellenbosch's language policy which was changed in response to the Fees Must Fall and Open Stellenbosch university movements.[281] Under the new policy, Afrikaans lost its position of primacy as a language of instruction to English.[282] The claimants, who were white-Afrikaans speaking, argued that this violated their constitutional rights including the right to education in mother tongue enshrined in section 29(2) and the right to equality and non-discrimination under section 9 of the Constitution. The Court rejected the challenge. It did so even though racial segregation such as in *AfriForum* was not an issue given that at least some students seeking tuition in Afrikaans were brown. Yet, the Court noted, there was 'a hard racial edge' to the facts in this case.[283] While most brown and white-Afrikaans speaking students could receive instruction in both Afrikaans and English, Black students could only receive instruction in English. A policy favouring Afrikaans was thus an obstruction for Black learners. The new policy disfavouring Afrikaans though was perceived to be an obstruction for brown and white-Afrikaans speaking students for whom access to Stellenbosch's learning and other opportunities was now not fully available in Afrikaans.[284] Meanwhile, the University declined to offer parallel tuition and other opportunities in both English and Afrikaans due to cost. Nevertheless, the Court was convinced that parallel tuition had the effect to 'peripheralise and stigmatise black students not conversant in Afrikaans'.[285] This, in addition to the significant cost of maintaining parallel tuition, was found to be 'a legitimate basis for upgrading English, while continuing to offer significant tuition in Afrikaans, even while sacrificing the previous primacy of Afrikaans'.[286]

In 2021, the Constitutional Court in *UNISA* considered a challenge to the discontinuation of Afrikaans as a medium of instruction at South Africa's largest university, UNISA. This time, a unanimous court upheld the challenge. Writing the unanimous judgment, Majiedt J first clarified that the Court's previous jurisprudence had not signalled 'an acceptance that the Afrikaans language must ineluctably be diminished as a language of teaching and learning'.[287] Indeed, Afrikaans had to be seen from a 'proper perspective', correcting the 'false myths' and 'simplistic narratives' of the language's origins, development, and present position.[288]

[280] ibid [55] (Mogoeng CJ).
[281] *Gelyke Kanse* (n 268) [4].
[282] ibid [7].
[283] ibid [27].
[284] ibid [29].
[285] ibid [40].
[286] ibid [41].
[287] *UNISA* (n 269) [4].
[288] ibid [4]–[5].

In what followed, Majiedt J gave Afrikaans its first 'Black' rendering in the South African Constitutional Court jurisprudence—resurrecting its shared history as a creole language of unique mixed origins where Afrikaans was spoken and developed by all racial groups and classes.[289] The white proprietorship of Afrikaans in the apartheid era belied this history.[290] The subsequent development of Afrikaans into 'a heterogeneous "rainbow" language, spoken today by more black people than white people'[291] reclaimed this history as well as the future of the language. Critiquing the unidirectional movement towards English language in South Africa, Majiedt J reminded that 'Universities as intellectual hubs of transformative constitutionalism must lead the charge for the decolonisation of language. The only way to achieve that is to ensure that all indigenous languages are progressively introduced as languages of teaching and learning, within the means reasonably available.'[292] It is in light of this that Majiedt J found that UNISA had failed, as required by section 29(2) 'to consider all reasonable alternatives' against the requirements of equity, practicability, and the need to ameliorate past racial injustice, in discontinuing Afrikaans as a medium of instruction. Furthermore, he distinguished previous cases from the present case on the basis that there was no racial segregation to be addressed in this present case. Unlike previous cases where the racial composition of classrooms was an important consideration, UNISA was a distance-learning institution, where the continuation of Afrikaans did not 'constitute a threat to racial harmony'.[293]

None of these four cases involved an allegation of racial discrimination. Yet, racial discrimination and in particular the history of structural racism and its link with language were crucial in interpreting the constitutional right to education in mother tongue.

Aside of the context of the right to education in mother tongue, other cases which too can easily be cast in the mould of racial discrimination—such as those challenging statutory provisions relating to police power which overwhelmingly affect Black people—are not examined directly under the constitutional prohibition of racial discrimination in section 9(3). For example, in *Residents of Industry House, 5 Davies Street, New Doornfontein, Johannesburg v Minister of Police*,[294] the Constitutional Court considered validity of section 13(7)(c) of the South African Police Service Act 1995 which authorized warrantless search. The applicants were 'poor and vulnerable people', overwhelmingly immigrants and Black people, who were subjected to invasive raids without authorization.[295] Even though the impact of warrantless searches was racialized it was not examined as such and instead

[289] ibid [6]–[9] [11]–[16] [19].
[290] ibid [10] [17] [18] [20].
[291] ibid [21] (reference omitted).
[292] ibid [22].
[293] ibid [62].
[294] [2021] ZACC 37.
[295] ibid [1].

only viewed in light of the right to privacy. Only in the partly dissenting opinion, Victor AJ, brought up the racialized aspect and found invalid not only warrantless searches under section 13(7)(c) but also the Commissioner's power to cordon off areas under section 13(7)(a)–(b) of the South African Police Service Act 1995. She paid heed to the applicants' argument that 'the raids were an occasion for state-sanctioned racism and xenophobia and the repeated humiliation of the poorest and most vulnerable members of our society'.[296] She confirmed that the selection of buildings to be raided was based on racial profiling.[297] She further recognized the intersectional impact of the raids on women and children who were 'poor and marginalised foreigners in South Africa'.[298] The overwhelming evidence of differential impact based on race, gender, origin, and class led her to conclude that the powers under section 13(7) could not be segregated lest they 'leave an inchoate power that would be open to abuse'.[299] Unlike the majority, she thus declared the entire provision unconstitutional. While the racialized impact of the exercise of police power was critical to her analysis, it was so as a matter of the general commitment to transformative constitutionalism and not the specific prohibition of racial discrimination under section 9(3).[300] The principle of anti-racism emerged as part of the broader commitment to transformative constitutionalism to inform the analysis under the right to privacy even where racial discrimination was not specifically alleged or examined.

In essence, the historical and contemporary recognition of structural racism as a reality, and the constitutional commitment to transform that reality, manifests concretely in constitutional rights jurisprudence other than in the context of the prohibition of racial discrimination under section 9(3) of the Constitution. The discussion above shows the interpretive moves made can be made with anti-racism as a legal principle, beyond racial discrimination law.

9.5 Conclusion

This chapter has shown that constitutional prohibitions of racial discrimination do not, by themselves, address structural racism. They need commensurate doctrine to activate their anti-racist potential. This doctrine is sparse. But where it does exist it shows that *both* the normative commitment to and application of a principle of anti-racism in constitutional doctrine *do* make a difference in addressing structural racism. It is important to disentangle both these lessons drawn from comparative law.

[296] ibid [166] (Victor AJ, partly dissenting).
[297] ibid [168] (Victor AJ, partly dissenting).
[298] ibid [171] [172] (Victor AJ, partly dissenting).
[299] ibid [179] (Victor AJ, partly dissenting).
[300] ibid [162] [220] (Victor AJ, partly dissenting).

First, constitutional text and spirit can signal a commitment to a principle of anti-racism. They do this primarily through the right to equality and non-discrimination which embodies a prohibition of racial discrimination. They do this secondarily as part of their constitutional values, principles, and goals. In the case of Canada, it is through the commitment to substantive equality; in India, it is through the commitment to anti-casteism; and in South Africa it is through a commitment to transformation. Individually and collectively, elements of the constitution and constitutionalism, broadly, can thus be interpreted to signal a strong and unequivocal commitment to anti-racism as a legal principle. This means that, normatively, constitutions can signal (i) resistance to structural racism, (ii) call for broad-based change, and (iii) commit to intersectional justice.

Second, this normative commitment needs to be practised in constitutional doctrine. Much of constitutional adjudication in comparative law however ignores this normative commitment. Thus, the bulk of the constitutional case law from Canada, India and South Africa, while it reiterates a symbolic commitment to anti-racism in addressing issues of indigeneity, caste, and colour, respectively, often does not apply anti-racism in *interpreting* the prohibition of racial discrimination. Doctrinally, this means two limitations in particular. First, the limitation as to the material scope of racial discrimination to exclude structural racism and its three elements—(i) the role of the state and state-like entities (ii) in racializing and (iii) instating a framework of racial disadvantage. Canadian, Indian, and South African constitutional doctrine is particularly good in recognizing the state's role in structural racism. But they fail in recognizing how processes of racialization instate racial order and especially racial disadvantage in a material sense. They thus fail to understand the two elements of 'racial' 'discrimination' in cases of structural racism. Second, evidentially, constitutional law, though open to a range of historical, sociological, testimonial, economic, and statistical evidence, places a high burden of proof on claimants of racial discrimination. Alongside a lower standard of review and a high degree of deference to the state as the respondent, the possibility of challenging the state constitutionally is actually rendered futile in practice.

Conversely, cases such as *Corbiere* in Canada, *Sukanta Shanta* in India, and *Mahlangu* in South Africa are befitting examples of how these limitations can be overcome. They hold the following lessons for the UK in realizing anti-racism as a legal principle.

First, the normative commitment to the principle matters. This does not mean explicit adoption of the locution 'anti-racism' as a legal principle. This means the normative commitment to anti-racism either in explicit standards such as a constitutional prohibition of racial discrimination or the prohibition of untouchability, or alongside broader normative commitments such as substantive equality, anti-casteism, transformation, and even decolonization. This holds an important lesson for the UK where the treatment of racial discrimination seems rudderless and based in no principled commitments. Articulation of normative commitments, or at least, the conceptual frameworks at play, in enforcing racial discrimination law, should be the baseline. In the absence of a single document in the form of a constitution in the UK, this baseline should be articulated in doctrine, in statutory and common law, and by the Parliament and the judges alike.

Second, doctrinally, an enlarged personal and remedial scope of racial discrimination is critical in allowing a range of claimants, and not just the individual claimants, from challenging structural racism and having it addressed in a broad-based as opposed to a piecemeal way. This in turn allows a broad range of perspectives and evidence to be considered in racial discrimination claims. Likewise, awareness of structural racism and its three elements is critical in understanding elements of racial discrimination, that is, what does it mean for something to be based on 'racial' grounds (processes of racialization which give rise to racial order and hierarchy); what does racial 'discrimination' in particular look like (racial disadvantage or the vast material gaps between racialized groups); and how does it come about (through structures) and who is responsible for it (state and state-like entities). Judicial awareness of this conceptual framework holds the key to an enlarged material and eventually evidential scope of racial discrimination.

10
Racial Discrimination in International Law

10.1 Introduction

So far this book has mainly considered anti-racism in the domestic context. Chapters 5–8 focussed on British law and Chapter 9 focussed on comparative law in Canada, India, and South Africa. Chapter 5 briefly mentioned that the UK's first foray into racial discrimination law as an anti-racist measure was inspired by the development of the International Convention on the Elimination of All Forms of Racial Discrimination ('ICERD').[1] Other than that, no mention of international law has been made.

But the question posed in this book: whether there is such a principle like anti-racism in law must also be answered in the context of international law. The reason being—international law, especially international human rights law, has a special relationship with states in that the field chiefly governs the behaviour of states. It thus seems primed for anti-racism, which, as this book defined, is about opposing structural racism that is wielded by the state. Is anti-racism reflected in the practice of international law?

The answer that emerges in this chapter is: partly.

Seen against the record of the Committee on the Elimination of Racial Discrimination ('CERD') under its individual communications procedure, the practice does not reflect anti-racism. That is, even though primed to scrutinize state responsibility, CERD fails to resist structural racism which is not only about being primed for scrutiny of states but also processes of racialization which give rise to race and eventually racial disadvantage. This is because, as this book has argued, structural racism is about how these three elements interact, that is, how (i) states (ii) racialize (iii) to instate a framework of racial disadvantage. The focus on states alone is thus insufficient in resisting structural racism if processes of racialization and the resulting framework of racial disadvantage are overlooked. Importantly, it is insufficient in enacting transformative anti-racism which, according to this book, is not only about (i) attending to structural racism, but also doing so (ii) in a broad-based and urgent rather than piecemeal and incremental way, and (iii) with a commitment to intersectional justice.

[1] International Convention on the Elimination of All Forms of Racial Discrimination, 660 UNTS 195 (signed in New York, 7 March 1996, entered into force 4 January 1969) [hereafter ICERD].

Anti-Racism as a Legal Principle. Shreya Atrey, Oxford University Press.
DOI: 10.1093/9780198947646.003.0013

In contrast, seen against the CERD's record under the state reporting mechanism and the inter-state communications procedure in the ICERD; and even the work of the Human Rights Council, especially the Office of the United Nations High Commissioner for Human Rights (OHCHR), international law reflects anti-racism better. In the final analysis, it appears that enforcement mechanisms—which notionally have greater influence and impact—are worse at reflecting anti-racism than monitoring mechanisms. It is perhaps exactly the lack of the ability to *effect* transformative change that makes the latter open to *ideating* transformative anti-racism.

That then is the central argument of this chapter. It is established as follows. First, Section 10.2 traverses through the practice of the CERD comparing its output in individual communications procedure (Section 10.2.1), inter-state communications procedure (Section 10.2.2), and state reporting mechanism (Section 10.2.3). Section 10.3 briefly considers the recent practice of the Human Rights Council ('the HRC') which has explicitly embraced transformative anti-racism. Section 10.4 concludes that the highly varied substantive engagement with anti-racism by the CERD and the HRC is likely dictated by the particular 'form' their engagement takes. The result is that, the more general the form (state reporting versus individual communications), the more dynamic is the engagement with anti-racism.

A word about the scope of this chapter is necessary before proceeding. International law, like municipal law, is a vast universe where every area within it can be tested for its engagement with anti-racism. From international law of the sea and international criminal law to international taxation law and international arbitration law—any area can be studied from an anti-racist perspective. Keeping with the theme of this book, this chapter focuses on racial discrimination law especially under the ICERD, which is 'the centerpiece of the international regime for the protection and enforcement of the right against racial discrimination.'[2] It especially focuses on the jurisprudence of the CERD—the specialist treaty body tasked with the monitoring and enforcement of the ICERD. This focus is justified for two reasons.[3]

First, unlike other norms in international human rights law, the norm prohibiting racial discrimination is considered a peremptory norm or *jus cogens* norm,

[2] Gay McDougall, 'The International Convention on the Elimination of all Forms of Racial Discrimination', UN Audiovisual Library of International Law <https://legal.un.org/avl/ha/cerd/cerd.html> (accessed 10 March 2025).

[3] This focus is inevitably narrow. It does not cover all of the CERD's practice, for example, the management of the early warning and urgent action procedure or the production of the general recommendations by the CERD. It does not include the jurisprudence of the International Court of Justice ('ICJ'). It does not cover racial discrimination law under other core human rights treaties such as the International Covenant on Civil and Political Rights ('ICCPR') or the International Covenant on Economic, Social and Cultural Rights ('ICESCR'), regional systems of human rights law such as the Inter-American or the African system, and other fields of law such as international refugee law or transitional justice. It is thus mainly focussed on the practice generated by the CERD monitoring and enforcement functions.

that is, a norm from which no derogation is permissible in international law.[4] Since *jus cogens* norms sit at the top of the hierarchy of norms in international law, the prohibition of racial discrimination sits at the top of the hierarchy of norms in human rights law. No other form of discrimination has this status in international law. The prohibition of racial discrimination is thus pre-eminent in international law.

Second, the norm was also the first to be considered pre-eminent in international human rights law. It was embodied in the ICERD which was the first international human rights treaty to be adopted in 1965—one year before the international 'bill of rights' was adopted in the form of the International Covenant on Civil and Political Rights ('ICCPR')[5] and the International Covenant on Economic, Social and Cultural Rights ('ICESCR')[6] in 1966. The ICERD is also more widely subscribed to than the ICCPR and the ICESCR, with 182 States Parties, as of 2025, as compared to 175 States Parties to the ICCPR and 172 States Parties to the ICESCR. As a treaty norm, the prohibition of racial discrimination is both the first human rights norm and one of the most widely accepted.

The chapter's focus on racial discrimination law, especially as developed by the specialist treaty body dedicated to the subject, speaks directly to this pre-eminence. It is in fact this pre-eminence which begs the question, if the norm prohibiting racial discrimination in international law is *so* important, it must *surely* be an anti-racist norm? The chapter shows that this surety may be an overestimation of the current practice of the CERD. In fact, the pre-eminence of the norm prohibiting racial discrimination in international law does not automatically lend itself to transformative anti-racism.

10.2 International Convention on the Elimination of All Forms of Racial Discrimination

The ICERD, as its name suggests, is a treaty dedicated to eliminating all forms of racial discrimination.

It defines 'racial discrimination' in article 1(1) as:

1. any distinction, exclusion, restriction or preference based on race, colour, descent, or national or ethnic origin which has the purpose or effect of

[4] Draft Articles on Responsibility of States for Internationally Wrongful Acts, with Commentaries (2001) 33 <https://legal.un.org/ilc/texts/instruments/english/commentaries/9_6_2001.pdf> (accessed 16 March 2025); *Barcelona Traction, Light and Power Company Limited* (New Application, 1962), *Belgium v Spain*, Judgment, Merits, Second Phase, [1970] ICJ Rep 3 (5 February 1970) [34].

[5] International Covenant on Civil and Political Rights (adopted 16 December 1966, entered into force 23 March 1976) 999 UNTS 171.

[6] International Covenant on Economic, Social and Cultural Rights (adopted 16 December 1966, entered into force 3 January 1976) 993 UNTS 3.

> nullifying or impairing the recognition, enjoyment or exercise, on an equal footing, of human rights and fundamental freedoms in the political, economic, social, cultural or any other field of public life.

There are two elements to this definition: the presence of racial grounds (race, colour, descent, or national or ethnic origin) and the impact on human rights (in purpose or in effect). First, 'racial' grounds are the five grounds that are listed in article 1(1) itself—race, colour, descent, or national or ethnic origin—and ostensibly exclude grounds like citizenship and nationality that are listed in article 1(2)–(3) which provide that:

> 2. This Convention shall not apply to distinctions, exclusions, restrictions or preferences made by a State Party to this Convention between citizens and non-citizens.
> 3. Nothing in this Convention may be interpreted as affecting in any way the legal provisions of States Parties concerning nationality, citizenship or naturalization, provided that such provisions do not discriminate against any particular nationality.

These 'restrictive general stipulations' may not be 'as exclusionary' as they seem 'superficially'.[7] In fact, the CERD has consistently developed standards narrowing the scope of these restrictive provisions and broadening the universal ambit of the prohibition of racial discrimination to 'everyone'.[8] Whether the CERD has succeeded is considered in Section 10.2.1.1 below.

Second, unlike domestic law where racial discrimination is not defined in relation to its impact on human rights, under the ICERD, racial discrimination is so defined. Thus, a distinction, exclusion, restriction, or preference, or simply, differential treatment without an objective justification,[9] is not sufficient to establish racial discrimination. Such differential treatment must also have a negative impact on the enjoyment of human rights.[10] The list of human rights though is not

[7] Patrick Thornberry, *The International Convention on the Elimination of All Forms of Racial Discrimination: A Commentary* (OUP 2016) 145 [hereafter Thornberry, *The International Convention*]; Theodor Meron, 'The Meaning and Reach of the International Convention of the Elimination of All Forms of Racial Discrimination' (1985) 79 American Journal of International Law 283, 311–313 [hereafter Meron, 'The Meaning and Reach'].

[8] ICERD, art 5; CERD, General Recommendation 11, On non-citizens, UN Doc A/48/18 (1994); CERD, General Recommendation 22, Refugees and displaced persons, UN Doc A/51/18 (1996); CERD, General Recommendation 30, Discrimination against Non-citizens, UN Doc CERD/C/64/Misc.11/rev.3 (2004); CERD, General recommendation 34, On racial discrimination against people of African descent, UN Doc CERD/C/GC/34 (2011).

[9] CERD, General Recommendation 14, Definition of Racial Discrimination, UN Doc A/48/18 (1994); CERD, General Recommendation 30, Discrimination against Non-citizens, UN Doc CERD/C/64/Misc.11/rev.3 (2004); CERD, General recommendation 32, The meaning and scope of special measures in the International Convention on the Elimination of All Forms Racial Discrimination, UN Doc CERD/C/GC/32 (2009).

[10] Meron, 'The Meaning and Reach' (n 7) 291.

confined to those enumerated in the ICERD and may be broadened based on context and future developments.[11]

Articles 2–7 of the ICERD prohibit racial discrimination. They contain extensive state obligations which go beyond prohibition as mere declaration and towards positive measures to prevent and address racial discrimination, including racial segregation and apartheid under article 3 and racist hate speech under article 4.

The three sections below parse through the practice of the CERD in enforcing, monitoring, and interpreting the state obligations contained in articles 2–7 in light of the definition of racial discrimination set out in article 1. The purpose is to understand the extent to which the practice reflects anti-racism as a legal principle especially in a transformative sense by: (i) addressing structural racism, in a (ii) broad-based and (iii) intersectional way.

10.2.1 Individual Communications

Article 14 of the ICERD provides that 'a State Party may at any time declare that it recognizes the competence of the Committee to receive and consider communications from individuals or groups of individuals within its jurisdiction claiming to be victims of a violation by that State Party of any of the rights set forth in this Convention'. Only about a third of the 182 States Parties allow individuals to bring claims to the CERD under article 14. The result is that the jurisprudence of the CERD under its individual communications procedure is modest, though considerably more substantial than under its inter-state communications procedure (Section 10.2.2). Thus, article 14 is considered one of the 'most underutilised' provisions of the ICERD.[12] The OHCHR jurisprudence database website returns 44 decisions on merits in individual communications considered by the CERD until 2024, since it first began to consider communications under article 14 in 1984. These decisions on merits are considered below in respect of the four limitations as to the scope of racial discrimination law that we have considered in the previous chapters (personal, material, evidential, and remedial).[13] It is useful to keep to this symmetry in testing how the CERD fares against these criteria and ultimately against anti-racism as a legal principle.

The analysis below shows that the totality of the CERD's practice under the individual communications procedure is far from what could be considered anti-racist in a transformative sense. Claimants in only 24 of the 44 communications

[11] Thornberry, *The International Convention* (n 7) 128.
[12] Theo van Boven, 'The Petition System under the International Convention on the Elimination of All Forms of Racial Discrimination: A Sobering Balance Sheet' (2000) 4 Max Plank UNYB 271, 272.
[13] Chapters 6 and 7 of this book.

have succeeded in establishing racial discrimination. Where claims fail, the failure seems to be explained by the ignorance of structural racism and in particular the role of the state in racializing and instating frameworks of racial disadvantage. Where claims succeed, they are still stymied by the lack of a transformative perspective which is open to intersectional justice and radical change.

10.2.1.1 Personal Scope

Although article 14 can only be invoked by individuals or groups of individuals who are 'victims', the CERD's interpretation of this requirement is not strict and can be proven in reference not to direct injury but to membership in a group which has been targeted. Thus, claims by interest-groups, organizations, and unions representing the cause of its members are readily admitted by the CERD.[14] This allows the CERD to go beyond interpersonal racism and entertain claims of institutional and structural racism.

Anna Kaptova v Slovak Republic[15] demonstrates this aptly. The communication concerned the plight of seven Romany families who had moved to a municipality to take up employment in an agricultural cooperative. When the cooperative ceased operations after about eight years, the Romany families lost their jobs and homes and were forced to move back to their municipality.[16] Here they were subjected to anti-Roma hostility by the authorities who had provided them temporary housing reluctantly and had declined to allocate space for trailers and torn down their temporary dwellings, forcing the families to flee to a different municipality.[17] Their fate did not improve. They were threatened and their dwellings were set on fire in the new municipality too. Several municipalities passed resolutions forbidding the Romany families from entering or settling in their villages.

The Kosice Legal Defence Foundation challenged these resolutions as acts of 'public discrimination' which infringed the rights and freedoms of Romany citizens at the Slovak Constitutional Court.[18] The challenge was dismissed for want of standing.[19] In response, the author, a Slovak citizen of Romany ethnicity, as the director of Legal Defence Bureau for Ethnic Minorities in Kosice, along with other Romany citizens who were targeted, made another submission to the Constitutional Court which too was dismissed for want of evidence of violation of rights resulting from the resolutions.[20]

[14] *TBB v Germany*, Communication No. 48/2010, UN Doc CERD/C/82/D/48/2010 (2013); *Zentralrat Deutscher Sinti und Roma et al v Germany*, Communication No. 38/2016, UN Doc CERD/C/72/D/38/2006 (2008).
[15] Communication No. 13/1998, UN Doc CERD/C/57/D/13/1998 (2000).
[16] ibid [2.1].
[17] ibid [2.2].
[18] ibid [2.5] [2.6].
[19] ibid [2.7].
[20] ibid [2.9].

Before the CERD, the claimant alleged a violation of the ICERD highlighting that the State Party had in particular 'failed to ensure that all public authorities and public institutions, national and local, refrain from acts or practices of racial discrimination'.[21] The claimant argued that she had victim status to bring this complaint because even though she had not lived in the municipalities that had passed the resolutions and did not intend to do so, she did intend to work and travel within these municipalities which had become impossible for fear of violence, discrimination, and expulsion.

The CERD agreed. It held that the claimant had victim status because she 'belonged to a group of the population directly targeted by the resolutions in question'.[22]

Likewise, claims in the nature of class action are also permissible and there is no requirement to prove that the individuals bringing the claim are all personally or identically affected. For example, in *Anne Nuorgam et al v Finland*,[23] the claim was brought by 23 individuals who were all members of the Indigenous Sami community. They challenged the inclusion of non-Sami persons on the electoral roll for the Sami Parliament on grounds that it 'promoted the inclusion of individuals who are not fully committed to the defence of Sami rights but rather supporting the State party's positions in Parliament ... [which could] result in the forced assimilation of the Sami people into the mainstream population in violation of article 1 of the Convention'.[24] The CERD held that this 'had the capacity to artificially modify the electoral constituency of the Sami Parliament, affecting its capacity to truly represent the Sami people and their interests'[25] and thus violated article 5(c) of ICERD which guaranteed equal enjoyment of political rights. The individuals were deemed entitled to claim the political rights of the Sami community as a whole.

In fact, collective claims concerning the Sami community have received the most robust analysis of structural racism by the CERD. *Lars-Anders Ågren et al v Sweden*[26] is an excellent example where the collective rights of the people of the Sami community provided a strong basis for intervention for the CERD. The case involved the grant of mining concessions to private companies on land which had been enjoyed by the Sami community. Sweden argued that since the land was not owned by Sami people the concessions did not violate the right to property enshrined in article 5(d)(v) of the ICERD. The CERD disagreed and held that 'a title is not a prerequisite for the recognition of indigenous people's property rights, as a

21 ibid [3.1].

22 ibid [6.5]. On merits, the CERD found that the resolutions, which had now been rescinded, had violated Article 5(d)(i) of ICERD which guarantees the right to freedom of movement and residence within the border of the State.

23 Communication No. 59/2016, UN Doc CERD /C/106/D/59/2016 (2023).

24 ibid [3.2].

25 ibid [9.14].

26 Communication No. 54/2013, UN Doc CERD/C/102/D/54/2013 (2020).

cardinal aspect of structural discrimination directed against indigenous peoples is precisely the lack of official recognition of rights over land'.[27] The Committee went on to state that:

> the close ties of indigenous peoples to the land must be recognized and understood as the fundamental basis of their cultures, spiritual life, integrity and economic survival. Their 'relations to the land are not merely a matter of possession and production but a material and spiritual element which they must fully enjoy, even to preserve their cultural legacy and transmit it to future generations'. In this regard, the realization of indigenous peoples' land rights may also be a prerequisite for the exercise of the right to life, as such, and to 'prevent their extinction as a people'.[28]

Inversely, when it is a claim brought by an individual (as opposed to a claim brought by a group [*Anne Nuorgam* and *Lars-Anders Ågren*] or on behalf of a group by an individual [*Anna Kaptova*]), the institutional or structural dimension of the claim is not explored even where apparent.

Consider the three claims against France alleging institutional racism at Renault. *Laurent Gabre Gabaroum v France*[29] concerned a French national born in Chad who had faced racial discrimination as an employee at Renault when he desired to move from his nightwatchman position to a management position. Eventually, despite the protestations and hurdles he faced, he became the first employee of African origin to hold a management position at Renault. Racial discrimination against him persisted. In addition to his own treatment, the claimant argued that France had failed 'to take effective measures to criminalize all forms of racist and xenophobic behaviour or to counter Renault's practice of stigmatizing and stereotyping French nationals of African origin on the basis of their colour, their national origin or their ethnic or racial origin'[30] and 'to acknowledge and take action against practices that could have negative repercussions on the employment of Africans by other firms'.[31] The CERD did not consider these arguments. Instead, it decided only on a point about the reversal of burden of proof that 'the employer should have presented proof that it had not used illegitimate criteria in order to justify

[27] ibid [6.3].

[28] ibid [6.6]. Citing Inter-American Court of Human Rights in *Case of the Mayagna (Sumo) Awas Tingni Community v Nicaragua*, Judgment, 31 August 2001 [149]; *Case of the Saramaka People v Suriname*, Judgment, 28 November 2007 [121]; *Case of the Sawhoyamaxa Indigenous Community v Paraguay*, Judgment, 29 March 2006. The same principles have been recognized at the African Court of Human Rights in *Centre for Minority Rights Development (Kenya) and Minority Rights Group (on behalf of Endorois Welfare Council) v Kenya*, application no. 276/03 (2009); *African Commission on Human and Peoples' Rights v Republic of Kenya*, application no. 006/2012 (2017).

[29] Communication No. 52/2012, UN Doc CERD /C/89/D/52/2012 (2016).

[30] ibid [3.1].

[31] ibid [3.2].

its unequal treatment of the petitioner' and that France had failed to reverse the burden of proof to have the employer prove this.[32]

Daniel Kotor v France[33] concerned a French national born in Togo who had worked with Renault from 1971 to 2004. He claimed discrimination on the basis of ethnicity in his career progression in comparison with that of other white European colleagues. He argued that the State Party was aware of widespread and systemic nature of discrimination against certain categories of employees at Renault and had failed to address it.[34] The CERD did not examine this claim and instead focussed solely on the State Party's failure to enforce the reclassification of the claimant's position at Renault which would have resulted in a higher monthly pension.

Stanislas Breleur v France[35] concerned an auto technician who worked at Renault from 1971 to 2003 until his retirement. He claimed that he had faced discrimination on the basis of ethnicity in career progression vis-à-vis other employees especially 'native European colleagues who were employed at the same grade and had a comparable professional profile.'[36] His complaints to the domestic courts were only partially successful. In particular, the claimant was never reclassified by Renault and that adversely affected the amount of pension he received. He argued that the State Party had failed to comply with the ICERD because:

> it was common knowledge that certain categories of employees within the company were discriminated against … [as] internal documents subsequently made public bear testament to the systematic nature of this discrimination, in particular the ESCADRE system, which introduced what can only be described as an 'ethnic codification' system, based on skin colour and ethnic origin, for internal use. The petitioner explains that, in an internal memorandum from Renault, it was mentioned that 'the worst offenders in terms of adapting to the company's work culture are undoubtedly the black Africans and the Algerians, Moroccans and Tunisians, closely followed by the workers from the [overseas departments]' and that 'the blacks are the most difficult to integrate into French society'.[37]

The claimant thus alleged a violation of article 2 as the State Party 'allowed discrimination to be practised against individuals or groups of individuals on the basis of their ethnic or geographical origin';[38] article 3 as the State Party 'failed to take measures to eliminate racial segregation within Renault';[39] article 4 as the

[32] ibid [7.2] [9].
[33] Communication No. 65/2018, UN Doc CERD /C/105/D/65/2018 (2022).
[34] ibid [3.2].
[35] Communication No. 66/2018, UN Doc CERD /C/107/D/66/2018 (2022).
[36] ibid [3.2].
[37] ibid.
[38] ibid.
[39] ibid [3.4].

State Party 'through its passivity, encouraged hatred and discrimination while it was a decision maker at Renault';[40] and article 5 as the State Party failed 'to ensure the protection of his fundamental rights, including his right to equal treatment without distinction as to race, colour or national or ethnic origin'.[41]

The CERD did not examine any of these allegations. It referred to its decision in *Kotor* and applied the reasoning directly to find a violation, only, of article 6 of the ICERD. But it made no connection with institutional racism even though at least three claims at this point had alleged it. The fact that these claims were brought independently and by individual victims seems to have thwarted the assessment of institutional racism at Renault.

Thus, although the CERD is generous about *who* can bring a claim under the ICERD, it is not similarly generous as to *which* type of discrimination the entity can claim. Unless individual victims or organizations explicitly bring claims of institutional and structural racism on behalf of their racial group or a group whose interests they represent formally, they cannot seem to claim institutional or structural racism. There is nothing in the text of the ICERD that ordains this. That is, there is nothing in article 14 specifically which ordains *who* can bring *which* type of claim: interpersonal, institutional, or structural racism. But in reality, individual victims seem not to be able to challenge institutional or structural racism. This then limits anti-racism, which, as Chapters 3 and 4 argued, is about addressing structural racism as it is the root cause of all racism.

10.2.1.2 Material Scope

The practice of the CERD under the individual communications procedure reveals two main limitations as to the material scope of the norm prohibiting racial discrimination under article 1(1) of the ICERD—first, the meaning of 'racial' grounds; and second, the meaning of 'discrimination'. These limitations stall the recognition and redressal of structural racism because they fail to capture how processes of racialization generate racial grounds and in turn racial disadvantage.

10.2.1.2.i Racial Grounds

The greatest hurdle in addressing structural racism results from the limited view of what the CERD considers racial grounds under article 1(1) and in particular its restrictive interpretation of the five grounds listed therein: race, colour, descent, or national, or ethnic origin. Claims which are based overtly on racial grounds listed in article 1(1) are deemed claims of racial discrimination. These include claims concerning obviously derogatory language or negative depictions of racialized groups,[42] or claims of 'exceptionally/manifestly offensive

[40] ibid [3.5].
[41] ibid.
[42] *Momodou Jallow v Denmark*, Communication No. 62/2018, UN Doc CERD/C/108/D/62/2018 (2024) (concerning negative depictions of Black people and Roma people); *Stephen Hagan v Australia*,

character'.[43] These succeed by the sheer force of their explicitness. In contrast, claims which are not explicitly based on one of the listed grounds—and are instead based on foreign status, citizenship, nationality, language, accent, appearance or religion—tend to fall outside the scope of article 1(1) and often fail as claims of 'racial' discrimination under the ICERD.

The distinction between explicit and inexplicit racial discrimination, however, should be irrelevant as no such distinction is supported by the text of article 1(1). Article 1(1) of the ICERD has been interpreted to include both direct and indirect forms of racial discrimination.[44] More importantly, there is a prior point to consider which is not about direct or indirect forms of *discrimination* but about what is considered *racial*, that is, the meaning of the five grounds listed in article 1(1) (race, colour, descent, or national or ethnic origin).

The following four sections consider statuses which have been argued as racial grounds listed in article 1(1): foreign status, citizenship or nationality, language, and religion. The discussion shows that claims based on these statuses rarely succeed given their lack of an explicit reference to listed grounds and the CERD's lack of a framework for understanding racial grounds on the basis of racialization explained in Part I of the book. It is thus the lack of awareness of the processes through which statuses *become* racial grounds which detains the CERD from interpreting article 1(1) appropriately. That is, from interpreting article 1(1) in a way that conforms to the object and purpose of the ICERD: to eliminate *all* forms of *racial* discrimination.[45]

10.2.1.2.i.a Foreign status The CERD's tryst with foreign status is perhaps the lengthiest and the knottiest. Successive claimants have argued that their treatment which was based on their status as a foreigner (as someone not belonging to the State Party, not only as a national or a citizen [considered in the next section below], but in a broader sense as someone either not resident in or not with ties to a State Party or with a particular visa status, etc) was in fact racial discrimination. Few such claims, however, succeed.

Communication No. 26/2002, UN Doc CERD/C/62/D/26/2002 (2003) (concerning the use of the 'N' word in naming a sports ground).

[43] *The Jewish Community of Oslo v Norway*, Communication No. 30/2003, UN Doc CERD/C/67/D/30/2003 (2005) [10.5] (concerning a march where statements such as the following were made: 'Every day immigrants rob, rape and kill Norwegians, every day our people and country are being plundered and destroyed by the Jews, who suck our country empty of wealth and replace it with immoral and un-Norwegian thoughts').

[44] CERD, General Recommendation 14, Definition of Racial Discrimination, UN Doc A/48/18 (1994) [2].

[45] ICERD, pmbl ('Resolved to adopt all necessary measures for speedily eliminating racial discrimination in all its forms and manifestations, and to prevent and combat racist doctrines and practices in order to promote understanding between races and to build an international community free from all forms of racial segregation and racial discrimination').

Some fail for good reasons. For example, in *BMS v Australia*,[46] the author, an Australian citizen of Indian origin, challenged the imposition of a quota on the selection of the number of foreign-trained doctors to be admitted in Australia for medical practice. The CERD rejected the challenge on the basis that the facts did not disclose any (i) detrimental treatment of foreign-trained doctors on the basis of any racial ground; or (ii) favourable treatment of Australian-trained doctors as they did not share a single racial, ethnic, or national origin.[47] Likewise, in *DF v Australia*,[48] the claimant was a New Zealand citizen residing in Australia who claimed racial discrimination due to Australia's withdrawal of entitlements to social security and citizenship from the claimant and all those who were not entitled to, or in possession of, "protected" Special Category Visas or permanent resident visas. The CERD found that the withdrawal was based not on a discriminatory distinction based on national origin but rather the removal of distinction between New Zealand citizens and other with the effect that New Zealand citizens now were on an equal footing with other non-citizens. It thus did not find a violation of ICERD.[49] Claims like *BMS* and *DF* seem to be justified by article 1(2) of the ICERD which allows 'distinctions, exclusions, restrictions or preferences made by a State Party to this Convention between citizens and non-citizens'.

Not all claims can be justified in this way. Take, for example, *AMM v Switzerland*[50] which concerned a Somali national living in Switzerland on a temporary 'F' status as an asylum seeker. The status came with limitations of work and travel which restricted the claimant to poorly paid and precarious jobs, and affected his ability to complete vocational training in maritime navigation which required mandatory travel and access to proper medical services. In addition, the claimant kept receiving several letters asking him to attend courses in 'Swiss life and customs' and 'living in an apartment' even though he had lived in Switzerland for many years. In light of the wider discourse in Switzerland which the claimant considered hostile to foreigners, he asked the CERD to determine 'to what extent the social, economic and cultural context in Switzerland is a factor in discrimination against particular groups of the foreign population'[51] and assess the validity of the 'F' status which was characterized by a high degree of surveillance, inability to access rights such as the right to work without

[46] Communication No. 8/1996, UN Doc CERD/C/54/D/8/1996 (1999).

[47] ibid [9.2].

[48] Communication No. 39/2006, UN Doc CERD/C/72/D/39/2006 (2008).

[49] *DR v Australia*, Communication No. 42/2008, UN Doc CERD/C/75/D/42/2008 (2009) (The claimant was a New Zealand citizen residing in Australia on a Special Category Visa (SCV), which allowed him to live and work indefinitely in Australia. He challenged a number of Australian laws as unlawfully restricting his rights to social security, education, and nationality, on the basis of his national origin. Applying its previous decision in *DF v Australia*, the CERD found that the distinctions in Australian laws were based not on national origin and were instead meant to eliminate the pre-existing distinctions that existed in favour of New Zealand citizens).

[50] Communication No. 50/2012, UN Doc CERD/C/84/D/50/2012 (2014).

[51] ibid [5.2].

permission of migration board or the right to non-emergency medical treatment. Although the CERD noted the abundance of examples of discrimination in accessing work, vocational training, and health services, it agreed with the State Party that such discrimination was simply because of the claimant's foreign status and not because of his ethnic or national origin. The CERD acknowledged 'the complexity of the issue raised in this case, which highlights the negative effects of the Swiss "temporary admission" status ('F' permit for foreigners) on some groups of foreigners who can also be distinguished by ethnic or national origin' and yet held that the claimant had 'not unequivocally established that the discriminatory acts ... were based on his ethnic origin or Somali nationality and not on his *status as a foreigner*'.[52] Thus, while the CERD admitted that there was a possibility of xenophobic discrimination based on the claimant's 'status as a foreigner', it required unequivocal evidence that that possibility coincided with racial discrimination on the basis of ethnic origin. But it made no effort to find such coincidence in light of the claimant's contention about the wider discourse of xenophobia in Switzerland.

In other claims, a state's failure to prosecute a statement such as: 'The State has given the foreigners work. They work in our slaughterhouses where they can easily poison our food and endanger the agricultural exports. Another form of terrorism is to break into our waterworks and poison the water', is deemed acceptable as the CERD considers that 'a general reference to foreigners does not at present single out a group of persons ... on the basis of a specific race, ethnicity, colour, descent or national or ethnic origin'.[53] The CERD has also rejected claims where claimants, such as Brazilians living in Denmark have demanded 'an investigation into the real reasons behind the "treatment" ... in order to ascertain whether or not criteria involving racial discrimination have been applied'.[54]

There are three outliers in the CERD's record on discrimination on the basis of foreign status. In *Habasi v Denmark*,[55] the Committee found a violation of the ICERD for the failure of the State Party to investigate whether a demand to show a Danish passport for obtaining a loan for an alarm set for a car was racially motivated. According to the CERD: 'financial means are often needed to facilitate integration in society. To have access to the credit market and be allowed to apply for a financial loan on the same conditions as those which are valid for the majority in the society is, therefore, an important issue.'[56] Failure to initiate a proper investigation into 'the real reasons behind the bank's loan policy visàvis foreign residents'[57]

[52] ibid [8.6] (emphasis supplied).
[53] *Kamal Quereshi* v *Denmark*, Communication No. 33/2003, UN Doc CERD/C/66/D/33/2003 (2004) [7.3].
[54] *MB* v *Denmark*, Communication No 20/2000, UN Doc CERD/C/60/D/20/2000 (2002) [3.1].
[55] Communication No. 10/1997, UN Doc CERD/C/54/D/10/1997 (1999).
[56] ibid [9.2].
[57] ibid [9.3].

was thus held to be a violation of rights guaranteed in the ICERD.[58] So while the discrimination was not explicitly based on racial grounds, the CERD imposed an obligation to investigate whether it was racially motivated.

The second outlier is *LK v The Netherlands*.[59] The claim was brought by a Moroccan citizen residing in the Netherlands. He was partially disabled. He and his family were offered a lease for a flat outside which there were about twenty people gathered at the time of viewing who shouted 'no more foreigners'. Others threatened to set fire to his car and apartment if he were to move in. His complaints against these facts were not investigated properly by the state authorities. The CERD found that the acts and the statements constituted incitement to racial violence which the State Party had failed to appropriately investigate and remedy. While the finding was brief, it was unambiguous that the explicit use of foreign status could be an inexplicit racial reference.

The final outlier is *SA v Denmark*.[60] The claim involved a Danish citizen of Bosnian origin who had applied for income support when he had failed to secure a job. He was denied income support because of his 'foreign sounding name' which led to a presumption that he did not have Danish nationality—a requirement for receiving income support.[61] The CERD concluded that the amount of compensation granted to the petitioner for racial discrimination was inadequate and did not reflect the mental anguish and humiliation faced by the petitioner who feared being deported to Bosnia—a country he had not lived in for years. While discrimination in this case was directly based on a 'foreign sounding name', the CERD had no objections in seeing it as a proxy for racial grounds. This was because the national authorities had seen discrimination in this light. But there was no real evidence of this. The Committee just assumed that the real reason for discrimination was not the apparent foreignness of the petitioner with a 'foreign sounding name', but racial grounds such as those enumerated in article 1(1) of ICERD.

There are two problems with the CERD's treatment of discrimination based on foreign status. First, claims, such as *Habasi*, *LK*, and SA, have succeeded and show that the CERD is not closed off to finding an overlap between foreign status and racial grounds. But there is no apparent principle as to when the CERD considers foreign status to overlap with racial grounds and when it does not. Second, what the CERD does seem to be averse to, is finding for xenophobic discrimination based on foreign status when it does not overlap with racial grounds. In fact, little attention has been paid to xenophobic discrimination which does not coincide

[58] Elspeth Guild, Stefanie Grant, and CA Groenendijk (eds), *Human Rights of Migrants in the 21st Century* (Routledge 2018) 9 ('There can be a human rights problem with the duty of non-discrimination when prohibited grounds of discrimination lurk behind a State's claim to the legitimacy of differential treatment between citizens and migrants or between migrants only on the basis of their nationality').

[59] Communication No. 4/1991, UN Doc A/48/18 (1993) 131.

[60] Communication No 58/2016, UN Doc CERD /C/97/D/58/2016 (2019).

[61] ibid [2.2].

with racial discrimination and the question whether it can be disproportionate under article 1(2)–(3) of the ICERD, as required by General Recommendation 30 which provides that:

> differential treatment based on citizenship or immigration status will constitute discrimination if the criteria for such differentiation, judged in the light of the objectives and purposes of the Convention, are not applied pursuant to a legitimate aim, and are not proportional to the achievement of this aim.[62]

Xenophobic discrimination inflicts the harm of disbelongingness or civic ostracization from a society or a nation.[63] It is a *sui generis* category of discrimination which relies not on a single specified ground (much like racial discrimination which could be based on race, colour, descent, or national, or ethnic origin) but on a combination of grounds, including, racial grounds, to create the category of 'foreigners' who can be excluded from social, cultural, economic, or political participation. A search of an exact overlap of foreign status with racial grounds misunderstands how the former is constructed fundamentally, intersectionally, in relation to the latter. The CERD seems entirely unaware of the processes of racialization at work here in the case of foreign status.

10.2.1.2.i.b Citizenship or nationality 'Citizenship' is absent from the list of racial grounds in article 1(1) but it is mentioned in article 1(2) which provides that: 'this Convention shall not apply to distinctions, exclusions, restrictions or preferences made by a State Party to this Convention between citizens and non-citizens.' 'Nationality' is also absent from the list of racial grounds in article 1(1) but it is mentioned in article 1(3) which provides that 'nothing in this Convention may be interpreted as affecting in any way the legal provisions of States Parties concerning nationality, citizenship or naturalization, provided that such provisions do not discriminate against any particular nationality'. As non-obstante clauses, these are not carte blanches for discrimination, as their scope cannot be broader than the main clause (the definition of racial discrimination under article 1(1)).[64] The CERD has thus interpreted the exceptions for legal provisions concerning citizenship and nationality to be lawful to the extent that they are proportionate.[65]

[62] CERD, General Recommendation 30, Discrimination against Non-citizens, UN Doc CERD/C/64/Misc.11/rev.3 (2004) [4].

[63] Shreya Atrey, 'Xenophobic Discrimination' (2024) 87 Modern Law Review 80.

[64] CERD, General Recommendation 30, Discrimination against Non-citizens, UN Doc CERD/C/64/Misc.11/rev.3 (2004) [1] [2]. On the specialized interpretation of international human rights treaties, consult James Crawford and Amelia Keene, 'Interpretation of the Human Rights Treaties by the International Court of Justice' (2020) 24 The International Journal of Human Rights 935.

[65] CERD, General Recommendation 30, Discrimination against Non-citizens, UN Doc CERD/C/64/Misc.11/rev.3 (2004) [4].

This means that citizenship or nationality discrimination should both be tested for its coincidence with racial discrimination under article 1(1) and for proportionality under article 1(2)–(3). Like foreign status, this is seldom the case for citizenship or nationality as well.

For example, in *Diop v France*,[66] the claimant was of Senegalese origin, domiciled in Monaco, and married to a French national. He was denied admission to the Bar Council in Nice as the right to practice law in France was restricted to French nationals. The CERD found that this restriction was lawful and did not constitute discrimination on racial grounds enumerated under article 1(1) of the ICERD. It did not consider whether such discrimination was proportionate under article 1(3).

Similarly, in *Ahmed Farah Jama v Denmark*,[67] the author, a Somali citizen living in Denmark, challenged the Danish authorities' refusal to investigate the following statement made by the leader of the Danish People's Party: 'Suddenly they came out in large numbers from the Somali clubs. There she is, they cried, and forced the door to the taxi open and then beat me … I could have been killed; if they had entered I would have been beaten up. It was rage for blood.'[68] The CERD found that 'the statement concerned, despite its ambiguity, cannot necessarily be interpreted as expressly claiming that persons of Somali origin were responsible for the attack in question.'[69] It held that the statement did not fall within the scope of the ICERD.

But in *Mohammed Hassan Gelle v Denmark*,[70] the following reference to Somalis *was* deemed to fall within the scope of the ICERD:

> why should the Danish-Somali Association have any influence on legislation concerning a crime mainly committed by Somalis? And is it the intention that the Somalis are to assess whether the prohibition against female mutilation violates their rights or infringes their culture? To me, this corresponds to asking the association of paedophiles whether they have any objections to a prohibition against child sex or asking rapists whether they have any objections to an increase in the sentence for rape.[71]

The CERD found that the statements could be understood as 'degrading or insulting to an entire group of people, i.e. persons of Somali descent, on account of their national or ethnic origin and not because of their views, opinions or actions regarding the offending practice of female genital mutilation' and 'generaliz[ing] negatively about an entire group of people based solely on their ethnic or national

[66] Communication No. 2/1989, UN Doc 10/05/91 CERD/C/39/D/2/1989 (1991).
[67] Communication No. 41/2008, UN Doc CERD/C/75/D/41/2008 (2009).
[68] ibid [2.1].
[69] ibid [7.4].
[70] Communication No. 34/2004, UN Doc CERD/C/68/D/34/2004 (2006).
[71] ibid [2.1].

origin and without regard to their particular views, opinions or actions regarding the subject of female genital mutilation'.[72] Importantly, the CERD held that the fact that the 'statements were made in the context of a political debate does not absolve the State party from its obligation to investigate whether or not her statements amounted to racial discrimination'.[73] In these circumstances, the failure to investigate whether an act of racial discrimination had taken place amounted to a violation of the ICERD.[74]

The difference between *Ahmed Farah Jama* and *Mohammed Hassan Gelle* is not apparent, other than as a matter of degree. The former concerned less extreme a statement as opposed to the latter. The CERD considered only the latter to fall within the scope of 'racial' grounds under article 1(1) and thus seems to imply a threshold of extremity in determining the material scope of 'racial' grounds under article 1(1). As Chapters 1 and 2 showed, race or racial grounds are categories which are produced and reproduced through racialization which is a qualitative exercise of ascription of racial categories to people, rather than an objective assessment. The CERD seems to selectively avoid this qualitative assessment of racialization in cases of citizenship or nationality discrimination.

10.2.1.2.i.c Language *Emir Sefic v Denmark*,[75] is the only example of a claim which implicated language as a ground of racial discrimination. It did not succeed. The CERD was reticent in testing whether language could be a racial ground and in turn in requiring the Respondent State to ask the same question. Instead, the CERD accepted the justification provided by the Respondent State that language was an objective, not a racial, ground of discrimination.

The claimant in *Sefic* was a Bosnian citizen, residing in Denmark, where he held a temporary residency and work permit. He was refused insurance for his car because he did not speak Danish. He alleged a breach of the State Party's positive obligations in ensuring adequate investigation of his complaint of racial discrimination before the domestic courts. In particular, he argued that 'the requirement to speak Danish as a prerequisite for the receipt of car insurance [was] not an objective requirement and that further investigation would have been necessary to find out the real reasons behind this policy'.[76] The CERD disagreed. It instead agreed with the reasons provided by the insurance company that 'the language requirement, including the ability to communicate with the customer, the lack of resources for a small company to employ persons speaking different languages, and the fact that it is a company operating primarily through telephone contact were

[72] ibid [7.4].
[73] ibid [7.5].
[74] *Saada Mohamad Adan v Denmark*, Communication No. 43/2008, UN Doc CERD /C/77/D/43/2008 (2010).
[75] Communication No. 32/2003, UN Doc CERD/C/66/D/32/2003 (2005).
[76] ibid [7].

reasonable and objective grounds for the requirement and would not have warranted further investigation.'[77]

The reason for not imposing an obligation on the Respondent State to investigate, as the claimant put it, 'the real reasons' behind the language policy seems non-obvious. It is only through a positive obligation on States Parties to investigate whether a *racial* ground was implicated that *racial* discrimination can be detected. Language seems to not trigger this positive obligation as a category which *could* be racialized.

As Part I of the book argued, in principle, any category is open to racialization. Such is the nature of racialization and in turn race or racial grounds. The CERD seems oblivious to this possibility as language is absent both from the list of grounds under article 1(1), and unlike references to citizenship and nationality, also from article 1(2)–(3), and thus finds no mention in the ICERD at all. In effect, this absence seems to permit racial discrimination through the proxy of language.

10.2.1.2.i.d Religion Religion is not a ground of racial discrimination under the ICERD. But as Part I of the book argued, religion is capable of being racialized, and when that is the case, it should be addressed as racial discrimination. Again, this requires the CERD to be open to processes of racialization which, as argued above in respect of other categories, it is not.

The most striking example is *AWRAP v Denmark*.[78] The author, a Danish citizen and a practising Muslim, challenged the lack of an effective investigation against the statements made in the Danish Parliament and in particular by members of the Danish People's Party, such as:

> The problem is that the country unfortunately has been flooded with Muslim so-called culture, and according to Islam it is the right of the male to beat his children and wife yellow and blue.[79]
>
> [A]ccording to Sharia and the Koran, a man has a special position requiring his wife and children to abide by his doings ... And if they don't, they'll be punished[80]

The CERD held that the impugned statements, though they referred to Koran, Islam, and Muslims, did not refer to any of the racial grounds mentioned in article 1(1) of ICERD, that is, race, colour, descent, or national or ethnic origin. It concluded that:

[77] ibid.
[78] Communication No. 37/2006, UN Doc CERD/C/71/D/37/2006 (2007).
[79] ibid [2.3].
[80] ibid [2.5].

no specific national or ethnic groups were directly targeted as such by these oral statements as reported and printed. In fact ... the Muslims currently living in the State party are of heterogeneous origin. They originate from at least 15 different countries, are of diverse national and ethnic origins, and consist of non-citizens, and Danish citizens, including Danish converts.[81]

The CERD recognized that 'the interface between race and religion' would render it 'competent to consider a claim of "double" discrimination on the basis of religion and another ground specifically provided for in article 1 of the Convention, including national or ethnic origin'.[82] However, it considered the present claim to be 'exclusively' based on religion.[83] It did not consider how religion may have been racialized in this case.

Essentially, what the impugned statements did was that they racialized actual or perceived Muslims as inherently violent. Religion thus operated *as* race because it served as grounds for stereotyping a group or a community as inherently or immutably predisposed to violence as a group. This is racialization which lies at the heart of Islamophobia (as explained in Part I of this book). It exceeds the use of religion as religion—to do with faith or belief—and extends to the use of religion as race in an intersectional sense where religion and race combine in indistinguishable ways. The CERD seems to lack such an appreciation of racialization in an intersectional sense which goes beyond a quantitative rendering of intersectionality as 'double' or 'dual' discrimination. The next section shows how this limited approach to intersectionality also prevents the CERD from appreciating the nature of intersectional discrimination as such, and not just racialization as an intersectional process which produces and reproduces racial grounds which are co-constituted by other grounds.

10.2.1.2.ii Racial Discrimination

Linked to the CERD's limited scope of 'racial' grounds is the limited scope of racial 'discrimination' under the ICERD. In particular, the CERD misses the nature of discriminatory harm when it exceeds obvious cases of racial violence or racist hate speech. To illustrate, the CERD misses the nature of discriminatory harm in at least two kinds of discrimination: xenophobic and intersectional.

First, consider *Mahali Dawas and Yousef Shava v Denmark*.[84] The claimants were Iraqi citizens who were recognized as refugees in Denmark. While they were being beaten as their family home was ransacked by a mob, one of the attackers shouted 'go home', while another spoke into his phone about 'problems with some

[81] ibid [6.2].
[82] ibid [6.3].
[83] ibid.
[84] Communication No. 46/2009, UN Doc ERD/C/80/D/46/2009 (2012).

perkere [foreigners]'.[85] A 'No Blacks allowed' sign was placed outside the house after the incident, forcing the petitioners to flee the municipality permanently due to fear of violence and discrimination. The claimants complained that the State Party had failed to interrogate the racist element of the attack and thus deprived them of an effective remedy for the violations. The CERD agreed that given the seriousness of the circumstances 'where the petitioners were subjected, in their own house, to a violent assault by 35 offenders, some of them armed, enough elements warranted a thorough investigation by public authorities into the possible racist nature of the attack against the family'.[86] As the State Party had set aside the criminal investigation, the CERD concluded that it had violated article 6 and article 2(1)(d) of the ICERD.[87] The claim was thus decided primarily as a *failure to investigate* racial discrimination rather than *as* racial discrimination.

The curious aspect of the decision is that the CERD had 'enough elements' that warranted a finding of racial discrimination itself. Epithets like 'go home' or 'problems with *perkere* [foreigners]' pointed to xenophobic discrimination against refugees in Denmark. The 'No Blacks allowed' sign pointed to both racial and xenophobic discrimination. But no finding of racial and/or xenophobic discrimination against Iraqi refugees was made.

Second, the CERD also misses intersectional discrimination when racism and xenophobia combine. *LG* v *Korea*[88] is an example of this. It concerned a foreign national working and living in Korea as a language teacher. The government introduced a requirement for all teachers who were not Korean nationals or who were not of Korean ethnicity to submit to mandatory HIV and drug testing as a precondition for approval or renewal of visa. The claimant argued that the requirement served to reinforce prejudice against non-ethnic Korean teachers.[89] Korean nationals of any ethnicity and ethnic Koreans were both exempt from such testing. The testing was thus drawn neither on the basis of nationality nor ethnicity alone but both of them at the same time. The CERD held that 'the mandatory testing policy limited to foreign teachers of English who are not ethnic Koreans does not appear to be justified on public health grounds or any other ground, and is a breach of the right to work without distinction as to race, colour, or national or ethnic origin'.[90] It further recommended that in addition to the State Party taking appropriate measures to address racial discrimination, it also 'counter any manifestation of xenophobia, such as stereotyping or stigmatizing, of foreigners'.[91] While the

[85] ibid [2.3] ('According to the petitioners, the attacker in that case was carrying a baseball bat and reportedly shouted at the victim "what are you looking at perker svine?" (Danish pejorative slang for "foreigner"')).
[86] ibid [7.4].
[87] ibid [8].
[88] Communication No. 51/2012, UN Doc CERD/C/86/D/51/2012 (2015).
[89] ibid [2.4].
[90] ibid [7.4].
[91] ibid [9].

CERD showed clear awareness of xenophobia in its recommendations, its finding was limited to racial discrimination alone. That is, it did not find for xenophobic discrimination or more precisely, xenoracism in this case where discrimination was directed against the claimant because of *both* her nationality and ethnicity, presumably because no particular nationality was being discriminated against.[92] Indeed, Korean nationals of non-Korean ethnicity were excluded from the testing requirements, making nationality inextricable from the ethnic discrimination at stake. The CERD showed no appreciation of this or the intersection of xenophobia and racism which was the crux of the xenoracist discriminatory harm here.

The CERD misses intersectional discrimination in other claims too, such as *Benon Pjetri* v *Switzerland*[93] which concerned discrimination based on race, disability, and nationality. The claimant in *Pjetri* was born in Albania and had lived in Switzerland since he was eighteen years old. He had a speech impairment and used a wheelchair. His application for naturalization was rejected by the municipal assembly because he was considered not to have integrated into the Swiss society. On evidence was a statement of one of the members of the municipal assembly (that decided such applications) that 'Kosovo-Albanians left a bitter taste in the mouth'[94] and a record of hostile environment targeting the claimant, including in the media. The claimant complained that the national authorities had failed to deal with 'double discrimination on the grounds of his origin and disability' experienced against 'the general xenophobic and racist atmosphere in the Rhine valley'[95] and had failed to adjust the criteria of integration to properly reflect the limitations of his disability.[96] The CERD was unconvinced. First, it held that the criteria for rejection of naturalization were based on lack of integration and not racial grounds and thus rejected the claim of racial discrimination. Second, it held that 'pursuant to article 1 of the Convention, it is not competent to consider the separate claim of discrimination on the grounds of disability'.[97] In essence, the CERD failed to: (i) scrutinize a criterion like 'integration' which essentially draws a line between 'us' and 'them' and thus has the potential not only for being applied along racial lines but also for excluding disabled migrants; and (ii) consider disability discrimination not as a 'separate claim' but as one entwined with other forms of discrimination such as in this context where disabled migrants from racialized groups would have found a requirement like 'integration' insurmountable in comparison with non-disabled migrants of racialized groups. The fact that the claimant's situation was intersectionally defined potentially by his race, disability, and nationality presented a hurdle the CERD neither confronted nor surmounted.

[92] ICERD, art 1(3).
[93] Communication No. 53/2013, UN Doc CERD/C/91/D/53/2013 (2016).
[94] ibid [2.2].
[95] ibid [4.5] [5.10].
[96] ibid [3.5].
[97] ibid [7.6].

10.2.1.3 Evidential Scope

Article 6 of the ICERD obliges the States Parties to 'assure to everyone within their jurisdiction effective protection and remedies, through the competent national tribunals and other State institutions, against any acts of racial discrimination which violate his human rights and fundamental freedoms contrary to this Convention, as well as the right to seek from such tribunals just and adequate reparation or satisfaction for any damage suffered as a result of such discrimination'.

The primary responsibility for the enforcement of the ICERD is thus on States Parties. This has led the CERD to lower its own standard of review to testing only whether the State Party has *not* acted *manifestly unreasonably* or *arbitrarily* in providing effective protection and remedies against racial discrimination.[98] This standard is evidently too low in acting as a bulwark against structural racism given that it is too lenient in what it expects of states. Under this standard, claims which succeed are claims which are patently or obviously racist claims because they involve, for example, use of racial slurs.[99] Otherwise, claims which succeed are those which evidently lack standards of enforcement which are in conformity with article 6,[100] such as a complete failure to investigate, outright dismissal of a claim without proper review, or the absence of a legislation for redressing racial discrimination.

For example, claims which succeed are of the kind such as *Dragan Durmic v Serbia and Montenegro*.[101] The claimant was of Romani origin and a citizen of Serbia and Montenegro who was denied access to a discotheque, while non-Roma persons were allowed, with 'the only apparent difference between them [being] the colour of their skin'.[102] The claimant's complaints were delayed, neglected, and dismissed by the domestic authorities on grounds that it appeared impossible to identify the personnel involved in the incident. The CERD found that it was unreasonable for the State Party to accept this reasoning.[103] It held that given that the claimant had presented an arguable case of racial discrimination, the State Party should have investigated the incident promptly, thoroughly,

[98] *Murat Er v Denmark*, Communication No. 40/2007, UN Doc CERD/C/71/D/40/2007 (2007) [7.2.2] ('it is not the Committee's task to decide in abstract whether or not national legislation is compatible with the Convention ... It is also not the Committee's task to review the interpretation of national law made by national courts unless the decisions were manifestly arbitrary or otherwise amounted to a denial of justice'); *TBB v Germany*, Communication No. 48/2010, UN Doc CERD/C/82/D/48/2010 (2013); *Zentralrat Deutscher Sinti und Roma et al v Germany*, Communication No. 38/2016, UN Doc CERD/C/72/D/38/2006 (2008) [7.7].

[99] *Murat Er v Denmark*, Communication No. 40/2007, UN Doc CERD/C/71/D/40/2007 (2007).

[100] *Grigore Zapescu v Moldova*, Communication No. 60/2016, UN Doc CERD /C/103/D/60/2016 (2021) (The claimant was of Roma origin and a national of the Republic of Moldova. He alleged racial discrimination in the handling of his complaint against the denial of employment due to his Roma ethnicity. While the claimant had brought a prima facie case of racial discrimination, the domestic courts had failed to shift the burden of proof to the company to show that the discrimination was justified. The CERD found that this violated article 6 of ICERD which guarantees effective remedies for racial discrimination).

[101] Communication No. 29/2003, UN Doc CERD/C/68/D/29/2003 (2006).

[102] ibid [2.2].

[103] ibid [9.3].

and effectively.[104] In the absence of such investigation, the State Party was found to have violated articles 5(f) and 6 of the ICERD.

Likewise, in *Kashif Ahmad v Denmark*,[105] the claimant, a Danish citizen of Pakistani origin, challenged the treatment of his complaint of racial discrimination when a high school barred him from joining his friend's graduation ceremony. The school referred to the claimant and his brother as 'a bunch of monkeys'.[106] The claimant's complaint was not examined properly by the national authorities and he obtained no apology or reparation. The CERD concluded that since no one denied that the claimant had been subjected to insulting racialized statements in public, the fact that the police had not investigated whether these statements were based on racial grounds constituted a violation of the ICERD which guarantees effective protection from discrimination and effective remedies for discrimination.[107]

Claimants bear a high evidentiary burden to prove racial discrimination in other instances where racism is less obvious or where enforcement measures exist and have been taken but are challenged for being inadequate or ineffective.[108] Take, for example, *Narrainen v Norway*.[109] The claimant was of Tamil origin, born in Mauritius, and of Norwegian nationality. He was detained in a penitentiary for being sentenced for a drug-related offence. He alleged that there was no case against him other than a testimony from a single individual which was later withdrawn; it was the investigating officer's and jurors' racist attitudes that had led to the prosecution and subsequent conviction.[110] These attitudes, in particular, of the jurors', had been investigated by the competent judicial bodies. Given that there were no obvious defects with the investigation and that the CERD's role was not to interpret Norwegian rules of disqualification of jurors or the disqualification in this particular case, the CERD found no violation of the ICERD.

In *BJ v Denmark*,[111] the claimant was a Danish engineer of Iranian origin who was denied entry into a discotheque because he was considered by the doorman to be a 'foreigner'.[112] It was undisputed that the act constituted an act of racial discrimination. The claimant challenged the Danish courts who refused to order the payment of compensation to the claimant as the act 'was not of such a grave or humiliating character as to justify the granting of pecuniary compensation'.[113] The CERD stated that in principle, refusal of entry to 'a place of service intended for the use of the general public solely on the ground of a person's national or ethnic

[104] ibid [9.6].
[105] Communication No.16/1999, UN Doc CERD/C/56/D/16/1999 (2000).
[106] ibid [2.1].
[107] Ibid [6.2].
[108] *UI and GI v Switzerland*, Communication No. 74/2021, UN Doc CERD/C/112/D/74/2021 (2024); *Hussain v Norway*, Communication No. 63/2018, UN Doc CERD/C/109/D/63/2018 (2003).
[109] Communication No. 3/1991, UN Doc A/49/18 at 128 (1994).
[110] ibid [2.2].
[111] Communication No. 17/1999, UN Doc CERD/C/56/D/17/1999 (2000).
[112] ibid [2.1].
[113] ibid [2.4].

background is a humiliating experience which … may merit economic compensation'.[114] It found that the facts had disclosed no violation of the ICERD in this case, but in future cases, pecuniary compensation should be considered even in cases which result in no physical injury. However, no assessment of whether pecuniary compensation was due *in this case* was made.

In a similar vein, *Miroslav Lacko v Slovak Republic*[115] concerned a Slovak citizen of Romany ethnicity. He was told to leave a restaurant where he had arrived for a drink with his friends. According to the waitress, the owner had prohibited her from serving Roma people as they had previously destroyed equipment on the premises. The claimant's request for prosecution was declined. The claimant argued before the CERD that the lack of a proper investigation into the matter reflected the absence of a Slovak legislation expressly and effectively outlawing racial discrimination. The CERD found no violation and simply asked the State Party to 'complete its legislation in order to guarantee the right of access to public places in conformity with article 5(f) of the Convention and to sanction the refusal of access to such places for reason of racial discrimination'.[116]

In *EIF v The Netherlands*,[117] the claimant, a citizen of the Netherlands of Surinamese origin, challenged his dismissal from the Netherlands Police Academy (NPA) on racial grounds. He was repeatedly targeted as resembling an ape, as a bad learner, as having insufficient proficiency in Dutch, as not modelling himself on white male police officers, etc.[118] He was dismissed from the NPA for bringing a complaint against the treatment of foreign students. The CERD found that while some of the allegations submitted by the claimant carried 'connotations of a serious nature', they had not been the subject of claims that were pursued at the domestic courts which considered only dismissal from the NPA which the CERD considered was not based on racial grounds.[119] The communication failed.

Similarly, in *ZUBS v Australia*,[120] the claimant, an Australian citizen of Pakistani origin, challenged his rejection from higher level positions at the New South Wales Fire Brigade because he lacked so-called local knowledge as a non-white person whose previous professional experience had been in Pakistan and Saudi Arabia. He claimed discrimination on racial grounds for being allocated work that was beneath his qualifications, which paid less, carried a heavier workload, and subjected him to continuous harassment. He also claimed discrimination in the handling of his complaints by the New South Wales Anti-Discrimination Board (ADB) first and by the Equal Opportunity Tribunal (EOT) on appeal. The CERD found

114 ibid [6.3].
115 Communication No. 11/1998, UN Doc CERD/C/59/D/11/1998 (2001).
116 ibid [11].
117 Communication No. 15/1999, UN Doc CERD/C/58/D/15/1999 (2001).
118 ibid [2.1].
119 ibid [6.2].
120 Communication No. 6/1995, CERD/C/55/D/6/1995 (2000).

against the claimant. It held that as a general rule, it was for the domestic courts 'to review and evaluate the facts and evidence' in a particular case of racial discrimination. The present claim failed since there was 'no obvious defect' in the judgment of the EOT.[121]

It is clear that the CERD leaves it for the States Parties to determine facts and ultimately the liability for racial discrimination in individual communications. It remains up to the States Parties to enforce the ICERD and to decide to investigate, prosecute, and make reparations in each case. Unless it is evident that the state wilfully or negligently failed to investigate a claim, no violation is found.[122] This standard of review fails against claims which require adequacy or efficacy assessments of the state machinery put in place to address racial discrimination. The structure of the state machinery for enforcing the norm prohibiting racial discrimination is assessed only superficially—for its existence rather than its operation. The CERD thus fails in opposing structural racism that may result from the operation of enforcement standards in a meaningful way.

10.2.1.4 Remedial Scope

Even though the CERD reviews state responsibility for human rights violations under the ICERD, the remedies it recommends to the states for the violations are perfunctory. Recommendations, confined to the final paragraph, are extremely terse and merely declaratory. The CERD rarely imposes remedies which are transformative or, as explained in Chapter 3, directed towards disrupting the drivers of racial disadvantage at their very source. Remedies under the individual communications procedure also do not require states to think about addressing racial discrimination intersectionally. The result is that even where structural racism is apparent on the face of the record, the remedial scope of the CERD reflects nothing more than liberal anti-racism in its focus on remedying racism as a one-off.

For example, in *Kashif Ahmad v Denmark*,[123] where a violation was found, the length of the recommendations was a single sentence: 'The Committee

[121] ibid [9.3].

[122] *Kamal Quereshi* v *Denmark*, Communication No. 27/2002, UN Doc CERD/C/63/D/27/2002 (2003). A decision to not prosecute for lack of evidence that statements that may have incited racial hatred or violence was defensible. The statements though were undisputed and were of the following variety:

> Cultural enrichments taking place in the shape of negative expressions and rapes against us Danish women, to which we are exposed every day ... Now it's too much, we will not accept more violations from our foreign citizens, can the Mohammedans not show some respect for us Danish women, and behave like the guests they are in our country, then the politicians in the parliament have to change course and expel all of them.
>
> Engage the military against the Mohammedan terror! ... Dear fellow citizen, it is that warlike culture these foreigners enrich our country with ... Disrespect for this country's laws, mass-rapes, violence, abuse of Danish women by shouting things like 'horse', 'Danish pigs' etc. And now this civil war-like situation.

[123] Communication No.16/1999, UN Doc CERD/C/56/D/16/1999 (2000).

recommends to the State party to ensure that the police and the public prosecutors properly investigate accusations and complaints related to acts of racial discrimination which should be punishable by law according to article 4 of the Convention.'[124] In *Anna Kaptova v Slovak Republic*,[125] the CERD directed the State Party to 'fully and properly' eliminate practices violating 'the freedom of movement and residence of Romas.'[126]

Brevity is not itself a problem, however. The problem lies with the reiterative nature of remedies as the CERD ends up repeating what it has already found as a violation.[127] Sometimes, the remedies are too general to even speak to the cause at hand. For example, in a claim prompted by the cancellation of a local authority's decision to provide low-cost housing for Roma people, the CERD only reminded the State Party of its 'obligation to provide the petitioners with an effective remedy. In particular, the State party should take measures to ensure that the petitioners are placed in the same position that they were in upon adoption of the first resolution by the municipal council. The State party is also under an obligation to ensure that similar violations do not occur in the future.'[128] The fact that the cancellation was resulted by racist public opposition to the local authority's decision, in an environment rife with hostility towards Roma people, was left unaddressed in remedies.

At other times, the CERD does not grant even those remedies which are specifically asked for by successful claimants. For example, when claimants asked for an apology for the use of the 'N' word in naming a prominent sports ground,[129] the CERD failed to ask the State Party for an apology.[130]

Lengthy and considered remedies are instead found in cases one suspects the least. Thus, in a claim which challenged the imposition of a requirement to prove

[124] ibid [9.2].

[125] Communication No. 13/1998, UN Doc CERD/C/57/D/13/1998 (2000).

[126] ibid [10.3].

[127] *Lars-Anders Ågren et al v Sweden*, Communication No. 54/2013, UN Doc CERD/C/102/D/54/2013 (2020) [8]–[9] ('The Committee recommends that the State party provide an effective remedy to the Vapsten Sami reindeer herding community by effectively revising the mining concessions after an adequate process of free, prior and informed consent. The Committee also recommends that the State party amend its legislation to reflect the status of the Sami as indigenous people in national legislation regarding land and resources and to enshrine the international standard of free, prior and informed consent. The State party is also requested to widely disseminate the present opinion of the Committee and to translate it into the official language of the State party, as well as into the petitioners' language. The Committee requests the State party to provide, within 90 days, information on the steps taken to give effect to the Committee's opinion.').

[128] *LR v Slovak Republic*, Communication No. 31/2003, UN Doc CERD/C/66/D/31/2003 (2005) [12].

[129] *Stephen Hagan v Australia*, Communication No. 26/2002, UN Doc CERD/C/62/D/26/2002 (2003) [3.5] ('the petitioner seeks the removal of the offending term from the sign and an apology, as well as changes to Australian law to provide an effective remedy against racially-offensive signs, such as the one in question').

[130] ibid [8] ('The Committee recommends that the State party take the necessary measures to secure the removal of the offending term from the sign in question, and to inform the Committee of such action it takes in this respect.').

discriminatory intent in order to prove employment discrimination based on ethnicity, the CERD made the following remedial order:

> The Committee recommends that the State party convey an apology to the petitioner and grant her adequate compensation for the damage caused by the above-mentioned violations of the Convention. The Committee also recommends that the State party fully enforces its Anti-discrimination Act: (a) through the enhancement of available court proceedings for victims of racial discrimination by ensuring, inter alia, that the principle of shifted burden of proof is applied in accordance with article 11 of the Anti-discrimination Act; and (b) through the provision of clear information about available domestic remedies in cases of racial discrimination. The Committee further recommends that the State party take all measures necessary to ensure that persons involved in education, at all levels, are periodically trained on the requirements to prevent and avoid racial discrimination, in accordance with the provisions of the Convention. In addition, the Committee recommends that the State party ensure the organization of adequate training programmes on equality before the law for law enforcement officials, including judges, focusing on the application of the Convention and the Anti-discrimination Act in the courts. The State party is also requested to [sic] widely disseminate the Committee's opinion, including among judicial bodies, and to translate it into the official language of the State party.[131]

Likewise, in a claim challenging the absence of reversal of burden of proof in handling a complaint of employment discrimination,[132] the CERD recommended that:

> the State party convey an apology to the petitioner and grant him adequate compensation for the damage caused by the above-mentioned violation of the Convention. The Committee also recommends that the State party fully enforce its anti-discrimination laws: (a) through the training of judges in anti-discrimination legislation, with a view to ensuring, inter alia, that the principle of shifting the burden of proof is fully observed; (b) through the provision of clear information about available domestic remedies in cases of racial discrimination; and (c) through strengthening of the monitoring of anti-discrimination labour standards. The State party is also requested to widely disseminate the present opinion of the Committee, including among judicial bodies, and to translate it into the official language of the State party.[133]

[131] *VS v Slovakia*, Communication No. 56/2014, UN Doc CERD/C/88/D/56/2014 (2015) [9].
[132] *Grigore Zapescu v Moldova* Communication No. 60/2016, UN Doc CERD/C/103/D/60/2016 (2021).
[133] ibid [10].

Lengthy remedies also followed in a case brought by an individual petitioner for the violation of his civil rights due to the non-recognition of his marriage which was officiated at a traditional indigenous ceremony.[134] The CERD recommended:

> the State party should, inter alia, (a) record the petitioner's marriage to Ms. Lavinas Picq in the civil register so that they may apply for a family reunification visa; (b) provide appropriate compensation to the petitioner for the harm caused; (c) apologize to the petitioner for the violation of his rights; (d) amend its legislation in keeping with the present opinion to provide for the recognition and registration of marriages officiated by traditional indigenous authorities in accordance with their customs and customary law that are not contrary to other international human rights obligations or to requirements under national law for the celebration of marriages; (e) establish a training programme for civil registry officials and the judiciary and other court personnel regarding the validity and recognition of indigenous marriages officiated by traditional authorities; and (f) disseminate this opinion widely and translate it into the Kichwa language.[135]

So, it is not as if the CERD cannot order remedies which are more considered and take into account the redressal of not just the immediate impact on the claimant but also that which caused the impact and that which can prevent it in the future. The examples above show that the CERD is capable of redressing structural racism by recommending transformative remedies which (i) address structural racism by attacking the drivers of racial disadvantage; (ii) effect broad-based change; and (iii) advance intersectional justice. But there is little guiding when it chooses to go down the route of transformative remedies. In fact, it seems to take this route where least apparent. Transformative remedies for structural racism thus seem entirely fortuitous.

10.2.2 Inter-State Communications

Articles 11–13 of the ICERD provide for an inter-state communications procedure. According to article 11(1), if a State Party considers that another State Party is not giving effect to the provisions of the ICERD, it may bring the matter to the attention of the CERD. CERD will then communicate with the State Party concerned and seek to clarify and remedy the matter in the next three months. Under article 11(2), if the matter is not adjusted to the satisfaction of both parties, either by bilateral negotiations or by any other procedure open to them, within six months after

[134] *Yaku Sacha Pérez Guartambel v Ecuador*, Communication No 16/2017, UN Doc CERD/C/106/D/61/2017 (2022).

[135] ibid [6].

the receipt by the receiving state of the initial communication, either state shall have the right to refer the matter again to the CERD by notifying it and also the other state. Article 11(3) obliges states to exhaust all local remedies before bringing proceedings under article 11(2). Article 11(4) empowers the CERD to demand any relevant information from the States Parties. When all the necessary information is collected and collated, article 12 empowers the CERD to establish an ad hoc Conciliation Commission ('Commission') for the settlement of the interstate dispute. Article 13 provides for the preparation, submission, and communication of the Commission's report embodying its findings on all questions of fact and such recommendations as it may think proper for the amicable solution of the dispute.

In contrast to the volume of individual communications under article 14 of the ICERD, the CERD has considered only three inter-state communications so far—*Qatar v Saudia Arabia*,[136] *Qatar v UAE*,[137] and *Palestine v Israel*.[138] This is still remarkable given that the inter-state communications procedures are mostly mythical under other human rights treaties either because they do not exist[139] or because they are not invoked.[140] The invocation of the inter-state communications procedure under the ICERD since 2018 is thus nothing short of iconoclastic. It provides an interesting opportunity to assess how the inter-state communications procedure fares against the principle of anti-racism outlined in this book.

Overall, the inter-state communications procedure appears relatively well suited to addressing structural racism for three reasons: first, its irrefutable nature, as that which cannot be subverted; second, its self-evident focus on structural racism; and third, its appreciation of a broad view of racial grounds and racial discrimination.

First, the CERD in *Palestine v Israel* conceived of the mandate of the inter-state communications procedure under the ICERD as 'automatic'[141] and 'compulsory'.[142] In that case, Palestine had brought a complaint against Israel for the violation of articles 2, 3, and 5 of the ICERD with regard to Palestinian citizens living in the Occupied Palestinian Territory, including East Jerusalem. Israel had argued that since it did not recognize the Palestinian entity, and did not have any treaty relations with it, the CERD lacked jurisdiction over Israel in the dispute. The CERD rejected the argument on two main grounds. First, it accepted that under general international treaty law, a State Party to a multilateral treaty could exclude treaty relations with an entity and hence the jurisdiction of mechanisms or courts in disputes with the entity. But the particular character of racial discrimination—which is 'insidious and pervasive', 'universally recognised as a scourge', and 'a matter of the

136 UN Doc CERD/C/99/5 (2019).
137 UN Doc CERD/C/99/3 (2019).
138 UN Doc CERD/C/100/3, UN Doc CERD/C/100/4, UN Doc CERD/C/100/5 (2019).
139 ICESCR does not have such a procedure. CRPD also does not.
140 CAT, arts 21, 30; CMW, arts 74, 92; ICCPR, arts 41–43; CEDAW, art 29; Ian Brownlie, *Principles of Public International Law* (OUP 1979) 641–650.
141 UN Doc CERD/C/100/3, UN Doc CERD/C/100/4, UN Doc CERD/C/100/5 (2019) [8].
142 ibid [9].

highest priority for the international community'—indicated that its prohibition under the ICERD pertained to 'interests of all the States parties' and occasioned an 'undisputable' concomitant obligation on all 'to act together against racial discrimination'.[143] Second, the Commission noted the unique character of the mechanism under articles 11–13, to which no State had made any reservations, as necessary or essential in 'ensuring the effective prohibition of racial discrimination, an erga omnes norm, for the common good of the whole international community which cannot be derogated from by the unilateral action of one State party, and which has no relevance to the existence of any prior bilateral relationship between States'.[144] Thus, the particular character of racial discrimination and its prohibition in the ICERD made the mechanism under articles 11–13 in turn indispensable and ultimately irrefutable by any State Party.

The extent of this irrefutability is reflected in *Qatar v Saudi Arabia* and *Qatar v UAE*, where the existence of parallel proceedings in the same dispute before the International Court of Justice did not stymie the inter-state communications procedure already triggered.[145] The CERD even remained 'seized of the matter' even though the procedure were eventually suspended following the Al Ila agreement reached by the States Parties to the dispute.[146]

The irrefutability of the inter-state communications procedure under the ICERD makes it particularly resilient to States Parties which seek to use sovereignty and state consent under international law to oppose charges of racial discrimination under the ICERD. This makes the inter-state communications procedure under the ICERD 'structurally' robust in comparison with other mechanisms of dispute settlement which can be subverted by state consent.[147] The lack of availability of the orthodoxy of international law to States Parties makes the inter-state communications procedure under the ICERD highly unusual and robust.[148]

Second, the inter-state communications procedure, as opposed to the individual communications procedure, is self-evidently focussed on structural racism in that it goes beyond individual instances of violations and instead is concerned

143 ibid [3.36].

144 ibid [3.43].

145 UN Doc CERD/C/99/3 (2019) [42]–[52].

146 Decision of the ad hoc Conciliation Commission on the request for suspension submitted by Qatar concerning the interstate communication Qatar v the Kingdom of Saudi Arabia; Decision of the ad hoc Conciliation Commission on the request for suspension submitted by Qatar concerning the interstate communication Qatar v the United Arab Emirates.

147 Scott Leckie, 'The Inter-State Complaint Procedure in International Human Rights Law: Hopeful Prospects or Wishful Thinking?' (1998) 10 Human Rights Quarterly 249, 252; Peter H Kooijmans, 'Inter-State Dispute Settlement in the Field of Human Rights' (1990) 3 Leiden Journal of International Law 87.

148 Rosana Garciandia and Jean-Pierre Gauci, 'Inter-State Communications before UN Human Rights Treaty Bodies: Testing the Waters for Collective Communications' (2024) 13 International Human Rights Law Review 160; Dai Tamada, 'Inter-State Communication under ICERD: From ad hoc Conciliation to Collective Enforcement?' (2021) 12 Journal of International Dispute Settlement 405, 425.

with how states racialize and enact racial disadvantage. This focus is not always possible given that international human rights law mainly governs the vertical relationship between states and individuals (where the states are the duty bearers and individuals the rights holders).[149] What perforce becomes the focus of individual enforcement mechanisms is the regulation of the specific instances of violations of individual human rights by states. A review of the state structures which instate racial order, and use that racial ordering to disadvantage and hence discriminate, is thus rare under the individual communications procedure, as evident in the discussion in Section 10.2.1.

In contrast, the inter-state communications procedure has been invoked in *Qatar v Saudi Arabia, Qatar v UAE,* and *Palestine v Israel* to challenge state actions *as* the drivers of racial disadvantage. *Qatar v Saudi Arabia* and *Qatar v UAE* concerned the large-scale expulsion of Qataris from Saudi Arabia and the UAE while *Palestine v Israel* concerned decades-long law and policy of Israel in the Occupied Palestinian Territory. These disputes essentially concerned, what the CERD called, 'generalised policy and practice' 'ordered and coordinated at the highest levels of government'.[150] There were two further implications of this. First, the CERD did not explicitly require the Applicant State, Palestine, to prove a prima facie case of 'generalised policy and practice' of racial discrimination in *Palestine v Israel.* Instead, it was satisfied with its own concluding observations for Israel which had successively noted evidence of a generalized policy and practice of racial discrimination against Arab citizens of Israel and Palestinians in the Occupied Palestinian Territory.[151] Second, given the acceptance of a prima facie case of a generalized policy and practice of racial discrimination, the CERD concluded that the Applicant State, Palestine, did not have to comply with the rule on exhaustion of domestic remedies.[152] With this, the CERD seemed to have accepted that 'structural deficits' in a Respondent State cannot be countenanced by pursuing either individual cases or remedies within the Respondent State itself.[153]

Third, the CERD has broadened the material scope of race and racial discrimination through the inter-state communications procedure. In *Qatar v Saudi Arabia* and *Qatar v UAE,* the CERD held that distinctions based on nationality are prohibited under the ICERD;[154] and in *Palestine v Israel,* the Commission found that

[149] Frédéric Mégret, 'International Human Rights Law Theory' in Alexander Orakhelashvili (ed), *Research Handbook on the Theory and History of International Law* (Edward Elgar Publishing 2011).
[150] Decision on the admissibility of the inter-State communication submitted by the State of Palestine against Israel, UN Doc CERD/C/103/R.6 (2021) [63].
[151] ibid [64].
[152] ibid.
[153] Jan Eiken, 'Breaking new ground – Again? The CERD Committee's decision on admissibility in Palestine v. Israel' (31 May 2021) <https://www.ejiltalk.org/breaking-new-ground-again-the-cerd-committees-decision-on-admissibility-in-palestine-v-israel/> (accessed 16 March 2025).
[154] Admissibility of the Inter-state Communication submitted by Qatar against the Kingdom of Saudi Arabia, UN Doc CERD/C/99/6 (2019); Admissibility of the Inter-state Communication submitted by Qatar against the UAE, UN Doc CERD/C/99/4 (2019).

Israel's action in the Occupied Palestinian Territory did not only constitute racial discrimination and racial segregation, but also constituted continued colonization of Palestine.[155] Neither view has been endorsed in similar claims adjudicated by the ICJ.[156] The ICJ has emphatically refuted nationality discrimination as prohibited under ICERD[157] and has not commented on colonization as a form of racism.[158]

This broadening of the material scope of race and racial discrimination has a knock-on effect on the range of remedies. Indeed, as a reconciliatory mechanism, the inter-state communications procedure is meant to be amicable as opposed to adversarial and hence is considered as having the 'potential for creative, structural remedies'.[159] Far from being unfriendly or threatening to states or state sovereignty,[160] it is meant to be a productive forum for states to co-generate the outcomes or recommendations of the Commission. Yet, the Commission can play a robust role where such a productive co-generation is not possible. The lengthy and substantive list of recommendations in *Palestine v Israel* confirms this possibility. The recommendations last two pages and are addressed to Israel, Palestine, all other states, Security Council, civil society organizations, and the CERD itself. An immediate end to and refrain from all attacks and hostilities is ordered. More importantly, forward-looking measures, such as the establishment of a national entity to address all violations, high-level interministerial body for international dialogue on the matter, a high-level contact group at the Security Council, a joint platform for human rights defenders, and a rapporteur or a working group to follow up on the present dispute, are also recommended.

However, not all substantive opportunities have been seized in the inter-state communications procedure. Much like the ICJ, the Commission lost an opportunity in *Palestine v Israel* to pronounce on apartheid specifically.[161] This has been

[155] Report of the ad hoc conciliation commission on the inter-State communication submitted by the State of Palestine against Israel under article 11 of the International Convention on the Elimination of All Forms of Racial Discrimination, Findings and Recommendations, UN Doc CERD /C/113/3 (2004) [48].

[156] Application of the International Convention on the Elimination of All Forms of Racial Discrimination (*Qatar v United Arab Emirates*), Preliminary Objections, Judgment of 4 February 2021 (ICJ); Legal Consequences arising from the Policies and Practices of Israel in the Occupied Palestinian Territory, including East Jerusalem, Advisory Opinion of 19 July 2024 (ICJ).

[157] Application of the International Convention on the Elimination of All Forms of Racial Discrimination (*Qatar v United Arab Emirates*), Preliminary Objections, Judgment of 4 February 2021 (ICJ); Kaijun Pan, 'Difference Between the ICJ and the CERD Committee: A Comment on the Application of the International Convention on the Elimination of All Forms of Racial Discrimination (Qatar v. United Arab Emirates) Case' (2022) 21 Chinese Journal of International Law 195.

[158] Legal Consequences arising from the Policies and Practices of Israel in the Occupied Palestinian Territory, including East Jerusalem, Advisory Opinion of 19 July 2024 (ICJ).

[159] David Keane, 'Towards an 'Amicable Solution' in the Universal Human Rights System: Inter-State Communications under the International Convention on the Elimination of Racial Discrimination', Völkerrechtsblog (28 April 2021) <https://voelkerrechtsblog.org/towards-an-amicable-solution-in-the-universal-human-rights-system/> (accessed 16 March 2025).

[160] Theodor Meron, *Human Rights and Humanitarian Norms as Customary Law* (Clarendon Press 1991) 152–153.

[161] David Keane, 'Palestine v Israel and the Collective Obligation to Condemn Apartheid under Article 3 of ICERD' (2022) 23 Melbourne Journal of International Law 1, 4.

long due given the vast developments in scholarship on and advocacy against apartheid in the Palestinian context.[162] The CERD neither considered the elements that make up apartheid under the ICERD nor considered whether Israel had violated its obligations under article 3 of the ICERD in relation to apartheid and not just racial segregation.

It is arguable that given that apartheid is considered the gravest form of racial discrimination under the ICERD,[163] even in the inter-state communications procedure, which is otherwise open to consideration of structural racism, CERD can be reticent in pronouncing on the gravest form of structural racism. No reason for this reticence is immediately apparent. The human casualty of this reticence in the case of Palestine is however too enormous to be reasoned away and only proves that the greater the casualty of structural racism, the harder it is to be called out in international law.

10.2.3 State Reporting

Article 9(1) of the ICERD provides that the States Parties submit for consideration by the CERD 'a report on the legislative, judicial, administrative or other measures which they have adopted and which give effect to the provisions of this Convention', first within one year after the State Party ratifies the ICERD and then every two years and whenever the CERD so requests.

Unlike the determination of specific disputes under the individual or inter-state communications procedures, the consideration of periodic reports submitted by the States Parties to the CERD is broader in at least two ways. First, the issues that are considered are not case-based or episodic and instead, by design, relate to the institutions and structures within states. After all, article 9 of the ICERD provides that the States Parties 'report on the legislative, judicial, administrative or other measures'. The concluding observations which result from the consideration of states reports thus inevitably focus on changes to the states institutions

[162] 'The Occupation of the West Bank and the Crime of Apartheid: Legal Opinion', Yesh Din (9 July 2020) < https://www.yesh-din.org/en/the-occupation-of-the-west-bank-and-the-crime-of-apartheid-legal-opinion/> (accessed 16 March 2025); 'Apartheid', B'Tselem: The Israeli Information Center for Human Rights in the Occupied Territories (12 January 2021) < https://www.btselem.org/apartheid> (accessed 16 March 2025); 'A Threshold Crossed: Israeli Authorities and the Crimes of Apartheid and Persecution', Human Rights Watch (27 April 2021) < https://www.hrw.org/report/2021/04/27/threshold-crossed/israeli-authorities-and-crimes-apartheid-and-persecution> (accessed 16 March 2025); 'Israel's Apartheid against Palestinians: Cruel System of Domination and Crime against Humanity', Amnesty International, Report No. MDE 15/5141/2022 (1 February 2022) < https://www.amnesty.org/en/documents/mde15/5141/2022/en/ > (accessed 16 March 2025); Michael Lynk, Report of the Special Rapporteur on the Situation of Human Rights in the Palestinian Territories Occupied since 1967, UN GAOR, 49th sess, Agenda Item 7, UN Doc A/HRC/49/87 (12 August 2022) [52] ('the political system of entrenched rule in the Occupied Palestinian Territory ... satisfies the prevailing evidentiary standard for the existence of apartheid').

[163] Thornberry, *The International Convention* (n 7) 236.

and structures. Second, the recommendations emerging in the concluding observations can often be quite blunt and forceful. So, in addition to being broad-based and directed at states institutions and structures, they can also signal disruptive and radical change, especially one which conceives racial justice intersectionally. Both these qualities enable the concluding observations to resonate with transformative anti-racism in spirit and its threefold emphasis on: (i) addressing structural racism as wielded by the state and state institutions; (ii) broad-based change; and (iii) commitment to intersectional justice. Indeed, it is only here, in the concluding observations of the CERD that we find the mention of *structural discrimination and inequalities*.[164]

The reason the concluding observations and the recommendations therein resonate with transformative anti-racism *in spirit* and may actually be limited in *enacting* transformative anti-racism is because they are neither self-enforcing nor can they be enforced by the CERD. All concluding observations can do is to censure the states formally and publicly to perform their human rights obligations. Like much of international human rights law, it is ultimately up to the states to act upon their human rights obligations. Given that this limitation applies not only to the CERD's state reporting mechanism but to all international law, it need not overshadow what is distinctive about state reporting from the standpoint of transformative anti-racism. In comparison to contentious (individual communications) and conciliatory (inter-state communications) mechanisms, state reporting in fact appears to go furthest in reflecting the principle of anti-racism in practice.

The point can be demonstrated by considering the CERD's concluding observations on over two dozen state reports submitted by the UK until 2024.[165] In its latest Concluding Observations from 2024 for the combined twenty-fourth to twenty-sixth periodic reports,[166] the CERD recommended that the State Party:

- 'systematically collect and publish comparable statistics on the enjoyment of rights by members of ethnic minorities in all fields of life ... harmonize data collection and to address any weaknesses related to the completeness, quality, consistency and comparability of the data collected ... improve the collection of data on the situation of ethnic minorities facing multiple and intersecting forms of discrimination'.[167]

[164] CERD, Concluding observations on the combined twenty-fourth to twenty-sixth periodic reports of the United Kingdom of Great Britain and Northern Ireland, UN Doc CERD/C/GBR/CO/24-26 (24 September 2024).

[165] This chapter considers only the concluding observations for the UK's twenty-six periodic reports submitted to CERD so far.

[166] CERD, Concluding observations on the combined twenty-fourth to twenty-sixth periodic reports of the United Kingdom of Great Britain and Northern Ireland, UN Doc CERD/C/GBR/CO/24-26 (24 September 2024).

[167] ibid [8].

- 'review and repeal all legislative provisions [such as the Illegal Migration Act 2023 and the Safety of Rwanda (Asylum and Immigration) Act 2024] that reduce the level of protection of the human rights under the Convention and that it ensures that any changes to the current human rights and migration framework strengthen the protection of human rights'.[168]
- 'ensure the adoption of comprehensive anti-discrimination and equality legislation in all jurisdictions of the State party, in particular in Northern Ireland and the overseas territories, containing a clear definition of racial discrimination, which includes direct, indirect, structural, multiple and intersecting forms of discrimination, covering all fields of law in the public and private domains and all prohibited grounds of discrimination, in accordance with article 1 (1) of the Convention'.[169]
- 'take adequate measures to combat the structural discrimination and inequalities faced by ethnic minorities, address the root causes of racial discrimination and inequalities, including colonialism and slavery, and eliminate all obstacles preventing these groups from fully enjoying their rights ... adopt a detailed action plan to eliminate structural discrimination and inequalities that has concrete targets, monitoring and accountability mechanisms and sufficient resources and includes special or affirmative measures'.[170]
- 'suspend the "prevent duty" and adopt robust measures to guarantee that, for as long as these counter-terrorism strategies remain in force, they do not result, in purpose or effect, in profiling and discrimination against ethnic and ethno-religious minorities'.[171]
- 'adopt the measures necessary to combat persistent poverty, which disproportionately affects ethnic minorities, in particular children, including by adopting a cross-governmental strategy against poverty and by effectively addressing unemployment, occupational segregation and discriminatory practices with regard to recruitment, salaries, promotions and other conditions of employment. It also recommends that the State party abolish policies that adversely impact ethnic minority households, such as the two-child limit and benefit cap'.[172]
- 'repeal or review legislative or policy measures that have an adverse impact on [Roma, Traveller and Gypsy] lifestyle, such as section 83 of the Police, Crime, Sentencing and Courts Act 2022, which criminalizes unauthorized encampments in England and Wales'.[173]

[168] ibid [12].
[169] ibid [14a].
[170] ibid [26].
[171] ibid [34].
[172] ibid [38].
[173] ibid [42].

- 'take effective measures to address structural inequalities and discriminatory barriers in the context of the social determinants of health, including climate change and environmental health hazards, improve health outcomes and ensure the accessibility and availability of culturally acceptable and gender-responsive quality health-care services for persons belonging to ethnic minorities, throughout its jurisdiction'.[174]
- 'redouble its efforts to acknowledge past wrongs and raise awareness of the legacies and impacts of colonialism and trafficking in enslaved people and their connection with present-day manifestations of systemic racism'.[175]
- 'consider making a formal apology for its role in chattel enslavement and the historic trafficking in enslaved Africans, adopt specific measures to address their lasting consequences and commit to reparations'.[176]

What stands out in these—albeit selective set of recommendations from the slew of recommendations made in the latest report—is both their scale and specificity. On the one hand, the concluding observations and the recommendations cover a vast array of themes: 'Statistics', 'Incorporation of the Convention into the domestic legal order', 'Human rights framework', 'Legislation against racial discrimination', 'National human rights institutions', 'Public policies and plans for combating racial discrimination', 'Paramilitarism and racism in Northern Ireland and ethnic and religious prejudice in Scotland', 'Racism in sports', 'Structural discrimination and special measures to address inequalities', 'Participation in political and public life', 'Right to freedom of peaceful assembly', 'Racial profiling, stop-and-search and excessive use of force by law enforcement officials', 'Counter-terrorism measures', 'Criminal justice system and juvenile justice system', 'Poverty, employment and social security', 'Housing and homelessness', 'Health', 'Education', 'Situation of migrants, asylum-seekers and refugees', 'Access to justice', 'Windrush generation', 'Forced assimilation of Gypsy/Traveller communities in Scotland', 'Forcible eviction of Chagossians from Diego Garcia', and 'Lingering effects of colonialism and the slave trade'. On the other hand, the report also makes specific recommendations such as suspending the prevent duty, repealing the section 83 of the Police, Crime, Sentencing and Courts Act 2022, abolishing the two-child limit and benefit cap for social security, and making a formal apology for its role in chattel enslavement. The scale and generality are accompanied by the precision of specific recommendations. The concluding observations thus issue broad-based calls for change, as opposed to piecemeal or incremental change directed at episodic or individual issues. They reflect the appreciation of the essence of transformative anti-racism which is in overhauling the entirety of socio-economic, political, and cultural

[174] ibid [44a].
[175] ibid [58a].
[176] ibid [58c].

relations between people. The fact that the concluding observations are targeted at states and state structures (such as its legislation and policy) and show awareness of intersectional justice completes their resonance with the three dimensions that make up transformative anti-racism and reflect anti-racism as a legal principle befittingly.

Concluding observations did not start out this way. They reflect anti-racism in a transformative sense only recently. The CERD's latest concluding observations from 2024 for the UK are its lengthiest ever. It repeats many of the enduring themes that have been reiterated in previous concluding observations, only confirming the lack of actual transformation that may be possible through a single or even successive concluding observations. These themes include statistics and data collection, the state of the national human rights institutions, racist hate speech and hate crimes, counter-terrorism measures, access to justice, discrimination against persons of African descent, Gypsies, Travellers and Romas, criminal justice, health, employment, and education. Yet, concluding observations have also tackled contemporary issues pertinent at the time of the particular cycle of state reporting. For example, the CERD concluding observations from 2016 expressed particular concern for the Haitians in the Turks and Caicos Islands[177]—a concern that was not reiterated in its next round of concluding observations in 2024—which instead focussed on a range of other new themes including structural racism, racism in sports, effects of colonialism and the slave trade, and issues pertaining to the Windrush generation that had erupted at the time. Likewise, in its concluding observations from 2011 for the combined eighteenth to twentieth reports, the CERD focussed on the riots and acts of vandalism that took place in the UK in August 2011.[178] The CERD was particularly scathing of the policy responses to the riots for their disproportionate impact on racialized minorities. It also noted the increase in virulent attacks on, and negative portrayal of, ethnic minorities, immigrants, asylum seekers, and refugees by the media in the UK.[179] Likewise, given the conditions of economic downturn at the time, the CERD reminded the UK of its responsibility that austerity measures and spending cuts do not exacerbate racial discrimination and inequality.[180] It expressed 'deep concern' about provisions, such as section 19D of the earlier Race Relations Act of 2000, which permitted public officials to discriminate on grounds of nationality, ethnic and national

[177] CERD, Concluding observations on the combined twenty-first to twenty-third periodic reports of the United Kingdom of Great Britain and Northern Ireland, UN Doc CERD/C/GBR/CO/21-23 (3 October 2016).

[178] CERD, Concluding observations on the combined eighteenth to twentieth periodic reports of the United Kingdom of Great Britain and Northern Ireland, UN Doc CERD/C/GBR/CO/18-20 (14 September 2011).

[179] ibid [11].

[180] ibid [13].

origin, and recommended its urgent removal.[181] It also showed scepticism towards the UK's position at the time of the enactment of the Equality Act 2010 which signalled 'moving away from treating inequality as principally concerning race and towards focusing on transparent frameworks to create opportunities for all' and thus recommended the development of a dedicated race action plan.[182] The CERD has consistently recommended the commencement of sections 1, 9(5), and 14 of the Equality Act 2010 concerning the socio-economic duty, caste discrimination, and dual discrimination.[183] This has not been achieved so far.

Successive concluding observations have thus been plain about the CERD's concerns but much briefer about its recommendations.[184] In fact, older concluding observations were, at relevant points, equally adulatory and withering of the government's efforts in combating racial discrimination.[185] For example, the recommendations for the UK's tenth and eleventh reports in 1992, which were just two paragraphs long, dedicated a paragraph each to praise and reprimand the government.[186] In contrast, the latest 2024 concluding observations last fifteen pages. The full text of the 2024 concluding observations stands out for its high level of detail both generally—in its appreciation of the bigger picture of the state of racism and racialized minorities in the UK—and specifically—in its assessment of the institutional and structural factors which contribute to the existing state of affairs. The emerging recommendations are thus some of the strongest that have been made in the history of UK's state reporting to the CERD, especially when assessed against the standard of transformative anti-racism.

It is quite another matter what these concluding observations actually achieve. This is because in the scheme of international human rights law, transformation is ultimately up to the states. What can be said, however, is that the practice of the CERD, in relation to its state reporting mechanism, has gone the furthest in comparison to its other mechanisms considered above (individual and

[181] ibid [16]; CERD, Concluding Observations on the sixteenth and seventeenth periodic reports of the United Kingdom of Great Britain and Northern Ireland, UN Doc CERD/C/63/CO/11 (10 December 2003).

[182] ibid [17].

[183] ibid [30].

[184] CERD, Concluding Observations on the fifteenth periodic report of the United Kingdom of Great Britain and Northern Ireland, UN Doc CERD/C/304/Add.102 (1 May 2001); CERD, Concluding Observations on the fourteenth periodic report of the United Kingdom of Great Britain and Northern Ireland, UN Doc CERD/C/304/Add.20 (23 April 1997); CERD, Concluding Observations on the thirteenth periodic report of the United Kingdom of Great Britain and Northern Ireland, UN Doc CERD/C/304/Add.9 (28 March 1996); CERD, Concluding Observations on the twelfth periodic report of the United Kingdom of Great Britain and Northern Ireland, including the dependent territories, Report of the forty-eighth session, UN Doc A/48/18 (15 September 1993) 82–84.

[185] ibid.

[186] CERD, Concluding Observations on the tenth and eleventh periodic reports of the United Kingdom of Great Britain and Northern Ireland, including the dependent territories, Report of the forty-sixth session, UN Doc A/46/18 (17 February 1992) 54–55.

inter-state communications procedures), in reflecting anti-racism as a legal principle. This is not to say that the CERD's practice on state reporting in the UK is now perfect. There is room for improvement especially in regards considering how non-state actors which act state-like (Meta, Google, Alphabet, X, Amazon, etc) affect state obligations and obligations of non-state actors under the CERD. There is also ample scope to develop a thoroughly intersectional perspective on racial discrimination in the concluding observations, going beyond the perfunctory references to intersectionality that have been made so far. So, while much is left to be desired under state reporting as a monitoring mechanism, it is still less than what is left to be desired vis-à-vis the CERD's record under its enforcement mechanisms.

10.3 Human Rights Council

Unlike domestic law, international law exceeds the boundaries of 'hard' law and includes the wider discourse or praxis of human rights, international relations, politics, diplomacy, advocacy, etc.[187] It is thus worth looking beyond what this chapter has considered so far—the practice surrounding a treaty—and towards the wider discourse in international law. While this wider discourse is perhaps too wide to be canvassed here exhaustively, a few notable examples from the work of the HRC, especially the OHCHR, stand out for their engagement with anti-racism as a legal principle.[188] Since engagement with anti-racism as a legal principle appears slight across domestic, comparative, and international legal doctrine, these other examples are instructive. They are especially instructive as they are examples from the HRC which is most proximate to the practice of international human rights law as it is tasked with overseeing all human rights activity at the United Nations (UN). Thus, though they may not be examples which are considered binding or enforceable in a traditional legal sense, they still constitute the practice of human rights, which is not confined to the grammar of law at the international level.

First, most prominently, transformative anti-racism has been taken up by the United Nations High Commissioner for Human Rights in their recent reports

[187] Arnold N Pronto, 'Understanding the Hard/Soft Distinction in International Law' (2015) 48 Vanderbilt Journal of Transnational Law 941; Christine Chinkin, 'The Challenge of Soft Law: Development and Change in International Law' (1989) 38 International and Comparative Law Quarterly 850; Gunther F Handl, W Michael Reisman, Bruno Simma, Pierre Marie Dupuy, and Christine Chinkin, 'A Hard Look at Soft Law' (1988) 82 Proceedings of the Annual Meeting 371.

[188] This section does not consider Universal Periodic Review and the Human Rights Council Complaint Procedure.

from 2021,[189] 2022,[190] 2023,[191] and 2024.[192] This was spurred by the murders of George Floyd and Breonna Taylor in 2020 and the ensuing mass protests worldwide that marked a watershed in the fight against racism. In response, the 2021 report set 'an agenda towards transformative change for racial justice and equality' with a fourfold objective: (i) reverse cultures of denial, dismantle systemic racism, and accelerate the pace of action; (ii) end impunity for human rights violations by law enforcement officials and close trust deficits in this area; (iii) ensure that the voices of people of African descent and those who stand up against racism are heard and that their concerns are acted upon; and (iv) acknowledge and confront legacies, including through accountability and redress.

The focus on fighting structural racism and bringing about broad-based or transformative change is obvious in this agenda. The report considers racism in a comprehensive sense and across social, cultural, economic, political, and psychological dimensions. The discussion of the reality of racism faced by people of African descent is thus not confined to a particular sphere or particular human rights. The report also transcends the discussion of the mental states of perpetrators and concerns the material reality of racial disadvantage. The report's agenda for change is thus the upturning of the stark racial disadvantages between groups—not in a minimal or incremental way but in an urgent and comprehensive way. This is reiterated in the 2022 report which urged 'measures to recognize and seek to address racism beyond the sum of individual acts and to begin to address past legacies ... [via] comprehensive evidence-based approaches—grounded in intersectional and intergenerational analyses—that address systemic racism, including structural and institutional factors, in State institutions, the private sector and societal structures across multiple interconnected areas'.[193]

[189] Human Rights Council, Report of the United Nations High Commissioner for Human Rights, 'Promotion and protection of the human rights and fundamental freedoms of Africans and of people of African descent against excessive use of force and other human rights violations by law enforcement officers', 47th session, A/HRC/47/53 (09 July 2021) [hereafter HRC, 2021 report].

[190] Human Rights Council, Report of the United Nations High Commissioner for Human Rights, 'Promotion and protection of the human rights and fundamental freedoms of Africans and of people of African descent against excessive use of force and other human rights violations by law enforcement officers through transformative change for racial justice and equality', 51st session, A/HRC/51/53 (2 August 2022) [hereafter HRC, 2022 report].

[191] Human Rights Council, Report of the United Nations High Commissioner for Human Rights, 'Promotion and protection of the human rights and fundamental freedoms of Africans and of people of African descent against excessive use of force and other human rights violations by law enforcement officers through transformative change for racial justice and equality', 45th session, A/78/166 (13 July 2023) [hereafter HRC, 2023 report].

[192] Human Rights Council, 'Promotion and protection of the human rights and fundamental freedoms of Africans and of people of African descent against excessive use of force and other human rights violations by law enforcement officers through transformative change for racial justice and equality', 57th session, A/HRC/57/67 (6 September 2024) [hereafter HRC, 2024 report].

[193] HRC, 2021 report (n 189), pmbl.

Equally, the agenda is framed in intersectional terms and in recognition of the fact that:

> people of African descent face interconnected, intersectional and compounded forms of racial discrimination, marginalization and exclusion that are shaped by historical legacies and mutually reinforced through cycles of structural inequalities that have lasted for generations, affecting the enjoyment of human rights in every part of life. Systemic racism persists, in large part, due to misconceptions that the abolition of slavery, the end of the transatlantic trade in enslaved Africans and colonialism, and measures taken by States to date, have removed the racially discriminatory structures built by those practices and created equal societies.[194]

In this regard, the report highlights the 'Black Lives Matter movement and associated groups, whose combined efforts offer a collective platform, characterized by integrated approaches and intersectional narratives, to respond to racism'.[195] The 2022 report spotlights an intersectional approach to the right to participation as a prerequisite to transformative change for racial justice and equality. It urges states 'to accelerate the pace of action and unveil multipronged comprehensive evidence-based approaches that encompass far-reaching legal, policy and institutional measures to dismantle systemic racism in all areas of life—developed, implemented and monitored with the meaningful participation of people of African descent'.[196] The 2023 report unpacks 'key elements of intersectionality as an essential framework to combat systemic racism and confront legacies of enslavement and colonialism'.[197] The High Commissioner concludes that intersectionality can be a 'game changer' and calls on 'a full shift in mindset, urging States to seize upcoming opportunities with renewed vigour and stronger political will to achieve transformative change for racial justice and equality for Africans and people of African descent ... responding to the full spectrum of lived experiences; alongside tackling the root causes and drivers of multiple and intersecting forms of discrimination, including structures, institutions, laws, policies and behaviours that perpetuate such discrimination.'[198]

The breadth of the High Commissioner's reports reflects the account of anti-racism as a legal principle set out in Part I of the book. In particular, it reflects a commitment to address structural racism by attacking the drivers of racial disadvantage wielded by the state and state-like entities to bring about broad-based change and intersectional justice. It is arguable that it is in the nature of these reports to allow for such breadth as they are not concerned with a single instance

[194] ibid [10] [14].
[195] ibid [49].
[196] HRC, 2022 report (n 190) pmbl.
[197] HRC, 2023 report (n 191) pmbl.
[198] ibid [70].

of racism (as enforcement mechanisms often are) or racism in a single country (as monitoring mechanisms often are). The general nature of these reports and the broad mandate of the UN Human Rights Council (and in turn the High Commissioner and the OHCHR) which concerns universal human rights issues across 193 UN member states enable anti-racism at scale.

But form does not dictate substance. In fact, nothing, prior to the spate of protests following George Floyd and Breonna Taylor's murders in the US, suggests that the HRC recognized anti-racism as a legal principle. Anti-racism was thus not pre-empted until 2021 other than perhaps in a liberal or cultural but never transformative sense. This confirms that in any context—local or regional, domestic or international, statutory or constitutional, legal or non-legal—anti-racism as a legal principle needs to be substantively engaged with in order to be engendered. It cannot simply be declared. So, even if the 'softer' form of some HRC measures enables this substantive engagement, other legal (statutory, common law, constitutional) or adjudicative (domestic or international courts, or treaty bodies) contexts should not be assumed to be closed off to it *simply* because of the difference in form between these contexts.

Recognition of anti-racism as a legal principle, however, does not ensure it being achieved. It is only a foot in the door for racial justice. In fact, the HRC needs to also *act* on anti-racism as a legal principle—something it has not been able to do fully. For example, as the joint statement made by the Special Procedures mandate holders before the HRC set out, the need of the hour, following the worldwide protests in 2020, was the establishment of the 'International Commission of Inquiry to Investigate Systemic Racism in Law Enforcement in the United States'.[199] No such accountability mechanism was established and no substantial resources were thrown behind other actors such as the several special procedures which could deal with racism more actively and independently, such as the Special Rapporteur on contemporary forms of racism, Special Rapporteur in the field of cultural rights, the Special Rapporteur on freedom of religion or belief, the International Independent Expert Mechanism to Advance Racial Justice and Equality in the context of Law Enforcement, and the Intergovernmental Working Group on the Durban Declaration and Programme of Action. So, while the Human Rights Council declared its commitment to anti-racism, its realization was left to the states, with the UN Human Rights system left to *do* little in that matter.

In sum, there is good reason to think that the form of international human rights law mechanisms makes them good enough only for rhetorical, conceptual, or

[199] 'Human Rights Council holds an urgent debate on current racially inspired human rights violations, systemic racism, police brutality and violence against peaceful protests' (17 June 2020) <https://www.ohchr.org/en/statements/2020/06/urgent-debate-human-rights-council-current-racially-inspiredhuman-rights?LangID=E&NewsID=25969> (accessed 16 March 2025).

declaratory recognition of anti-racism.[200] Recent evidence shows that it is possible for the UN human rights system to be able to ideate, iterate, and insist on anti-racism (something that had not been done previously). The same evidence though shows that it does not or cannot give effect to anti-racism by itself and rather leaves it to states to be inspired to do so. States, however, seem slow in embracing anti-racism as a legal principle, as demonstrated in Chapters 5–9.

10.4 Conclusion

Much like domestic law, international law has taken 'a firm stance against racism' through the prohibition of racial discrimination.[201] Yet, when considered against the record of the practice in international law, the stance does not automatically translate into anti-racism. While there is evidence of anti-racism as a legal principle being recognized in international law, much of the practice appears wanting in giving effect to the principle. What seems to explain the differing responses to anti-racism in international law is the type of mechanism or form of engagement under consideration. Treaty body monitoring mechanisms seem to fare better than enforcement mechanisms in recognizing anti-racism. Likewise, non-treaty body engagement with anti-racism reflects a strong commitment to anti-racism. In the final analysis, even though international law may be limited in activating the actionable component of anti-racism as a legal principle and to actually give effect to the principle, it may nevertheless be considered as recognizing the principle conceptually.

[200] Robert Knox, 'Marxism, International Law and Political Strategy' (2009) 22 Leiden Journal of International Law 413.

[201] Geir Ulfstein, 'Qatar v United Arab Emirates' (2022) 116 American Journal of International Law 397, 401.

Conclusion

So, is there anything like a principle of anti-racism in law?

Conceptually, yes, there can be. As this book argued in Part I, anti-racism as a legal principle is a commitment to address structural racism and to transform the very drivers of racial disadvantage. The principle was derived in four stages.

As Chapter 1 argued, the first step towards anti-racism was broadening the meaning of racism from animus or ideology to include racial disadvantage. This shift in focus to the material conditions of racism is critical in understanding the sources or roots of racism and in turn for crafting responses to racism.

The roots of racism lie in structural racism. Structural racism is to do with how (i) state and state-like entities (ii) racialize (iii) to instate a framework of racial disadvantage. Chapter 2 showed that at the heart of all racism is structural racism without which no racism can exist or be explained. It developed a source-based typology of racism which includes interpersonal or individual, institutional or systemic, and structural racism. It argues that since it is structural racism which underlies all these other forms of racism, structural racism should be at the centre of all anti-racist efforts.

Chapter 3 developed a complementary typology of anti-racism which included liberal, cultural, and transformative anti-racism. While liberal anti-racism is concerned with changing individual behaviours and minds, cultural anti-racism is concerned with changing the collective experience of racism in communities. Both leave structural racism intact and thus respond to racism only at a superficial level. Liberal and cultural anti-racisms are thus inadequate in attacking the sources or roots of racism. The adequate version of anti-racism is transformative anti-racism because it attacks (i) structural racism (ii) in a broad-based and (iii) intersectional way. 'Anti-racism' in a complete sense is thus simply a shorthand for transformative anti-racism and not liberal or cultural anti-racism.

The lynchpins between Parts I and II of the book were Chapters 4 and 5. They connected the conceptual accounts of racism and anti-racism with norms and standards in law.

Chapter 4 argued that anti-racism fits the mould of a legal principle because it provides general guidance for all action rather than determine a particular outcome (as is excepted of legal rules), ordain the achievement of a socio-economic goal (as policies do), or state a virtue (as values do). Anti-racism as a legal principle thus guides the imagination and operation of all law and policy to address

Anti-Racism as a Legal Principle. Shreya Atrey, Oxford University Press. © Shreya Atrey 2026.
DOI: 10.1093/9780198947646.003.0014

structural racism. Anti-racism as a legal principle though need not be legislated or declared. Instead, it transpires in the practice of law.

While Part I offered a conceptual account of anti-racism as a legal principle, Part II explored how anti-racism transpired in practice.

The empirical case for anti-racism as a legal principle was thus made in Part II of the book.

Empirically, the answer to the central question posed in this book depends on whether one prefers a quantitative or a qualitative view of the doctrine presented in Part II of the book. Quantitatively, bearing in mind only a handful of cases where structural racism is addressed, the answer may be in the negative. Qualitatively, bearing in mind the strength of reasoning in these handful of cases, the answer may be in the affirmative. Equally, the qualitative difference, which anti-racism as a legal principle *could* have made in cases of structural racism where it was not applied, also furnishes a clear argument for its adoption in such cases in the future. This position emerged in six stages.

Chapter 5 took the first step towards connecting anti-racism and racial discrimination law. It showed that though racial discrimination law is often deemed anti-racist, the sixty-year strong trajectory of British racial discrimination law reflects mainly liberal, and previously cultural, but never genuinely transformative, anti-racism. This is because racial discrimination law has not been imagined for addressing structural racism. But nothing explicitly bars the use of racial discrimination law to address structural racism either. As Chapter 4 argued, anti-racism is neither legislated nor self-activating. It can only be gleaned at in the actual practice of racial discrimination law and how it addresses structural racism. The next chapters thus tested the extent to which the current practice in racial discrimination law reflected anti-racism as a legal principle.

Chapter 6 argued that case law under Britain's single consolidated equality legislation, the Equality Act 2010, hardly scratches the surface of structural racism. It appears effective only against interpersonal racism, that too of the most obvious kind. This is despite their being no obvious limitation to addressing structural racism in the statute. Instead, the limitation is in how law is practised and in the particular doctrinal moves made in law which limit the personal, material, evidential, and remedial scope of racial discrimination law to exclude structural racism.

Thus, first, racial discrimination law is mostly limited to individual claims of episodic or discrete nature. It is ill-disposed to claims brought by entities (other than individuals) which are often better capable of mounting challenges of structural racism against the state. Second, its material scope, that is, the subject matter it applies to, is limited both in terms of the type of 'racial' grounds it applies to and also the type of 'discrimination' it considers racial discrimination. Racial grounds are those which fit grounds explicitly recognized as racial, namely, colour, nationality, and ethnic or national origins. Language, accent, immigration status, asylum status, refugee status, or religion are thus outside the scope of racial discrimination even though, as Part I of the book explained, they are as capable of being racialized as other attributes such as colour or descent. Likewise, structural racism, which is to do with background conditions or structures rather than the most proximate cause of discrimination, is often excluded from the ambit of what is considered 'discrimination', as is intersectional discrimination. Underlying causes or patterns of racialized disadvantage even when directly challenged slip through the cracks of both direct and indirect discrimination. Third, the requirements of proving structural racism appear insurmountable in practice. This is especially so for claims of indirect discrimination where evidence of racial disadvantage is treated triflingly, and the bar for passing the proportionality test is set too low for the state. Fourth, remedies in discrimination law are highly constrained and rarely transformative. They thus respond to the outward effects rather than the underlying causes of structural racism, even where the latter are evident.

Case law under the UK's Human Rights Act 1998 is not much different. But, as Chapter 7 argued, it does seem more open to challenges against the state and, occasionally, has also successfully resisted structural racism. These occasional successes—such as the *Belmarsh* case—prove instructive in how anti-racism as a legal principle emerges, not in name or as a label, but in the way in which the doctrine is applied to address structural racism (how state and state-like entities racialize to produce racial disadvantage) in a transformative way (broad-based and intersectional).

A similar result follows in common law as Chapter 8 showed. While there is no general common law principle of equality or non-discrimination in the UK, there is yet a special status of prohibition of racial discrimination within the existing grounds of judicial review, which can reflect anti-racism as a legal principle. Common law judicial review thus remains a viable mechanism for giving effect to anti-racism as a legal principle. However, it is underutilized even when it is principally geared towards addressing excesses of state power and hence particularly suitable for addressing structural racism.

Chapter 9 turned to comparative constitutional case law in countries with seemingly strong commitments to racial equality or racial justice. Perhaps surprisingly, even constitutional prohibitions of racial discrimination do not automatically align with anti-racism unless doctrine is attentive to it. Examples of attentiveness of doctrine to the frameworks of structural racism and transformative anti-racism reflect anti-racism as a legal principle befittingly—such as *Corbiere* in Canada, *Sukanya Shanta* in India, and *Mahlangu* in South Africa.

As Chapter 10 argued, international law is no different and requires no vocal or textual adoption of a so-called legal principle of anti-racism. Instead, it requires conceptual awareness of anti-racism and the translation of that awareness into the granularities of legal practice. Here, the form of practice in international law matters. The more formal a mechanism in international law—such as treaty-body enforcement mechanisms—the more resistant it is to giving effect to anti-racism. The less formal mechanisms—such as treaty-body monitoring mechanisms and non-treaty body mechanisms—are more open to adopting anti-racism as a legal principle, in principle, though less capable of giving effect to the principle as these mechanisms often are neither binding nor enforceable.

Part II of the book thus revealed a rather sparse reflection of anti-racism as a legal principle across British, comparative, and international law. Yet, in subjecting the doctrine to the conceptual account of anti-racism as a legal principle developed in Part I, it showed that anti-racism *can* and occasionally *does* make a difference to how law is practised.

The book thus progressively worked towards a normative case for anti-racism as a legal principle, a case which the conclusion reinforces.

Normatively, anti-racism as a legal principle *should* exist in law—whether British, comparative, or international law—for three reasons.

First, there is often no 'racism' or 'anti-racism' in law. Neither international instruments nor domestic constitutions and statutes mention these locutions.[1] What is mentioned however is 'racial discrimination'. Indeed, as Chapter 5 argued, racial discrimination law is considered the legal response to racism and hence an expression of anti-racism. Though this justification is popular, it is unsubstantiated in practice because, as this book has shown, the doctrine of racial discrimination law does not quite address the full range of racism, especially racism which is the antecedent of all forms of racisms, that is, structural racism.

This revelation presents two options: (i) to abandon the anti-racist justification of racial discrimination law; or (ii) to insist on it and to insist on the practice reflecting it in turn. The former is not really an option as it leaves the field of racial discrimination law without any connection to racism and anti-racism. As Part I argued, this is not how the field of discrimination law was conceived, and as Part II argued, discrimination law seems to operate rudderless, as erratic and as lacking direction, when its link with anti-racism is severed. The only real option is the latter. The ideal position is thus not to abandon the anti-racist credentials of racial discrimination law but to reinforce them as racial discrimination law is meaningless without them. We risk making racial discrimination an entirely artificial legal category if it loses its links with racism, which in turn is about structural racism. A commitment to the legal principle of anti-racism which is about addressing structural racism is thus not only the normatively desirable but also the normatively expedient option for racial discrimination law.

[1] As the introduction mentioned, a notable exception is Brazil where the Constitution of 1988 in Article 4, Section VIII mentions the 'repudiation of terrorism and racism' as a guiding principle for Brazil's international relations and Article 5, Section XLII declares racism a crime for which bail is not available, and which is punishable by imprisonment. Further, 'The Anti-Racism Act', Law No. 7,716/89, prohibits discrimination based on race, colour, ethnicity, religion, or national origin.

Second, there is no normative bar to anti-racism in law either. Law is not complicit with racism in any normative sense.[2] Law's complicity with racism and indeed its active part in generating and regenerating racism as a 'structuring structure'[3] is doctrinal not normative. At the normative level, law, especially discrimination law, is indeterminate.[4] It is neither liberal nor conservative *as such*. Even if law's indeterminacy is deemed facile,[5] it still generates conditions for subversion towards more radical, progressive, or transformative ends.[6] These conditions can emerge because law or any other structuring structure is not one thing but instead represents numerous social, political, economic, cultural, psychological, familial, religious, and other networks of interrelationships.

This, as Chapter 3 explained, is the very essence of structures. It is the disparate nature of structures which gives rise to both the possibility of their reproduction and transformation. That is, as structures are essentially made up of a network of relationships that are not fully coordinated, the possibility of structural change exists in structures themselves. In the legal context, this means that different parts of how legal structures operate in practice generate the conditions for both their *re*production and *de*production. It is thus the structure of law itself—its extensive doctrinal intricacies—that make structural change possible. A clear appreciation of the nature of structures helps appreciate law's normative compatibility with anti-racism as a legal principle which is meant to transform the very structures in which racism and anti-racism may be located.

Third, following above, if limitations to anti-racism as a legal principle are doctrinal not normative—that is, they are a bug not a feature of the legal system—then they can be addressed or debugged. This book has tried to show how this can be done. The normative case for anti-racism as a legal principle emerges in the application of the principle to the doctrine of racial discrimination law. The analysis in Part II showed not only how the principle is ignored, but also what its appreciation can do in effectively addressing structural racism through law. The analysis showed this not just through the discussion of the few successful cases, but through the numerous failed cases. It was in reading the failed cases through the lens of anti-racism that the normative appeal of anti-racism as a legal principle was confirmed.

The discussion in Part II was clear that any broader critique of law in terms of its adjudicatory model of ex-post individual enforcement was unnecessary. In fact, no model of discrimination law, whether based on negative versus positive duties,

[2] Cf Peter Fitzpatrick, 'Racism and the Innocence of Law' (1987) 14 Journal of Law and Society 119; Laurence Lustgarten, 'Racial Inequality and the Limits of Law' (1986) 49 Modern Law Review 68.

[3] Pierre Bourdieu, *Outline of a Theory of Practice* (Cambridge University Press 1977) 72.

[4] Kimberlé Williams Crenshaw, Race, Reform, and Retrenchment: Transformation and Legitimation in Antidiscrimination Law (1988) 101 Harvard Law Review 1331.

[5] Cf Sara Ahmed, *On Being Included: Racism and Diversity in Institutional Life* (Duke University Press 2012) 53 (considers racial discrimination law to be a 'containment strategy').

[6] Bharat Malkani, *Racial Justice and the Limits of Law* (BUP 2024).

or litigation versus regulation, or individual versus the collective, will function effectively without a fundamental commitment to anti-racism.[7] It is the lack of anti-racism as a principle that limits what law does in addressing structural racism. Law thus requires anti-racism as a legal principle in order to function optimally.

This does not mean that law *only* requires anti-racism as a legal principle and that rules prohibiting racial discrimination, policies advancing racial justice, and values promoting diversity can be done away with. In fact, a complex phenomenon like racism requires a range of legal norms and standards including rules, policies, values, and principles.[8] Anti-racism can thus exist in all of these forms. Further, as Chapter 3 showed, anti-racism in liberal and cultural forms can also exist *alongside* transformative anti-racism. But their existence *without* transformative anti-racism is futile in addressing racism in any meaningful way, that is, for addressing not just the symptoms but the causes of racism.

In order for anti-racism to actually do what its content prescribes—to address structural racism—anti-racism *must* exist as a legal principle which is capable of guiding action at the broadest level. That is, anti-racism as a legal principle guides how law and policy are imagined, drafted, interpreted, and enforced. As Chapters 3 and 4 explained, it is in the nature of anti-racism itself that it exceeds platitudes and declarations and insists on action.[9] Given that its actionable component is diverse and context-sensitive, its guidance for action too is general, and best expressed in the form of a principle.

The normative commitment to anti-racism as a legal principle is thus a commitment to the highest-level fundamental principles around which societies are organized, viz. democracy and rule of law. That is, it is a basic or primordial commitment through which every other more specific commitment in law and policy emerges and makes sense. Indeed, in postcolonial capitalist societies such as Canada, India, South Africa, and the UK, which are shaped by racism, a commitment to undo that racism must exist at the highest level. This is because structural racism in these postcolonial contexts continues to shape the social, political, economic, cultural, religious, familial, and other structures in a fundamental sense.[10] Anti-racism too must thus (re)shape these structures in a fundamental sense.

[7] Colm O'Cinneide, 'Fumbling Towards Coherence: The Slow Evolution of Equality and Anti-Discrimination Law in Britain' (2006) 57 Northern Ireland Legal Quarterly 57, 64 (describing the Equality Act 2010 as a 'combination of agreement about mid-level operating principles, and strong disagreement about foundational and guiding principles').

[8] John Braithwaite, 'Rules and Principles: A Theory of Legal Certainty' (2002) 27 Australian Journal of Legal Policy 47 ('consistency in complex domains can be even better realised by an appropriate mix of rules and principles than by principles alone').

[9] Michel Wieviorka, 'Is it So Difficult to be an Anti-Racist' in Pinina Werbner and Tariq Modood (eds), *Debating Cultural Hybridity: Multicultural Identities and the Politics of Anti-Racism* (Zed Books 2015) 152 ('[anti-racism] cannot be satisfied either with the easy conscience that moralising speeches or expressions of goodwill induce, or with the idea that racism ... ought to decrease with education or with the forward march of reason').

[10] See Jodi Melamed, 'Racial Capitalism' (2015) 1 Critical Ethnic Studies 76; Nancy Leong, 'Racial Capitalism' (2013) 126 Harvard Law Review 2151; David Theo Goldberg, *Racist Culture: Philosophy*

The normative commitment to anti-racism as a legal principle is fundamental but simple. To be an anti-racist is to address structural racism. No other form of opposition to racism, such as in the form of liberal or cultural anti-racism, is adequate in addressing racism centrally. Law is anti-racist only when it actually addresses structural racism. Law is not anti-racist when it opposes structural racism theoretically or rhetorically. As this book has argued, anti-racism is anti-racism only in practice. This means that it is neither necessary nor sufficient for anti-racism to be written down in constitutions, statutes, treaties, or case law. The adoption of anti-racism as a legal principle does not require law reform. It requires action; and precursively, it requires reasoning about action through the principle. It cannot be declared *done*. Instead, it inheres in how we go about *doing* law. Anti-racism is a process forever in motion to preventatively and proactively resist structural racism, even if anti-racist utopias are achieved. It is thus a timeless principle which perpetually guides how state and state-like entities govern.

and the Politics of Meaning (John Wiley & Sons 2009); Tayyab Mahmud, 'Colonialism and Modern Constructions of Race: A Preliminary Inquiry' (1999) 53 University of Miami Law Review 1219.

Index

For the benefit of digital users, indexed terms that span two pages (e.g., 52–53) may, on occasion, appear on only one of those pages.